The Insubordinate
and the Noncompliant

The Insubordinate and the Noncompliant

CASE STUDIES OF CANADIAN MUTINY AND DISOBEDIENCE,
1920 TO PRESENT

Edited by Howard G. Coombs
Foreword by Major-General P.R. Hussey

CANADIAN DEFENCE ACADEMY PRESS
KINGSTON

THE DUNDURN GROUP
TORONTO

Catalogue No. D2-201/1-2007E

Published by The Dundurn Group and Canadian Defence Academy Press in cooperation with the Department of National Defence, and Public Works and Government Services Canada.

Editor: Michael Carroll
Copy-editor: Nigel Heseltine
Designer: Jennifer Scott
Printer: Transcontinental

Library and Archives Canada Cataloguing in Publication

Coombs, Howard G.
    The insubordinate and the noncompliant : case studies of Canadian mutiny and disobedience, 1920 to present / Howard G. Coombs.

Includes index.
ISBN 978-1-55002-764-8

    1. Mutiny — Canada — History — 20th century. 2. Military offences — Canada — History — 20th century. 3. Military discipline — Canada — History — 20th century. 4. Canada — Armed Forces — History — 20th century. 5. Canada — History, Military — 20th century. I. Title.

FC226.A632 2007   355.1'3340971   C2007-904663-0

1   2   3   4   5   11   10   09   08   07

Conseil des Arts du Canada   Canada Council for the Arts   Canadä   ONTARIO ARTS COUNCIL / CONSEIL DES ARTS DE L'ONTARIO

We acknowledge the support of the **Canada Council for the Arts** and the **Ontario Arts Council** for our publishing program. We also acknowledge the financial support of the **Government of Canada** through the **Book Publishing Industry Development Program** and **The Association for the Export of Canadian Books**, and the **Government of Ontario** through the **Ontario Book Publishers Tax Credit** program and the **Ontario Media Development Corporation**.

Printed and bound in Canada
www.dundurn.com

Canadian Defence Academy Press
PO Box 17000 Station Forces
Kingston, Ontario, Canada
K7K 7B4

Dundurn Press
3 Church Street, Suite 500
Toronto, Ontario, Canada
M5E 1M2

Gazelle Book Services Limited
White Cross Mills
High Town, Lancaster, England
LA1 4XS

Dundurn Press
2250 Military Road
Tonawanda, NY U.S.A.
14150

Contents

FOREWORD

I~T GIVES ME GREAT PLEASURE~ to present the third book in a series discussing individual and collective aspects of military misbehaviour and protest. *The Insubordinate and the Noncompliant: Case Studies of Canadian Mutiny and Disobedience, 1920 to Present* builds upon the scholarship of the previous two Canadian Forces Leadership Institute (CFLI) volumes, *The Unwilling and the Reluctant: Theoretical Perspectives on Disobedience in the Military* and *The Apathetic and the Defiant: Case Studies of Canadian Mutiny and Disobedience, 1812–1919*, to form a collection of material that elaborates on the theory and historical interpretations of these topics within a Canadian context over the past two centuries. As such, this book represents another step towards the CFLI Strategic Leadership Writing Project's goal of creating a distinct body of professional material that captures the experiences of Canadian military leadership.

Themes of mutiny and disobedience may seem of little value to the study of the profession of arms. On closer examination, however, they demonstrate that sailors, soldiers, and aviators have ways to commune with formal military authorities outside of the hierarchical channels of communication that are normally bounded by authority and discipline. We need to understand the precursors to these acts of protest so that the root cause rather than the result can be addressed in a timely and effective manner.

Examination of incidents of mutiny and disobedience can provide a perspective on military leadership that is seldom considered: the view from below. Leaders at all levels should take into account how their actions and decisions are perceived by those they lead and manage. This volume, along with the others in this series, provides material for introspection on this sometimes challenging viewpoint.

Within the realm of military education one must approach topics of this nature with an open mind, critically scrutinizing content and context for the lessons that may be found there. I hope this work is enjoyed by its readership and that it helps to foster discourse regarding facets of leadership and management within the Canadian Forces. When reviewing this book, pay heed to the words of the philosopher George Santayana: "Those who fail to learn the lessons of the past are condemned to repeat them."

MAJOR-GENERAL P.R. HUSSEY
Commander, Canadian Defence Academy

PREFACE

LEADERSHIP IS A MULTIFACETED AND multidisciplinary topic, and the Canadian Forces Leadership Institute has, through the Strategic Leadership Writing Project, attempted to capture the full extent of the subject within a Canadian framework. This is part of CFLI's commitment to the creation of professional military knowledge. Our aim is to collect, analyze, synthesize, and disseminate insights and experiences, historical and contemporary, in regards to Canadian operational leadership. All of this is with a view to producing a compilation of knowledge for Canadian Forces educational, training, and professional development institutions, as well as for increased public awareness. The constituent material is being assembled through the contributions of serving and retired military personnel, academics, researchers, professional writers, and CFLI staff. This volume, *The Insubordinate and the Noncompliant: Case Studies of Canadian Mutiny and Disobedience, 1920 to Present*, is part of that undertaking and builds on two other works of a similar nature that have been published through this initiative.

The three-volume collection examines the phenomena of mutiny and disobedience from a theoretical and historical perspective. The first book, *The Unwilling and the Reluctant: Theoretical Perspectives on Disobedience in the Military*, addressed the reasons that account for the occurrence of such acts, while the second volume, *The Apathetic and the Defiant: Case Studies of Canadian Mutiny and Disobedience, 1812–1919*, and this text provide historical examples of military personnel resisting lawful authority, but not without perceived cause. Therein lies the value of this research: rather than simply catalogue cases of ill discipline, this book and the others in the series present the idea of mutiny and individual disobedience as an *in extremis* attempt to communicate with those in authority.

While this premise is borne out through the body of material that has been assembled in all three manuscripts, the current volume, being contemporary, may seem to have greater relevance. However, I would like to note that the themes within these volumes are consistent across time and space. In fact, the rebellious activities and disobedient behaviour of today share many of the same precipitating factors of those from 200 or more years ago. As such, study of this work is necessary to gain insight into those unchanging elements of human nature that Canadian military leaders must understand to exercise effective command and leadership within the profession of arms in the context of today's challenges.

Colonel Bernd Horn
Deputy Commanding Officer
Special Operations Forces Command
Canadian Forces

ACKNOWLEDGEMENTS

Tᴴɪꜱ ᴡᴏʀᴋ ᴡᴏᴜʟᴅ ɴᴏᴛ ʜᴀᴠᴇ taken form without the contribution of many people, particularly the chapter authors. Mutiny and disobedience, while fascinating topics, require a great deal of effort and persistence to research, in part because nations and their militaries balk at the detailed examination of incidents of internal dissent, perhaps fearing what can be discovered.

Normally, mutinies and acts of disobedience are punished summarily, without addressing the roots of the problem. Consequently, written sources of information about incidents and their aftermath are at times difficult to find, making a rigorous examination of these past occurrences challenging in the extreme. Nevertheless, the contributors have dealt with these subjects with fairness and balance, avoiding both emotionalism and sensationalism, using primary and secondary source materials to support their perspectives. There is no doubt their stellar work will stand the scrutiny of time. For that reason, any credit for this book rests wholly with them, with responsibility for omissions or errors falling solely on my shoulders.

I would also be remiss if I did not thank the Canadian Forces Leadership Institute for giving me the opportunity to edit this volume. It has been an adventure, and I have learned an enormous amount because of it. Colonel Bernd Horn's mentoring has been appreciated and invaluable, as has the outstanding support provided to me by the staff of the institute.

The efforts of Craig Mantle deserve credit as well. While concurrently editing two volumes of a similar genre, he ensured, with great humour and tolerance, that there would be no redundancy or overlap between this work and the other books. His diligence helps make these three volumes a comprehensive package of theory and history concerning Canadian military protest.

Dr. Allan English, my supervising professor, deserves my gratitude for his perspectives and ongoing advice, which proved invaluable throughout the process. Moreover, it is essential to acknowledge the tolerance and support of my bride of 16 years, Donna, who, with my children, Leo and Lindsay, made sure that I kept balance and perspective in my life — whether I wished to or not.

Finally, I owe a debt of appreciation to those soldiers, non-commissioned officers, and officers I have been privileged to know over the past three decades. Their insights into human behaviour helped me better understand the unspoken and normally unstudied dimensions of military mutiny and disobedience. Without them this work would not have been possible.

HOWARD G. COOMBS
Kingston, Ontario

INTRODUCTION
Howard G. Coombs

$\mathbf{M}$Y INTEREST IN MUTINY AND disobedience originally stemmed from research conducted to fulfill the requirements of my undergraduate degrees at Memorial University of Newfoundland during the mid-1980s. During that time, I had the privilege of studying with noted Canadian labour historian Dr. Greg Kealey. It was he who introduced me to concepts of collective and individual protest. The result of that collaboration was an essay entitled "Collective Action During the Newfoundland Election Disturbances of 1861."[1]

Subsequently, before leaving full-time military service, I served with many Canadian Army units and came to the realization that those nineteenth-century concepts of protest remained valid, more so in the closed and ordered environment of the military than in the larger Canadian society. It seemed as if the structured agrarian forms of protest discernible during the Newfoundland Election Riots almost 150 years ago had analogous manifestations within actions of mutiny and disobedience committed by the members of the post-modern Canadian military.

In the Newfoundland of 1861, groups and individuals engaged in activities against different elements of society and the ruling elites that appeared to lack structure or reason. On closer inspection, however, the activities proved to be part of escalating patterns of protest. In the context of the epoch they were meant to communicate clearly defined messages expressing the collective and individual interests of those people.

British social historian E.P. Thompson plainly articulated the underpinnings of this idea when he wrote of class consciousness in his seminal work, *The Making of the English Working Class*. In this social history Thompson suggested that "class happens when some men, as a result of common experiences (inherited and shared), feel and articulate the identity of their interests as between themselves, and against other men whose interests are different from (and usually opposed to) theirs."[2] In a similar fashion the incidents of seeming ill discipline that are contained within this volume, *The Insubordinate and the Noncompliant: Case Studies of Canadian Mutiny and Disobedience, 1920 to Present*, represent a form of dialogue between military personnel and their leadership analogous to that of the disenchanted settlers of Newfoundland and the colonial hierarchy. The contributors to this volume, the third of a series, examine this discourse to dissect the underlying causes of such events.

Such rigorous study of military protest is long overdue. Few official attempts have been made to systemically analyze military rebellion, or mutiny, in a comprehensive fashion. Regrettably, information from sources other than authorized records is lacking, because those involved with the processes of the military bureaucracy maintained accounts of mutiny from the viewpoint of the institution but avoided personal records of the misbehaviour that might be incriminating and consequently not in their best interests. Accordingly, the job of reconstructing all facets of incidents of collective and individual protest is challenging.

Challenges aside, there has been some impetus to construct meaning within these forms of rebellion. Historian Lawrence James proposes that mutiny is a collective action undertaken by members of the military when they feel they have no other recourse. James's study *Mutiny: In the British and Commonwealth Forces, 1797–1956* indicates that mutineers viewed their participation in this act completely justified given the nature of their complaints. The most prevalent sources of discontent were rooted in aspects of military routine and quality of life. James writes that although the genesis of a mutiny could be attributed to trivial matters, the form and level of the resultant collective action could be completely disproportionate to the original cause.[3]

James's interpretation minimizes the role of military leadership in the genesis of a mutiny and his focus is upon the conditions of service and the reaction of authorities to the event rather than the prior activities of informal leaders. However, his explanation of mutiny as a group response of last resort to perceived intolerable circumstances seems to be accurate.

For an examination of the role of duly constituted leaders in the origins of mutinous behaviours one can turn to Joel E. Hamby in "The Mutiny Wagon Wheel: A Leadership Model for Mutiny in Combat." Hamby hypothesizes that leadership, training, and military discipline are tools necessary to prevent mutiny. It is my contention, that of these factors, leadership is the most important. Although Hamby focuses on mutiny among units engaged in combat, aspects of his model are useful when examining the elements of collective action in all types of mutinies and suggest what commanders could have done to mitigate the conditions that are precursors to mutiny. Similar to James, Hamby views mutiny as the practical expression of soldiers' concerns, not the cause.

Hamby sees eight influences in the genesis of a mutiny: Alienation, Environment, Values and Hope, Combat Experience, Training, Discipline, Primary Groups, and Leadership. These influences impact on one another and, as a whole, shape the unit's willingness to engage in combat. They can cause integration or disintegration. Mutiny is more likely when leadership is not used to mitigate negative influences. A positive command climate can moderate instances of ineffective leadership and reduce the impact on those factors that, taken together, sap the morale of a combat unit and lead to a mutiny.[4]

After a mutiny, efforts to maintain cohesion must be aimed at primary groups, which are the reason soldiers fight.[5] The bonds of loyalty to one another, the will and determination to live, and the expectations of comrades keep individuals motivated in combat. The primary group forms and regulates accepted standards of behaviour. Hamby notes that a divergence in primary group goals from that of the organization will result in a lessening of efficiency and contribute to a mutiny.[6]

In my opinion, informal and formal mechanisms of candid communication are of the utmost importance to the maintenance of organizational cohesion in this leadership model. Hamby's work neglects the criticality of this relationship in mitigating conditions that manifest themselves through mutinous acts. Although the establishment of such discourse is not a panacea, its absence seems to be a key determinant in the initiation of such military protest.

While studying these chapters, one must be aware that similar to the patterns of dissent discerned by social historians like Thompson, the military legacy is also the result of a clearly articulated tradition that has provided a voice to those who would have no other recourse.

In the Canadian Forces these conventions stretch well back and were well established before the first cases contained in this book. During the First World War, collective and individual disobedience were relatively common tactics used to demonstrate dissatisfaction. Canadian historian Bruce Cane, in *It Made You Think of Home: The Haunting Journal of Deward Barnes, Canadian Expeditionary Force: 1916–1919*, provides a number of examples of these behaviours from the period. In his journal Deward Barnes, a soldier in the 19th Battalion of the Canadian Expeditionary Force, described instances of both types of disobedience. Barnes noted that on 11 July 1916 before embarking for England from the training camp at Borden, Ontario:

> The camp was inspected by Maj.-Gen. Sir Sam Hughes and we had a march past. It was a terrible, hot day. When we arrived we were hot and dirty and they didn't allow us any water. The idea was to get us used to little water. We started our march past in column, no one was in step and carried their rifles any old way. When we all got the command to eyes right, we booed General Hughes and said, "Take us out of this rotten hole." The march past was a failure, but there was nothing done about it.[7]

Later, on 8 May 1917, following one of his first combat engagements in France, which included almost 36 hours with no sleep, great physical exertion, and hitherto unknown levels of violence, Barnes declined a direct order to join a group searching the battlefield for two wounded Canadians. He refused on the pretence that he was a Lewis gunner (light machine gun operator) and could not leave his post:

> Lieutenant Harmon … detailed me and I would not go. I told him I was a gunner and was not to leave my post (that was before I noticed who he was) and that was our training — which was all bosh. He sent me to get the Sergeant-Major, who was down a big dug out. I got him and he told the Sergeant-Major that I was to go and lead the six men over the barricade and up to these wounded men. When I knew I had to go I was satisfied. I knew it was war and I never shirked

once in any duty. It was about seven o'clock and he
could see I was all in, but I had to go.[8]

Of great interest to us today is the reaction of the leadership to
these events. The first event Barnes details is group insubordination,
which was simply ignored. In the second incident Barnes is given time
to reconsider his refusal before issue is made of his negative response
to a legitimate order.[9] In both cases it seems as if the unspoken
message was understood by those in authority.

This theme of establishing communication is introduced by
Bernd Horn in Chapter 1. He examines the 1st Canadian Parachute
Battalion hunger strike at Bulford, England, in October 1944 to show
that even units considered elite are not immune to mutinous acts. In
this case the Canadian parachutists, recently bloodied at Normandy,
used a refusal to eat to communicate their displeasure over what
was perceived as a needlessly harsh training regime. Horn examines
the role of unit and formation leaders in precipitating and resolving
these events.

In a similar vein Rick Walker establishes that even high-ranking
officers can demonstrate resistance when they believe their advice
must be heeded. In Chapter 2 Walker dissects the role of the senior
leadership of the Canadian Army in precipitating the conscription
crisis of 1944. By challenging the government on its reluctance to
implement conscription fully, the Army generals hoped to expand
the Canadian commitment and establish the foundation of a national
Army — created in the crucible of war by conscription and sustained
in peacetime by universal military service. In the aftermath of this
debacle Walker suggests that not only were the results underwhelming
but the Army condemned itself to a state of organizational perdition
in the eyes of the elected leadership of the nation. One can see
that even if the message being communicated is heeded, extremely
negative consequences can follow.

Allan English suggests that some outwardly mutinous behaviour
can communicate issues concerning leadership as well as psychological
distress. Chapter 3 looks at leadership and command styles in the
Royal Air Force's Bomber Command during the Second World War
and their impact on the crews who constituted this formation and
endured great mental stresses while carrying out extremely hazardous
missions. English also scrutinizes the manner in which what was
euphemistically termed "lack of moral fibre" or LMF manifested itself
as an extreme reaction to conditions that were no longer tolerable.

In Chapter 4 David Bercuson examines incidents of non-compliance in a Canadian element of Bomber Command during 1943 at the height of the bombing campaign. An assessment of aborted bombing missions originating from Number 6 Group of the Royal Canadian Air Force not only delineates constructions of LMF but also scrutinizes methods of resistance by Canadian bomber crews who, for one reason or another, did not complete assigned tasks. Bercuson suggests that this rebellion against the imperatives of air combat took an almost undetectable form of "grey" insubordination.

Chapter 5 by Dean Black is a study of the expression of mutiny and indiscipline in Canada's Second World War Air Force, focusing specifically on incidents pertaining to pilots in fighter squadrons. Black puts forward that these Canadian "knights of the air" could also be prone to rebellion; however, given that the means of expression involved the aircraft they flew, these incidents were more violent and direct in nature than the behaviours outlined by English and Bercuson. Black suggests that in extreme cases fighter pilots might have created the circumstances leading to the death of other pilots who had violated what was considered "acceptable."

In keeping with this theme of communication, Chapter 6 offers an excellent overview of disobedience in the Canadian Air Force after both world wars. Rachel Heide shows how mass refusals and demonstrations were methods members of the air service used to communicate their unhappiness, but with significant differences from their comrades in the Navy and Army. Although Heide believes that all services reacted through collective action when they felt justified in establishing and upholding a moral economy, she suggests there were important differences in the issues under protest. Unlike Army and Navy mutinies, which were normally connected with internal matters relating to conditions of life and poor leadership, Air Force dissension manifested concerns pertaining to civil governance. The political themes of confrontation in 1919 involved perceived obligations vis-à-vis owed pay and in 1946 related to a desire for timely repatriation from Europe to North America. Although these air personnel did not dispute the existence of the Canadian government, they wanted it to live up to the compact they had established by enrolling in the Air Force during the conflict and provide the post-war benefits that should have resulted from their sacrifices. The protests were intending to draw attention to seemingly unjust governmental policies so that they would be rectified.

Michael Whitby, in Chapter 7, discusses the largest Canadian naval mutiny in the history of that service and perhaps that of the Second World War. In 1943 the crew of HMCS *Iroquois* refused to leave their mess decks until their complaints were listened to by senior naval officers. Although this disobedience was ostensibly about a disliked captain who had cancelled all shore leave, the precipitating causes were much deeper, relating to the rapid expansion of the wartime Canadian Navy and a corresponding clash of civilian and military cultures. In this case a number of contributing elements exacerbated the situation onboard the *Iroquois*. Whitby points out that naval mutiny follows a centuries-old tradition of giving voice to those who have no other recourse. This naval mutiny was neither the first nor the last of that decade.

Such sea-going discourse took unexpected forms, like that described by Richard Mayne in Chapter 8. Mayne explores incidents of crew sabotage aboard ships of the Royal Canadian Navy (RCN) between 1942 and 1945. He suggests that these events were likely the result of individual grievances against the leadership of the ships in question. Such acts of sabotage were, perhaps, a means of addressing wrongs that could not be resolved in any other fashion. In effect, the impairment of the ship's functioning communicated individual unhappiness with aspects of naval service aboard that vessel.

Chapter 9 by Robert Caldwell examines the riotous Victory in Europe celebrations that took place in Halifax during 7–8 May 1945. He proposes that these disturbances resulted from an amalgamation of cultural and command issues. In a similar fashion to the tensions noted by Whitby, the culture of the RCN Volunteer Reserve (RCNVR) included undesirable traits produced by the rapid growth of the wartime RCN. In combination with this was a lack of effective naval leadership in the Halifax region. Caldwell puts forward that the Halifax riots were the result of this explosive mix signalling the unhappiness of RCNVR sailors of that time and place.

The culmination of this period of naval protest occurred in 1949 with a number of separate mutinies aboard ships of the RCN. In Chapter 10 Richard Gimblett scrutinizes these incidents and examines how they brought about the landmark *Mainguy Report*. Gimblett contends that the naval tradition of mutiny coalesced with post-war dissatisfaction concerning conditions of service on ship and ashore to produce grievances that had no other recourse but mutiny. These protests led to governmental direction to form a commission of inquiry under the direction of Rear-Admiral E. Rollo Mainguy and from the resultant report came many of the recommendations that enabled the construction of an effective post-war Navy.

Although perceived ill treatment and injustice could mobilize sailors to give protest through collective action, Defence Minister Paul Hellyer's efforts to integrate and unify Canada's military services produced a comparable reaction with high-ranking officers. In Chapter 11 Daniel Gosselin dissects the controversies surrounding unification and delves into the controversies of 1966. He argues that the conflict over unification was not a battle over uniforms and service customs but a genuine civil-military crisis that set Hellyer against his top military advisers. This was a crisis that had been brewing since at least the 1950s and perhaps earlier if one re-examines the ideas presented by Rick Walker in Chapter 2.

Moving from resistance to governmental direction by senior military leaders, Randall Wakelam considers the apparent casual disobedience of flying regulations by aircrew in the 1970s and 1980s and advocates that this noncompliance resulted from a culture of tolerance. According to Wakelam, this culture was neither one of disregard for legal orders and regulations nor resulted from a laissez-faire approach to discipline, but instead was the product of sanctioned risk-taking. This was an attempt to provide aircrew with an environment that lent itself to producing flexible and adaptable aviators who would be prepared to fight in a complex environment.

Correspondingly, Chapter 13 by Gordon Sharpe looks at a comparable example of flexibility and adaptability by the Army through examining the dilemmas of Canadian soldiers in the Balkans during 1993–1994. He studies the activities of the Second Battalion of Princess Patricia's Canadian Light Infantry, with a special emphasis on the actions of their commander, Lieutenant-Colonel Jim Calvin, during their deployment in that war-torn region. Sharpe puts forward that Calvin disregarded accepted doctrinal principles concerning military employment during peace operations and uses contemporary command and control theory to explain the underlying factors that precipitated Calvin's decision. In doing so Sharpe shows that commanders must demonstrate courage and initiative by disregarding inappropriate guidance, and offers an analytical paradigm that can assist with making that decision.

Completing this examination of insubordination and non-compliance is an assessment of the systemic issues that eventually resulted in the disbandment of the Canadian Airborne Regiment. In Chapter 14 Bernd Horn analyzes disobedience in the Airborne from 1968–1995 and concludes that most of the problems resulted from externally controlled factors. Furthermore, he argues that the Regiment was reflective of the Canadian Army as a whole and, as such, was representative of disciplinary problems within the whole institution. Together the issues combined to generate a culture of disobedience that resulted in the destruction of Canada's only airborne unit.

There are many threads linking the chapters of this volume. Prominent among them is the idea of mutiny and disobedience as communication. Spanning all Canadian services during times of war and peace, the chapters demonstrate that military leadership has formal and informal dimensions. Formal leaders have *de jure* authority vested in them by legislation. Informal leaders have *de facto* influence that can arise from many sources. The formal leadership of any organization must always ensure that it minimizes the divergence between the actions of informal leadership and organizational aims. When this separation transpires, mutiny is sometimes the result. *The Insubordinate and the Noncompliant* examines this idea and many others to dissect the Canadian experience of military mutiny and disobedience over the past 90 years.[10] Consequently, at the beginning of the twenty-first century, with Canadians engaged in theatres of operations at home and around the world, one should heed the manifold lessons drawn by the contributors to this volume to ensure that sailors, soldiers, and air personnel are provided leadership that will ensure mission success wherever elements of the Canadian Forces are deployed.

NOTES

1. Howard Gerard Coombs, "Collective Action During the Newfoundland Election Disturbances of 1861" (Unpublished B.A. [Honours] Essay, Memorial University of Newfoundland, 1986).

2. E.P. Thompson, *The Making of the English Working Class* (London: Victor Gollancz Ltd., 1963; reprint, Harmondsworth, Middlesex, England: Penguin Books Ltd., 1976), 9–10.

3. Lawrence James, *Mutiny: In the British and Commonwealth Forces, 1797–1956* (London: Buchan & Enright, Publishers, 1987): 13–15.

4. Joel E. Hamby, "The Mutiny Wagon Wheel: A Leadership Model for Mutiny in Combat," *Armed Forces & Society* 28, No. 4 (Summer 2002): 575–78.

5.   "A primary group is a typically small social group whose members share close, personal, enduring primary relationships ..." *Wikipedia: The Free Encyclopedia*, available at *http://en.wikipedia.org/wiki/Primary_group*.

6.   *Ibid.*, 587–88.

7.   Bruce Cane, *It Made You Think of Home: The Haunting Journal of Deward Barnes, Canadian Expeditionary Force: 1916–1919* (Toronto: Dundurn Press, 2004), 32.

8.   *Ibid.*, 85–86.

9.   *Ibid.*, 86.

10. These thoughts are captured in the newest leadership manuals for the Canadian Forces. *Leadership in the Canadian Forces: Conceptual Foundations* and *Leadership in the Canadian Forces: Doctrine* were published by the Canadian Defence Academy in 2005 and are accessible through the Canadian Forces Leadership Institute Website at *www.cda.forces.gc.ca/CFLI/engraph/leadership/leadership_e.asp*.

Good Men Pushed Too Far?
The First Canadian Parachute Battalion
Hunger Strike, 20–23 October 1944

Bernd Horn

W HAT DRIVES MILITARY UNITS, OR large parts thereof, to commit acts of mass disobedience? Several reasons such as unacceptable living or working conditions, as well as draconian and inhuman treatment, rise to the surface as potential causes. Justifiable as these reasons may be, in the face of deprivations and the demands placed on troops during operations, or in a wartime setting, large scale acts of disobedience are almost invariably seen as unacceptable, because the environment is severe and the unit's security could be compromised.

Mass acts of disobedience that are actually committed can often be attributed to units that are green, inexperienced, ad hoc, and/or have poor cohesion and strained morale. Furthermore, the leadership component of these organizations is also normally a contributor to the problem. It is often weak, inexperienced, transient, and relatively new to the organization. A catalyst — a traumatic event, fear, a major disappointment, or a combination of factors is then added to the mix to set the whole thing off.

In the face of such challenges and circumstances a break down of discipline is not overly surprising, but what could be the trigger for an act of disobedience by a specially selected, arguably elite combat hardened unit in a garrison setting? What could prompt such a seasoned group of cohesive and experienced soldiers to undertake such action, particularly in wartime? Was the case of the 1st Canadian Parachute Battalion (1 Cdn Para Bn) hunger strike in Bulford, England from 20–23 October 1944, a case of good men pushed too far? Or, was it a matter of "unreasonable" expectations based on a reputation that was earned from their contribution and achievements during the Normandy campaign?

To properly assess the case study it is necessary to briefly examine the history of 1 Cdn Para Bn up to the event. During the early years of the war, Canadian commanders and politicians dismissed the idea of airborne forces as a luxury that the Canadian Army could not afford and frankly did not need. However, the continuing American and British development of these forces and their subsequent belief that paratroopers were a defining element of a modern army led the Canadians, in July 1942, to form a similar capability, but on a much smaller scale.

Despite the Army's initial resistance to the idea of airborne soldiers, it now undertook an all out effort. In fact, the parachute battalion was given elite status and was widely advertised as such.[1] It was granted "the highest priority."[2] The Army also attempted to provide it with the best available personnel. "Only the best men," directed the Army commander, "will do."[3] Although only limited experience was available on which to base selection, it was clear that paratroopers needed characteristics such as resourcefulness, courage, endurance, and discipline.[4] The *Canadian Army Training Memorandum* explained that "parachute training is tough … It needs young men, alert and clever young men, who can exploit a chance and who have the guts necessary to fight against overwhelming odds and win."[5] Nevertheless, it was also evident to the Army leadership that the airborne soldier required a level of intelligence above the normal infantry requirement. "Only physically perfect men of high intelligence and good education were admitted," explained Captain F.O. Miksche, a renowned military writer of the time.[6]

Senior commanders acknowledged the higher standards required of paratroopers. They knew that the paratroopers would require "greater stamina and powers of endurance than is generally asked of an infantry soldier." The director of military training succinctly asserted, "'guts all along the line" was a necessity.[7] Brigadier F.G. Weeks, the deputy chief of the general staff (DCGS), elaborated, "the Dominion's aim was to develop such a hard striking unit that it would have an efficiency excelled by no other such group in the world."[8]

Army leadership also decided that all serving members should be of the rank of private and they made it mandatory for all volunteers to revert prior acting or substantive rank to that of private before proceeding for training.[9] As a result, many senior non-commissioned officers rejoined the ranks. The conceptual model was such that one journalist quipped, "You've practically got to be Superman's 2IC [second-in-command] in order to get in."[10]

Significantly, the Army tried to make certain that theory was backed up with practice. A complex and discerning screening process was undertaken to ensure that only the finest candidates were selected for further training. Army psychiatrist, Dr. A.E. Moll, developed a rating system that was used to grade volunteers during selection boards. His system ranked an individual from a range of A (outstanding) to E (rejected).[11] Only those who achieved an "A" score were kept for airborne training.[12]

The requirements imposed on the volunteers demanded an exceptionally high standard of mental, physical, and psychological fitness. Criteria were quickly developed and promulgated.[13] Initially soldiers were required to be fully trained before they could qualify to apply for parachute training. However, within three months this restriction was lifted and volunteers needed only to be "basically trained." This ensured that there was a larger pool of talent to draw from.[14]

All volunteers were required to pass a rigorous selection process. Once an individual volunteered for parachute training he was put through a personality appraisal consisting of a review of the individual's service record and qualification card data, the completion of a questionnaire, administration of a word association test, and a self-description test. Finally, a psychiatric interview needed to be passed. The examiners deemed the psychiatric interview essential to determine not just whether the volunteer would "take the jumps" but if he would "become an efficient paratrooper in every sense of the word."[15]

Early on in the process military commanders and examiners agreed that "only those whose suitability is beyond reasonable doubt are to be recommended."[16] A rigorous application of the selection criterion was imposed despite the understanding that this would make it difficult to meet the quota requirement.[17] By December 1942, a report from the director of personnel selection said that approximately 50 percent of those volunteering were rejected.[18]

The Army and medical examiners, as well as the psychiatrists, however, were but the first obstacles aspiring paratroopers had to deal with. Those who demonstrated fear of heights, water, or closed places were automatic rejections. So were those with showing symptoms such as palpitation, nocturnal dyspnoea, stomach disorders, frequent headaches, low back pains, and urinary frequency, as well as psychotic or psychopathic tendencies. In addition, reports noted, "the seclusive, lonely type of individual appears to do poorly with this unit."[19] However, even if an individual passed the initial stages of the selection process, he still had to be accepted by the commanding officer (CO) of the parachute battalion.[20]

In sum, screening was severe. As said earlier, it averaged a rejection rate of 50 percent. And this was just the beginning. A further 35 percent of successful volunteers were lost to normal parachute training wastage rates.[21] However, the process ensured that 1 Cdn Para Bn had the cream of the Canadian Army. On the whole, they were some of Canada's fittest, most motivated, and capable soldiers. A great many were former NCOs with years of experience.

Not surprisingly, the strenuous selection and training, led to the Army hierarchy deciding that the "Parachute Corps must be considered an elite Corps in every sense."[22] The *Canadian Army Training Memorandums* aptly summarized that "Canada's paratroop units are attracting to their ranks the finest of the Dominion's fighting men ... these recruits are making the paratroops a 'corps elite.'"[23]

The media was even more complimentary in their description of the new airborne unit. "The army picked them out of thousands of fit young Canadian soldiers," wrote journalist Robert Taylor, "who sought berths in the Canadian army's newest and already its elite corps, the first parachute battalion."[24] Other reporters and newspapers were equally impressed. They described the paratroopers as "action-hungry and impatient to fill their role as the sharp, hardened tip of the Canadian army's 'dagger pointed at the heart of Berlin.'"[25] With unanimity, newspapers invariably described the parachute volunteers as "hard as nails" representing the toughest and smartest soldiers in the Canadian Army.[26] One journalist wrote: "They are good, possibly great soldiers, hard, keen, fast-thinking and eager for battle," while another asserted that they were "Canada's most daring and rugged soldiers ... daring because they'll be training as paratroops: rugged because paratroops do the toughest jobs in hornet nests behind enemy lines."[27] Others painted a picture of virtual super-men. "Picture men with muscles of iron," depicted one writer, "dropping in parachutes, hanging precariously from slender ropes, braced for any kind of action ... these toughest men who ever wore khaki."[28] Another simply said, "your Canadian paratrooper is an utterly fearless, level thinking, calculating killer possessive of all the qualities of a delayed-action time bomb."[29]

Once established the unit began a tough training regimen, which combined with the element of parachuting, created a cohesive unit. As training progressed, the senior command at National Defence Headquarters struggled with the issue of 1 Cdn Para Bn employment. Clearly, a collection of aggressive and offensive-minded paratroopers would be wasted on home defence tasks, particularly as there was no direct threat to Canada. Consequently, even before the paratroopers were considered operationally ready, they were offered up to the commander of Home Forces in England. The British quickly accepted the offer, so in March 1943, 1 Cdn Para Bn was added to the establishment of a second British airborne division that was forming.

In late June 1943, the Battalion's 31 officers and 548 other ranks deployed to England for overseas duty. They were subsequently attached to the 3rd Parachute Brigade (3 Para Bde), as part of the 6th Airborne Division (6 AB Div). The Battalion rapidly settled into their quarters at Carter Barracks at Bulford Camp, where the second and more gruelling phase of their training began in earnest.

Their new brigade commander was the incomparable Brigadier James Hill. He was an experienced airborne commander who saw action in Tunisia, North Africa during Operation Torch, as the CO of the British 1st Parachute Battalion. While in North Africa he was severely wounded and evacuated to England.

Hill, based on his operational experience, believed that the unforgiving nature of airborne warfare was such that the survival of his paratroopers depended to a great extent on their physical fitness. Therefore, he set demanding standards. Hill expected a unit to cover 50 miles in 18 hours with each soldier carrying a 60 pound rucksack and weapon. Ten mile marches within a two-hour time period were also considered the norm.

The brigadier welcomed the Canadians. He saw in them the making of great warriors. "As the days passed," wrote Hill, "General Gale [6 AB Div commander] and I realized what a unique and interesting Battalion had joined us as brothers."[30] However, he was not blinded by their strengths. Hill consistently "kept a tight rein" on his Canadians. Although he admired their spirit he also felt that they were neither well disciplined, nor adequately trained when they first joined the Brigade.[31]

Their shortcomings were quickly addressed by Hill's rigorous training regimen and demanding standards. By spring 1944, it was merely a matter of time before the Canadians would be tested in battle. The planning and preparation for the invasion of Europe was now in the final stages. Missions had already been assigned. The 6th Airborne Division was responsible for protecting the left flank of the 3rd British Infantry Division that was to land on a beach west of Ouistreham. In turn, 3 Para Bde was given the daunting tasks of destroying the coastal defence battery at Merville, demolishing a number of bridges over the River Dives, as well as controlling the high ridge centred on the small village of Le Mesnil that dominated the landing beaches.

Brigadier Hill assigned 1 Cdn Para Bn the responsibility of covering the left flank of the brigade's drop zone (DZ) and protecting its movements within the DZ. The Battalion was also given three primary missions — the defence and protection of 9 Parachute Battalion's left flank during its approach march and attack on the Merville battery; the destruction of two bridges spanning the River Dives; and the of destruction of German positions and a headquarters, as well as a bridge at Varaville.

The Battalion crossed the channel and jumped into France between 0030 hours and 0130 hours, 6 June 1944. The drops were badly scattered over a wide area owing to a lack of navigational aids, and thick dust and smoke, which drifted over the drop zones from the heavy bombing of nearby targets. Intense enemy anti-aircraft fire also contributed, because it panicked many of the pilots who immediately took evasive action that only magnified the difficulty of delivering the paratroopers accurately onto their objectives. On the first drop, only 30 of 110 paratroopers of "C" Company landed on the DZ. The subsequent drops were no better. The second group, made up of the main body of the Battalion, was scattered over an area 40 times greater than planned. To add to the problems, many leg kit bags ripped open, scattering the unit's vital heavy machine guns, mortars, and anti-tank weapons across the Normandy countryside. This significantly reduced the firepower available to the airborne soldiers in the critical days that followed.

In the midst of the growing chaos, the physical and psychological toughness, honed by careful training, showed its importance and value. The paratroopers, as individuals and a collective unit, not only persevered but flourished despite the unexpected situations and setbacks. By the end of the day, the resiliency of the Canadian paratroopers enabled them to attain all their assigned objectives with less than 30 percent of the troops and equipment originally allocated to the tasks. Their missions completed, they grimly dug-in to hold the ground they had won. Despite heavy losses, the Battalion held off all German counter attacks until the eventual Allied break-out.

By mid-August, the tide had finally turned and 1 Cdn Para Bn, as part of 3 Para Bde, for the first time since the Normandy drop, was back on the offensive. Commencing on 16 August, and continuing for the next 10 days, the unit participated in an advance and series of attacks against the German rearguard until finally being pulled from the line. On 4 September, the Battalion began its departure from France and returned to its adopted home in Bulford three days later.

Unquestionably, 1 Cdn Para Bn distinguished itself in its first combat action. However, this came at great cost. During the three month period between 6 June and 6 September 1944, the Battalion sustained heavy losses. Of the original 544 paratroops dropped, 83 were killed, 187 were wounded and 87 became prisoners of war. In regard to 1 Cdn Para Bn's performance on D-Day, Brigadier James Hill wrote: "They really put up a most tremendous performance on D Day and as a result of their tremendous dash and enthusiasm they overcame their objectives, which were very sticky ones, with considerable ease ..."[32] Hill was justifiably proud of his Canadians. "The battle," he wrote, "carried on for three months till the Germans were driven across the Seine. In this period, the 6th Airborne lost some 4,457 men killed, wounded, and missing. Throughout that time, the Canadian Parachute Battalion had never been out of the line. They won their spurs and glory ... and paid the price. Nearly half the Battalion were either killed, wounded or missing ... It had been a bloody battle with high stakes. No quarter asked or given."[33]

The unit's return to England provided the opportunity to reconstitute itself and prepare for its next mission. The Battalion's first priority was bringing itself back up to strength through the integration of reinforcements from the 1 Cdn Para Training Company. The general feeling that prevailed recalled Sergeant R.F. "Andy" Anderson was one of "tremendous relief and of great success and of having survived a most harrowing experience."[34] During the next four days, activities were mostly administrative in nature consisting of clothing, pay, and medical parades. Although discipline remained high, the officers and the senior NCOs still made an effort to ensure that the tempo of activity was relaxed and that the men were not rushed. Everyone knew that these first few days would prove difficult. Many familiar faces had vanished. "Out of my company's 120 men," recalled John Kemp, "there were 22 of us that returned to Carter Barracks."[35]

The base staff went out of their way to welcome the paratroopers back home and great care was taken to prepare excellent meals. Many day passes were issued enabling the paratroopers to go out on the town, dance and have a few pints. For those who preferred to stay in camp, they had the option of taking in a movie or show. On 11 September, the paratroopers were given a well-deserved 13-day furlough. Before heading off to their various destinations, the paratroopers were warned that the day following their return, training would start once again in earnest.[36]

As promised, on 26 September 1944, Acting Lieutenant-Colonel Jeff Nicklin, the Battalion's new CO had the unit formed up for a special parade.[37] His address was short and to the point. He wanted to command the best battalion in the Division. Accordingly, he insisted that training would be demanding.[38] His previous "in your face," harsh disciplinary style as the unit's deputy commanding officer (DCO) had been tolerated by the untested troops in the training leading up to Normandy. However, it now annoyed the hardened combat veterans. Nonetheless, Nicklin's command approach was fully endorsed by Brigadier Hill who believed that strong leadership was necessary to ensure that the paratroopers put forth full commitment and effort during training. In fact, Hill's Evaluation Report of Nicklin stated:

> An officer of the highest integrity who possesses unusual drive and determination. He sets a very high standard in the Battalion and is prepared to accept no compromise. He is a stern disciplinarian, but takes infinite trouble to safeguard the welfare of the men. He is a good trainer of troops and is tactically sound in his ideas. He requires further experience in the tactical handling of his Battalion.[39]

Part of the problem, however, also lay in the difference between the old and the new CO. Lieutenant-Colonel G.F.P. Bradbrooke, before D-Day, had been judged by most, including his superiors, as acceptable given that he commanded a unit that had not seen combat. Brigadier Hill rated Bradbrooke as "a good administrator, a very good CO in peacetime and an intrepid parachutist."[40] However, in Normandy, Bradbrooke's leadership during the defence of the Le Mesnil crossroads and the subsequent pursuit of the retreating German forces was not up to Hill's, or the unit's, expectations. As the Normandy Campaign progressed, Hill noted that Bradbrooke lacked

LIEUTENANT-COLONEL G.F.P. BRADBROOKE (LEFT) AND
MAJOR JEFF A. NICKLIN POSE AT BULFORD, ENGLAND, 1944.
(Department of National Defence, Sergeant Elmer R. Bonter, Library and Archives Canada PA 179151)

the aggressive leadership required to lead his men during combat. Soldiers noted that the CO was seldom seen on the front lines.

In contrast, the behaviour and demeanour of the Battalion's DCO, then Major Nicklin, caught Hill's attention. Nicklin had been active throughout the entire course of the campaign. The ex-Canadian Football League star regularly visited his soldiers in their forward positions. Furthermore, he enjoyed the action and even took part in reconnaissance patrols. "Jeff Nicklin," observed one senior NCO, "was one who almost seemed indestructible, six feet three inches tall, football hero back home, a stern disciplinarian, physical fitness his specialty."[41] Those who played football with Nicklin back home "rated him almost immortal."[42] Unquestionably, Nicklin was a rugged physical individual, who was feared and could sense fear, recalled Brigadier Hill.[43] In this officer, Hill discerned the leadership qualities that could prove useful to supervise the Battalion's post campaign training.

Although Hill respected the accomplishments and sacrifices of his Canadian paratroopers, he had nevertheless learned a valuable leadership lesson while commanding soldiers during the Battle of France, in 1940 and paratroopers later in North Africa, in 1942. The brigadier had observed that "blooded" veterans who returned from combat duty to resume daily training routine showed unwillingness to "snap to it" and put up with various aspects of garrison duties and discipline. For that reason, he believed that a strong hand was required to once again motivate, closely supervise, and control battle hardened troops. Hill was right. Having faced death and survived, many veterans now thought that they were better than their new untested comrades. Hill identified this type of combatant as, "heroes and crooked berets that had to be knocked on the head and have discipline reimposed."[44]

This post operational mind-set was seemingly now developing within 1 Cdn Para Bn. "Here we have very tough chaps, heroes," explained Hill, "They had to be disciplined. So, I popped in Jeff Nicklin."[45] In the end, regardless of what the paratroopers had accomplished, Hill would not compromise his two airborne tenets — discipline and physical fitness. There was still much to accomplish and the war was far from over.

Nicklin now focused on correcting the deficiencies and shortcomings experienced during the Normandy Campaign. He paid special attention to those skills required for offensive operations. As a result, the new training plan emphasized weapons handling, physical fitness, rapid clearance of drop zones, the efficient execution of offensive and defensive battle drills, and, especially, street fighting.

The Battalion had its work cut out. It was a long way from its pre-D-Day level of operational readiness. Nicklin accepted this challenge without hesitation. The men immediately noted the change in the tempo. "The training got more severe," recalled Sergeant John Feduck, "and nothing was let go. Nothing was overlooked." He added that "Nicklin was the type of guy, who did everything strictly by the book, and he had his own way of training, making sure you went for your runs. There was no slacking off." Nicklin's training schedule was simple. "You trained all the time," stated Feduck. "You had no time for yourself," he added, "Leaves were a little shorter and you worked harder."[46]

Physical training under Nicklin "was a hell of a lot tougher," recalled Sergeant Harry Reid, "He wanted us to become linebackers."[47] The new CO's objective was clear. "He wanted to have the best battalion in the Brigade," said Sergeant Andy Anderson. "Nicklin had us out on the parade square at six o'clock in the morning, and worked us till dark." Anderson noted that "Brigadier Hill was thrilled and he did not object to that." Nicklin really enjoyed the physical part of the training. He personally led the bimonthly 10-mile forced march. As the paratroopers arrived at the finish line, "he [Nicklin] and the RSM [regimental sergeant-major] would stand at the gate with a clipboard," recounted Anderson, "and took down the names of the stragglers." No quarter was given. "If they could not keep up," stated Anderson, "they were gone."[48] Nicklin wanted each platoon to arrive at the finish line as a group.

Nicklin's Normandy experience had confirmed in his mind that a well-trained group that worked skilfully together could inflict greater damage than a few isolated paratroopers. Since the Battalion's return from France, Nicklin stressed the importance of teamwork in all training, for veterans and reinforcements alike. He had personally experienced the benefits and results of this concept as well as the close-knit camaraderie that it fostered during his tenure with the Canadian Football League's Winnipeg Blue Bombers. He knew that teamwork was vital in wining football games. Nicklin knew that it would also enhance the effectiveness of his paratroopers.

Furthermore, Nicklin insisted that all his officers become team players. They were now ordered to take part with their men in all training activities. Under Nicklin there were no exceptions. "He started pushing them hard," recalled Sergeant Roland Larose, "He ordered all the officers to take part in these runs and physical training exercises."[49] This was a Nicklin training directive that the troops appreciated.

The hard training and demanding exercises assisted in integrating the reinforcements that the unit received. Nonetheless, the first few weeks proved difficult for the new men. "That's when the BS [bull shit] started, the attitude of some of veterans was, 'We were there [Normandy] and you weren't,'" explained Major Hilborn.[50] The new men had to prove to the veterans that they could indeed fit in and, more important, keep up.

Nicklin had anticipated this situation and told his officers he would not put up with such behaviour. "There was no lording over others," recalled Lieutenant Alf Tucker. Nicklin insisted that all veterans use "their experience to show the replacements how to react and protect themselves or how to act in a manner that was in their best interest. I remember," said Tucker, "that the officers took that to heart."[51]

"The problem," conceded Hilborn, "now became one of reintegrating the old with the new. They all had to be taught to think alike."[52] A redeeming factor was that the reinforcements were all qualified paratroopers. They had also undergone advanced weapons and fieldcraft training similar to that given to 1 Cdn Para Bn. The men had a good handle on their basic skills. Now, they just had to be accepted by the veterans. The integration of the new members eventually worked itself out. By mid-October 1944, the Battalion's training program was progressing well and the undesirables had been weeded out. Corporal Richard Creelman commented that "There were quite a few that did not come up to what they were expected to and they were replaced. They [battalion headquarters] found out quickly who were the leaders and who weren't." Those who chose to remain knew that they would have to work hard. "We had some experience by now," said Creelman, "and we knew what was expected of us. We knew what it was like getting shot at."[53]

It was also easier to keep the men in line. "All you had to do," explained Sergeant Larose, "was to tell them to smarten up, or they'd be back to the Canadian Army. That was it."[54] Even though the training was difficult, the pride of wearing the distinctive maroon beret and the unique Canadian Parachute Qualification Badge combined with the knowledge that they were the first to take the fight to the enemy were reasons enough for the paratroopers to dig deeper and find the energy to keep up with the unrelenting tempo.

Those who remained were extremely professional. They were self-motivated and possessed good leadership skills and initiative. "In the Nicklin regime, we had to be prepared and were expected to take on a lot of initiative," revealed Andy Anderson. "Certain phases during the exercises were especially prepared to evaluate candidates [all ranks] and their use of initiative," he explained. "You would be briefed and once you landed [during an exercise], referees would black arm band [identification system used during an exercise to simulate casualties and wounded personnel] a certain percentage of your stick." A paratrooper would then be designated by the referees to carry on with the unit's task. "You had to know where

A PARATROOPER OF THE 1ST CANADIAN PARACHUTE BATTALION
ADVANCES IN AN OPEN FIELD AT BULFORD, ENGLAND, 1943.
(Department of National Defence, Library and Archives Canada PA 209697)

you were," stated Anderson, "who was missing, what you had to do and what resources were at your disposal. This was a new part of the training that had been derived from our Normandy experience." He concluded, "This training really paid off." Quick thinking and adapting to any situation resulted in the mission's success. It also kept casualties to a minimum.

Despite the challenging training the paratroopers were becoming increasingly disgruntled with certain aspects of the CO's uncompromising level of discipline. Roland Larose recalled one particular case. "Sometimes NCOs, had to give drill exercise to defaulters [paratroopers who had committed infractions or had not performed up to expectation]. He [Nicklin] got them to wear a smock with a big yellow stripe down their back. That really cheesed us off," said Larose. "You can only push a guy so far … They weren't yellow, that's the part we didn't like."[55]

Even the smallest detail did not escape Nicklin's watchful eye. "We used to have to blanco [colour] our stripes [rank insignia] white," stated Corporal Ernie Jeans. He went on, "I didn't do that because I wasn't on parade much. However, one day, Nicklin noted my stripes and hollered at me from across the parade square. I had to race over and I had a lot of explaining to do."[56] By all accounts the CO was unrelenting. "[Lieutenant-] Colonel Nicklin," wrote Anderson, "was a by the book commander, absolutely no quarter given and he had no compassion for defences that were mounted." He added, "the number of soldiers punished severely for what might be minor infractions gave the colonel the unkind title of the 'Tyrant.'"[57] By late October, a group of paratroopers decided that they would no longer put up with this excessive discipline and organized a hunger strike.

The Battalion War Diary entry for Friday, 20 October 1944, simply reads: "On evening supper parade great confusion was caused when the men refused to eat." It explained, "The complaint lay not in the food but in the treatment of the men by the commanding officer."[58] What in fact transpired was a refusal by some 70 to 80 men to eat their meal. The following day, the War Diary simply noted "Personnel still not eating." However, what it failed to highlight was the fact that the hunger strike had now spread through the whole battalion, including the training company.[59] On Sunday, 22 October, the War Diary reported, "Personnel in camp refused to eat again today." Clearly, the hunger strike was meant to pass a serious message. The troops, however, "were observing all orders meticulously and were actually attending meal parades but were not eating."[60]

The protest, argued some of the senior leadership, was organized by a group of malcontents to complain about what Captain Madden described as "a parade square type discipline."[61] Madden explained that "The men saw it as chickenshit … They knew that so many of the manifestations of this parade square discipline were unessential to getting the job done in war."[62] Private Jan de Vries added that "Many paratroopers were uncomfortable with this course of action." However, he conceded, "we were put in a position that we had to show solidarity and go with the flow."[63]

Whereas discipline was an integral element of a military life, Nicklin enforced it with an iron hand, affecting every facet of the daily lives of his men. "He [Nicklin] imposed such requirements," complained Madden, "that when they went to the canteen at night, they couldn't go casually dressed. They had to go with their battledress jacket buttoned up. They couldn't wear their fatigue shoes; they had to wear proper ammunition boots, and that sort of thing."[64]

The hunger strike came at an inopportune moment. With the influx of a large number of new paratroopers, NCOs, and officers, the incident threatened to cause irreparable damage to the unit's cohesiveness and morale. Many officers were concerned by this turn of events. Although some backed the CO's actions wholeheartedly, others thought that Nicklin was unnecessarily hard on the men. "It was disconcerting," lamented Madden, "in that you were expected to go back to battle with these guys and here they had, you know, dug in their heels and shown that they weren't prepared to obey orders or do what was required...."[65]

Lieutenant William Jenkins, agreed. "It was an unpleasant experience around camp," stated Jenkins, "because morale was usually very very high. But, now whose part do you take." Jenkins added, "You could not condemn them [the men] for what they did. The position that most of us [officers] took, was that it was your business and do whatever you like ... It was a tense period for a while."[66] The strike went on for three days and further strained the relations between the men, the NCOs, and the officers.[67]

Its impact threatened to reach even beyond the unit. The press was soon on the story. Colonel W.G. Abel at Canadian Military Headquarters impressed on Rear-Admiral G.P. Thomson, the chief press censor at the Ministry of Information to kill the story. But the story was not a threat to security, therefore, editors could only be requested to suppress the story. However, Abel argued that the "hunger strike amounted to mutiny and it would be valuable for the enemy to know that a Canadian formation was not at present battle worthy because of incipient mutiny."[68] The War Office was of the same frame of mind and they were intent that "every possible step will be taken on the highest level necessary to prevent it [publication]."[69] After all, the senior leadership was concerned of the "possible serious effect if publicity were to encourage the spread of the hunger strike as an instrument of protest in the Army."[70]

On Saturday afternoon (22 October 1944), the news editor of the *London Daily Mail* called Brigadier Hill to ask whether he could come and take a look at the "hunger strike." Hill responded, "Look there is a war on. The war has to be won. Give me until Monday and if that strike isn't settled on Monday you can come and see me and look into it."[71]

Brigadier Hill monitored the situation and finally on 23 October decided to intervene. Hill was revered by the men. "Brigadier Hill was a tremendous officer," remembered Sergeant Flynn, "He was out every morning and did all the things he expected us to do. He had a smile all the time. I was certainly impressed with him."[72] Sergeant Anderson agreed. "I can hardly think of any general officer that the men could feel any affection for, except Hill," he added, "He is always up front, he has been wounded at least six times, he is totally without fear, and what I always imagine as a great leader, however you measure it."[73]

Hill ordered the entire Battalion to be assembled in the base auditorium. Upon Hill's arrival all officers and warrant officers were asked to leave. The men were then given a few minutes to present their concerns. The brigade commander then interjected, "Look, you are letting the whole party down." He then appealed to their sense of pride. "More importantly," he chided, "you are letting Canada down."[74] The meeting was short and to the point. Deep down, the paratroopers knew that the brigadier was right. He was a professional soldier and would not tolerate such nonsense. Hill ended the meeting abruptly. "Now," he emphatically asserted, "I am making it absolutely clear I am giving you an order, and you are going back to eat your lunch."[75] A few hours later, Brigadier Hill was informed that the Canadian paratroopers had done as they were told.

The following day, six paratroopers requested to meet with the brigadier. They identified themselves as the ring leaders and apologized for their behaviour. Hill was impressed by this show of character:

> I accepted their apologies and thanked them very much for coming in. I always loved those Canadians and that made me love them more and more. That couldn't have happened to any other battalion except a Canadian battalion. It was wonderful. Of course, really, that I had the grip on them to some extent was that I loved them, literally. If you love people you are commanding and, lead, they will always reciprocate.[76]

A Canadian Army investigation into the hunger strike concluded that a number of factors caused the protest. These were reported as:

(a)   The battalion was being reconstituted and that roughly two-thirds of the men were new since the operation in Normandy.

(b)   Most of the junior officers were new.

(c)   The former CO had not been a strict disciplinarian and the men had been getting away with a lot, though discipline as a whole was not bad.

(d)   The new CO was an exceptionally strict disciplinarian and in his enthusiasm had been punishing minor offences on a much too severe basis and in some respects had produced regulations, particularly concerning dress within the camp area, which were not entirely reasonable ones.

(e)   Many of the new junior officers have not grown to know their men as they should.

(f)   It appears that a number of the new men in the Battalion were among those at Camp Shilo, Canada, who staged a similar hunger strike successfully there some time earlier this year

Paratroops, as a whole, appear to be somewhat over-pampered and temperamental primadonnas, and they dislike going through the training process again after their operations in Normandy.[77]

No action was taken against the soldiers or instigators. Hill believed that the incident "had pretty well burnt itself out" and he felt it would be "unwise to exaggerate the importance of the whole matter by digging them out at this stage and making examples of them."[78] Part of the problem was also the rationale behind the protest. Although both Hill and Divisional Commander, General Richard Gale, expressed complete confidence in Nicklin, both were "satisfied that the main cause was the slightly excessive enthusiasm for perfection in disciplinary matters by the CO."[79]

Despite the belief shared by Hill and Gale that "the CO's appreciation of the disciplinary situation is cured," in the end, whereas the men had given in, Nicklin refused to change his rules.[80] "Major Eadie, the Battalion's Second in Command," remarked Sergeant Anderson, "told me after the war that on many occasions he asked Nicklin to back off on certain issues regarding discipline. But he refused to do so."[81]

With the hunger strike behind them, everything returned back to normal at Carter Barracks and the Battalion began its November training. In the end, the hunger strike did not seem to adversely affect the Battalion's later performance. Their record of action and accomplishments in the aftermath of the hunger strike were commendable. They distinguished themselves when they were rushed to Belgium to assist the Allied effort at stopping the Germans during their Christmas offensive in the Ardennes in December 1944, commonly called the "Battle of the Bulge." They also performed admirably in Holland in the aftermath of the German attack during one of the coldest winters on record. In addition, they demonstrated their professionalism and effectiveness during Operation Varsity, the airborne assault across the Rhine in March 1945 and the subsequent pursuit of the German forces across North West Europe. The Battalion ended the war in Wismar on the Baltic Sea, the only Canadian troops to link-up with the Russians.

Lieutenant-Colonel Nicklin, however, was killed in battle, on 24 March 1945, in the parachute assault during Operation Varsity. In response to rumours and supposition, the Canadian Army sent an investigative team to determine whether Nicklin's death was as a result of enemy action or *fragging*, to use a contemporary term. In the end, his death was attributed to enemy action. He had landed in a tree directly above an enemy machine-gun nest — he never had a chance. Ironically, normally Nicklin jumped in the middle of the stick so that he could have half of his headquarters on either side of him upon landing. However, for this operation he wanted to be the number one jumper so that he could lead his troops into battle.[82] That decision cost him his life.

On 30 September 1945, the 1 Canadian Parachute Battalion was officially disbanded. The nation's first airborne soldiers had earned a proud and remarkable reputation. Their legacy would become the standard of excellence that would challenge Canada's future paratroopers and imbue them with a special pride. The Battalion never failed to complete an assigned mission, nor did it ever lose or surrender an objective once taken. The Canadian paratroopers were among the first Allied soldiers to have landed in occupied Europe, the only Canadians to have participated in the "Battle of the Bulge" in the Ardennes, and by the end of the war had advanced deeper into Germany than any other Canadian unit. "The Battalion," wrote Field Marshal Sir Allan Brooke, chief of the imperial general staff, "played a vital part in the heavy fighting which followed their descent onto French soil in 6 June 1944, during the subsequent critical days and in the pursuit to the Seine. Finally, it played a great part in the lightening pursuit of the German Army right up the shores of the Baltic. It can indeed be proud of its record." Unquestionably, the paratroopers of 1 Canadian Parachute Battalion, as well as their supporting airborne organizations, the 1 Canadian Parachute Training Company/Battalion and the A-35 Canadian Parachute Training Centre, established, at great cost and personal sacrifice, the foundation of the Canadian airborne legacy.

In the end, the 1 Cdn Para Bn hunger strike provides interesting lessons and considerations. First, discipline and "grounding" of combat/operationally experienced troops is necessary to ensure they maintain their focus and continue to develop and hone the skills required for future operations. Second, soldiers, even those who are highly trained, professional, and combat experienced, will accept rigid discipline and high tempo training, but it must be seen as appropriate, fair, and reasonable. Although they may grumble and complain, as long as a commander's actions meet the above criteria, group disobedience is not likely to occur. However, if these expectations are not met, individuals inculcated with Western democratic values, who are products of Canadian society, can be expected to take the action that they deem necessary to address the injustices they feel they face.

This case study also highlights a number of challenges that commanders at various levels face. Initially, what role should junior leaders/commanders play in providing feedback to their superiors in regards to soldier discontent. How hard do subordinate commanders press their superior to "ease up." This is not an easy question. Of course it depends on the personalities of all concerned. Nonetheless, leaders have an obligation to their subordinates to represent their concerns; as well as an obligation to their superiors to keep them informed and provide an accurate account of affairs within the unit. However, the balance between appearing to be a whiner, or non-supportive of the chain of command and representing valid grievances is not always easy or clear. It is even more difficult if the commanding officer or superior refuses to accept criticism or comment.

The challenge for the commanding officer is no less straight-forward. Invariably, subordinates at all levels complain. It would seem that physical training, operational training, and discipline are always too difficult, too demanding, too time consuming, and so on. But the CO is responsible for the effectiveness and efficiency of the unit. Its overall operational effectiveness determines its success and inherently the survival of its members. So how much is too much? Getting this wrong is costly. Finding out too late is not an option.

Finally, challenges exist for a CO's superior as well. Inevitably rumours of discontent circulate. The difficulty is determining how much is valid and how much is simple grousing. Moreover, if the CO is achieving the overall effect his superior desires, should one interfere? What if the CO is implementing what he believes to be direction from his higher authority? How easy is it for a superior commander to recognize his influence, or whether it is being interpreted correctly?

In the case of 1 Cdn Para Bn, Hill's involvement is curious. Despite deep affection for "his Canadians," he believed they were a wild-spirited bunch who needed careful, constant, and discipline. As such, he was a big fan of Nicklin and even after the hunger strike, there is absolutely no evidence of Hill counselling the airborne CO to change his ways, which would seem to be tacit if not direct continuing support for Nicklin's style of leadership. But, then again, he never disciplined the instigators or ring leaders of the hunger strike either.

For these reasons, the 1 Cdn Para Bn hunger strike of 20–23 October 1944, provides an excellent case study of what can happen when good men are pushed too far. Surprisingly, it had no real consequence. No disciplinary action was taken and the CO seemingly refused to change his ways, though lack of time may have played a part because he was killed in action just five months later. The incident, however, has remained a bit of an embarrassment to the veterans. Nonetheless there are lessons that military leaders at all levels should consider.

NOTES

1. Library and Archives of Canada (henceforth LAC), Record Group (henceforth RG) 24, Series C-1, Vol. 21, Parachute Troops. Organization, Training 1941– 45, File HQS 8846–1, Memorandum, DND HQ MD No. 2, "Serial 1351 — 1st Parachute Battalion," 27 November 1942, Microfilm C-5278.

2. *Ibid.*, Vol. 12, File HQS 8846–1, Letter, Major-General H.F.G. Letson (Adjutant General), "1st Parachute Battalion — Serial 1351," Microfilm C-5278. As early as 29 July 1942, the DCGS declared that "the formation and individual training of the 1st Canadian Parachute Bn is an urgent matter and [I must] stress the importance of eliminating any delays in this regard." Canadian Airborne Forces Museum (henceforth CAFM), AB 1, Vol. 2, File 19, 1 Cdn Para Bn, Letter, DCGS to District Officers Commanding, "Canadian Parachute Battalion," 29 July 1942.

3. Draft letter, Air Chief Marshal C.F.A. Portal, Air Ministry to GHQ Home Forces, January 1942. Air Ministry: Army Cooperation Command: Registered Files. Airborne Forces Organization, February 1941–43. Public Records Office (PRO) AIR 39/26.

4. CAFM, AB 1, Vol. 6, File 21, 1 Cdn Para Bn, Major General R.N. Gale, Pamphlet — "To All Officers in the 6th Airborne Division," June 1943.

5. "Training Paratroops," *Canadian Army Training Memorandums*, No. 20, November 1942, 10.

6. Captain F.O. Miksche, *Paratroops — the history, organization and tactical use of airborne formations* (Faber and Faber Ltd, 1942), 133.

7. Directorate of Heritage and History (henceforth DHH), File 112.3M300 (D99), Memorandum, DMT to DCGS, "1st Canadian Parachute Battalion," 22 October 1942.

8. LAC, RG 24, Series C-1, Vol. 17, File HQS 8846–1, Letter, The Secretary DND (Army), "1st Canadian Parachute Battalion — Accounting of Personnel," 17 December 1942, Microfilm C-5277; *Ibid.*, Vol. 1, Memorandum, A.P. 3, "1st Canadian Parachute Bn — Documentation, Relinquishment of N.C.O. Appointment, 11 February 1943; and LAC, RG 24, Series C-1, File HQS 8846–8, No. 3, Letter, Military Attache Canadian Legation to the Secretary, Department of National Defence (Army), "Organization — 1st Canadian Parachute Battalion," 20 February 1943. File HQS 8846–8, Promotions 1 Cdn Para Bn, 1942–43, Microfilm C-8379.

9. LAC, RG 24, Series C-1, Vol. 17, File HQS 8846–1, Letter, The Secretary DND (Army), "1st Canadian Parachute Battalion — Accounting of Personnel," 17 December 1942, Microfilm C-5277; *Ibid.*, Vol. 1, Memorandum, A.P. 3, "1st Canadian Parachute Bn — Documentation, Relinquishment of N.C.O. Appointment, 11 February 1943; and LAC, RG 24, Series C-1, File HQS

8846–8, No. 3, Promotions 1 Cdn Para Bn, 1942–43, Letter, Military Attache Canadian Legation to the Secretary, Department of National Defence (Army), "Organization — 1st Canadian Parachute Battalion," 20 February 1943. Microfilm C-8379.

10. "Canada's Jumping Jacks!" *Khaki. The Army Bulletin*, Vol. 1, No. 22, 29 September 1943, 1.

11. 1 Cdn Para Bn Assn Archives, Letter, A.E. Moll, "Selection of Airborne Personnel," 52/Psychiatry/4/3 S.P.5. — 24 November 1943..

12. Moll was certain that the "A" candidates were clearly the best material. He was equally sure that the "E" personnel should not be considered. However, he conceded some uncertainty in regards to the 80 percent who fell into the grey area in between. But Moll and his staff decided that as long as the supply of volunteers remained strong they would continue to accept only the best. CAFM, Letter, 15 November 1985, from Dr. Bill McAndrew (DHH Historian) to Brigadier General E. Beno.

13. As of 10 July 1942, the initial physical requirements for paratroops were:

Alert, active, supple, with firm muscles and sound limbs: capable of development into aggressive individual fighter with great endurance.

Age: officers — not over 32 years of age for captains and lieutenants and not over 35 years for majors; other ranks (ORs) 18–32 inclusive.

Physically qualified as follows:

- Weight — maximum, not to exceed 185 pounds.
- Height — maximum, not to exceed 72 inches.
- Vision — Distant vision uncorrected must be 20/40 each eye.
- Feet — Greater than a non symptomatic 2nd degree pes planus to disqualify.
- Genito-urinary system — recent venereal disease to disqualify.
- Nervous system — evidence of highly labile nervous system to disqualify.
- Bones, joints and muscles — Lack of normal mobility in every joint, poor or unequally developed musculature, poor coordination, asthemic habitus [thin-muscle type], or lack of at least average athletic ability to disqualify.
- Medical History — History of painful arches, recurrent knees or ankle injuries, recent fracture, old fractures with deformity, pain or limitation

of motion, recurrent dislocation, recent severe
illness, operation or chronic disease to disqualify.

Other than listed above, the physical standards to be the same as
Army Standard "A.1."

DHH, File 171.009/D223, Letter, Adjutant-General to All District Officers
Commanding, "Parachute Battalion, Serial No. 1351," 10 July 1942. The
Army definition of "A.1." category was: "The man shall be able to see to shoot
or drive, and can undergo severe strain without defects of locomotion and with
only minor remediable disabilities. Age — between 22 and 32 years of age;
Height — usual heights — minimum 5'2," max 6'; Weight — minimum 125
1bs, maximum 196 lbs; Visual Standards — 20/40 both eyes without glasses.
Colour vision should be "defective safe;" Hearing W.V. — 10 ft. both ears,
i.e., a man standing with his back to the examiner and using both ears, must
be able to hear a forced whisper 10 feet away. Must have patent Eustachian
Tubes; Dental — Men must not drop with false teeth, consequently there must
be eight sound or reparable teeth (including two molars) in the upper jaw in
good functional opposition to corresponding teeth in lower jaw; Injuries of
limbs — it was agreed that men with old fractures of the lower limbs or spine,
however well recovered, were not suitable. Flat-feet not acceptable. Must have
full movements in all joints of lower limbs; Mental and intelligence standard:
It was agreed that men with alert minds are required for these duties and that
men with doubtful intelligence should be eliminated by an intelligence test."
LAC, RG 24, Series C-1, Vol. 15, File HQS 8846–1, Medical Standards for
Paratroops, Microfilm C-5277.

14. LAC, RG 24, Series C-1, Vol. 12, File HQS 8846–1, Letter, Adjutant General
to Commanders, "1st Parachute Battalion — Serial 1351," 2 October 1942,
Microfilm C-5277. There were those who were ineligible to volunteer for
the paratroops. They were: tradesmen who have completed trade training;
personnel under instruction in Army trade schools, technical schools or
vocational schools; and personnel earmarked for trades such as surveyors,
instrument mechanics, wireless mechanics, radio mechanics, electrician sigs
and fitters.

15. 1 Cdn Para Bn Assn Archives, Letter, Major A.E. Moll, "Selection of Airborne
Personnel," 52/Psychiatry/4/S.P.5. 24 November 1943, 3.

16. DHH, File 163.009 (D16), Memorandum, Colonel W. Line, "Selection of
Personnel — 1st Parachute Battalion," 23 December 1942; and LAC, RG 24,
Series C-1, Vol. 16, File HQS 8846–1, Microfilm C-5277.

17. Examiners reported that the chief non-physical causes for rejection were lack
of enthusiasm for parachute work, which often became evident once individuals
learned in more detail what they had volunteered for, and evidence of emotional
instability that was defined as:

   • Sociability: unfriendly, reclusive, lacking in social skills.

- Adjustment to army life: discontented, complaining.
- Occupational History: frequent changes, little responsibility or pay in relation to ability.
- School History: poor progress, truancy, bad conduct.
- Family History: home broken by death or divorce, foster parents, alcoholism, juvenile delinquency or crime, nervous disorders in relatives.
- Personal Health and History: tremors, sweating extremities, stammering, nightmares, pounding heart, cold sweats, dizzy or fainting spells, nail-biting, alcoholism, vague stomach or nervous ailments, fear of dark or high places, sex problems, drug addiction, juvenile delinquency or crime, frequent visits to Medical Inspection Room (MIR).

18. LAC, RG 24, Series C-1, Vol. 16, File HQS 8846–1, Memorandum, Colonel W. Line, "1st Parachute Bn. (Serial 1351), 26 December 1942, Microfilm C-5277. An independent assessment of 613 personnel appraisals provides additional detail. Of the cases examined, 322 of the 613, or 52.5 percent were accepted. The personnel assessments consulted were found primarily in LAC, RG 24, Series C-1, Vol. 19, File HQS 8846–1, Microfilm C-5277. They spanned the period September 1942 to early 1943. It became evident that the cases in January -March 1943 were less rigidly assessed then those in 1942. The major categories for rejection were nervousness or "tremulous hands for 29 percent;" "instability" accounting for 13 percent; "family background" (broken home, parental or spousal disagreement with joining paratroops, family health history) for 12 percent; and "lack of aggressiveness" for 11 percent. The remainder of the reasons were: health reasons — 10 percent; voluntary withdrawal — 9 percent; mentally slow — 7 percent; non-swimmer — 1 percent; poor military record — 2 percent; and other — approximately 6 percent.

19. LAC, RG 24, Series C-1, Vol. 24, File HQS 8846–1, Letter, Adjutant General to GOCs, "Selection of Personnel — Canadian Parachute Troops," 11 May 1943, Microfilm C-5277.

20. *Ibid.* Often, it took mere appearances to dash the hopes of a volunteer. "This soldier is young," assessed the CO, "slight in build and does not appear rugged enough to be a paratrooper." In the end, he had the last word — and his veto ended a candidate's career in the paratroops.

21. In January 1943 the medical criteria for screening were amended in response to feedback provided by the initial intake of volunteers and their success rates (italics indicate amendments):

- Alert, active, supple, with firm muscles and sound limbs: capable of development into aggressive individual fighter with *GREAT* endurance.
- Age: *18–32, both inclusive.* [In June 1943, the lower end was amended to 18-1/2.]
- Physically qualified as follows:

- o Weight — maximum, not to exceed *190* pounds.
- o Height — maximum, not to exceed 72 inches.
- o Vision — Distant vision uncorrected must be 20/40 each eye.
- o *Feet and Lower Limbs: Flat feet not acceptable. Better than average bone structure and muscular development of lower limbs.*
- o Genito-urinary system — recent venereal disease to disqualify.
- o Nervous system — evidence of highly labile nervous system to disqualify. *History of nervous complaints to disqualify.*
- o Bones, joints and muscles — Lack of normal mobility in every joint, poor or unequally developed musculature, poor coordination, asthemic habitus, or lack of *better than average* athletic ability to disqualify.
- o *Hearing: W.V.-10 ft. both ears, i.e., a man standing with his back to the examiner and using both ears must be able to hear a forced whisper 10 ft. away. Must have patent Eustachian Tubes.*
- o *Dental: Men must not drop with false teeth; consequently there must be eight sound or reparable teeth (including 2 molars) in the upper jaw, in good functional opposition to corresponding teeth in lower jaw.*
- Medical History — History of painful arches, recurrent knees or ankle injuries, recent fracture, old fractures with deformity, pain or limitation of motion, recurrent dislocation, recent severe illness, operation or chronic disease to disqualify *(unless recurring, properly healed fractures not to disqualify)*.
- *Mental and Intelligence Standard: It was agreed that men with alert minds are required for this type of training and that men with doubtful intelligence should be eliminated by intelligence test.*

Other than listed above, the physical standards to be the same as Army Standard "A.1."

It was also a reflection of the fact that as the war progressed the rigorous selection process became an impediment in reaching the necessary quotas. By May 1944, the criteria were severely relaxed. The new standards for "Parachutists (Operational)" were forgiving:

Physical

- PULHEMS: 1112111.
- Age: 18-1/2 — 32 years inclusive.
- Max Height 6'2", max wt. 220 lbs. A proper correlation of height and weight will be required.

- Teeth: must have a sufficient number of second teeth to masticate food reasonably well if dentures should be broken or lost.
- Must be in good physical condition. A history of part-icipation in rugged sports, or in a civilian occupation or hobby demanding sustained exertion, is desirable.

Other Qualifications

- Should be emotionally stable, well-motivated, self-reliant, and relatively aggressive.
- Must be General Service prior to despatch for paratroop training.
- Must have completed Basic Training.
- If non-English speaking, must be sufficiently bilingual to take all instruction in English.
- Must have at lest the equivalent of Gr. VI Education.
- Must be genuinely interested in paratroop training after having been thoroughly informed concerning the strenuous physical requirements and the emphasis on Infantry training.

But the loosening of the criterion was not enough. The director of personnel selection stressed to his examiners that a psychiatric examination was no longer required at the time of initial nomination. Furthermore, he reminded them that any personnel who met the minimum PULHEMS requirement and was otherwise suitable, would be eligible for paratroop service. In fact, Army examiners were prodded to ensure that whenever a suitable recruit was encountered they should be immediately briefed on paratroop service. PULHEMS stood for: P — physique; U — upper limbs; L — lower limbs; H — hearing; E — eyes; M — mental; S — stability. Soldiers were graded from 1 to 5 for each of these factors, 1 being fit for any military employment, 5 being fit for none. Major-General F.M. Richardson, *Fighting Spirit. A Study of Psychological Factors in War* (London: Leo Cooper, 1978), 165. See 1 Cdn Para Bn Assn Archives, "Physical Standards and Instructions for the Medical Examination of Serving Soldiers and Recruits for the Canadian Army — 1943,"; and LAC, RG 24, Series C-1, Vol. 19, File HQS 8846–1, "Medical Standards for Paratroops — All Ranks," 18 January 1943. 1 Cdn Para Bn Assn Archives, Letter, Adjutant General to GOCs, "Selection of Paratroops — Specifications General Instructions," 17 May 1944, Microfilm C-5277; 1 Cdn Para Bn Assn Archives, Letter, Director of Personnel Selection to All District Army Examiners, " Selection of Paratroops — Specifications General Instructions," 22 May 1944; DHH, File 163.009 (D16), Letter, Director of Personnel Selection to All District Army Examiners, " Selection of Paratroops," 2 March 1945; and DHH, File 112.21009 (D197), Folder 6, "A.35 Canadian Parachute T.C.," 19 November 1943. Sergeant R.F. Anderson stated that, based on his discussions with others, a minimum of 60–70 percent of volunteers failed the selection/training process. Interview with Bernd Horn, 11 June 1998. This is consistent with the recollection of other veterans.

22. *Ibid.*

23. "Training Paratroops," *CATM*, November 1942, No. 20, 10.

24. Cdn Para Bn Assn Archives, Lockyer, Mark, File 10–31, Robert Taylor, "Paratroop Van Eager to Be Tip of Army 'Dagger,'" *Toronto Daily Star*, 12 August 1942.

25. *Ibid.*

26. Cdn Para Bn Assn Archives, Firlotte, Robert, File 2–11, James C. Anderson, "Tough, Hard-as-Nails Paratroopers Arrive to Open Shilo School," 22 September 1942, 1; *Ibid.*, File 2–111, "Toughest in Canada's Army Back for Paratroop Course," *The Star*, 21 September 1942; and Ronald K Keith, "Sky Troops," *Maclean's*, 1 August 1943, 18–20 and 28. This is simply a representative sample. Virtually every article in newspapers nationwide used similar adjectives to describe Canada's "newest corps elite."

27. LAC, "Assembling Paratroopers At Calgary," *Globe and Mail*, Vol. 99, No. 28916, 18 August 1942, 13, Microfilm N-20035; and 1 Cdn Para Bn Assn Archives, Lockyer, Mark, File 10–3, Robert Taylor, "Paratroop Van Eager to Be Tip of Army 'Dagger,'" *Toronto Daily Star*, 12 August 1942.

28. LAC, "Assembling Paratroopers at Calgary," *Globe and Mail*, Vol. 99, No. 28916, 18 August 1942, 13, Microfilm N-20035.

29. LAC, James C. Anderson, "Canada's Paratroopers Don't Have Stage Fright," *Saturday Night*, No. 11, 12 December 1942, 11, Microfilm 56A.

30. Jean E. Portugal, *We Were There — The Army. A Record for Canada*, Vol. 2 of seven (Toronto: The Royal Canadian Institute, 1998), 944.

31. DHH, 1 Cdn Para Bn, File 145.4011 (D2), Letter Brigadier James Hill to the Honourable P.J. Montague, Cdn Military HQ, 9 April 1945.

32. *Ibid.*

33. Portugal, 943–44.

34. R.F. "Andy" Anderson, interview with Michel Wyczynski, 7 February 2002.

35. Harold Johnstone, *Johnny Kemp, DCM, His Story with the 1st Canadian Parachute Battalion, 1942–1945* (Nanaimo, BC: Private Printing, 2000), 17.

36. LAC, RG 24, Vol. 15299, 1 Cdn Para Bn War Diary, 11–24 September 1944. Battalion personnel boarded three trains on 11 September for Scotland, London and the Midlands. All personnel were ordered to return by 24 September 1944. September 1944.

37. Bradbrooke was transferred to a staff position in the Canadian Military Headquarters in London. Nicklin was promoted to the rank of acting lieutenant-colonel on 8 September 1944. LAC, RG 24, (2) Appointments — Promotions, Part II Orders, No. 37, 8 November 1944.

38. *Ibid.*, 26 September 1944.

39. 1 Cdn Para Bn Assn Archives, Evaluation Report, Nicklin, Major Jevon, Albert. Prepared by Brigadier S.J.L. Hill, 17 February 1945.

40. 1 Cdn Para Bn Assn Archives, Brian Nolan Fonds, Brigadier James Hill file, Brigadier James Hill, interview with Brian Nolan, 33–34.

41. 1 Cdn Para Bn Assn Archives, Anderson, R.F., File 11–2, Sgt R.F. Anderson, "From the Rhine to the Baltic."

42. 1 Cdn Para Bn Assn Archives, Joe Ryan, "Old Manager Pays Tribute to Nicklin," newspaper clipping, unknown date or publication.

43. *Ibid.*, 41.

44. *Ibid.*, Brigadier James Hill's speaking notes, November 1993, 22.

45. 1 Cdn Para Bn Assn Archives, Brian Nolan Fonds, Brigadier James Hill file, Interview of Brigadier Hill by Brian Nolan, 37.

46. John Feduck, interview with Michel Wyczynski, August 2002.

47. Harry Reid, interview with Michel Wyczynski, 24 January 2002.

48. R.F. Anderson, interview with Michel Wyczynski, 7 February 2002.

49. Roland Larose, interview with Michel Wyczynski, 10 January 2002.

50. Richard Hilborn, interview with Michel Wyczynski, 14 December 2002.

51. Alf Tucker, interview with Michel Wyczynski, 12 December 2001.

52. Richard Hilborn, interview with Bernd Horn, 27 April 2001.

53. Richard Creelman, interview with Michel Wyczynski, 27 December 2001.

54. Roland Larose, interview with Michel Wyczynski, 10 January 2002.

55. *Ibid.*

56. Ernie Jeans, interview with Michel Wyczynski, 22 January 2002.

57. Sergeant Andy Anderson, letter to author, 4 August 2005.

58. LAC, RG 24, Vol. 15299, 1 Cdn Para Bn, War Diary, October, 20 October 1944. Another version of this story that has been circulating throughout the years inferred that the men were protesting the quality of the food. Most paratroopers agreed that the food wasn't the best, however, it was not the cause of this hunger strike. This is borne out by the official report on the incident. See Memo, LAC, RG 24, War Diaries, Series C-3, Vol. 15,299, Cdn Para Bn, Cdn Liaison Section, 3 Para Bde, "Refusal to Eat," 23 October 1944. Appendix 18, 1 February 1944-January 1945.

59. LAC, RG 24, Vol. 12,721, File 2011, Para Battalion, Memo, "1 Cdn Para Bn," AAG to MAG, 24 October 1944.

60. *Ibid.*

61. DHH, Biography File, John Madden, Telephone interview with Jan de Vries, 8 December 2002. John Madden, 1st Canadian Parachute Battalion. Taped recollections, non-dated, 21.

62. *Ibid.*, John Madden.

63. Jan de Vries, telephone interview with Michel Wyczynski, 8 December 2002.

64. DHH, Biography File, John Madden, 21.

65. *Ibid.*

66. William E. Jenkins, interview with Michel Wyczynski, 19 December 2001.

67. Many of the veterans that were interviewed confirmed that they did not go hungry during this period. They were provided with rations from other units, or had built up their own personal food stashes or had light lunches or snacks at the NAFFI.

68. LAC, RG 24, Vol. 12,721, File 2011, Para Battalion, "Hunger Strike Story," DDPR to MGA, 24 October 1944.

69. LAC, RG 24, Vol. 12,721, File 2011, Para Battalion, Memo, "1 Cdn Para Bn," AAG to MGA, 24 October 1944.

70. LAC, RG 24, Vol. 12,721, File 2011, Para Battalion, Memo, "Hunger Strike Story," DDPR to MGA, 24 October 1944.

71. Quoted in Brian Nolan, *Airborne* (Toronto: Lester Publishing, 1995), 123–24.

72. Sergeant Denis Flynn, Interview with Bernd Horn, 18 April 2001; During the German breakthrough at the village of Bréville on 11 June 1944, Brigadier Hill gathered up a reserve force and personally led the counterattack to re-establish the Allied line. Major Murray Macleod stated: "The counter-attack went in led by Brig Hill, and his personal bravery was said to do a lot for the stiffened stand

of all the troops there. His apparent lack of concern for the hail of bullets and shellfire about him as he walked back and forth between the defensive positions gave heart and the position held." Portugal, 963.

73. 1 Cdn Para Bn Assn Archives, File 11–2, Anderson, R.F., Sgt R.F. Anderson, "From the Rhine to the Baltic.". He also stated: "In line of march and in any attack, you could always find the Brigadier at your elbow. His courage and leadership inspired our men, and to this day, he holds 'his Canadians' as special in his heart and prayers."

74. Brigadier James Hill, interview with Brian Nolan, April 25, 1994, 40. 1 Cdn Para Bn Assn Archives, Brian Nolan Fonds. Brigadier James Hill file. The War Diary notes, "General training in the morning and a lecture from Brigadier Hill who promised that there would be an investigation into all grievances."

75. *Ibid.*

76. *Ibid.*

77. LAC, RG 24, Vol. 12,721, File 2011, Para Battalion, Memo, "1 Cdn Para Bn," AAG to MGA, 24 October 1944; and LAC, RG 24, Series C-3, Vol. 15,299, War Diaries, 1 Cdn Para Bn, Memo, Cdn Liaison Section, 3 Para Bde, "Refusal to Eat," 23 October 1944. Appendix 18, February 1944-January 1945.

78. LAC, RG 24, Vol. 12,721, File 2011, Para Battalion, Memo, "1 Cdn Para Bn," AAG to MGA, 24 October 1944.

79. *Ibid.*

80. *Ibid.*

81. R.F. "Andy" Anderson, interview with Michel Wyczynski, 7 February 2001.

82. Alf Tucker, interview with Bernd Horn, 23 June 2001. Tucker, the signals officer, was normally the number one jumper. Interestingly, a newspaper article at the time stated, "the men who loved him as seldom a leader has been loved" was completely off the mark. The hunger strike, or more accurately, the causes for it, drove an irreparable wedge between the soldiers and Nicklin. Many veterans to this day still voice their criticism of their former CO. See 1 Cdn Para Bn Assn Archives, Joe Ryan, "Old Manager Pays Tribute to Nicklin," newspaper clipping, unknown date of publication.

2

THE REVOLT OF THE CANADIAN GENERALS, 1944: THE CASE FOR THE PROSECUTION

Richard J. Walker

> *The present situation could not continue. The national training scheme was pure window dressing and worthless, and the government must know it ... Unless his views on this matter of organization were accepted He [Crerar] would have seriously to consider his position ... By the way he talked he is alert for a case upon which to bring this matter to the test. He wants a showdown. The essence of his talk was: "Soldiers are soldiers — they know about war. Politicians are politicians — they have their undeniable uses but planning and carrying on war is not one of them. Politicians in times like these, must clear out of the way of the men who know what must be done and how to do it.*

> — Chief of the General Staff,
> Major-General H.D.G. Crerar, as noted in conversation with
> Grant Dexter, September 13, 1940[1]

FROM THE ARRIVAL OF GENERAL HUTTON in 1898 to 10 June 1940, the evolving Canadian Army struggled to achieve two objectives; to establish a societal contract with a government that would accept the Army as an autonomous military profession, and to force that government to cede to the Army a pride of place within Canadian society.

Though these objectives had been denied in the past, the nature of the military disaster that faced Canada in 1940 created a strategic context within which Army leadership could now achieve both.

The fall of France and the German threat to Britain was a shock to the defenders of the empire. One cannot overstate the impact of this event on Canada's political leadership and how quickly it transformed government thought and action. As a writer in *Maclean's* observed on 1 July 1940:

> The quietest war capital in Christendom has become a cauldron of excitement; disillusioned, shocked from its complacency. Day by day, as the shadow of the Swastika lengthens across the English Channel, old shibboleths, old comfortable delusions, go overboard. Where once reigned smugness, self-satisfaction, there is now a wholesome fear; with it fortunately, more of war stir and vigour.[2]

From a civil-army perspective, this transformation created a new working relationship. In governmental terms, the fear that civilization was on a precipice looking into the abyss of defeat created a realization that there was now no burden too great or price too high in assuring victory. This new reality meant that, although government maintained ultimate responsibility for the war effort, it had to devolve authority in a variety of directions. C.D. Howe's domination of the Department of Munitions and Supply and his network of "dollar-a-year men" was a dramatic example of the degree to which this delegation of authority was aimed at getting the job done. The Army received the same license, to which was added the necessity of secrecy.

The Army responded in two ways. The first was a professional expression of military expertise in providing advice to the government and on building an Army to meet the need, or as J.L. Ralston phrased it, serve as a "dagger at the heart of Berlin."[3]

The second was for Army leadership to seize the opportunity to affirm its autonomy and to advance its agenda. Army leadership believed the objectives of winning the war and building a national Army were complementary. Therefore, though one can claim that the Army was opportunistic in exploiting the advantages that devolved authority presented, within the context of the times, Army leadership viewed their initiatives as simply shedding the now irrelevant political constraints of the past and affirming their societal contract in the defence of the state.

The challenge of representing both sides in this civil-army duality fairly or rendering full justice to both is to comprehend the strategic context in which initiatives and decisions were taken and to appreciate that though both elements were sincere in advancing separate agendas towards a common goal, they were not freed from the political constraints of the past. For example, the Army had to grow in size to meet its operational requirement. That growth also complemented its corporate need for a substantial standing force that would logically take its post-war pride of place within Canadian society.

Conversely, the government principle of proportionality was based on a "win the war only" constraint. This was not a Robert Borden style of wartime government. Though the cabinet was forced to relinquish control of certain functions, the control of personnel and its historic link to the threat of wartime conscription was to be the exception to the rule.

Though Army leadership can be seen as logical, sincere, and well intentioned, its link to personnel put it immediately at odds with the cabinet on how to proceed. Since the Army's needs lay beyond just winning the war, a conflict pitting civil expectations against those of the Army was inevitable. The actions of the participants in this conflict can only be judiciously assessed within the strategic context of the period. In spite of Prime Minister Mackenzie King's limited liability strategy, Army leadership had fixed designs on expanding to a full national commitment well before the fall of France in June 1940.

Part One

Though General McNaughton assured King that he was content with a single division, he immediately conferred with the War Office on how best to grow to meet both Army and War Office expectations of a full national commitment. King's statement that the government "intends to see that a second division is sent overseas as soon as may be possible," triggered both staff planning and a warning from King that the Canadian Government had not approved the formation of a Canadian Corps and that:

> Your discussions with War Office should proceed only on basis of offers and commitments actually and expressly made by Canadian Government. Discussions regarding any further commitments

involve major matters of policy and ought to be initiated by Governments.[4]

This is not to suggest that cabinet was opposed to the corps concept in principle. To the contrary, it had political, morale, and fiscal merit. On 2 April 1940, the cabinet debated the issue of authorizing a Canadian Corps of two divisions and ancillary units.

Ironically, it was J.L. Ralston, minister of finance, who argued with Norman Rogers, minister of militia, against a corps on the grounds of need and expense. As he pointed out, he could buy 10 destroyers "with what we would be paying for equipment for ancillary services."[5] Yet King supported Rogers's pragmatism that he could maintain a modest corps of two divisions, "whereas if this were not done we might have a third division on our hands. More than that he felt it might not be possible to raise voluntarily."[6] King appreciated the politics of national morale and was sympathetic to troop morale:

> The Canadian public would wish to have a Corps, that the pride of the nation would demand that; also, that we owed it to McNaughton and the men who were prepared to give their lives, to let them have, in the way of formation, what they most desired. The people would expect us to be prepared to incur additional expense if need be for this national expression to our forces overseas.[7]

Norman Rogers intended to pre-empt the call for a third division when he confronted McNaughton and his Canadian military headquarters staff on 22 April 1940. In dismissing McNaughton's claims, "he had at no time pressed for the formation of a Canadian Corps, though he thought that a corps was probably the smallest organization through which the Canadian forces in the field could be effectively administered and fought." Rogers made cabinet concerns over voluntary recruiting crystal clear.[8] He warned "that the question of organizing a 3rd Canadian Division might prove to be undesirable, as the limiting factor was the maximum force Canada could maintain in the field on the basis of voluntary recruiting."[9] The Army experts concurred with their minister "that a balanced Canadian corps of two divisions and ancillary troops might prove to be the maximum which Canada could maintain by voluntary recruiting in a war of long duration."[10] Similarly, McNaughton assured Rogers, "from a military point of view it was much more effective to have a smaller formation promptly maintained to full establishment than a larger formation under strength by reason of a failure to have reinforcements immediately available."[11] Ironically, it was Major-General H.D.G. Crerar, the future architect of the "Big Army," who served as secretary to the consensus "that before any action was taken to form a 3rd Canadian Division the factors of existing commitments on manpower in the land and in the air forces, the requirements of industry, etc., would need to be carefully weighed."[12] Based on his clear direction to McNaughton to structure a Canadian Corps of only two divisions, Rogers advised cabinet that a "Canadian Corps could be formed with little additional cost to present military commitments."[13]

This was Norman Rogers at his best. He dominated all proceedings, and the cabinet imperatives of limited liability and voluntary service punctuated all discussion.

His death in June 1940 was a watershed in civil-army relations as King at first felt fortunate to be able to turn to Colonel James Layton Ralston for relief. King committed to his diary that he would nominate Ralston as prime minister "tomorrow" if he had to and "without a moment's hesitation. He is the most unselfish man I have met."[14] Ralston's savaging of the 1939 Department of National Defence (DND) estimates served to reassure King of his suitability as a bulwark against Army expansion. King's sense of security now rested on the compatibility and the fitness of two men, Ralston and General McNaughton.

The strategic context inspired a new generation of ambitious and innovative officers prepared to make a clean break with the past. Major-General H.D.G. Crerar matched this profile and he moved quickly to secure a shift of power away from Ottawa and into his own hands. In his capacity as Senior Staff Officer, Canadian Military Headquarters (CMHQ) in London, Crerar was able to get Rogers to agree in principle "that the General Officer Commanding [GOC] Canadian Forces in the theatre of war should have the final word in recommendations to the Department of National Defence regarding operations, organizations, appointments, and military business generally."[15]

This realignment not only made the chief of the general staff (CGS) and his Army Council a secondary appendage, but it also gave McNaughton direct access to the minister. This was the direct link of expert military advice that in peacetime had always been denied.

Crerar wrote personally to Rogers on 10 June 1940. Though grieved by Rogers's death on that same day, Crerar wasted no time in attaching a copy of his letter to Rogers to a secret and unauthorized letter to the new minister, Ralston, on 17 June 1940:

> It is evident that your primary and immediate advisers on C.A.S.F. [Canadian Army Special Force] operations and requirements in this theatre of operations must be G.O.C. Canadian Forces and the senior officers of this Headquarters.
>
> Distasteful or not, in the nature of things it cannot be the Members of the Defence Council in Ottawa whom you can regard as your "experts" in such matters. Time, space and the rapidity of events prevent this function from being performed by these officers, no matter how able and keen they may be. Believe me, these remarks are purely objective.
>
> Request for authority to do this or that from this Headquarters, if within the bounds of Departmental power, should have priority of consideration over other matters, and if not deemed within the power of immediate approval by the several members of the Defence Council, should be at once referred to you.
>
> Also, if further explanation or clarification is needed, this should be requested from here within hours (not days or weeks, as at present). Hitler just does not wait on anybody and delay in obtaining authority for action which I know [sic] to be sound is imperilling our war effort in this part of the world. Frankly, unless the Minister and the overseas portion of the Department of National Defence (which this Headquarters, in fact, is) are in intimate and sensitive touch with one another, misfortune, or worse, lies ahead. But if you trust me, provide me with the means to act, legitimately and with effective speed.[16]

The wartime relationship between Canada's soldiers and statesmen turned on this single letter and on the shift of real power from Ottawa to McNaughton's headquarters. In tolerating this act of insubordination, Ralston sent the signal that the CGS now served as a factotum for the overseas commander, and the minister as his cabinet agent.

Within the month, Crerar became Ralston's new CGS and it was clear that he would brook no civilian or military interference in the Army mission. As McNaughton stressed in his letter of 7 August 1940, "I am firmly convinced that from this position you will be able to reorient and redirect Canada's war effort onto the proper lines and we here will have that understanding support which is necessary if our efforts are to be worthwhile." [17]

The Allied military reversals of 1940 played into the hands of the conscriptionists. In light of the emergency and the National Resources Mobilization Act (NRMA) men legislated for compulsory military training, it was reasonable for Army leadership to link both as cause and effect. Crerar understood that he had been returned to Canada "in order to undertake constructive action in respect to the development of its land forces." Within days of his appointment as CGS, he articulated both the Army's wartime and post-war expectations in his seminal work, "Observations on Canadian Requirements in Respect to the Army." His immediate focus on the Army's post-war structure, for example, helps to explain the continuity of the Army's motives and initiatives during the war. As early as July 1940, therefore, corporate structure became the critical ingredient in laying the groundwork for both the wartime and post-war armies:

> While the urgency of the moment forces us to utilize a Militia system and organization which looks to the past, rather than to the present and to the future, we must not lose a moment in undertaking a thorough analysis of Canada's probable post-war military requirements and in planning a defence organization which will produce our future Service needs with a maximum of efficiency and a minimum of expense. Unless this is done it will be impossible to ensure the progressive adoption of policies which will advance us in the desired direction. And we must be clear in our minds as to that destination, for the future Militia organization should be settled before demobilization of the present C.A.S.F. commences.[18]

Crerar's concern for the post-war future for the Army was made clear in his memorandum to Ralston of 3 September: "It is also necessary to look further to the future, and plan, still on the basis of compulsory training and service, the outlines of the Canadian Army we shall need for our security after the war." If conscription for the defence of Canada remained a firm policy carried over into a postwar environment then "it will be possible to formulate a reasoned plan for the organization of a Canadian Army." Yet he warned the minister, "If, however, the defence of this country is to be dependent in large part on the voluntary or "go-if-you-please' system, then it will be impossible to plan and develop the future defence of Canada in an ordered and economical way, and an uninformed public opinion pressing for 'action' may force our war effort into unproductive channels."[19]

Consolidating Army power and future expansion were also the themes of Crerar's letters to McNaughton. His inference of continued growth was clear: "shortly after the Canadian Corps is formed, and a going concern, your elevation to Army Command would, I believe, give similar satisfaction to Canada, if that is of interest to you."[20]

Crerar understood that his role in Army expansion was "to obtain acceptance of a national policy which would lead towards a balanced and progressive development of the maximum military effort we could produce."[21] His pursuit of this "maximum" military effort, while resisting the restrictions of proportionality and voluntarism, was basic to his belief in the inevitability of a showdown with government:

> On my arrival I found the Government happily committed to compulsory training and, indeed, service but with a very superficial scheme for training [NRMA] and utilizing the manpower so called up. I stressed to the Minister that this scheme must be regarded as purely an interim measure and that in the course of the next few months the Government would need to face the entire problem of the future organization of military service for Canada. (Memo submitted) I believe that it will bring matters to a head.[22]

Part Two

The McNaughton Clique was now in control of the department, and a few months after his appointment as CGS, Major-General

H.D.G. Crerar felt compelled to vent to the journalist Grant Dexter that he regarded the existent war organization "as most inefficient and unsatisfactory." In his view, it had been largely "botched" because of an NRMA scheme that was militarily very costly and completely useless. "We now had in Canada a direct conflict in policy — compulsion at home, voluntary enlistment for overseas. These were mutually destructive." He made it clear that there must be a showdown on this policy within a few months: "Either the policy must be abandoned as wasteful and useless or we must adopt a real policy of compulsory training and call men and really make soldiers out of them."[23] It was clear to Grant Dexter that Army leadership anticipated a showdown over conscription, and that, in Crerar's inference of having "to consider his position," resignation in wartime was a possible tactic in that confrontation.[24]

The Army's commitment to conscription never deviated for a moment. The difference was that a pliable minister and restructured Army council combined to give Crerar the opportunity to reshape government policy. This fact became clear to Grant Dexter when he and Ralston discussed the growing criticism of the Army's recruiting campaign. When Dexter suggested that the most certain effect of this campaign was to hasten the conscription crisis, Ralston rationalized, "he was minister but must act upon the advice of his staff of professional soldiers. Being a civilian, he could not set aside his advisers simply because he disagreed with what they said. They knew; he did not know. As a fact, Crerar refused to give him any advice which would enable the present trainees to be usefully used."[25] As Dexter noted, Ralston had been skilfully cornered:

> He is perpetually the amateur civilian dealing with the expert. If he overrules the expert on points of major policy, he must assume that he is better qualified to decide. This is a very difficult position for a Minister to take. If he accepts the advice — suspending his own judgement because he lacks military training — he has ceased to be minister, the generals are in charge and Cabinet control has been forfeited. He tends, and rapidly, to become the Cabinet representative of the general staff.[26]

Throughout Ralston's conversation with Dexter, he left little doubt that his deference to Army advice now equated to Army control of the Department. Curiously, Ralston made no effort to conceal his hatred of Crerar, while displaying an inability to deal with him.[27] In Grant Dexter's analysis, "his problem is that wherever you turn to escape from the conscription crisis — calling more trainees, releasing men now on coast defence for overseas by breaking up units — the general staff refuse to advise and thus turn him back in on the trouble. The last thing he [Ralston] said was very interesting. 'You know,' he said, 'the war committee of the cabinet could decide to do any of these things, and I would simply have to tell Crerar that these were my orders as well as his."[28] It became obvious to the lay East Block observer that civil-army relations within the DND were dysfunctional.

Though cabinet suspicions loomed, Ralston remained blind to the scale or detail of Crerar's grand design. Apart from the armoured and infantry divisions, there were hundreds of ancillary units that consisted of administrative and supply bases, reinforcement depots, and corps troops of many descriptions and functions. As Victor Sifton, master general of ordnance (MGO), suspected, "Crerar is steadily increasing the establishment without Ralston getting on to it. He adds corps troops, special columns of one kind or another- always boosting the establishment. McNaughton is doing the same thing in Britain." Sifton simply could not make Ralston see "that the gang are putting it over him by increasing establishments surreptitiously."[29] More to the point, Sifton revealed that there was a plot afoot to double the size of the Army:

> The plotters are McNaughton and Crerar with Price Montague as a consenting party. Both staffs of course are in it (McNaughton's and Crerar's). These people want 2 Corps of 3 divisions each plus 1 armoured division and 1 tank brigade, each. There you have 8 divisions and 2 brigades. As we know, the [Ogdensburg] defence agreements bind us to maintain 2 divisions at home. You might raise these by conscription, of course, but the voluntary end would be nearly 9 divisions instead of nearly 5 as at present.[30]

The plan had been hatched in early 1941. Emboldened by the government's policy to extend the NRMA service from four months to an indefinite period, the general staff cemented their view that the "trainees" were for all practical purposes reserves for overseas service and that the imposition of conscription was inevitable. Crerar asserted his confidence in this eventuality in a letter to McNaughton:

> The decision to retain the "trainees" in the Service for an indefinite period after they have finished their four months in the Training Centres has been well received. I believe that a high proportion of these 21-year olds will volunteer for overseas and those which do not will be introduced into Coast Defence and Internal Security Battalions. All these rather represent several bites at the cherry, the cherry being Conscription for service anywhere. On the other hand, this progressive process is educating the public to what may well be inevitable and I believe that if this comes to pass, the final stage will be taken with a minimum of fuss by all concerned.[31]

Victor Sifton's short career as MGO provides invaluable insights into the impending civil-military confrontation over personnel. Sifton was the voice in the wilderness in his warnings of the fiddling of personnel statistics and the unauthorized packing of ancillary units and Army establishments that laid the secret foundation for the "Big Army." He warned the minister as early as 1 October 1941 of the personnel fiddle.

As a lieutenant-colonel himself, he empathized with those who pined for conscription but warned Ralston that this panacea would imperil national unity and was unconscionable as a department goal. "It appears to me that we are permitting ourselves to drift into a position with respect to manpower for the armed services which may bring about a very serious political crisis in the next six to eight months if recruiting fails to keep up … To carry out the proposals [recruiting] that I suggest would require a degree of enthusiastic driving force on the part of all senior officers in this country which hitherto has not made its appearance."[32] He warned that in the last war recruiting dropped off sharply once full employment was reached and that full employment was now imminent.[33] One month later his warning materialized as the *Vancouver Sun* declared "Canada Nearing End of Manpower" and the Dominion Bureau of Statistics revealed that with the Armed Forces' need for personnel at 14,000 men per month and the expansion of industry at 28,000 per month, "our unemployed have disappeared." The only major source of personnel left was, "those who have never worked and married women."[34]

Ralston agreed with everything Sifton put forward and confessed that he "knew for an absolute certainty that King will never waver or yield in his opposition to conscription. He knows King well and there can be no mistaking his attitude. He simply will not discuss conscription. When the time of breakdown comes, our man [Ralston] will quit and seek other war work."[35] This was a strange self-indictment of a cabinet minister who was prepared to foment an anticipated civil-army "breakdown." This helps to explain why Ralston ignored the failed recruiting campaign in the summer of 1941 and the charge by his own executive assistant, Colonel Magee that Crerar sabotaged recruiting across the country. As the consensus of Dexter's informants made clear:

> Crerar's vanity is such that he must get control of everything and having done so, he smothers all new ideas, won't cooperate. He has killed off half a dozen good ideas re: helping recruiting. Too much trouble. Interfere with the training of the army, etc. Ordinarily he could do this with impunity. But the consequences this time are so grave that the lads are taking their complaints to Ralston. Col. Magee [executive assistant to the minister] has tried to resign because the general staff vetoes every suggestion he makes and he feels he is wasting his time … Victor [Sifton] has gone to town against Crerar twice in the past week. Ralston *hates* [sic] Crerar: despises the general staff from top to bottom … It is a mess.[36]

Part Three

The product of Crerar's labours came to light in the form of the *Army Programme 1942–43* on 18 November 1941, as Army designs on this maximum strength now collided with King's principle of proportionality. While drawing on Army-controlled personnel studies and the now evident downturn in recruiting, Crerar revamped the backfill rationale for growth as originally sold to Rogers and the cabinet since 1940. Ralston pitched his version to cabinet along the same line:

It is true that in recent weeks the numbers of voluntary enlistments have been below the totals which the Adjutant General has called on Military Districts to produce. On the other hand ... we have opportunity and reason to induct into Army formations and establishments in Canada some 40,000 "Home Service" personnel, called up under the provisions of the NRMA Act. This action will release close to an equivalent number of "General Service" [GS] volunteers, now in Home Formations and establishments, for use in the mobilization of new units for overseas, or for reinforcements.[37]

Once again, the intention to "induct" the NRMA men to backfill Home Defence duties so as to "release" GS men as reinforcements was the ramp for Crerar's expansion of the Canadian Army overseas. It did not appear incongruous to Ralston that Crerar, who had refused to "advise" on just such a course of action repeatedly up to that point in 1941, now assured him that "induction" was the cornerstone for this unprecedented expansion to full Army status.

The imprecision and arguably the insincerity of this understanding cannot be overstated. It was not a promise to induct, so much as a statement of an "opportunity and reason" to induct. Based on past practice, there was no reason to believe that the Army would voluntarily adopt this course of action in lieu of conscription. Or, in the spirit of R. MacGregor Dawson's observation, this was a general staff "who so far as it is known, had never at any time in any place advocated a small army if there was any conceivable chance of obtaining a large one."[38] It would be an insult to the intelligence of these officers to suggest that this stratagem was anything less than a brilliant stroke in refuting the criticism that expansion would raise the issue of conscription for overseas service.

Both Crerar and his replacement as CGS, General Kenneth Stuart, continued to use this induction rationale in their questionable assurances that the Big Army was somehow compatible with the voluntary system.

The War Committee discussions of early December 1941 featured three conflicting agendas. The first was King's view that Army expansion was dependent on an Army guarantee that it would never lead to overseas conscription and his assertion that he would never lead a conscriptionist government if it should. The second was that Ralston was prepared to support the Army's attempts to comply with the first, but that "he could not guarantee that conscription might not be necessary, that he always kept himself free to advocate it, if it became necessary, though he would try his utmost to get the men without conscription."[39] The third was that if directly challenged by the prime minister, Army leadership was prepared to offer a politically acceptable response while giving no indication of their ulterior motive in doing so.

During the Committee meeting of 3 December, King quizzed the new chief of the general staff, Major-General Kenneth Stuart, and his adjutant general, Major-General B.W. Browne: "Could the Army Staff give assurances that their proposed programme could be carried out by the voluntary method; further, was this programme being presented as an effective maximum Army contribution on Canada's part, or would it be subject to increases later on?"[40] In responding to the prime minister's challenge, Stuart stated disingenuously, "that the programme had been worked out so as to fit into the Government policy of voluntary enlistment for overseas. That is what the Staff had aimed at, had worked for, and what he believed would be accomplished in that way."[41]

Stuart's confidence reassured King that the Army was sensitive to "the difficulty that has been the only real one which presents itself, namely that of resorting to conscription to get the numbers required."[42] The veracity of that assurance must be viewed within the context of general staff actions and motives. To contemplate that Stuart was not playing politics on behalf of the Army is to demean the intelligence of the Army's senior leadership. The Army's belief in the inviolability of a voluntary system in war, Crerar's claim that the NRMA programme had been "botched," the belief that conscription at home and voluntary enlistment for overseas were "mutually destructive," and that a civil-army showdown over Crerar's "cherry of conscription for service anywhere" was inevitable — all underpinned Stuart's obfuscation.

King accepted Stuart's assurance and his claim that this represented "a complete organization for fighting purposes" and "the last demand."[43] It was implied to be a complete Army or, as Stuart described to the *Free Press*, "the kind of army a soldier dreams of commanding, hard-hitting, beautifully balanced, incredibly powerful."[44] Hardhitting it would prove to be, but its "beautifully balanced" structure proved illusory. As E.L.M. Burns pointed out in his seminal work, *Manpower in the Canadian Army, 1939 — 1945,*

LIEUTENANT-GENERAL KENNETH STUART IN ENGLAND
DURING THE SECOND WORLD WAR.
(Canadian War Museum AN 19890296 005)

the fighting arms in the Canadian Army made up only 34.2 percent of the Army while the "Headquarters and overhead" elements constituted 28.2 percent, as compared to the 11.6 percent within the American Army.[45] At this ratio, to keep one Canadian division in the field required 93,150 soldiers as compared to 71,000 for an American division and 84,300 for a comparable British division. Therefore, to maintain a mere five divisions overseas required, by November 1944, a staggering 465,750 soldiers, or 110,750 more than the Americans and 44,250 more than the British.[46]

Part Four

Cabinet exasperation centred on its inability to modify the Army's war plans. In King's view, the "trouble was with Ralston and the general staff. Ralston stood up for the generals, fought the Cabinet in their behalf ... The true ambition of our general staff was to build an army in Britain not particularly for the defence of Britain but to be the spearhead of the attack on Germany ... all our generals were concerned about was to be in at the kill. I have talked to him again and again. I have asked not once but many times why he does not tell the generals what we, the cabinet, think instead of continually telling us what the generals think. Generals are almost invariably wrong."[47] Held in check by Ralston's threatened resignation, King let matters drift with the health of the voluntary recruiting system serving as his barometer for crisis.

The generals were correct in assuming that most public opinion at the time of Bill 80 supported the implied commitment to compulsion if "needed." The voluntary system was expected to continue as an imposed political requirement, but in the Army's viewpoint Bill 80 validated their assumption of unlimited conscription. Brigadier James Mess, the deputy adjutant general and director of recruiting, made this key assumption evident in his resignation in December 1944. His press release to the *Montreal Gazette* confirmed Army leadership's pre-crisis expectations:

> He and 75 percent of the 5,000 civilian recruiting advisors had from the start shared strong views favouring total conscription, he says. But they had carried on because the Army had to have men, because the stated requirements were being met by the voluntary system by which, under previous government policy, the men could be raised. But this support had been given, he insists, on the distinct understanding that should the voluntary method fail

to supply the Army's needs, the reserve of draftees at home would be promptly available for overseas service through invocation of full-unlimited conscription.[48]

Part Five

Military historians have focused on the shortage of infantry reinforcements as the root cause of the November 1944 conscription crisis. They identify an error in computing the infantry battle casualty rate, as confirmed in Major-General E.L.M. Burns's *Manpower in the Canadian Army 1939–1945*, as the glitch in staff planning that exonerates Army leadership from any duplicity in forcing conscription onto an unwilling government. A different line of inquiry reveals that the "miscalculation" of casualty rates may have been the least relevant of the author's findings. Burns determined that the actual shortage of infantryman averaged only 5 percent and that it was not the critical factor that Army apologists attempted to portray. On the contrary, the Burns analysis reveals an engorged and unbalanced structure "which was over organized; it had too many high formations and administrative headquarters for the number of fighting troops." This was Crerar's purpose-built Army and, in his "most important lesson," Burns linked Bill 80 and the Army's expansion to the Army's belief that the government would eventually be compelled to do the right thing. As Burns concluded, "We have seen by the statistics assembled in this book that the major waste of manpower was not in the casualties incurred in battle, but in extravagant use of men for administrative purposes, born of the idea that 'there are plenty more where the first lot came from.'"[49] The key point was that, in the spirit of Robert Borden's support of the Canadian Corps, when Ralston and the Army of 1944 demanded that the Canadian Army be kept up to full strength, they meant the same full administratively bloated strength that Burns deprecated. The political issue was about saving the Army's current and post-war structure, and not about reinforcements.

In consequence and unbeknownst to the minister, his Army was attempting to finesse a political time bomb. General Stuart's role and General Crerar's influence in this intrigue is enigmatic. During Ralston's visit to Britain in April 1944, he met with both Crerar and Stuart. His deputy minister, Lieutenant-Colonel G.S. Currie, kept minutes of those meetings. On 7 April General Crerar stated to the minister that he wanted the "postwar policy as to the strength of the Canadian Army decided on as soon as possible."

In pressing the issue Crerar explained, "We must realize that there are a large number of our men who have been trained only as purely professional soldiers, not tradesmen in civil life, and they want to know what they can expect of the Army." He also pressed the minister: "Are we to have compulsory service and what is to be the strength of the [post-war] standing Canadian Army?" Crerar made his feelings apparent as he produced a telegram from Ottawa asking him to make a public statement favouring a volunteer Army in order to aid recruiting. He declared that it was "impossible for him to make any such statement at this time. It would be of danger because it might be considered as taking sides on a political question. His men would vote almost solidly for conscription."[50]

King therefore, hosted the Quebec Conference of September 1944 secure in the false confidence that, as reported by T.A. Crerar, "casualties have been fantastically light and the Army is embarrassed with an over supply of men."[51] Yet, what King did not know was that, based on Crerar's 1940 direction, the Army had fixed on a plan for its post-war structure and role since 1943. It was no coincidence that in the midst of an imminent crisis over infantry reinforcements, General Murchie, the new CGS, was signing off on Plan-G, a Top Secret blueprint that defined the Army's post-war role and secured a standing peacetime Army based on a system of universal military training. Similarly, the text of Plan-G laid bare the Army's contempt for voluntary service and debunks any claim of Army impartiality during the crisis of November 1944. If the generals could not get King to impose unlimited conscription during a wartime crisis, then the Army's post-war assumptions and their corporate survival, as reflected in Plan-G, were threatened.

Two issues dominated Murchie's submission of the full contents of Plan-G to Ralston in September 1944. The first was the repudiation of the voluntary system. As the document made clear:

> In two wars, Canada has found it necessary to adopt a system of compulsory military service to provide adequate manpower. The voluntary system in wartime cannot therefore produce the nation's maximum war effort. The voluntary system is haphazard and costly in method, uncertain in result, incapable of yielding a steady stream of reinforcements, inequitable in

incidence and disturbing to industry. In future wars, it may again be anticipated that some form of compulsory military service will be required, thereby giving effect to the obligation imposed by the Militia Act upon all male citizens of 18 to 60 to serve in the defence of Canada.[52]

The second was General Murchie's spur to Ralston, "May I point out also the degree of urgency which now exists in regard to arriving at a decision as to the adoption of a system of universal military training." Timing was now everything, as Ralston was being asked to support a policy of post-war conscription before the urgency of the imminent crisis dissipated. As Murchie made clear, "Our requirements under such a system in staffs, equipment and accommodation can best be found, and with the least confusion and disruption, from amongst our presently serving personnel (who may wish to continue their Army career) before demobilization, and from our existing properties before disposal."[53] The immediacy of the conscription issue was being leveraged to secure the Army's post-war future.

Part Six

The cabinet had no inkling of the maelstrom that was about to sweep over them. The opening salvo of what C.P. Stacey called "one of the most violent and bitter public controversies in Canadian political history" began on 19 September 1944, with the *Globe and Mail's* partisan support for Connie Smythe's claim that Canadian divisions were being bleed to death due to a lack of infantry reinforcements.[54] Similarly, long-service leave became a serious issue in troop and home front morale. The deputy adjutant general advised the minister on 14 October 1944 that any possibility of a leave program was effectively "blocked by the reinforcement situation," and General Murchie referred to the "insistent and justifiable demands of the soldiers serving overseas for leave" and the fact that 11,000 soldiers in Italy had four years overseas service.[55] That was the message that the minister received from the troops when he arrived in Italy on his first leg of his well-documented fact-finding mission on 26 September 1944.

Although deeply moved by the soldiers' appeal for leave, Ralston was deluged in controversy over Premier George Drew's inflammatory speeches about government insensitivity to the plight of the soldier and he took Drew's charge that he [Ralston] was "the man who bears the heaviest load [of guilt] for he has betrayed that trust," as a slight to his personal honour.[56] The official CMHQ rebuttal showed clearly that there was no deficiency of reinforcements on paper, that the Army was at 94.91 percent of War Establishment (WE), and that the Infantry was at 90.77 percent of WE, with an additional 10.80 percent of WE in reinforcements behind them. The undisputed problems at the front had been caused by the sheer inability to get reinforcements forward. As the deputy chief of the general staff confirmed, "It was simply the gigantic problem of actually moving reinforcements from the U.K. to the front Line. The front moved hundreds of miles in a few weeks. But the enemy held all the ports outside of Normandy and the railways were not working. There have been times when the units at the front have been short of men simply because, with all the energy in the world, the reinforcements could not be moved forward any faster. Young regimental officers fighting the enemy are prone to overlook such difficulties ... and to criticize accordingly."[57] Clarity was only achieved after the fact by General E.W. Samson's March 1945 report that pointed out that an actual shortage of infantry reinforcements was only felt at the front in North-West Europe "during the period August to early October 1944." Or, as C.P. Stacey confirms, the "actual shortage *in units* had been overcome before the decision was taken to send NRMA soldiers overseas."[58]

These were the essential questions discussed by Stuart and Ralston during their dinner meeting of 12 October 1944. After dinner, Colonel H.A. Dyde, Ralston's military secretary, walked home with General Stuart and "we had a chat about the reinforcement situation. I felt that when I left General Stuart he had not fully made up his mind what recommendation he was going to make."[59] The next day, 13 October, Stuart presented Ralston with a memorandum in which he reversed himself on casualty rates, indicating the situation to be nearer 60,000 than 40,000 in losses and that he was nearing the bottom of the barrel for francophone infantry units. Yet his theme in this memorandum was that "the question of leave can no longer be delayed." In a detailed argument Stuart pressed issues of morale, the link between no leave policy and reinforcements, and spoke for the men: "They just can not understand why they should keep going in to battle practically every day and living constantly in the greatest danger and discomfort when trained replacements are available in Canada and living in comparative safety and luxury."[60] What the minister did not know was that throughout September,

General Stuart and General Crerar were already preparing to put a leave scheme into operation. This helps to explain why Stuart emphasized the leave issue as a critical determinant in defining the "need" for compulsion. It was also significant that the plan was to be presented for ministerial approval on 1 November, but was lost to the Army because of Ralston's dismissal.[61] The calculus was simple: no conscripts, no leave program.

The entire crisis now turned on the fact that Ralston accepted Stuart's claim of an imminent shortage without any challenge to Stuart's projected numbers. Ralston clearly felt compelled to honour the promise that he made to the soldiers: "He reiterated that if the military commanders were not satisfied with the reinforcement situation, then the government was prepared to give the matter of dispatching NRMA personnel overseas the most careful consideration."[62] In Ralston's view, General Stuart "was not satisfied," be the issue leave, morale, reinforcements, or equality of sacrifice.

Ralston stunned cabinet on 19 October with his disclosure of Stuart's projected infantry shortfall of 15,000 men. Though the projection was for early 1945, Ralston demanded that because of the Army's administrative requirement for transport, the cabinet remedy the situation within 60 days. A standoff ensued as all government proposals to address the reinforcement issue were parried by the Army, and where all roads intentionally led to the only acceptable military option, of converting the terms of service of NRMA personal. As General Stuart made clear in his letter to Ralston of 19 October, "It is apparent, of course, that I am leading up to a recommendation that the future effective maintenance of our Canadian Forces in two theatres requires that additional personnel be made available from Canada for service overseas. Actually such is my belief today."[63] Army leadership had now declared that the need for unlimited conscription had been realized. Although Stuart's memorandum of 19 October is well known, his memorandum of 30 October, in which he cites many errors in his earlier projections, was of great significance: "I stated that our casualties in 21 Army Group have been at an intense rate continuously. A careful subsequent analysis of our casualties shows that this statement is not correct. Our casualties since "D" day have been above normal but under the intense rate."[64] In spite of this error, Stuart did not adjust his stand that the reinforcement pool must remain at the intense rate projection.

In his formal "Appreciation of the Situation," the Chief of the General Staff, General Murchie, provided the government with a limited series of alternatives. All of them, not surprisingly, led either to a reduction in the effectiveness of the Canadian Army, or would materially affect the contribution to the Canadian war effort or a resultant negative effect on morale. The CGS dug in his heels and "based on purely military considerations the adoption of para 7. c. [Option for NRMA compulsion] would in my opinion meet the requirement ... both as to numbers and without disruption of the organization and fighting efficiency of the Canadian Army."[65]

Perhaps the most significant element in this chain of events was that General Murchie discussed his alternatives with Ralston before his presentation to the Cabinet War Committee. During their 23 October meeting, the CGS suggested two possible courses of action to Ralston and "stated a number of weighty objections to either of these courses; but he pointed out that adoption of either of them was a matter of government policy" and by inference not military necessity. Ralston generally agreed with Murchie's objections but added, "I considered further that, when trained NRMA men were available, Canada's duty at this crucial period of the war was to support our men in the line; that our obligation to them and to ourselves and to our Allies was not to relax, but to go on with the task to help shorten the war." In this critical admission, Ralston had the opportunity to avert the crisis but instead abrogated his ministerial responsibility "for a matter of government policy," and in doing so encouraged Army leadership to harden their position of no compromise with civil authority.[66]

At the end of the day, the cabinet issue was not about accounting but about how to deal with the Army's stonewalling. Though Norman Robertson, Arnold Heeney, and others came back with numerous options, such as financial inducements, to meet the problem of reinforcements, neither Stuart nor Ralston would entertain any alternative to unlimited conscription.[67] Or, as King acknowledged, "The truth of the matter is that the Defence people want the NRMA men forced to go overseas without further consideration."[68] With calculated stoicism Stuart and Army leadership bided their time, knowing that time was something that King did not have. Ralston's dismissal from cabinet on 1 November 1944 was as decisive and as dramatic a performance as King had ever given. At the critical moment of decision, King produced one of Ralston's previous letters of resignation, which he held in abeyance until he was now forced to accept it. Though much distressed in having to offend Ralston, this was an act of statecraft that could have no other result. "I cannot forget that he was prepared to have me and the government destroyed politically." Such was the consensus of Liberal Party opinion, that after the fact Ralston received only one telegram of commiseration.[69]

With equal assertion, King then poached the recently retired General McNaughton from the Conservative camp, appointed him Ralston's successor, and counselled him on the inviolability of his definition of "conscription if necessary":

> General, let me make perfectly clear what I mean about the need for conscription. I have always used it in reference to the winning of the war, not in reference to keeping the Army formations up to strength. I would not want to be understood as considering conscription as necessary in any other sense but if it were necessary to win the war, I would not hesitate to put it in force.[70]

McNaughton now declared himself in full agreement with his new chief, and recommended both the immediate sacking of Stuart and Murchie as being untrustworthy, and a major shake-up of the officers of the Army Headquarters.

Part Seven

The rapidly unfolding events of the first 22 days of November not only triggered an unprecedented crisis in Canadian political history but also sealed the fate of the post-war Canadian Army. King's innate ability to manage crises and the source of his cunning leadership lay in the application of two unusual principles. The first can be expressed as the "Homuth Principle," as identified by Karl K. Homuth in his House of Commons (House) analysis, "The Prime Minister has always been adroit in his leadership of the Liberal Party. He has never stepped into any place yet without leaving both front and back doors open so that there would always be a way of escape."[71] The second can be expressed as the complementary "Pickersgill Principle," as observed by King's secretary, Jack Pickersgill, "Mackenzie King genuinely believed and frequently said that the real secret of political leadership was more in what was prevented than what was accomplished."[72] It was upon these defensive principles that King relied in his political management of

Army leadership and his calculated efforts to save the nation from the threat of a conscription crisis.

As King played for time, McNaughton fared less well. Once he had revenged himself on Ralston and sacked Stuart, it was left to his vanity to mask his true predicament. He was an anachronism who could no longer relate to the public or to his younger generation of officers. As the adjutant general, Major-General Henry Letson, reflected later in life, "I shall go to my grave wondering at the unbelievable arrogance of Andy in thinking that he could solve a problem which so many able men had attempted to do without avail."[73] Although his public appeals for the "maintenance of our long traditions of voluntary service" stalled, McNaughton's blue ribbon "Special Cabinet Committee on Army Enlistments for General Service" was rapidly organized, enthusiastically launching its manifesto on 6 November 1944. This Top Secret cabinet document had a compound aim: "we want reinforcements and unity." This impressive collection of initiatives was wholly dependent on two critical variables: that there would be sufficient time to execute this innovative program; and that Army leadership would support inducements that promised a "new deal" for the NRMA men. The Army, as the document directed, "should be told that this was top priority and should be asked to submit a programme for Cabinet backing." Similarly, the committee erred in its belief that the "reputation of General McNaughton is the biggest weapon we have."

Yet the committee was not so naïve as to realize that the Army was inherently resistant to the program. "No doubt many officers believe that the NRMA should be sent overseas. Their loyal sympathetic support should be sought." Inevitably, the Committee's goals and the supporting text of King's nationally broadcast "Race of Noble Warriors" speech of 8 November 1944 ran counter to the Army's desire to have the government capitulate on the conscription issue. To support this initiative was to bail out a Liberal administration bent on reneging on a perceived promise and responsibility.

Should King's effort fail and the government fall as a logical result, the Tories were waiting in the wings to carry through the Army's agenda.[74]

General Officer Commanding Pacific Command, Major-General Pearkes, now became the willing catalyst in a fateful sequence of events. It is little known that his corps commander, Lieutenant-General Crerar, sacked Pearkes in May 1942 for errors in judgment. In his confidential report, Crerar wrote: "Although he reaches decisions quickly, he is inclined to do so without adequate consideration to the full result.

I do not therefore hold that his judgment on larger issues is to be relied upon."[75] Playing to this weakness, Pearkes encouraged an impromptu press conference of 20 November as the *Vancouver Province* reported, "General Pearkes told the assembled officers that they had a duty to the public to inform it of the situation. He declared that he had no objection to the officers stating their ideas of the reaction of the NRMA recruits to the appeals of the prime minister and the minister of national defence."[76] When the *Globe and Mail* picked up the story a day later it turned into a national press firestorm. The officers held none of their scepticism back and their candid criticism of government policy created the real impression of an Army defying its own government. Their public "message" was that the men would only serve if conscripted. The national reaction to the boldness of the Army "messenger" was electric.

King, though he held a tenuous grip on cabinet unity, felt confident enough to launch a surprise recall of Parliament for 22 November. The plan was Machiavellian in construct. King was content with the deadline for McNaughton's latest recruiting campaign, the end of November, and he remained determined to do nothing to interfere with a justifiable need for reinforcements. The endgame was that if there was to be conscription, be it limited or unlimited, it simply could not happen on his watch nor could the Liberal Party be tainted in the process. King's aim was to protect the party and, through its social agenda, protect the interests and unity of the country. The sequencing of his plan was highly calculated. He would go to the House and seek a vote of confidence in the administration. Should he be defeated, any replacement government would face disaster in imposing full conscription. They would be forced to hold a general election and "would have to either adopt our social policy or repudiate it. If they repudiate it, we would certainly win. Even if they adopt it, the country would have more faith in myself to carry it out than they would in any other leader."[77]

The harsh counter-scenario came in the form of McNaughton lecturing his cabinet colleagues on the implications of a martial imposition of conscription. Ironically, the soldiers who would be expected to maintain peace, order, and good government would be for the most part NRMA men. They would find themselves in the untenable position of having to collect, press into service, or arrest those of like ilk. McNaughton expressed his fear of "situations that might arise with the possibility of bloodshed. Once that sort of thing started it might spread like a prairie fire throughout the country."[78] He added, ominously, that he felt there was a real conspiracy in the department itself not to have the voluntary system work. He believed that it could still work but "instead of helping, everything possible was being done from different sources to enforce conscription"[79] In this siege mentality, the Pearkes news conference story that broke with the CBC News broadcast of 21 November simply confirmed to King a pattern of military resistance:

> It is quite apparent that there is a conspiracy there [Vancouver].One after the other has been coming out and saying that the N.R.M.A. men were just waiting for the Government to do its duty and send them overseas. That looks like the Army defying the civil power. These men in uniform have no right to speak in ways which will turn the people against the civil power.[80]

Events moved quickly as the Army appeared to align itself to the Tory agenda and the defeat of the King government. Such was the highly charged mood on 21 November, as King prepared to face the House the next day. Unbeknownst to the prime minister, Brigadier R.A. MacFarlane, officer commanding Military District 10, tendered his resignation to McNaughton that day in protest against government policy. Inexplicably, McNaughton reveals neither record of having acknowledged receipt of this critical development on 21 November, nor any explanation why he did not warn King.

Part Eight

Still unaware of MacFarlane's resignation, King entered the House on the morning of 22 November ready to face the Tories to his front and the coterie of cabinet plotters to his rear. Confident in his mastery of the "Homuth Principle," King felt secure in facing the House with one door blocked by the cabinet dissidents but his escape through the vote of confidence still available. King was preparing to execute his "Pickersgill" avoidance strategy, whereby the destruction of the Liberal Party would be neatly averted and the genuine need for reinforcements addressed, albeit at someone else's political expense.

Though C.G. Power had earlier alluded, in conversation with King, to "some of the Army taking matters into their own hands" and having a sort of "Curragh Incident" over the reinforcement question, the thought that the Army would overtly resist cabinet policy, intervene

PRIME MINISTER WILLIAM LYON MACKENZIE KING VOTES IN THE
CONSCRIPTION PLEBISCITE, OTTAWA, ONTARIO, 1942.
(Department of National Defence, Library and Archives Canada C 37127)

in politics, or appeal directly to the public was never considered by King's strategists in any of their prior policy sessions.[81]

There is no denying that Brigadier MacFarlane's resignation on 21 November was purposely timed for best effect on the opening of Parliament. It was not only an unprecedented public act of a wartime resignation in protest to civil authority, but the tenor of his press statement of 24 November spoke volumes about the motivation underlying the actions of the military members of Army Council on 22 November.

Brigadier MacFarlane made it clear that reinforcements had never been the issue and that unlimited conscription was the real issue. He declared that most of the Army leadership was opposed to government policy on both the voluntary system and on any qualified Order in Council that reflected less than unlimited conscription for overseas service. The principle of equality of sacrifice was prominent in his declaration: "over-all conscription is necessary as the only fair way to ensure the necessary reinforcements for the Canadian Army overseas." He went on to confirm that "if a poll of Army officers were taken across Canada you would find 99 percent of them would consider overall conscription the only way to handle an army."[82] He could have added that it was the only way to save the future of the Canadian Army.

MacFarlane's claim that he "could not conscientiously do his job as a soldier under the existing system" gives credence to the long-smouldering desire for unlimited conscription as identified earlier by Brigadier James Mess, deputy adjutant general and director of recruiting. The Army Council had, for example, recalled Brigadier Mess from a European visit during the final days of the crisis. His bomber flight back to Canada had been delayed by weather and he was therefore not available to join his Army Council colleagues for their collective action against the minister on 22 November. His equally high profile resignation of 29 November, confirmed King's suspicion that the Army's true aim had never been the provision of emergency reinforcements. In his press release, Brigadier Mess declared that he had resigned in protest of the government's policy of limited conscription as being simply "inadequate ... and not good enough."[83]

As the deputy adjutant general "C" at National Defence Headquarters (NDHQ) and director of recruiting, Mess was responsible for the recruiting campaign that McNaughton claimed had not been given a fair trial. As an integral military member of

Army Council, Brigadier Mess was well positioned to advance his strong support for conscription. His press release also made clear that his colleagues were not focused on the simple provision of reinforcements but in securing the Army's future well-being.

With the agreed civil-army deadline for the final recruiting campaign set for the end of November, King's recall of Parliament for 22 November caught the conscriptionist forces off-balance. The military members of Army Council quickly realized that the surprise recall of Parliament now made the results of the recruiting campaign superfluous. As General Murchie later described Pearkes's antics to Angus Macdonald, "the generals only exercised their right to express their opinion. Obviously, their intention was to embarrass the government into acquiescing to their demand for conscription, a dubious proposition even in peacetime." With the end of November deadline now immaterial, the military members of Army Council were forced to act precipitously. In conversation with King's biographer, R. MacGregor Dawson, General Hugh Young, quarter-master-general, pleaded guilty to the Army Council's rejection of the recruiting campaign in favour of putting direct pressure on McNaughton and King.

Their final memorandum to McNaughton had been precisely timed to impact on the proceedings of Parliament on 22 November. Young's explanation for the Army Council having turned on its civilian masters was grounded in their collective frustration that "nothing was happening." He kept saying, "Nothing was being done ... no results."[84]

Similarly, Army Council was fully aware of the structural imbalances within the overseas Army. General Walford, adjutant general, identified as early as March 1944 that the Army was all out of proportion and he recommended that the structure be altered.

He admitted to Dawson that the crisis could have been averted, as the civil element had maintained throughout, if action had been taken on his recommendations. A case in point was the adjutant general's 27 May 1944, recommendation that the 8,500 fully trained GS soldiers, in the range of 18 years and 6 months and simply biding their time in Canada waiting to turn 19 be "authorized service in an operational area." The recommendation died as the Army Council meeting of 8 June 1944, directed the adjutant general to study the entire question of the minimum suitable age for operations and to prepare a recommendation for the minister.[85] Therefore, those same unemployed 8,500 soldiers were accounted for in the October tally within the 67,000 as being underage for service. General Walford also acknowledged that the "PULHEMS" factor for "stability," for example, was far too strictly applied: "if a man got damp palms he was downgraded, he would not do in battle.... 40 percent of the men who passed physically were turned down on stability." Similarly, "all Allies (and Germans) were in the same box re: reinforcements and all had made the same re-adjustments: U.S. turned a large number of divisions into reinforcement drafts when they left the U.S. [sic] British did the same."[86]

Yet, since General Murchie and the military members saw their role as a subordinate agency serving the needs of the overseas Army, there was simply no desire to avoid a civil-army showdown. It was all part of General Crerar's "bites at the cherry — the cherry being conscription for service anywhere." Crerar predicted that the Army's "educating the public" would make the process of confrontation or conversion "inevitable" and that "the final stage will be taken with a minimum of fuss by all concerned." He was being proved correct, as the Army's power to influence Canadian policy had never been as potent as at that moment. The demand for unlimited conscription was now endorsed by the Tories and their Committee of 200, a frustrated public, the individual soldier at the front, and a fractured cabinet balancing on the razor edge of capitulation. All that appeared needed was a well-timed nudge to tilt King's administration into either doing its duty or facing defeat. If Army leadership hesitated King's exposed flank would be lost, the war ended, and the Army's post-war ambitions cashiered.

This well-timed nudge came in the form of an unsolicited telephone call and subsequent visit by the military members of the Army Council to McNaughton on the morning of 22 November. The question of what was said, how it was expressed, and how received by the minister has been shrouded in a secrecy that has masked its historical significance. R. MacGregor Dawson's 1953 interview notes of his discussions with the key players provide clarity only if the answer to those questions can be appreciated contextually.

As General Hugh Young confirmed, they informed the minister, "they would not assume responsibility for continuing in their jobs unless reinforcements were sent overseas."[87] Although no explicit threat of mass resignation was made to McNaughton, as identified in the statements of generals Murchie, Walford, Gibson, Young, and the minister himself, the option had been candidly discussed among the military members.

"Young had the definite impression that they were all prepared to stand by their memo to that extent, if necessary;" most certainly, "it was considered." General Hugh Young made it clear that "McNaughton did take the memo as an ultimatum," and that he was genuinely shaken by the encounter; "they apparently had given him no warning whatsoever." When General Young's story is woven through the testimony of his colleagues, a consensus on the potential for mass resignation clearly emerges. General Walford, for example, confirmed, "They thought there was a chance that McNaughton might fire them." This helps to explain why they waited as a group in the Woods Building until midnight, when, the story is told, one of their number rose and said "I'm going home. If they want to fire me, they can fire me just as well in bed." When asked what would have happened had McNaughton fired his council, General Young admitted "that there might have been resignations all across Canada."[88]

On the morning of 22 November, King believed all was in hand and that he remained in control of events. He was well aware that his cabinet conspirators, now six in number (Macdonald, Ilsley, Howe, Gibson, Mulock, and T.A. Crerar), had decided on mass resignation. King accounted for almost every contingency and he was confident that the longer-term interests of his Party (Liberals) and the nation were secure. He never wavered in his determination to go "right through" on the voluntary principle. He had no doubt that the country would support him if he had the benefit of a unified cabinet. Despite cabinet dissension, he still had his one escape door left open to him. He might lose power temporarily, but with the conscriptionists falling victim to their own short-term success, his quick return to power would be unsullied by conscription and his social platform would survive intact.

King's meticulous planning was torn asunder with McNaughton's phone call. There are partial versions of that conversation available, but the text of what King heard and his interpretation of McNaughton's tone were the critical elements in King's split-second analysis. McNaughton had also believed himself in control of events until 21 November, when Brigadier MacFarlane's resignation appears to have stunned him into silent paralysis. General Murchie's telephone call and the unsolicited visitation from his generals bearing their ultimatum were clearly unsettling. When King took the receiver he was likely overpowered by McNaughton's sense of urgency. McNaughton's own cryptic record of the call sets the tone of imminent crisis: "MacF resign. Military end disintegrating." The gist of the message was that "the Chief of the General Staff and the Adjutant-General were now convinced that the voluntary methods of recruiting could no longer be effective. There had been incidents on the West Coast and in Quebec. One officer had resigned over the issue and, if other senior officers did the same, military control would disintegrate and finally disappear."[89] This message to King was presented as an ultimatum.

King instantly recognized the situation that faced him. The Army had reneged on the November deadline of the campaign. Because of King's perceived vulnerability, the Army now discriminated between the needs of the State, the welfare of the Army, and the correct direction of Government policy. This ultimatum was designed to shift government policy to the Army's advantage. It was by definition direct military intervention in politics, that intervention taking the form of corporate blackmail with the implied threat being political ruin. Apologists who misrepresent Canada's wartime generals as being politically inept and duty-bound plodders do them a great disservice. The military members of Army Council knew exactly what they were doing and why. As General Walford acknowledged, "they knew that if one of them resigned he might bring down the government and they were conscious of their responsibility."[90] This reality was not lost on King. Therefore, should they all resign, the resulting disintegration would ensure the government's fall in disgrace and chaos, the consequences of which, both international and domestic, were too catastrophic to contemplate. The unasked question remains, "conscious of their responsibility" to whom? In this political gamble, the military members of Army Council were prepared to sacrifice themselves in the act of political intervention. In their view, the needs of the state and the needs of the Army had finally coalesced. King's immediate priority was to regain control of the situation. This was the Pickersgill Principle incarnate-"prevention and not accomplishment." First, there would be no *volte-face* on conscription. He would, on the other hand, make a measured concession as a preliminary move in suppressing each of these revolts, one at a time. The epiphany that lifted "an enormous burden" from King's mind was not that he now had the Army to scapegoat his policy reversal, but that he had during that day devised a winning strategy to turn the flank of both his attackers. Genuinely believing in the magnitude of the threat posed by the ultimatum, King called in St. Laurent and briefed him in detail. As King later described to Grant Dexter, "St. Laurent insisted that there must be no question of the supremacy of the civil power. The military must be resisted ... After some difficulty, St. Laurent came round to the point that the civil supremacy must be maintained, if necessary by the pretence of agreeing with the military. Between them they worked out the formula of conscription for 16,000 ... McNaughton was told not to report to cabinet the military revolt but to make his recommendation along the lines agreed to."[91]

In suppressing each revolt in sequence, King made reinforcements the single issue that all factions were compelled to support. King's instrument was a one-time draft of 16,000 emergency reinforcements provided by an Order in Council not unlike the amended terms of NRMA service previously used in Order in Council P.C. 5011, of 18 June 1943, for the Aleutian Island and Kiska campaigns. It was the application of the new P.C. 8891 that offered the greatest room for manoeuvre.

McNaughton's role in King's "pretence of agreeing with the military" became a curious blend of personal vanity and *realpolitik*. He was ordered to keep the matter secret and to fix the Army in place, while King dealt with the Tory opposition and his cabinet conspirators. Accordingly, McNaughton met with his full Army Council of both civilian and military members on the morning of 23 November. His short address not only served King's intent but also created the self-serving myth that his generals had not ambushed McNaughton. The cover story, as reflected in the minutes, that he had actively sought their official advice, which they tendered in a constitutional manner, went a long way in salvaging his reputation. This rationalization appeared to be in the best interests of both parties. With the civilian members of Army Council having no foreknowledge of events and the military members in attendance knowing the background to be patently untrue.[92]

This sanitized version of events was a relief to all present but it said nothing about any further drafts of "extended service." It was the realization of having been duped that drove Brigadier James Mess to his highly public resignation of 29 November and his claim that King had reneged on his promise to the Army of unlimited conscription.

On the political front, King appealed for party loyalty and focused his stratagem on the sole issue of reinforcements. He deftly avoided any hint of unlimited conscription in his vote of confidence challenge to the House: "It is not the question of conscription; it is the question of whether the present Government should continue to conduct Canada's war effort, or whether the direction of that effort should be handed over at this stage of the war to another administration."[93] Playing on the uncertainty of all Liberal members, but particularly in an attempt to quiet the fears of his Quebec caucus, King dramatically turned his back to the opposition, looked his colleagues in the eye, and, in conjuring up the spectre of Laurier's commitment to national unity, took his mentor's near sacred text as his own:

> If there is anything to which I have devoted my political life, it is to try to promote unity, harmony and amity between the diverse elements of this country. My friends can desert me, they can remove their confidence from me, they can withdraw the trust they have placed in my hands, but never shall I deviate from that line of policy. Whatever may be the consequences, whether loss of prestige, loss of popularity, or loss of power, I feel that I am in the right, and I know that a time will come when every man will render me full justice on that score.[94]

The high drama worked to perfection. By holding the core of his Quebec ministers, King neutered the opposition, stifled cabinet dissent, and crushed the Army's gamble. There would be no conscription, then or in the Army's post-war future. Ironically, the Army's corporate demise was embedded in Laurier's eloquence as King declared "That a time will come when every man will render me full justice on that score."

King's triumph was complete. As he confided to his diary of 7 December, "I shall never forget the last hours of the sitting. The intense silence of the House while I was speaking. The power that I was able to put into my utterances and the readiness with which words came. The ovation and the greetings at the close, all of this on top of having been obliged to take a course which was quite opposite of what I had believed would be necessary up until the moment the officers of the Department of Defence made it pretty clear that the military machine might disintegrate entirely and the Government itself dissolve unless I took the step I did."[95]

Conclusion

The well-documented cases of the NRMA "mutiny" at Terrace, B.C. and other incidents across the country fuelled King's fears. "Here was exactly what McNaughton had told cabinet would happen if we had to resort to conscription. The officers had lied by saying that the men were ready to go and were anxious to go but wanted to be ordered by the Government." McNaughton confessed to King that as in the Terrace incident, if troops "began to resist he had not the soldiers or the men to enforce law and order. And that the Department of Defence had nothing prepared in the way of plans to meet this contingency and by calling out the Militia in aid of the Civil Power, whom he thought could be trusted to do their entire duty, but it was a matter of trust."

King had every reason to believe that McNaughton's "prairie firestorm" was possible: "Here indeed would be a state of anarchy, not merely in the philosophical sense of no government existing, but as well in the actual sense of civil strife. One can only pray to God that we may be spared anything of the kind. I believe we will, but if we are it will be because of the belief that the people of Quebec still have in myself and now also in McNaughton. It makes clear that had I not taken the course I did, and the Government passed into the hands of conscriptionists, that a measure of civil war would have been inevitable."[96] This appeared to King to have been proven in fact as 2,000 of the first 5,000 NRMA conscripts deserted by 5 January and more than three-quarters of the first 10,000 had followed suit by March, when only about 2,500 of the total actually reached operational units.[97]

King neither forgave nor forgot, and retribution was swift. The first to go was McNaughton. Though King remained loyal to McNaughton and supported him through his Grey North election defeat, St. Laurent sensed him more the military leader than the civilian manager and he expressed the fear that when directed to cut the Army he would resist. When McNaughton began counselling King about keeping the goodwill of the Army and "also keeping it to a considerable size," the bonds of loyalty evaporated and McNaughton was let go with dignity.[98] King, on the other hand, held his generals in open contempt. The chiefs of the services were summarily banished from the Cabinet War Committee sessions as of 13 December 1944, at which time King noted with satisfaction "the proceedings made it apparent that they were not needed and by their not being present, the discussions were shortened."[99] Retribution was also a key theme in the election of 11 June 1945, when the "Soldier's Vote" led to King's personal defeat at the polls. The irony of that rejection was not lost on King. "It does seem cruel that it should be my fate, at the end of the war, in which I have never failed the men overseas once, that I should be beaten by their vote and this, particularly, by a C.C.F. [Co-operative Commonwealth Federation] man whose party at the outbreak of the war were unwilling to even have our men participate at all."[100]

St. Laurent's suspicions about McNaughton proved warranted, for unbeknownst to cabinet, the minister had previously met with the CGS Committee and approved the Army's secret post-war structure based on a system of compulsory peacetime military service. The final version of Plan-G surfaced in June 1945 and envisaged a Permanent Force of over 55,000 supported by a standing conscript Army of 48,000, all of which was underpinned by a militia strength of 178,000. J.L. Granatstein's comment that Plan-G "died a forlorn death, a victim of the past" was apt in that it embodied the figurative death of the Army's post-war ambitions and corporatism. Declaring Plan-G and all such paper schemes as "perfectly outrageous," King arbitrarily cut the Army to a total strength of 20,000–25,000, little appreciating that in doing so he had authorized the largest peacetime Army in Canadian history.[101]

The story of the November 1944 crisis, which climaxed the 48-year evolution of civil-army relations in Canada, lay dormant because of the self-imposed silence of the antagonists. With the threat to the country well past, King, as promised, invited Max Freedman, senior editorial writer at the *Winnipeg Free Press*, to write his memoirs. Freedman's review of the evidence revealed that King firmly believed that he faced an ultimatum from Army leadership and the potential of civil war during the November crisis. Based on this revelation, Richard S. Malone confronted King on this specific point and received King's unqualified confirmation that it was the threat of an Army revolt that forced him to bring in conscription.[102] This confirmation not only served as the missing link in solving the mystery of King's apparent policy reversal but it also fuelled the controversy surrounding the work of King's early biographers Bruce Hutchison and Robert MacGregor Dawson.

The refusal of King's critics to entertain the notion that Canadian generals could have used the implicit threat of resignation as a political stratagem in forcing a reversal of cabinet policy has stifled academic debate. Remarkably, even J.L. Granatstein, who, in his many works, such as *Canada's War*, professed the "Army as scapegoat" theory, has shifted ground slightly. His standard interpretation ("But for the Prime Minister, only a revolt could suffice. He had to find some way of making his *volte-face* appear credible, and only extreme urgency could justify his course both to himself and to his ministers"[103]) has now evolved to the observation that "District Commanders and other senior officers signed a memorandum that might have been read as a threat to resign. Certainly Mackenzie King took it that way ... the "generals' revolt" tipped the scales."[104]

MacGregor Dawson's interview notes can be challenged, but it remains likely that it was General Hugh Young who chose to break with his colleagues and that he was the anonymous general who eventually confirmed Bruce Hutchison's story. In his memoirs, *The Far Side of the Street*, Hutchison maintains that Prime Minister St. Laurent was so disturbed by the public impression that he had been duped, that in exchange for correcting the public record, Hutchison was provided with a credible if anonymous witness who confirmed:

> In brief, the members of the Army Council, he amongst them, had met on the morning of November 22, 1944, and decided to resign if the government did not impose conscription immediately. I gasped. The general was telling me that King and St. Laurent had indeed faced, with Defence Minister A.G.L. McNaughton, a crisis far more alarming than they had dared to discuss in Cabinet.
>
> While the nation may not have been in danger of anarchy, or anything like it, as King later hinted to Parliament, clearly the resignation of the men who commanded the defence forces at the climax of the European war would have destroyed the government. If that was no great matter the convulsion following it would have shattered both the war effort and the brittle partnership of the two Canadian communities.[105]

Armed with the biggest scoop of his life, Hutchison and the editors of *Maclean's*, who "through other, and confidential, sources ... were able to verify the information in all its main particulars," went to press and discovered that the "great scoop had been received by the public with a great yawn."[106] One of the greatest civil-army secrets of the war remained buried and guarded by a "circle of three ministers and a few soldiers who had so long and so honourably sealed their lips."[107]

The needs of a divided nation dictated that this delicate brinkmanship remain secret. Though Laurier tutored that "it does not do to cherish resentments in public life," King never forgave Army leadership.[108] He simply compiled his documentary evidence and as he had dramatically expressed in the House, "I know that a time will come when every man will render me full justice on that score." That justice has been long in coming. The irony of General Crerar being hosted by his nemesis, Mackenzie King, during his Army's victory parade through Ottawa was not lost on King. Crerar's Army, though crafted as the "Dagger Pointed at the Heart of Berlin," had recently posed, in King's view, a much greater threat to Ottawa. Neither the irony of that fact nor the coincidental link to the day of 7 August 1945, escaped King. It was on this his 26th anniversary of his election as the Leader of the Liberal Party of Canada, that King felt vindicated:

> It had fallen to my lot to have the honour of greeting the Commander of the Canadian Army, the first General of a Canadian Army, on his return from the battles he had fought in Europe and to drive with him through the streets of the capital ... To share with him on the drive accounts in detail of much that related to the war and to hear from his lips that the army had been denied nothing that they needed. That he could think of nothing which had not been done by the Government in the course of the course of the whole war. I told Crerar I had made up my mind that the men who were fighting at the front would never suffer for anything that the Government could do on their behalf. We spoke at luncheon of the anxious time I had had last November. He told me it was a very anxious time for them as well. That everything had worked out splendidly. I said it might all so easily have gone in the opposite direction and Canada would have been without any government at all.[109]

Crerar's ceremonial moment as Canada's last true Army general was the defining symbol in the process of building a national Army.

Like its predecessor, the Canadian Corps, Crerar's Army was to be powered by unlimited conscription in war and sustained as a peacetime standing Army through a program of universal military training. Little did Crerar realize that the showdown he sought and the gamble that "worked out splendidly" would lead to the emasculation of his Army's corporatism — a state of institutional perdition from which the Canadian Army has yet to recover.

NOTES

1.   Queens University Archives (henceforth QUA), AArch 2142, ULM 75–207, Box 3, Sec C, Folder 22, Grant Dexter Papers, 13 September 1940.

2.   C.P. Stacey, *Canada and the Age of Conflict Vol. 2: 1921–1948* (Toronto: University of Toronto Press, 1981), 298–99.

3.   Library and Archives Canada (henceforth LAC), Manuscript Group (henceforth MG) 26, J17, Vol. 6, File 8, Statement from General McNaughton that the metaphor "A Dagger Pointed at the Heart of Berlin" originated in a public speech by Ralston, which he later attributed to General McNaughton. King Papers, McGregor Dawson Conscription Interviews.

4.   Document No. 854, Telegram 165, 14 February 1940, in David R. Murray ed., *Documents on Canadian External Relations (DCER) 1939–1941 Part 1*, Vol. 7 (Ottawa: Department of External Affairs, Information Canada, 1974), 740.

5.   University of Western Ontario (henceforth UWO), Microfiche No. 146, King Diaries, "Meeting War Committee of the Cabinet," 3 April 1940, 348.

6.   UWO, Microfiche No. 146, King Diaries, 2 April 1940, 345.

7.   *Ibid.*

8.   Memorandum by Senior Officer, Canadian Military Headquarters, Minutes of the Meeting, London, April 22, 1940, *DCER*, 764.

9.   *Ibid.*

10.   *Ibid.*

11.   *Ibid.*

12.   *Ibid.*

13.   *Ibid.*, 763.

14. Irving Norman Smith, "How Mackenzie King Fought the War," *Saturday Night* 75, No. 21 (October 15 1960), 25–26.

15. LAC, MG 30, E157, Vol. 1, File 958.009 (D12), Crerar Papers, Memorandum-Notes on Discussion Between the Minister of National Defence and Major-General Crerar, Senior Officer C.M.H.Q., 26 April 1940, paragraph 3, Letter Crerar to Ralston, 17 June 1940.

16. *Ibid.*, Letter Crerar to Ralston, 17 June 1940.

17. *Ibid.*, Letter McNaughton to Crerar, 7 August 1940, Re: C.G.S. Position.

18. LAC, MG 30, E157, Vol. 1, File 958c.009 (D13), Crerar Papers, "Observations on Canadian Requirements in Respect to the Army," 15 July 1940.

19. LAC, MG 27, Series III B II, Vol. 37, Ralston Papers, C.G.S. Memorandum to the Minister Ralston, "The Canadian Army," 3 September 1940, 7.

20. LAC, MG 30, E157, Vol. 1, File 958c.009 (D12), Crerar Papers, Letter Crerar to McNaughton, 8 August 1940.

21. *Ibid.*

22. *Ibid.*

23. QUA, Box 2, Sec C, Folder 18, Dexter Papers, 13 September 1940.

24. *Ibid.*

25. QUA, Box 2, Sec C, Folder 20, Dexter Papers, 10 October 1941.

26. QUA, Box 19, Folder 177, Dexter Papers, Explanation on the History and Function of the Army Council.

27. *Ibid.*

28. *Ibid.*

29. Dexter Papers, 12 June 1941, Folder 19, Sec C, Box 2, QUA.

30. *Ibid.*, Major-General P.J.Montague was the senior combat officer, Canadian Army Overseas.

31. LAC, MG 30, E157, Vol. 1, File 958.009 (D12), Crerar Papers, Letter Crerar to McNaughton, 14 May 1941.

32. QUA, AArch 2144, Series 1, Box 4, Sifton Papers, Letter Sifton to Ralston, 01 October 1941.

33.   QUA, Box 2, Sec C, Folder 20, Dexter Papers, October 1941.

34.   LAC, MG 27, Series III B II, Vol. 52, Ralston Papers, *Vancouver Sun* clipping, 23 September 1941.

35.   QUA, Box 2, Sec C, Folder 20, Dexter Papers, 9 October 1941.

36.   QUA, Box 2, Sec C, Folder 17, Dexter Papers, 12 June 1941.

37.   LAC, MG 30, E157, Vol. 1, File 70, 958.009 (D12) H.Q.S.- 20–1-9, Crerar Papers, To Minister: Army Programme 1942–43, 18 November 1941. As of 5 November 1941, there was a total Army strength of 241,530 (121,332 in the U.K.) and 173,640 in Canada, not including NRMA personnel; and LAC, MG 27, Series III B II, Vol. 38, Ralston Papers, "Army Programme 1942–43," 18 November 1941.

38.   R. MacGregor Dawson, *The Conscription Crisis of 1944* (Toronto: University of Toronto Press, 1961), 28.

39.   J.W. Pickersgill, *The Mackenzie King Record Vol. 1 1939–1944* (Toronto: University of Toronto Press, 1960), 303; reflects a King Diary entry for 2 December 1941.

40.   QUA, AArch 2150, Box 38, Folder 11-A, C.G. Power Papers, Minutes of War Cabinet Committee, 3 December 1941.

41.   Pickersgill and Forster, eds., *The Mackenzie King Record: Vol. 1 1939–1944*, 304.

42.   *Ibid.*, 304; and see King Diary entry for 3 December 1941.

43.   *Ibid.*, 304.

44.   QUA, Box 3, Sec C, Folder 21, Dexter Papers, 12 January 1942.

45.   E.L.M. Burns. *Manpower in the Canadian Army, 1939–1945* (Toronto: Irving and Company Limited, 1956), 18.

46.   *Ibid.*, 6 and 14.

47.   QUA, Box 3, Sec C, Folder 21, Dexter Papers, 28 February 1942.

48.   QUA, AArch 2208, Box 5, King Papers, Press Clippings, *Montreal Gazette*, 22 December 1944.

49.   Burns, *Manpower in the Canadian Army*, 166.

50.   LAC, MG 27, Series III B II, Vol. 43, Ralston Papers, Memorandum of notes Made by Lieutenant-Colonel G.S. Currie, 28 April 1944.

51. QUA, Box 3, Sec C, Folder 26, Dexter Papers,17 September 1944.

52. Crerar Papers, Post War Army Planning Top Secret HQS 24–1 (DSD), To the Minister, 7 September 1944, paragraph 16. For a complete copy of Post War Plan-G, see LAC, MG 30, E133, Vol. 264, Directorate of History, National Defence Headquarters, D/Hist 112.35 2009 (D302) Post War Plan-G.

53. *Ibid.*, Paragraph 41.

54. Brian Nolan, *King's War: Mackenzie King and the Politics of War 1939–1945* (Toronto: Random House, 1988), 119; and C.P. Stacey, *The Canadian Army 1939–1945: An Official Historical Summary* (Ottawa: King's Printers, 1948), 235.

55. LAC, MG 27, Series III B II, Vol. 86, Ralston Papers, D.A.G. Memo, 14 October 1944; and Memorandum from Lieutenant-General Murchie to Minister, 21 October 1944, Vol. 84.

56. *Ibid.*, Vol. 62, Cable King to Ralston re: George Drew Hamilton Speech.

57. *Ibid.*, Vol. 62, Memo DCGS to Chief of Staff, Overseas Trip File September-October 1944.

58. Stacey, *Arms, Men and Governments*, 481.

59. LAC, MG 27, Series III B II, Vol. 62, Ralston Papers, Diary Sep-23-October 18 1944, Overseas Trip Colonel H.A. Dyde.

60. *Ibid.*, Vol. 63, Memo General Stuart to Ralston,13 October 1944.

61. Stacey, *Six Years of War Volume I*, 430. Leave Policy.

62. LAC, MG 27, Series III B II, Vol. 62, Ralston Papers, Diary Overseas Trip Colonel H.A. Dyde, 23 Sep-18 October 1944.

63. LAC, MG 30, E520, Vol. 1, File CMHQ 1944, Stuart Papers, Letter Stuart to Minister 19 October 1944 at a.

64. QUA, Series II A, Box 38, C.G. Power Papers, Memorandum to the Minister by Lieutenant-General Stuart, 30 October 1944.

65. LAC, MG 30, E520, Vol. 1, File CMHQ 1944, Stuart Papers, Memo to Minister From C.G.S. "Appreciation of Options."

66. LAC, MG 27, Series III B II, Vol. 85, Ralston Papers, Statement on Retirement File, 23 October 1944, 18.

67. LAC, MG 30, E520, Vol. 1, Stuart Papers, Memo to P.M. from A.D.P.H [Arnold Heeney] Re: Army Reinforcements, 23 October 1944.

68. Pickersgill and Forster, eds., *The Mackenzie King Record: Volume 2*, 143. The full details of the many alternatives presented in *The Reinforcement Crisis, Phase 1*, 1944 portion of this volume.

69. R.S. Malone, *The World in Flames 1944–1945* (Don Mills, ON: Collins, 1984), 155; and Henry Borden Memo.

70. *Ibid.*, King Diary entry for 1 November 1944, 183. The Ralston reference is found on page 196.

71. Statement by Mr. Karl K. Homuth (Waterloo South), *House of Commons Debates*, Vol. 3, July 31, 1940, 2225.

72. Pickersgill and Forster, eds., *The Mackenzie King Record: Volume 1 1939–1944*, 10; and quoted in Nolan, *King's War*, 3.

73. QUA, AArch 2150, Box 17, File 1-E, C.G. Power Papers, Letter Major-General Henry Letson to Power, 25 April 1967.

74. QUA, Box 38, File II A, C.G. Power Papers, *Top Secret Report of Cabinet Committee on Army Enlistments for General Service*, 6 November 1944. This high-powered committee was chaired by McNaughton, and included Ian A. Mackenzie, J.G. Gardiner, W.P. Mulock, Colin Gibson, General L.R. Laflech, Brooke Claxton, and A.D.P. Heeney as secretary.

75. LAC, MG 30, E157, Vol. 1, File 958.009 (D12), GOC 10–0-2, Crerar Papers, Special Confidential Report Major-General G.R. Pearkes (by Lieutenant-General Crerar, Comd 1 Cdn Corps), 6 May 1942.

76. LAC, MG 26, J17, Vol. 6, King Papers, File (6) Clippings — *Vancouver Province*, 20 November 1944; and the rebuttal argument and an attempt to vindicate General Pearkes can be found in Dr. R.H. Roy, "Major-General G.R. Pearkes and the Conscription Crisis in British Columbia, 1944." Published in *BC Studies*, No. 28, (Winter 1975–76), 53–72. Also held as D/Hist 75/273, or *Canadian Historical Association* (June 1975), 68; and "Highly Trained Draftees Ready to Go Overseas, but Not as Volunteers," *Globe and Mail*, 21 November 1944, 1.

77. King Diary entry for 14 November 1944, Pickersgill and Forster, eds., *The Mackenzie King Record: Vol. 2 1944–1945*, 216. For the confirmation on King's support in the West, see page 293.

78. *Ibid.*, 222.

79. *Ibid.*, 223.

80. *Ibid.*, 224.

81. Pickersgill and Forster, eds., *The Mackenzie King Record: Vol. 2 1944–1945*, 148.

82. "Brig. R.A. MacFarlane Says Most Officers Opposed to McNaughton," *Globe and Mail*, 25 November 1944, 13; "Brigadier MacFarlane Resigns in Protest," *Winnipeg Free Press*, 24 November 1944, 1; Similarly, see *Globe and Mail*, 24 November 1944, 1. All reports support MacFarlane's claim that he tendered his resignation on 21 November. It was only made known to King on 22 November and officially accepted on 23 November 1944.

83. QUA, AArch 2208, Box 5, King Papers Press Clippings, *Toronto Telegraph*, 23 December 1944; and *Ottawa Morning Journal*, 23 December 1944. Brigadier Mess resigned on 29 November, and his resignation was accepted on 20 December. The MacFarlane quotation comes from the *Montreal Gazette*, 24 November 1944.

84. Library and Archives Canada (henceforth LAC), Manuscript Group (henceforth MG) 26, J17, Vol. 6, File 8, King Papers, MacGregor Dawson Conscription Interviews II, General Hugh Young No. 2, 19 January 1953. The reference to General Pearkes entreating with the Conservatives is found in a letter from General Samson to Richard S. Malone and quoted in *A World in Flames*, 291. The General Murchie reference is quoted in Bernard Charles Leblanc, *A Reluctant Recruit: Angus L. Macdonald and Conscription 1940–1945*. Unpublished M.A. Thesis (Kingston, ON: Queen's University, 1987), 97.

85. DHH, 112.1 (D88), Office File Army Council Memo to C.G.S. "Reduction of Age Limit for Despatch Overseas, 27 May 1944, Minutes of Army Council 8 June 1944, paragraphs 3 and 4.

86. LAC, MG 26, J17, Vol. 6, File 8, King Papers, MacGregor Dawson Conscription Interviews II , General Walford interview, 2 February 1953.

87. *Ibid.*, General Hugh Young interview No. 1, 19 January 1953.

88. *Ibid.*, General Young interview. The general officer's Woods Building anecdote comes from R. MacGregor Dawson, *The Conscription Crisis of 1944*, 91.

89. John Swettenham, *McNaughton, Volume 3: 1944–1966* (Toronto: Ryerson Press, 1969), 59.

90. LAC, MG 26, J17, Vol. 6, File 8, King Papers, MacGregor Dawson Conscription Interviews, General Walford interview, 2 February 1953; and see also J.L Granatstein, *The Generals: The Canadian Army Senior Commanders in the Second World War* (Toronto: Stoddart Publishing Co., 1995), 345 (Notes to Chapter 8, Note 137).

91. QUA, Box 4, Sec C, Folder 27, Dexter Papers, 9–10 January 1945.

92. DHH, 112.1 (D145), C.G.S. Office File of Minutes of Meeting of Army

Council, 23 November 1944.

93.   *House of Commons Debates*, 27 November 1944, Vol. 6, 6611.

94.   *Ibid.*, 6617–18.

95.   Pickersgill and Forster, eds., *The Mackenzie King Record: Volume 2*, 271. King Diary entry for 7 December 1944.

96.   *Ibid.*, 252–53. King Diary entry for 28 November 1944.

97.   Pickersgill and Forster, eds., *The Mackenzie King Record: Volume 2 1944–1945*, 284; and see also Whitaker, *Tug of War*, 234–35.

98.   *Ibid.*, 437. King Diary entry for 17 July and 16 August 1945, 462.

99.   Stacey, *Arms, Men and Governments*, 129; and quote from the King Diary of 13 December 1944.

100.   Pickersgill and Forster, eds., *The Mackenzie King Record: Volume 2*, 415. King Diary entry for 14 June 1945.

101.   J.L. Granatstein, *Broken Promises: A History of Conscription in Canada* (Toronto: Oxford University Press, 1977), 247.

102.   Malone, *A World in Flames:* 288–89.

103.   J.L. Granatstein, *Canada's War: the Politics of the Mackenzie King Government* (Toronto: Oxford University Press, 1975), 367; and QUA, Box 82, Series III, C.G. Power Papers, C.G. Power's notes to a Postscript by Bruce Hutchison, *Maclean's*, May 15, 1953, 20.

104.   J.L. Granatstein, "Canadian Generals in the Second World War: Better Than Expected" in Bernd Horn and Stephen Harris, eds. *Generalship and the Art of the Admiral: Perspectives on Canadian Senior Military Leadership* (St. Catharines, ON: Vanwell, 2001).

105.   Bruce Hutchison, *The Far Side of the Street* (Toronto: Macmillan, 1976), 225–26; and QUA, Box 6, Series I-C, C.G. Power Papers, Letter Hutchison to Power,1 March 1953, Series I-C, Box 6, QUA.

106.   C.G. Power Papers, QUA, Box 82, Series III, *Maclean's*, May 15, 1953, C.G. Power's notes to a postscript by Bruce Hutchison, 20.

107.   Bruce Hutchison, *The Far Side of the Street*, 229. All of Hutchison's work on the crisis was done in close collaboration with C.G. Power. Much is revealed in the series of letters found in the QUA, AArch 2142, Box 6, Series I-C, C.G. Power Papers, 1952–1953; and QUA, Box 8, Series I-C, series of letters between Power and Ralston's son, S.B. Ralston, 1952.

108.   Pickersgill and Forster, eds., *The Mackenzie King Record: Volume 2*, 463.

109.   *Ibid.*, 452–53.

3

Leadership and Lack of Moral Fibre in Bomber Command, 1939–1945: Lessons for Today and Tomorrow

Allan English

Introduction

Two recent Canadian Forces (CF) publications have codified and described in detail, for the first time, what it means to be a leader in the CF. As well as providing doctrinal guidance for members of the CF today and in the future, *Duty with Honour* and *Leadership in the CF: Conceptual Foundations* (henceforth *Conceptual Foundations*) also provide frameworks and theoretical models to analyze Canadian military leadership. This chapter takes advantage of these frameworks and theoretical models to analyze leadership in the Royal Air Force's (RAF) Bomber Command in the Second World War with a view to providing lessons, based on both historical experience and current CF leadership doctrine, for CF leaders of today and tomorrow.

I have chosen to focus on Bomber Command because it was the fighting force that the Royal Canadian Air Force (RCAF) contributed to more than any other in the Second World War, and Canadians serving in Bomber Command were subject to British policies and practices governing leadership, morale, and discipline, including those related to lack of moral fibre (LMF). In 1944, about 40 percent of all RCAF aircrew posted overseas were sent to Bomber Command. By January 1945, 46 percent of Bomber Command's pilots came from Canada, Australia, or New Zealand, and 55 percent of these Dominion fliers were Canadian.[2] Unfortunately for these aircrew, Bomber Command suffered the highest losses of any of the RAF's formations. By the end of the war, Bomber Command had lost 47,268 of its complement on operations, representing over two thirds of all RAF fatal casualties.[3] Of this number, 9,919 were RCAF aircrew serving in Bomber Command.[4] This figure accounts for more than one half of the total of RCAF personnel killed in the Second World War, and about one fifth of the fatal casualties suffered by all Canadian forces in that conflict. From an individual's perspective, even though operational tour lengths were designed to give aircrew a 50–50 chance of survival, in reality losses were often higher, and, at times, as many as 75 percent of the bomber crews perished.[5]

Some in certain disciplines take a proprietary view of subjects like leadership, believing that their discipline is uniquely qualified to study it. I advocate a multi-disciplinary approach to subjects like leadership and command because the nature of these topics makes an examination of them from the perspective of various disciplines more effective. Historians, I believe, have an important contribution to make to the study of leadership, and yet there are few analytical historical studies of Air Force leadership. An important tool of analytical historical leadership studies is to use historical experience to create analogies that can be applied to present and future challenges. Although no two leadership experiences are identical, history can be seen as sort of Aircraft Operating Instructions (AOIs) for those Air Force activities with historical precedent. However, in some fields the historical AOIs are as lacking as instruction manuals were in the earliest days of aviation.

This is particularly true in the field of human behaviour, a discipline usually acknowledged as the preserve of scientists. While some can question the relevance of studying human behaviour using "the battlefield as [a] laboratory, and history as its instrument,"[6] there are good reasons for doing so. Those disciplines that depend on numerical data for their inquiries have serious problems to contend with in the fog of war. Many of the factors that contribute to combat performance, for example, morale, motivation, luck, and timing, are not easily quantified. In addition, information that is gathered during hostilities often suffers from enough errors to make "any conclusion based on statistics alone of very doubtful value," according to one Second World War investigator.[7] Peacetime studies, on the other hand, though apt to gather more reliable data, frequently must restrict or simplify the number of variables under investigation to make numerical analyses more manageable. This is not to deny the importance of statistics, rather it emphasizes that scientific studies of war cannot stand alone. History has a place: it "sets the numbers in a context which helps us to understand them."[8]

And it is incumbent upon us to get this right, or risk being among those who, having forgotten their history, are doomed to repeat the mistakes of the past.

This chapter begins by summarizing the theoretical frameworks and models that will be used to analyze leadership and lack of moral fibre in Bomber Command 1939–1945. The second part of this chapter describes certain challenges faced by Bomber Command leaders during the Second World War. The chapter concludes by analyzing those challenges using the theoretical frameworks and models presented in part one. This chapter argues that while position power may be the foundation of military leadership, Air Force leaders must develop personal power bases, especially expert and referent power, to be effective in combat operations.

Theoretical Models and Frameworks

Duty with Honour asserts that strong and effective leaders are at the heart of military professionalism, and that their tasks include ensuring that the profession is constantly evolving to effectively meet new challenges; setting and maintaining high professional standards; demanding excellence in performance; and ensuring that all members of the CF have the ability to improve their professional competencies. Above all, according to *Duty with Honour*, effective leaders exemplify the military ethos, and especially the core military values that are the essence of military professionalism. They make sure that all understand that their duty to country and colleagues is central to the profession of arms, and they demonstrate that loyalty can and must be applied both upwards to superiors and civil authority and downwards to subordinates.[9]

Duty with Honour also recognizes that the military profession in Canada includes individuals, such as doctors or lawyers, who are members of other professions. It argues that while in uniform they must accept the duties and responsibilities of membership in the profession of arms. However, because they must also adhere to the codes and ethics of their primary profession, there is a potential for a conflict of interest between doctor/patient confidentiality and the operational readiness of a unit, for example, as exemplified in the practice of military medicine as opposed to practising "medicine in the military."[10] Resolving these potential conflicts between competing professional requirements is one of the key functions of the officers

AN AVRO LANCASTER 2 BOMBER FLIES LOW OVER THE COUNTRYSIDE.
(Department of National Defence, Library and Archives Canada PA 145613)

who lead these specialist branches.[11] Therefore, another theme of this chapter will be to examine the role of members of other professions, like the medical profession, who serve their country in uniform.

Conceptual Foundations holds a values-based leadership model for CF leaders where mission accomplishment and operations primacy are key dimensions of leadership.[12] However, *Conceptual Foundations* cautions us that too much emphasis on any single value dimension (e.g., mission accomplishment, efficiency, cohesion, obedience, and so on) can be counter-productive, and that effective leaders must be able to reconcile or balance competing values rather than resorting to trade-offs of convenience.[13] As we shall see, during bomber operations in the Second World War, dealing with competing values was a major challenge for leaders, and how they dealt with them provides us with valuable lessons.

Leaders rely on various sources of power to influence others and to accomplish their missions. *Conceptual Foundations* describes two major classes of social power that leaders use: "[P]osition power, which reflects attributes of an appointment or rank within a larger social structure of authority and power; and personal power, which reflects the socially valued or useful qualities of an individual. Position power is conferred, and is, therefore, temporary. People gain and lose position power on occupying and leaving certain positions, appointments, or ranks. But appointed leaders can also compromise their legitimacy by improper conduct or ineffective performance, and, in some cases, can be relieved from duty as a result of such conduct or performance. Personal power, on the other hand, is earned entirely by individual effort and adaptive learning, and therefore is highly portable. However, like position power, it too is maintained by effective conduct and performance."[14]

Position power is the foundation of military leadership and it is often divided into five sub-classes: legitimate, reward, coercive, information, and ecological. However, almost all military leaders also rely on personal power to effectively carry out their duties. Personal power includes three sub-classes, expert, referent, and connection, and effective Bomber Command leaders were particularly reliant on expert and referent power. *Conceptual Foundations* describes expert power as "the capacity to provide others with needed knowledge or advice." It comes from knowledge, skill, or experience, and as we shall see, expertise in operational flying was a prerequisite to becoming a credible leader in Bomber Command. Referent power is the ability "to provide another with feelings of personal acceptance, approval, efficacy, or worth," according to *Conceptual Foundations*. It is generally based on the respect and esteem of followers for a leader, but it can also derive from the desire of a follower to identify with and emulate a leader. *Conceptual Foundations* tells us that the "[q]ualities that increase referent power include friendliness and likeability, concern for and loyalty to others, courage, authenticity, integrity, and other forms of selfless and benevolent behaviour."[15] In Bomber Command, effective leaders depended on referent power to get their followers to persevere in difficult circumstances, especially when casualty rates were high and chances of survival for their crews were low.

The leadership styles or influences used by effective Bomber Command leaders generally could be described as what *Conceptual Foundations* calls "transformational leadership," and involve such leader activities as exemplifying personal, sometimes self-sacrificing, commitment to the mission, and their ethical ideals; facilitating the performance and achievement of followers; and providing intellectual stimulation and inspiration through persuasion, support, appropriate delegation, and individualized consideration.[16] According to *Conceptual Foundations*, there are three different ways subordinates can respond to a leader's attempts to influence them: commitment, compliance, or resistance.[17] However, transformational leaders aim to foster commitment in their followers and "regard respect and trust as necessary conditions of follower commitment and resilient performance."[18] This latter point was particularly true of successful Bomber Command leaders, as we shall now see.

Leadership and Lack of Moral Fibre in Bomber Command 1939–1945

My discussion of leadership and LMF in Bomber Command during the Second World War begins by tracing the origins of these phenomena in the First World War. Many direct parallels between Air Force experiences in the two conflicts can be drawn, and the ordeal endured by some of those who survived the first war had a direct effect on their actions in the next. For example, almost all the RAF's senior Air Officers were veterans of aerial combat in the First World War, and as squadron commanders they had witnessed the effects of "flying stress" on front-line aviators. Among the RAF's specialist consultants in the Second World War, its senior neuropsychiatrist had served as a medical officer (MO) in the Great War. He applied his wartime experience directly to problems of psychological disorders among aircrew after 1939, and he understood that "flying stress" was inextricably linked with LMF.

The term *lack of moral fibre* was used in print as early as 1884. Although it has not yet been established how the term originated in the RAF,[19] the labels *LMF*, *waverer*, *W*, and *loss of confidence* or *lacking in confidence* came to be synonymous in everyday RAF usage.

These expressions conveyed particular assumptions about life and human behaviour, some of which still have currency today, that were widely held in the first half of this century. In this era, "physicians' judgements were often heavily value laden," diseases of the mind were often equated with immorality,[20] and a peculiar fusion between moral and medical judgments ensued.[21] This was to have an important effect on the treatment of aircrew who were diagnosed as suffering from psychological disorders. The first opportunity to observe, on a large scale, the consequences of these assumptions and the relationship between "flying stress" and leadership was provided by the First World War.

Air forces were tiny in 1914, but four years of war demanded enormous expansion. The British air services alone had 22,171 aircraft on charge at the armistice, and had expanded from 2,073 all ranks in 1914 to 291,175 in 1918.[22] As the size of the air forces increased, their casualties grew correspondingly. For example, during a five-month period of intense fighting in 1916, the Royal Flying Corps' (RFC) 21 Squadron lost 19 aviators killed or wounded and 6 labelled "neurotic," a turnover of more than 100 percent.[23] This wastage continued unabated, so that by the end of the war the RAF estimated it would need almost 1,300 pilots per month to keep its squadrons at full strength.

Besides the problem of finding replacements, these losses affected the survivors of combat as well, and "flying stress" or "getting the wind up," as it was called by First World War aviators, took its toll on even those with the highest awards for bravery. One Victoria Cross winner, Lanoe Hawker, recorded in his diary an example of this when he described an incident that occurred over enemy lines on 29 March 1915. He had switched off his engine to discuss artillery ranging with his observer when a near miss by enemy anti-aircraft fire "… put [the] wind up me properly, switched on and fled at 100 m.p.h."[24] This incident demonstrated that even the bravest of men could react in less than courageous ways when exposed to unexpected terror in the air.

Another cause of "flying stress" was fatigue. However, early in the war, little provision was made for the regular rest of aircrew, and it was not until "the widespread toll caused by nervous strain" forced a decision, that a regular leave policy was introduced.[25]

For those who did succumb to "flying stress," the RFC established, in October 1917, a special treatment centre for its aviators on the Western front. Major (later Lieutenant-Colonel) James L. Birley, who served in France from 1916 to 1919[26] and was head of the RFC medical organization there, arranged that all aviators suffering from "flying fatigue" be sent to a designated hospital "for study and treatment."[27] The treatment was based on the accepted medical practices of the day, and combined limited military duties with occupational therapy and rest.[28]

In 1920 Birley summarized much of what the Air Force had learned about "flying stress" in the First World War. He suggested that aviators went through three successive stages: inexperience, experience, and stress. He noted that 70 percent of casualties occurred during the period of inexperience, especially in the first three months of active service. Once past this stage, the aviator was at the "zenith" of his effectiveness. This was followed by the period of stress when the flier became "stale" or burnt out. Birley believed it was the MO's job to prolong the second stage as long as possible by resting the aviator "at the critical moment," before burnout occurred.[29] However, the MO was not expected to act alone; he usually co-operated closely with those who led the squadron.

The best of these were perceived to be aggressive, skilled fliers who led by example. Among them, those who were most admired carried out their orders intelligently and used their expertise to minimize the risks to the lives of their charges.[30] While ability as a combat pilot was important, exceptional commanding officers (COs), such as Hawker, were also noted for the personal interest they took in the well-being of their subordinates.

But sometimes more heroic measures were needed to preserve squadron morale. Hawker's unit was the first to be equipped with DH2 aircraft, which had been rushed into service to counter the "Fokker scourge." The DH2 suffered from a number of manufacturing and technical problems, and it was soon dubbed the "Spinning Incinerator" by the pilots who flew it. On 13 February 1916, two of Hawker's best pilots were killed in accidents involving spins on their own side of the lines. Rumours quickly circulated among his pilots that these machines were death traps. A complete collapse in squadron morale seemed imminent, and Hawker had to act quickly. Immediately after the fatal accidents, he took a DH2 up on his own and recovered from every possible spin condition. He then described the proper manoeuvres to his pilots, and they all practised until they were proficient in spin recoveries. After that, while Hawker was in command, his squadron did not lose another flier from spinning into the ground. Thus, a potentially serious morale problem was avoided by a CO demonstrating his flying competence and by taking a personal risk.[31]

The publication of accounts by Hawker and many others, combined with the scientific literature on "flying stress," left a valuable legacy in the realm of leadership and human behaviour in aerial combat during the First World War. However, this material was largely neglected between the wars, and in 1939 British authorities decided that fresh studies on "flying stress" would have to be conducted. Most of the new research was guided by the senior RAF consultant in neuropsychiatry, Group Captain (later Air Vice-Marshal) Charles P. Symonds. More than any other person, Symonds defined RAF medical policy on aviation psychology as it related to "flying stress."[32] In recognition of his contribution to this field of inquiry, in 1949, Symonds received a prestigious award from the

Aero-Medical Association of the United States.[33] Both Canadian and American Air Force authorities, particularly those involved in the strategic bombing of Europe, were influenced by Symonds's work.

However, at the beginning of the Second World War, many practices from the previous war still remained in place; "flying stress" was treated solely as a medical problem, in the same way that "shell shock" had been at the start of the First World War. Symonds believed this to be "unjustified and dangerous to morale," as he thought that a "fit man should not be able to escape the hazards of operational flying through a medical back door."[34] To rectify the situation a number of changes to medical and administrative procedures were initiated.

On the medical front, in 1942, Symonds helped to prepare two reports, which reflected the RAF medical branch's understanding of psychological disorders in aircrew. In the first, a summary of the existing literature found that the "most important single predisposing cause of psychological breakdown in flying personnel [was] fatigue," and, though noting the effects of in-flight physical factors, it stated that the main cause of fatigue was fear. Reflecting prevailing attitudes about human behaviour in combat, the report claimed that the most important cause of fear was "individual predisposition … [which is] largely dependent upon temperament." Although it was understood, as Birley had observed in the First World War, that it was the MO's duty to rest aircrew "at the crucial moment," most hopes for reducing the incidence of psychological disorders among aircrew were pinned on better selection methods assumed to eliminate those temperamentally unsuited for operations.[35]

The second report summarized the experiences, up to March 1942, of various RAF MOs, both specialist and non-specialist. It began by expressing concern over the "great confusion of thought as well as the nomenclature adopted among those concerned with the psychological welfare of aircrews in the RAF."[36] The report was thorough and discussed all the main ways of moderating psychological casualties, including leave, operational tour limits, alternate employment, and physical amenities for aircrew. However, the tone of the opinion of the senior medical officer of Bomber Command, Air Commodore F.N.B. Smartt, predominated. He said, "the importance of temperamental unsuitability in causing psychological disorders in members of air crew" necessitated the "radical elimination of those unsuitable individuals."[37] Although Bomber Command medical advisers recognized the importance of the cumulative effects of the strain of training and of operational missions in precipitating "flying stress" among "normal" aviators, they held that there was an identifiable group of people who broke down more easily under pressure. These men were, by virtue of their genes and family background, unfit to be aircrew, and were, therefore, to be treated with no sympathy. These views were supported by data that estimated that, by contemporary neuropsychiatric standards, approximately 22 percent of aircrew were predisposed to psychological disorder. It was admitted that it would be "uneconomical" to reject this entire number, but it was suggested that eliminating the 3 percent who comprised "severely predisposed individuals" would be useful.[38]

From a scientific point of view, the greatest weakness in these data was that they were almost exclusively based on the examination of persons already diagnosed as suffering from a psychological disorder. Although it might have been true that "two-thirds of the individuals who failed to withstand the stress of flying were predisposed to nervous breakdown," as one wartime study concluded,[39] little research was done to estimate how many of those who might have been predisposed did not break down. It could have been the case that many of those who were predisposed to break down did admirable work.[40]

Perhaps Bomber Command's severe attitude can be partially explained by the number of psychological casualties it was suffering even early in the war. By January 1941, it had recorded "an annual total of five percent of operational air crews [who] developed psychological illness of sufficient severity to lead to admission to hospital or disposal by [the RAF's Central Medical Establishment]." Because this figure only included those who were admitted to hospital or formally disposed of, Air Commodore Smartt concluded that "the total number of psychological disorders in aircrew ... must be much higher than this."[41] These mounting losses represented a worrying situation to a command that was already suffering severe personnel problems because of expansion and operational attrition.

To address these problems, new administrative policies were devised by the British Air Ministry. Definite tour lengths were introduced in March 1941, and regular leave was also granted to operational aircrew.[42] By 1943, the Air Ministry's goal was to maintain the "efficiency and confidence" of aircrew over the course of one operational tour, an instructional tour, and a second operational tour. "Tired men" could be given a break, in the form of special leave or early posting, without recourse to formal medical channels if a squadron commander judged that the individual had been "exposed to exceptional stress or if his stamina appear[ed] to be subnormal."

Most cases were to be handled locally, but this led to varying standards among units. Symonds acknowledged that MOs disposed of cases differently depending on their "sagacity and enthusiasm,"[43] and that there was also real "difficulty in making the distinction between lack of confidence and neurosis."[44] If a case was referred to a specialist, evidence was required "that the fear state [was] so persistent or recurrent that it [was] disabling" before a diagnosis of neurosis could be made.[45]

In an attempt to resolve some of these difficulties, what came to be known to as the "LMF Memorandum" was issued in September 1941, and revised in 1943 and 1945 in relatively minor ways.[46] The memorandum dealt with "members of air crews who forfeit the confidence of their Commanding Officers in their determination and reliability in the face of danger in the air, owing either to their conduct or to their admission that they feel unable to face up to their duties ..." It classed aircrew who were "found unable to stand up to the strain of flying" into three categories: (i) those who were medically fit, but who had forfeited the confidence of their COs "without having been subjected to any exceptional flying stress"; (ii) those who were medically unfit "solely on account of nervous symptoms and without having been subjected to any exceptional flying stress"; and (iii) those who were medically unfit for other reasons. The memorandum emphasized that, even though it was not easy, cases coming under the terms of category (i) had "to be *proved* to be lacking in moral fibre" [my emphasis]. If there was any question of medical disability, the man was to be placed in either category (ii) or (iii) as appropriate. For these two categories, the unit MO, or a specialist if the case was referred to one, had to decide if there was "evidence of physical or nervous illness." If there was none, the case was to be dealt with by the executive branch. Despite the minimal amount of psychological training given to RAF doctors, the MO was, in most cases, "encouraged to take the responsibility of the decision on himself."[47] With this procedure, the Air Ministry put much of the burden of classification onto the medical profession. The official history of the RAF Medical Services claimed that the onus was placed on physicians because the "executive were often loath to accept responsibility and preferred disposal ... through medical channels whenever possible."[48]

Beginning in February 1943, no one could be categorized LMF on a second tour. However, for those individuals whom the Air Council branded LMF, the consequences could be serious. Officers were required to resign their commissions. Non-commissioned aircrew were usually demoted to the lowest rank in the Air Force for at least three months and assigned to the most menial jobs, often cleaning latrines. From 1944 on, any LMF case released from the Air Force could be called up to work in the coal mines or drafted into the Army. In all cases permission to wear the flying badge was withdrawn for categories (i) and (ii), and for category (i) personnel, their service documents were "marked in the top right-hand corner with a large red "W," signifying "waverer."[49]

The LMF procedure has been represented by its defenders as carefully designed to weigh all the factors in what was recognized as a difficult situation, and there is some truth in this view.[50] The LMF label did inspire fear in fliers, and it did keep some of them at their stations. We are led to believe by supporters of the system that many aircrew were generally happy with a procedure they felt was necessary to keep up the bombing effort.[51] Before rejecting LMF policies out of hand, one should consider the opinion that it was less harsh than a court-martial, and an appropriate way of dealing with those who would not or could not face the strain of operations.[52]

However, from the individual's point of view, the most serious weakness of these policies was that the method used to make the distinction between a psychological disorder and "lack of confidence" was unreliable. Unfortunately, for those who were branded LMF, it was not accepted until late 1944 that psychiatric opinion was not dependable in individual cases, and by that time most of these men had already been dealt with according to the harsh standards of the day.

Symonds was aware of these difficulties, and he declared, as early as 1943, "In the distinction between anxiety neurosis and cowardice expediency usually in the end counts more than scientific judgment. This should surprise no one who has reflected upon the part played by group opinion in deciding when individual behaviour should be regarded as pathological."[53] He recognized that there was no clear line between an anxiety neurosis and a normal emotional reaction to stress; however, he maintained "that in the interests of morale, a line must always be drawn." Symonds explained that the position of this line varied according to the group attitude towards danger, and that the medical profession in these cases was often called upon to make an "arbitrary" decision as to "whether the man had tried hard enough to satisfy group standards."

Near the end of the war, a study on the reliability of psychiatric opinion in the RAF was conducted that showed that these were indeed arbitrary decisions. It found that, in over 5,000 cases of aircrew referred to two or more specialists, even experts in the field of human behaviour had "only an even chance" of agreeing upon the determination "lack of confidence" or some other diagnosis. Symonds's experience as an infantry battalion MO in the First World War had led him to a similar conclusion, as he had been "long convinced that the dividing line between anxiety neurosis and normal fear in combatants is artificial and related to circumstance."[54] And one of the most influential circumstances was the state of squadron leadership.

Much of the literature in military psychology today suggests that "strength of leadership and unit cohesion are the only factors with demonstrated merit in reducing [combat stress] casualties."[55] Examples from Bomber Command lend some support to this view, and show a remarkable consistency with Air Force leadership styles in the First World War. The case of one of the RAF's most celebrated leaders, Leonard Cheshire, CO of 76 Squadron for the first four months of 1943, illustrates this point. Some COs got the derisive nickname "François" from their subordinates because they usually only participated in relatively safe raids on France. Not Cheshire. He deliberately elected to fly as second pilot "with the new and the nervous" on dangerous raids. In this way he demonstrated competence and risk-taking to his followers. By the end of the war, Cheshire had earned a VC, 3 DSOs, a DFC, and had become "a legend." His replacement had a much different experience. Rarely flying on dangerous ops, and plagued with "bad luck" early returns, the new CO saw the unit's efficiency and morale deteriorate alarmingly. By the spring of 1943, 76 Squadron's early return rate sometimes exceeded 25 percent of the aircraft dispatched. At the end of 1943 this CO was replaced. His successor, "Hank" Iveson, resumed the custom of the CO flying dangerous missions, and he broke up crews with persistent early return records. This resulted in better unit performance, which significantly improved morale, but a CO had to be constantly alert to maintain it at a high level. When the squadron was re-equipped with the new Mark III Halifax, which had a "fearsome reputation for accidents," Iveson and his three flight commanders flew on the first operational mission with this aircraft to demonstrate their confidence in the squadron's equipment.[56]

The example of 76 Squadron shows how aircrew would follow charismatic leaders. Crews could not be driven to their tasks in

Bomber Command; there were too many ways to shirk them, especially on night operations, if they felt their leaders were letting them down. For example, they could "deliberately sabotage" their aircraft to avoid going on ops,[57] they could "boomerang" (return early), or become "fringe merchants" (those who bombed on the edge of the target to avoid defences). And as the bombing campaign penetrated further into Germany, in order to get above the defences, crews could jettison their bombs in the sea or over occupied Europe.[58] Good Bomber Command leaders inspired their men to press home the attack in the face of overwhelming odds against survival. But no matter how inspirational the leadership, there was a limit to what anyone could endure. Until operational limits were introduced, as one Bomber Command Senior MO remarked, "Flying personnel used to say that they flew till it was 'coffin or crackers.'"[59] In other words, they flew, without hope of survival, until they were killed or went mad.

Senior leaders in Bomber Command acknowledged that, under these circumstances, everyone had the "wind-up," but that training, discipline, morale, and confidence in equipment, as well as good leadership, allowed most aircrew to overcome their fears. Squadron commanders knew that operational conditions, especially bad flying weather and improving enemy defences, contributed to stress. However, they believed some factors were controllable, and they specifically underscored the disastrous effects upon morale of repeated cancellations of missions, especially late cancellations. From a morale point of view they felt that it was better to go on a sortie in bad weather than to cancel late. The instance of one "freshman" was cited who "scrubbed" 17 times before his first trip; when he finally got to fly on ops, he quit after three trips. Some sympathy was expressed for this pilot, as he had endured as much stress, before he got airborne against a real target, as someone who had gone on many sorties.[60]

These issues were a source of great concern to senior RAF officers, and, in 1942, Symonds was asked to enquire into the relationship between leadership and psychological disorders in Bomber Command fliers. After interviewing 44 aircrew, mostly station, squadron, and flight commanders, and 37 Bomber Command MOs, Symonds concluded that good leadership was "vital" to helping men "accept and carry the load of operational flying." Though no one type of personality appeared to ensure good leadership,[61] Symonds identified a number of characteristics and behaviours that were displayed by successful leaders. The first task of the good leader, who was new to a squadron, was to establish his flying expertise. If he had no operational experience in Bomber Command, he had to demonstrate that he was "an efficient operational pilot" as soon as possible. While he was proving his proficiency to the squadron it was also important that he shared its risks by going on "difficult raids," especially "when losses [were] heavy or morale low." On ops, crews wanted their CO to set an example of steadiness under pressure. Subordinates, like superiors, also appreciated a keen commander who displayed initiative and drive. They wanted to believe that a CO's "whole interest" was in the squadron. This would be demonstrated by "a personal knowledge of all the crews," and by being accessible to them when required. However, aircrew expected a CO to be hard but fair "in all matters" of flying and duty. Above all, he had to be *perceived* to be a leader by his followers, and it was recognized that even a " good pilot may be a bad leader." To foster a perception of good leadership a CO was expected, particularly "when things [were] going badly," or after " heavy casualties" to be active, organizing "intensive training." Speaking "quietly and with confidence" and taking a trip when the squadron had a run of poor luck further built an image of the concerned, effective leader.[62]

The importance of leadership was such that "the fortunes of the squadron" were often described in terms of its COs. One station commander remarked that cases of lack of confidence "usually occur in epidemics, and when an epidemic occurs it is usually due to a bad squadron or flight commander." In one case, when "it became known that a squadron commander wouldn't fly operationally," five cases of LMF occurred in the first fortnight. Men cracked "because they had no confidence" in their leaders.[63] It is an ironic twist that senior officers directing Bomber Command operations observed that LMF cases proliferated when COs had lost the confidence of their subordinates — precisely the opposite of what was provided for in the LMF memorandum.

Symonds's study confirmed that good leadership often reduced losses and psychological casualties. In numerical terms the relationship between combat losses and psychological casualties, can be illustrated using the concept of the "neuropsychiatric (NP) ratio." Copp and McAndrew have explained how the NP ratio was used by land forces in the Second World War to show the proportion of neuropsychiatric casualties to total battle casualties (killed and wounded), and as a measure of the stress each unit had experienced.

The NP ratio for Canadian infantry units engaged in combat in Italy from late 1943 to mid-1944 averaged about 23 percent.[64] By way of comparison, Bomber Command had an NP ratio of about 20 percent, which comes close to the 23 percent for the Canadian Army in Italy. Of course these known cases of "neurosis" only accounted for those diagnosed as such by the medical branch. There is no way of knowing how many of Bomber Command's fatal casualties may have had psychological factors as a cause in their demise, since 88 percent of them were listed as "Presumed dead," and met their fate in an unknown way.[65]

In terms of total losses, Bomber Command suffered grievously compared to other formations, on what has been called the "cutting edge of battle." Canadian rifle companies fighting the early campaigns in Italy, and British and American infantry in Normandy experienced casualty rates of 50, 76, and 100 percent of unit strength respectively.[66] Bomber Command's rate was 250 percent of unit strength. From this perspective, the Bomber Command NP ratio seems acceptable in relation to the heavy casualties it suffered.

Lessons about human behaviour and leadership were acquired at a terrible price in both world wars, and it our responsibility to make use of information gained at such a cost. Therefore, I will conclude by highlighting some of the conclusions of this chapter that may be of use to today's Air Force leaders.

Conclusions

Three general conclusions stand out from this examination of leadership and lack of moral fibre in Bomber Command. First, experience from the First and Second World Wars teaches us that psychological casualties among combat aircrew are inevitable, and that they will increase as losses and sortie rates increase. Second, it is extremely difficult to distinguish between those who are suffering a combat stress reaction and those who just think they cannot go on. Both leaders and medical personnel need to be knowledgeable and observant to be effective in winnowing out those who can no longer sustain an operational effort. Third, good leadership can not only improve operational efficiency, but also significantly reduce losses caused by "flying stress." Good Air Force leaders should exhibit above average flying skills, and can, to a certain extent, be trained to display behaviours that inspire confidence in their subordinates.

More specifically, though position power may be the foundation of military leadership, Air Force leaders must develop personal power bases to be effective. In the case of Bomber Command, expert power was required to have credibility as a leader and referent power was necessary to get followers to accomplish their missions, especially when casualty rates were high and chances of survival for crews were low. A key leader behaviour required to establish referent power was for leaders to share the risks with their subordinates by going on dangerous missions when heavy casualties were anticipated. It is noteworthy that squadron COs or other senior leaders were not expected to lead all missions, particularly early in their tours, but that they were expected to share the risks with their subordinates. This sharing of risks with subordinates was key to building the trust and commitment that was vital to the transformational leadership style used by successful Bomber Command leaders.

In summary, the best Bomber Command COs were bold, skilled aviators who led by example. Successful COs set an example of steadiness under pressure, displayed initiative and drive, and showed a personal interest in the welfare of squadron members. However, they were also expected to be hard but fair "in all matters" of flying and duty. To be perceived to be a good leader COs were also expected to be active, organizing intensive training, speaking "quietly and with confidence" to their subordinates, and going on missions when things were not going well for the squadron. Good Bomber Command leaders inspired their personnel to press home the attack in the face of overwhelming odds against survival. And those who were most admired carried out their orders intelligently and used their expertise to minimize the risks to the lives of their charges. But no matter how inspirational the leadership, there was a limit to what anyone could endure, and this was where specialists had an important role to play.

Another theme of this chapter was to examine the role of specialists who as members of other professions, like the medical profession, serve their country in uniform. As we have seen, doctors, psychologists, and other experts had an important role to play in advising and supporting Bomber Command leaders. Many of these experts were civilian specialists who served in uniform during the war. They played key roles in devising and applying those policies related to LMF and other issues associated with leadership in stressful environments. In some cases, these experts felt that Bomber Command leaders had abdicated their responsibilities and had made medical officers responsible for determining if aircrew were fit to go on operations. In other words, specialists were asked to become more than advisers to the leadership and to actually take decisions that were properly the responsibility of the leadership, after receiving expert advice. The most effective specialists worked closely with the leadership, and provided advice based on both their professional expertise and the experience they gained working with operational units.

Specialists also conducted a number of ground breaking studies during both World Wars. One of their most relevant findings related to this analysis is that the state of squadron leadership was the key to squadron performance in Bomber Command. Many other factors contributed to squadron performance, and for short periods of time could even predominate, but in the long run, how leaders dealt with adversity and how they did or did not inspire their charges was the greatest predictor of how effective any particular squadron would be on operations.

In 1994, when I first wrote the essay upon which this chapter is based, I concluded with these words:

> [N]ow is the time to act on these lessons, lest we be caught unawares in a crisis, as some of our predecessors were. In the First World War, James Birley recalled afterwards, he and his colleagues had been "thrown into the rush of war, to be deluged by surprises, confronted with undreamt of situations, and expected at a moment's notice to pronounce expert opinions on subjects concerning which [they] would sometimes have preferred to confess a profound ignorance."[67] Birley and his contemporaries, pioneers at the dawn of powered flight, may be forgiven their shortcomings. Those of us working at the dawn of the 21st century, with the experience of the past available to us, will not.

Over 10 years after these words were written, it is encouraging to see that the CF have published books like *Duty with Honour* and *Leadership in the CF: Conceptual Foundations* that have provided an intellectual foundation for the study and the teaching of leadership in the CF. However, it is discouraging to see that in more than a decade the Canadian Air Force has made no discernible progress in learning, let alone teaching, the leadership lessons from its past.[68]

One can only hope that with the stand up of the CF Aerospace Warfare Centre in the fall of 2005 that this lack will be remedied, otherwise the Air Force will be forced to re-learn painful lessons that were once acquired at tremendous cost.

NOTES

1. This chapter is based on Allan English, "Leadership and Lack of Moral Fibre in Bomber Command 1939–1945," in William March and Robert Thompson, eds., *The Evolution of Air Power in Canada*, Vol. 1 (Winnipeg: Air Command History and Heritage, 1997), 67–75. Some of the issues raised here are discussed in more detail in Allan English, *The Cream of the Crop: Canadian Aircrew 1939–1945* (Kingston, ON: McGill-Queen's University Press, 1996), especially Chapters 4, 5, and 6.

2. John Terraine, *The Right of the Line* (London: Hodder and Stoughton, 1985), footnote 18, 765.

3. *Ibid.*, 682.

4. Charles Webster and Noble Frankland, *The Strategic Air Offensive Against Germany 1939–1945*, Vol. 4 (London: HMSO, 1961), 440. This number does not include Canadians serving with the RAF.

5. Terraine, *The Right of the Line*, 522; and Air Vice-Marshal D.C.T. Bennett, leader of the Pathfinders, in Walter Thompson, *Lancaster to Berlin* (Toronto: Totem Books, 1987), foreword [no page number].

6. Richard E. Ruggle, review of *Battle Exhaustion: Soldiers and Psychiatrists in the Canadian Army, 1939–1945*, by Terry Copp and Bill McAndrew, *Canadian Defence Quarterly* 20, No. 5 (Spring 1991), 46.

7. Dr Burdett McNeel, commander of No. 1 Canadian Exhaustion Unit in Normandy, 1944, in *Ibid.*, 46.

8. *Ibid.*, 46.

9. Canada, Department of National Defence (DND), *Duty with Honour* (Kingston, ON: Canadian Defence Academy, 2003), 55.

10. For a discussion of military medicine and "medicine in the military" in a Canadian context, see Canada, DND, "The Mission and Medical Ethics: Is There a Conflict?" Ethics in Operation, Proceedings of the Conference on Ethics in Canadian Defence Ottawa, 2–3 November 1999, sponsored by the Defence Ethics Program, Chief Review Services, 19–26 available at *www.dnd. ca/ethics/archives/documents/conf1999_e.pdf.*

11. *Duty with Honour*, 12.

12. Canada, Department of National Defence, *Leadership in the Canadian Forces: Conceptual Foundations* (Kingston, ON: Canadian Defence Academy, 2005), 20.

13. *Ibid.*, 25.

14. *Ibid.*, 58–59.

15. *Ibid.*, 58–60.

16. *Ibid.*, 68.

17. *Ibid.*, 72–73.

18. *Ibid.*, 74.

19. John McCarthy, "Aircrew and 'Lack of Moral Fibre' in the Second World War," *War and Society* 2, No. 3 (September 1984), footnote 2, 88.

20. Andrew Scull, "The Social History of Psychiatry in the Victorian Era," in Andrew Scull, ed., *Madhouses, Mad-Doctors, and Madmen* (London: Athlone, 1981), 25.

21. Michael J. Clark, "The Rejection of Psychological Approaches to Mental Disorder in Late Nineteenth-Century British Psychiatry," in Scull, ed., *Madhouses, Mad-Doctors, and Madmen*, 273.

22. H.A. Jones, *War in the Air, Appendices* (Oxford: Clarendon Press, 1937), appendices 39 and 41.

23. Brereton Greenhous, ed., *A Rattle of Pebbles: The First World War Diaries of Two Canadian Airmen* (Ottawa: Canadian Government Publishing Centre, 1987), xx.

24. Tyrrel Mann Hawker, *Hawker, V.C.* (London: Mitre Press, 1965), 70.

25. Edward Mannock, *The Personal Diary of Major Edward "Mick" Mannock*, annotated by Frederick Oughton (London: Neville Spearman, 1966), footnote 67, 159.

26. "The Medical Service of the Air Force," *Lancet* (16 March 1918), 419; and *Who Was Who*, Vol. 3, (London: Adam & Charles Black, 1947), 115–16.

27. Douglas H. Robinson, *The Dangerous Sky: A History of Aviation Medicine* (Seattle: University of Washington Press, 1973), 90, 101.

28. Barbara Sicherman, "The Paradox of Prudence: Mental Health in the Gilded

Age," in Scull, ed., *Madhouses, Mad-Doctors, and Madmen*, 221; and Isaac Jones, *Flying Vistas* (Philadelphia: Lippincott, 1937), 200–01.

29. J.L. Birley, "The Principles of Medical Science as Applied to Military Aviation, Lecture I," *Lancet* (29 May 1920), 1149.

30. Jean Beraud Villars, *Notes of a Lost Pilot*, trans. by Stanley J. Pincetl, Jr., and Ernest Marchand (Hamden, CT: Archon Books, 1975), 97, 146–47, 169, 200; Roger Vee, (Vivian Voss), *Flying Minnows: Memoirs of a World War I Fighter Pilot from Training in Canada to the Front Line, 1917–1918* (London: Arms and Armour Press, 1976), 239; and Curtis Kinney with Dale M. Titler, *I Flew a Camel* (Philadelphia: Dorrance and Company, 1972), 88.

31. Hawker, *Hawker, V.C.*, 125, 129, 135, and 140–43.

32. D.D. Reid, "Historical Background to Wartime Research in Psychology in the RAF," in E.J. Dearnaley and P.B. Warr, eds., *Aircrew Stress in Wartime Operations* (London: Academic Press, 1979), 1.

33. Charles P. Symonds, *Studies in Neurology* (New York: Oxford University Press, 1970), 21.

34. *Ibid.*, 18–19.

35. C.P. Symonds and Denis Williams, "Psychological Disorders in Flying Personnel, Section 1. A Critical Review of Published Literature," Flying Personnel Research Committee (FPRC) Report 412(c), January 1942, Public Records Office (PRO) AIR 57, 1, 5, 7, and 8–11.

36. C.P. Symonds and Denis Williams, "Psychological Disorders in Flying Personnel, Section 2. Review of Reports Submitted to Air Ministry Since the Outbreak of the War, April 1942," FPRC Report 412(d), [1942], PRO AIR 57, 4, 6.

37. *Ibid.*, 7 and 10.

38. Denis J. Williams, "Predisposition to Psychological Disorder in Normal Flying Personnel," FPRC Report 516, February 1943, in Air Ministry, Great Britain, *Psychological Disorders in Flying Personnel of the RAF*, Air Publication 3139 (London: HMSO, 1947),192.

39. Air Ministry, *Psychological Disorders in Flying Personnel of the RAF*, i.

40. Studies since the Second World War have concluded that there are no predisposing traits to psychological breakdown in combat, Shabtnai Noy, "Combat Stress Reactions," in Reuven Gal and A. David Mangelsdorff, eds., *Handbook of Military Psychology*, (Chichester, Eng.: John Wiley, 1991), 514.

41. Symonds and Williams, "Psychological Disorders in Flying Personnel, Section 2," 5.

42. Air Historical Board, Great Britain, "Flying Training-SFTSs 1934–42," unpublished narrative, n.d., PRO AIR 41/4, 20.

43. C.P. Symonds and Denis Williams, "The Probability of Return to Full Flying of Men Who Have Broken Down Under the Strain of Operational Duties," FPRC Report 561, November 1943, PRO AIR 57, 1.

44. C.P. Symonds and Denis Williams, "Investigation of Psychological Disorders in Flying Personnel by Unit Medical Officers," FPRC Report 412(k), February 1945, PRO AIR 57, 6.

45. C.P. Symonds and Denis Williams, "Clinical and Statistical Study of Neurosis Precipitated by Flying Duties," FPRC Report 547, August 1943, in Dearnaley and Warr, eds., *Aircrew Stress in Wartime Operations*, 34.

46. Terraine, *The Right of the Line*, 533.

47. "Memorandum on the Disposal of Members of Air Crews Who Forfeit the Confidence of Their Commanding Officers," S.61141/S.7.C(1), 19 September 1941, PRO AIR 2/8591, 2–3.

48. S.C. Rexford-Welch, ed. *The Royal Air Force Medical Services*, Vol. 2 (London: HMSO, 1955), 133.

49. "Memorandum on the Disposal of Members of Air Crews Who Forfeit the Confidence of Their Commanding Officers," S.61141/s.7.C(1), 3–4; Max Hastings, *Bomber Command* (New York: Dial Press, 1979), 249; McCarthy, "Aircrew and 'Lack of Moral Fibre' in the Second World War," 88–89, 96; and "Minutes of a Meeting Held on the 20th October 1944, to Discuss the 'W' Procedure," PRO AIR 2/8592.

50. See, for example, Charles Messenger, *"Bomber" Harris and the Strategic Bombing Offensive, 1939–1945* (London: Arms and Armour Press, 1984), 205–07.

51. Murray Peden, *A Thousand Shall Fall* (Stittsville, ON: Canada's Wings, 1979), 416; and Norman Longmate, *The Bombers* (London: Hutchinson, 1983), 188.

52. Interview with General (Retired) Chester Hull, CO of 428 Squadron in the Second World War, Ottawa, 28 May 1992.

53. Symonds and Williams, "Clinical and Statistical Study of Neurosis Precipitated by Flying Duties," 34.

54. Symonds and Williams, "Investigation of Psychological Disorders in Flying Personnel by Unit Medical Officers," 6.

55. Noy, "Combat Stress Reactions," in Gal and Mangelsdorff, eds., *Handbook of Military Psychology* 520–21.

56. Hastings, *Bomber Command*, 247–48, 252.

57. Some examples are given by Hastings, *Bomber Command*, 248 (deliberately fouling the magnetos while running up the engine); and Longmate, *The Bombers*, 184 (tampering with gun-turret hydraulic systems).

58. The number of bombs "jettisoned" during the Battle of Berlin has been described as "enormous," Webster and Frankland, *The Strategic Air Offensive Against Germany 1939–1945*, Vol. 2, 195–96. Harris was aware of these problems. The policy of having tour lengths defined by successful sorties, where possible confirmed by photos taken at bomb release, was designed to discourage "fringe merchants" and "boomerangs." Messenger, *"Bomber" Harris*, 90; and Terraine, *The Right of the Line*, 524.

59. Symonds and Williams, "Psychological Disorders in Flying Personnel, Section 2," 19.

60. This effect had been noted in early 1940 by flying personnel medical officers in Fighter and Coastal Commands. Being on standby could generate 25–80 percent as much stress as actual combat flying. This created so much fatigue that there were "several cases of pilots falling asleep in the air," H.W. Corner, "Flying Duties at a Fighter Squadron," FPRC Report 122, 24 March 1940, PRO AIR 57, 1–2.

61. Hastings, *Bomber Command*, 159–60; and interview with Donald M. Schurman, who served in Bomber Command, Kingston, 17 December 1992. Schurman added that COs who attempted to minimize losses "one way or another" were respected by their squadrons.

62. Symonds and Williams, "Personal Investigation of Psychological Disorders in Flying Personnel of Bomber Command," FPRC Report 412 (f), August 1942, in Air Ministry, *Psychological Disorders in Flying Personnel of the RAF*, 32, 53.

63. *Ibid.*, 53–54.

64. Terry Copp and Bill McAndrew, *Battle Exhaustion: Soldiers and Psychiatrists in the Canadian Army, 1939–1945* (Montreal: McGill-Queen's University Press, 1990), 57–58, 81, 114.

65. C.P. Symonds and Denis Williams, "Occurrence of Neurosis in Royal Air Force Air Crews in 1944 and 1945," FPRC Report 412(L), April 1945, in Air Ministry, *Psychological Disorders in Flying Personnel of the RAF*, 178, 180. Webster and Frankland, *The Strategic Air Offensive Against Germany 1939–1945*, Vol. 4, 440. Of 47,268 Bomber Command casualties lost on operations, 41,548 were "[p]resumed dead."

66. John A. English, *On Infantry* (New York: Praeger, 1984), 138.

67. Birley, "Principles of Medical Science as Applied to Military Aviation," 1147.

68. See Allan English, "Survey of Current Leader Development in the Air Force," report written for Defence Research and Development Canada, 17 March 2004 for a discussion of problems with research into and teaching of leadership in the Canadian Air Force.

4

ERRANT AIRCREW: A CASE FOR "GREY" INSUBORDINATION IN No. 6 GROUP (ROYAL CANADIAN AIR FORCE), BOMBER COMMAND IN 1943

David Bercuson

IN ONE OF THE DARKEST periods of a twentieth-century war, one combatant wrote:

> The line between the living and the dead was very thin ... if you live on the brink of death yourself, it is as if those who have gone have merely caught an earlier train to the same destination. And whatever that destination is, you will be sharing it soon, since you will almost certainly be catching the next one.[1]

The passage evokes the melancholia of an infantryman serving on the Western Front during the darkest days of First World War. But it is not. It was written by Flight Lieutenant Denis Hornsey, a pilot of No. 76 Squadron of Bomber Command in the fall of 1943. Ironically, Hornsey's Halifax bomber was shot down shortly after he penned those words. He survived the crash and escaped across France to return to the United Kingdom. Shortly after that, Air Chief Marshal Arthur Harris, commander-in-chief of Bomber Command, launched his six month-long "Battle of Berlin." It was a campaign that brought death to thousands of Bomber Command aircrew, and nearly broke the back of the British Bomber offensive.

The comparison of the fates of soldiers on the Western Front in the First World War with the flyers of Bomber Command in the Second is not far fetched when survival rates of both are compared. In the First World War, for example, Britain, with its empire and the dominions, mobilized 8,904,467 soldiers; 10.2 percent were killed in action or died on active service, 23.47 percent were wounded and 2.15 percent were categorized as "missing" but can be presumed dead. The approximate overall casualty rate was 35.82 percent.[2] This was almost 50 percent lower than the loss rates suffered by Bomber Command aircrew in 1939–1945. One source records that for any given 100 aircrew in Bomber Command over the course of the war, 51 were killed on operations, nine were killed in crashes in the United Kingdom, three were seriously injured, 12 became prisoners, one was shot down but evaded capture, and 24 survived unharmed.[3] According to Martin Middlebrook and Chris Everitt's authoritative *The Bomber Command War Diaries*, Bomber Command aircrew sustained a casualty rate of some 60 percent in almost 390,000 sorties over the course of the Second World War.[4] There is no reason to believe that the casualty rate of aircrew flying with No. 6 Group Royal Canadian Air Force (RCAF) Bomber Command, or of Canadian bomber squadrons that were formed before the establishment of No. 6 Group, or of squadrons that were occasionally detached from the group, was significantly different. Volume 3 of the *Official History of the RCAF in the Second World War* puts the total number of Canadian aircrew — in fighter, bomber, transport, or coastal command squadrons — at some 50,000 of whom some 30 percent became casualties on operations over the course of the war.[5] Given the nature of bomber operations, it must be assumed that Canadian bomber aircrew sustained a casualty rate much higher than that.

Many studies have demonstrated that warriors who find themselves in constant danger of imminent death, for long periods, and who are all too aware of growing death tolls around them, do not have a limitless supply of courage.[6] As British historian John Terraine puts it:

> it is simply not possible to take large numbers of young men abruptly out of civil life, and subject them to most unnatural stress for a long period, without problems (something serious) arising ... Fear of operational flying was something that few escaped. Bomber Command's 8,000 aircrew killed in training or accidents supply a sufficient reason.[7]

The vast majority of aircrew got through the fear somehow whether they showed symptoms of that fear or not. And if certain individuals did from time to time show the unmistakable signs of fear before, during, or after missions, most of them also found the courage to continue. But a number of aircrew did not. In their cases fear of operational flying could produce severe symptoms associated with combat fatigue, battle exhaustion, shell shock, or the more modern post-traumatic stress disorder (PTSD). In his study of Canadian aircrew, Allan English chooses to use the term *Combat Stress Reaction* (CSR) for aircrew whose fear drove them to avoid further combat.[8] The definition he proffers encompasses "all soldiers who negotiate evacuation with a reason other than being hit by a direct enemy projectile or explosive ..."[9] In the particular case of bomber aircrew, English describes them as "any airman who asked to be relieved of flying duties, or was prevented from flying on exhibiting symptoms of physical or mental illness for which no organic cause could be found. It would also include those who, on bombing operations, deliberately failed to press home their attack on the target, the "fringe-merchants," the "boomerangs," and those who jettisoned their bombs en route to the target to avoid the defences by gaining altitude."[10] This is a large grab bag ranging from the certifiably ill to those who might be categorized as, essentially, insubordinate.

VARIOUS BOMBS MAKE UP THE TOOLS OF THE TRADE.

(Department of National Defence, Library and Archives Canada PA 213867)

In ground forces, there were several options open to those whose fear surpassed their coping ability. They could be treated as psychiatric casualties, in which case they were either returned to their units when they recovered or dismissed from the service. They could refuse to obey orders to enter combat and eventually be charged with insubordination. Or they could desert. Foot soldiers can resort to desertion in two ways; by finding relatively safe ways of surrendering to the enemy or by simply disappearing, usually into rear areas and sometimes by finding ways to return home. In the British Empire/Commonwealth armies in the First World War, desertion rates per 1,000 men-under-arms ranged from 20.7 percent in 1914–1915, to 7.41 percent in 1917 and 1918.[11] Terraine counts 7,361 *official* charges of desertion in the imperial, Commonwealth, and empire forces over the course of that war, a number that may well hide truer (and higher) desertion rates.[12]

Desertion is difficult for flyers, especially bomber aircrew who most likely must decide as a unit that they have had enough and will seek refuge in a neutral country. Over the course of the war a tiny number of Royal Air Force (RAF) aircraft came down in neutral Switzerland or Sweden; most of them crash landed or were forced to land because of damage suffered after attack by enemy fighters.[13] If there were any that landed in neutral countries due solely to their crew making a collective decision to desert, the number in both absolute and percentage terms must be so small as to be virtually non-existent.

Fearful aircrew had alternatives to desertion. They could demonstrate an inability to fly because of psychological factors or they might outright refuse to fly. In the Royal Air Force (RAF), aircrew who could not, or would not, fly because of fear could find themselves categorized as men who had "forfeited the confidence of their Commanding Officers in the face of danger in the air."[14] That forfeiture of confidence was usually referred to as Lacking Moral Fibre or "LMF." Some RAF commanders considered LMF equivalent to "cowardice" as it had been defined by the British Army in the First World War.[15] Max Hastings claimed that "in 1943 most cases of men relieved of operational duty for medical or moral reasons (i.e., LMF) were treated by the RAF with considerable harshness." He attributed this to two related factors. The first was the Air Ministry belief that "gentlemen made the best aircrew"[16] but that the exigencies of war had unfortunately forced the RAF to take in all types of men, including large numbers who were not socially or psychologically "fit" to fly.

The second was that if these unfit men were not dealt with quickly or harshly, LMF "would go through a squadron like wildfire."[17]

John Terraine does not quite agree with Hastings. He observes that by 1939, the British defence establishment had learned that "Citizen Forces, raised by conscription, cannot — at any rate, in democracies — be treated like regulars." One result of this realization was that only four British Army soldiers were shot for "cowardice" in the Second World War as opposed to 346 in the First World War. Terraine points out that the diagnosis of LMF was often arbitrary and sometimes influenced by class attitudes (a much smaller percentage of officers were classified as LMF than non-commissioned-aircrew). There was also disagreement as to what to do about LMF; was it a temporary phenomenon that could be quickly cured by rest or a crime to be punished? If men taken off flying duties were assigned to ground tasks, wasn't that simply playing to their fears?[18] That was an ongoing dilemma.

In *The Bomber War: The Allied Air Offensive Against Nazi Germany*, Robin Neillands suggests that the line between simply carrying on and being categorized as LMF was not as clear cut as some have suggested:

> Those who were unable to continue or had done more than their share or had a particularly distressing experience, or simply did not have the temperament for this sort of work, were usually treated with sympathy and posted to other work. In most cases a spot of leave, a chat — pleasant or direct — from the group captain or, in extreme cases a short spell at the Air Crew Correction Centre at Sheffield for a dose of discipline put an end to the problem or at least enabled the man to finish his tour.[19]

Allan English treated LMF extensively in his history of the selection and preparation of Canadian aircrew for Bomber Command and pointed out that the RCAF took a somewhat different view of LMF than did the RAF. RCAF squadron commanders and medical officers were sometimes more reluctant to use the classification. The RCAF itself insisted that when dealing with RCAF personnel serving in RAF squadrons, the Canadian minister of national defence for air be given the final word on the disposition of an LMF case. This insistence was probably more because of the Canadian government's desire to be the ultimate authority in the disposition of those serving in Canadian uniforms than leniency towards hesitant flyers. But there was another factor at work — the RCAF's attitude to LMF reflected the overall Canadian tendency to treat aircrew as flying units who were designated not by class, or even by commission, but by what they did — face the enemy in the dangerous night sky over Germany.[20] Eventually all Canadian aircrew were commissioned — a reflection of this attitude.

It is hard to pinpoint how extensive the LMF phenomenon was. When Hastings wrote his history of Bomber Command in the late 1970s, he was unable to obtain any precise statistics from the judge advocate general of the British Armed Forces about the extent of the problem as it might have been revealed through disciplinary courts martial. Hastings concluded from the rough evidence of his own interviews with aircrew that about one in every seven was lost to operations at some point because of being classified as LMF.[21] Other estimates are much lower. Terraine cites a report prepared by Wing Commander J. Lawson of the Air Ministry personnel department that estimates "that less than 0.3 per cent of the total aircrew have been classified [LMF]. This [was] indeed a grand record."[22] Indeed it was, but Terraine also pointed out that LMF could not be measured by way of numbers of aircrew court-martialled since the "requisite papers do not exist." Although it is known that approximately 16,000 courts-martial of aircrew took place over the course of the war, no record is available that breaks these procedures down by category.[23] Richard Overy, in *Bomber Command: 1939–1945*, notes: "Over the war an estimated 200 cases a year were classified as LMF, or slightly less than 0.4 per cent of all bomber crews."[24] This would indicate that few of the cases mentioned by Terraine were LMF and that most LMF cases were simply not officially prosecuted as such.

As English points out in his definition of CSR, however, refusal to fly was not the only alternative available to aircrew whose fear was getting the best of them. A far more attractive alternative was to avoid a mission, or fail to press it home, for reasons that were ostensibly mechanical. In No. 6 Group, for example, the "turnback" rate alone for the year 1943 (not counting missions that were aborted even before takeoff) ranged from a low of zero on the night of 10–11 August 1943 for a mission of 41 aircraft taking part in a main force attack on Nuremberg to a high of 62.5 percent or 10 returns out of 16 sorties on the night of 25–26 February 1943 to the same target.[25] That was in a year that saw the group mount 67,233 sorties, drop 12,630 tons of bombs, and lose 341 aircraft — a loss rate of 4.7 percent. Dunmore and Carter observed of 1943: "The Group's losses and its dismal early return rate combined to give it an unenviable reputation in Bomber Command."[26] Thus, although the turn-back rate for the group varied greatly, with absolute numbers ranging from zero to 34 (on the night of 29–30 March in a raid to Berlin) aborts or turn-backs obviously involved considerably larger numbers of aircrew in 1943 than those classified LMF. Put simply, failure to fly at all, or failure to press home an attack, was far more common than failure to fly for psychological reasons.

Historical researchers have not studied the question: was failure to press home an attack for reasons other than mechanical difficulty a form of insubordination? As was shown above, courts martial records of aircrew do not reveal how many aircrew were charged with insubordination. Insubordination is not mentioned as a possible factor for failure to press home a mission in any of the secondary works consulted for this study on Bomber Command or the air war.[27] A high return rate was almost always taken as a sign of low morale but the explanation was never drawn out to its logical conclusion — that a bomber crew that deliberately returned from a mission without bombing the target, and that had experienced no undue mechanical difficulty, was in effect declaring "tonight we decided to disobey orders." It may never be possible to prove that a certain percentage of early returns — or outright aborts — was insubordination, but the prospect should be considered nevertheless.

If failure to press home an attack, by way of an aborted or uncompleted mission, was genuinely the result of mechanical failure, no implication can be drawn as to aircrew morale. A high rate of genuine aborts or returns because of genuine mechanical malfunctions can most certainly be taken as an indication of problems with ground crew — or persistent faults with certain types of aircraft. If, however, aborts or returns (or for that matter any failure to press home an attack as ordered) were not rooted in mechanical failure, they could have constituted a type of "grey" insubordination. Grey insubordination will be defined here as failure or refusal to follow orders to bomb a particular target, at a time and from an altitude that was pre-assigned, by means of visual or mechanical target identification, and by aiming for markers or other target indicators as ordered, when not caused by mechanical malfunction.

In an often overlooked study of No. 6 Group, "Canadianization and the No. 6 Bomber Group RCAF," Leslie Nuttal observed: "The success of RAF–RCAF bomber operations depended totally upon the integrity, honour, and courage of the aircrews. They flew at night, alone, unseen either by their commanders or their peers. If a crew chose to avoid doing its duty it could easily do so. Crews with low morale might return early from an "op" with mysterious mechanical difficulties. Or they might drop their bomb loads over the North Sea and fly on to the target with a significant height advantage over their more dedicated comrades. More commonly, they became "fringe merchants," dropping their loads on the outer edges of a target so they could get out of the danger zone more quickly. Crews with high morale struggled on to their assigned target and dropped their bombs to the best of their ability."[28] As with others who have written about Bomber Command, Nuttal does not refer to insubordination at all, but to morale, which was well recognized as a cause of failure to complete mission.

Morale was " difficult to assess using statistics," Nuttal notes, though Group headquarters constantly tried to do so by analyzing operational failure data.[29] There were two main types of such failures; aircraft that did not sortie and aircraft that returned early. Procedures were in place to reduce the former by having aircrew air test their aircraft the morning before an operation and report all mechanical difficulties to the ground crew. It was the latter's job to ensure that the aircraft was ready before takeoff time. Sometimes aircraft checked out in the morning and certified ready by the ground crew were still mysteriously found to be deficient by the flight crew on run-up to takeoff. If no spare aircraft were available, the crew then missed the mission.

After takeoff there were many ways an aircraft might be made to experience mechanical failure. Nuttal describes one recurring problem:

> A common form of self-induced failure involved the "magneto drop." Before takeoff, all pilots were trained to boost their engines to takeoff revs and check the power loss with first one, and then the other magneto turned off. (Magnetos in aero engines performed a similar function to distributors on car engines). Switching off a magneto always involved a drop in engine revolutions but the line between a normal, and therefore acceptable drop and a severe drop was sometimes fine. With aging engines the

normal mag drop would often exceed air force specifications. A good skipper would accept the drop and get on with it. A less keen type would — legally — shut the engines down and report his aircraft as unserviceable.[30]

If already on the mission, he might turn back. Or he might turn back for a number of other reasons — deficiencies in the oxygen system, radios that didn't work, turrets that would not revolve, et cetera. But where was the line between one crew suffering low morale but pressing on regardless, another suffering low morale and detecting a mechanical problem that didn't exist, and a third with a pilot or flight engineer who actually induced a mechanical problem during a flight whether or not it was found after landing? The last was surely insubordination, grey or not.

No. 6 Group was formally stood up on 1 January 1943 with eight existing RCAF squadrons that were "hastily assembled"[31] to meet a deadline that had been determined largely by political considerations.[32] Five were based in Yorkshire, three in nearby County Durham. These were the most northerly bases in Bomber Command. Those in Yorkshire were located inland, in the Vale of York, behind a range of hills that loomed between their bases and the North Sea. They flew twin-engine Wellingtons, which were nearing obsolescence for the sort of mass heavy missions that Harris was about to lay on, and older Halifax four-engine bombers. For most of 1943 their location, their equipment, their very newness at a time when Bomber Command was itself in a period of rapid transition, created mechanical, operational, and morale problems. Location could not be helped. Bomber groups were supposed to fly similar types of aircraft for reasons of logistics. Their squadrons were also supposed to be based pretty much together for reasons of logistics and morale. In 1943 the Vale of York was the only area in the U.K. where new bases could be created for the new group that were not impossibly far from potential targets.

Nevertheless the Vale of York created problems of its own. Ground fog plagued early morning landings. Aircraft from the bases flew so far to the north to join the main force bomber stream that they were often in range of German night fighters based in Northern Germany or Southern Denmark before they could join the protective anonymity of the bomber stream. The hills of York were themselves an obstacle to many take offs of heavily laden aircraft. And many

RCAF aircrew were convinced that their squadrons did "not get such good aircraft as other [RAF] squadrons and that consequently they would be unwise to join RCAF squadrons if they could avoid it."[33]

Problems with higher loss rates and early returns began to surface as early as March 1943. Nuttal writes: "6 Group Staff found these early returns, many of which were later found to be 'OK on Test,' very disheartening," and in worried tones requested that "... Captains. Before turning back please ask yourself this question: 'Is my return really necessary?'"[34] The plea did not help much. As the *Official History* notes: "April was a cruel month for No. 6 Group." The Group had the lowest percentage of crews claiming to have attacked their primary target, about 15 percent of all aircraft returned early (lower than March but still high), and the loss rate rose to 8 percent, the highest in Bomber Command.[35] The next three months were "worse ... even than April" though the percentage of early returns abated somewhat from about 19 percent in March to about 11 percent in July. The improvement in the return rate was chalked up to better work by ground crews resulting in a reduced number of technical failures.[36]

It is probable that many, if not most, early returns were truly because of mechanical problems. Operational Research Reports written at the time by the Operational Research Section of Bomber Command pointed to numerous "teething troubles"[37] besetting the Group from frequent changes of aircraft types to the consolidation of Group squadrons on new bases as causes for lowered morale and below average performance. Inexperience of individual aircraft ground crew, lack of time working together, introduction of new equipment, modification of existing equipment, or having to work at a break-neck pace during a period when the Bomber Command chief Arthur Harris was pushing his aircrews to hit the enemy ever harder, all took their toll on aircraft maintenance.[38]

In the second of three reports — that done on 10 July 1943 — the Operational Research Section compared performance statistics for No. 6 and No. 4 Group. The latter was located almost as far north as No. 6 Group and flew similar aircraft. A comparison of abort rates in No. 4 Group and No. 6 Group for the period February to May 1943 showed that 8.7 percent of Halifax missions were aborts compared to 13.3 percent in No. 6 Group. The figure for Wellingtons was similar in the two groups but the Canadian group was marginally higher (No. 4 Group = 12.2 percent; No. 6 Group = 14.5 percent).[39] The OR staff reported that for No. 6 Group Wellingtons and Halifaxes, "the increase in the abortive rate coincided in time with the sharp relative increase in the 6 Group loss rate." The report noted as well that the abortive rate was consistently greater than the return rate for No. 4 Group but that "there is no one cause to that the greater part of the difference ... is due. The most common cause, engine defects, has had a very similar incidence for the two groups." The only conclusion that the report drew about this difference was that there must have been "some lowering of the standard in either training of crews or maintenance of aircraft."[40] The report did not draw the obvious conclusion that when loss rates mounted, crews must have either found, looked for, or created reasons to return early at a higher rate.

In late May 1941 the air officer commanding No. 6 Group, Air Vice-Marshal George E. Brookes touched indirectly on the problem of early returns in a letter to Arthur Harris. Brookes was actually discussing the related question of when not to give a crew credit for a mission and this had great importance as 30 missions comprised an operational tour. He noted that Group staff had "intensified ... efforts to work out a satisfactory solution to the question of the cancellation of sorties when there are sufficient grounds for believing that crews have unjustifiably failed to press home their attack." Sometimes crews were not credited for missions, or were given half credit, by station or squadron commanders where there was "good reason," but the problem was "the difficulty of getting definite evidence." He went on:

> Not more than 2% of sorties have been cancelled solely on the grounds that the crew has failed to press home its attack. The decisions in these instances have been based on such photographic evidence as is available, combined with careful interrogation of the crews. This percentage does not include the considerable number of sorties which have been cancelled due to aircraft returning early from operations for various reasons, chiefly mechanical failure of equipment. In these latter instances the chief factors considered are the experience of the crews, weather, and the distance to which the sortie penetrated before turning back.[41]

Brookes made no mention of lower morale or insubordination

as a possible cause of what he himself termed the "considerable" number of early returns.

By the summer of 1943, No. 6 Group reached a low point. The Official History states: "Serviceability hovered around 60%; the number of crews lacking in moral fiber and declared to be 'waverers,' although only .45% in June, was the second highest in the command ... while the number of crews reporting they had attacked the primary objective ... rose slowly and steadily from 83% in April to 89% in July, all other main force groups did better."[42] By then Bomber Command had grown to the point where it routinely dispatched 500 or more aircraft almost every night. Invariably there were high abort rates right across the Command. To take one example, No. 6 Group dispatched 73 Halifaxes and Wellingtons to bomb Hamburg on the night of 2–3 August 1943; 23 of those aircraft or 31.5 percent aborted. The crack No. 5 Group, flying the much better and newer Lancaster sent 128 aircraft to bomb Hamburg of which 18 or 14 percent aborted. That was just below the mission average abort rate of 14.3 percent across the entire Command.[43] The rate of aborts in No. 5 Group was much lower than that of No. 6 Group on that particular mission, but when the inexperience, the "teething troubles," and the inferior aircraft of No. 6 Group is taken into consideration, the abort rate for No. 5 Group still seems high, especially since the abort rates that caused so much alarm in No. 6 Group in March 1943 were comparable. In a number of other randomly selected missions in 1943, however, the No. 6 Group abort rates were consistently higher than the Bomber Command average, though they did improve towards the end of 1943.

Date in 1943	Bomber Command Abort Rate	No. 6 Group Abort Rate
28–29 March	7.2%	11.3%
29–30 March	26.1%	34.2%
12–13 May	8.2%	16.7%
27–28 May	4.1%	12.0%
22–23 June	9.7%	22.4%
29–30 July	6.0%	10.8%
17–18 August	3.8%	24.2%
16–17 September	11.7%	21.4%
3–4 October	6.1%	9.3%
22–23 November	8.7%	9.0%[44]

There is one piece of evidence that indicates that No. 6 Group was improving its early return and/or aborts towards the end of 1943. In an appendix to the last of the three Operational Research Reports done on No. 6 Group, the missing and abort rates for November 1943 to January 1944 were compared for Halifax aircraft of the six squadrons of No. 6 Group (419, 427, 428, 429, 431, 434) and the seven squadrons of No. 4 Group (10, 76, 77, 78, 102, 51, 158). The No. 4 Group squadrons averaged an abort rate of 10.1 percent while the Canadian group averaged 10.6 percent.[45] The Operational Research Section had (in its October 1943 report) characterized the No. 6 Group squadrons as not having had time to "settle down and develop a good team spirit with its attendant high morale"[46] because of the group's newness, but such an observation could not have been made about the older and completely established No. 4 Group.

By most measures, No. 6 Group performance drew even with Bomber Command averages in losses, sorties attacking the target successfully, and aborts sometime in late 1943 and early 1944. A number of factors have been cited to explain the improvement including a change of command from Brookes to C.M. "Black Mike" McEwen, a First World War ace who was a stickler for training and discipline.[47] It is especially noteworthy that the Canadian Group greatly improved its performance at about the time that Harris launched the Battle of Berlin — surely the most harrowing period of the entire war for bomber aircrew. But how to explain the mystery that this paper raises — that at any given time in the critical year of 1943, a significant number of sorties launched by No. 6 Group squadrons either never left the ground or returned early without attacking the main target ostensibly for mechanical reasons, but in many cases probably for induced or imaginary mechanical reasons? And how to explain that, with rare exceptions, only a tiny fraction of aircrew were ever labelled as LMF or charged for dereliction of duty?

There can be only one answer. Station and squadron commanders knew well that many aborts were not caused by mechanical failure but were a form of insubordination best ignored in first and possibly even in second instances. If a pattern appeared to emerge with a particular pilot or crew, that was one thing. Otherwise, treat the phenomenon as the pink elephant in the room and ignore it. Consequently, a pattern of aborts over an entire group was the result of newness, or mechanical problems, or a transition in aircraft, or ineffective tactics, or lack of training, or inexperience. It was rarely LMF and it was never insubordination. There are indications that such leniency was more the norm and not the exception for Canadian squadrons, where a very Canadian view of aircrew solidarity could be found instead of the more class conscious perspective of some RAF squadrons. But Bomber Command as a whole clearly shied away from the "I" word as well. "Grey" insubordination, after all, was not mutiny, not revolt, not a four square turning against officers and authority. It was a human reaction to the specific nature of this new type of warfare — home every day, likely to die on any given night. Maybe Grey insubordination, and the willingness to all but ignore it, it was the necessary lubrication that allowed the aircrew of Bomber Command to press on. If it was, it worked. Without closer and more intense study, we may never know for sure.

Notes

1.   Quoted in Max Hastings, *Bomber Command* (London: Pan Books, 1981), 263.

2.   Figures taken from "1914–1918 Casualty Figures," available at *www.worldwar1. com/tlcrates.htm.*

3.   "Statistical Summary of Bomber Command's Operations," available at *www. lancastermuseum.ca/commandlosses.html.*

4.   Martin Middlebrook and Chris Everitt, eds., *The Bomber Command War Diaries: An Operational Reference Book, 1939–1945* (Lancaster, Eng.: Midland Publishing, 1996), 708.

5.   See Appendix A to Brereton Greenhous, Stephen J. Harris, William C. Johnston, and William G.P. Rawling, *The Crucible of War 1939–1945: The Official History of the Royal Canadian Air Force Volume 3* (Toronto: University of Toronto Press, 1994), 912.

6.   The two best Canadian studies are Allan D. English, *The Cream of the Crop: Canadian Aircrew, 1939–1945* (Montreal: McGill-Queen's University Press, 1996) and Terry Copp and Bill McAndrew, *Battle Exhaustion: Soldiers and Psychiatrists in the Canadian Army, 1939–1945* (Montreal: McGill-Queen's University Press, 1990).

7.   John Terraine, *The Right of the Line: The Royal Air Force in the European War, 1939–1945* (London: Hodder and Stoughton, 1985), 521.

8.   English, *The Cream of the Crop*, 91.

9.   *Ibid.,* 91–92.

10. *Ibid.*, 92.

11. "Stephen's Study Room: British Military and Criminal History in the period 1900 to 1999," available at *www.stephen-stratford.co.uk/desertion.htm*.

12. Italics from author. Terraine, *The Right of the Line*, 521.

13. *Ibid.*, 535–36.

14. *Ibid.*, 528.

15. *Ibid.*, 535.

16. *Ibid.*, 254.

17. *Ibid.*, 253.

18. *Ibid.*, the discussion in Terraine is from 527–37.

19. Robin Neillands, *The Bomber War: The Allied Air Offensive Against Nazi Germany* (New York: Overlook Press, 2001), 93.

20. English, *The Cream of the Crop*, 113ff.

21. Hastings, *Bomber Command*, 253.

22. Terraine, *The Right of the Line*, 535.

23. *Ibid.*, 521.

24. Richard Overy, *Bomber Command: 1939–1945* (London: HarperCollins, 1997), 174.

25. This data was compiled from the statistics contained in reports produced by Bomber Command after each night's missions. See United Kingdom National Archives (henceforth UKNA, formerly Public Records Office), AIR 14/3410 (microfilm).

26. Spencer Dunmore and William Carter, *Reap the Whirlwind: The Untold Story of 6 Group, Canada's Bomber Force of World War II* (Toronto: McClelland & Stewart, 1991), 194.

27. Those include: Dunmore and Carter, *Reap the Whirlwind*; English, *The Cream of the Crop*; Hastings, *Bomber Command*; Robin Neillands, *The Bomber War*; Leslie Nuttal, "Canadianization and the No. 6 Bomber Group RCAF" (Ph.D. Dissertation, University of Calgary, 1990); Overy, *Bomber Command*; Henry Probert, *Bomber Harris: His Life and Times* (London: Greenhill, 2001); Denis Richard, *The Hardest Victory: RAF Bomber Command in the Second World War* (New York: W.W. Norton & Company, Inc, 1995); James Taylor and Martin

Davidson, *Bomber Crew* (London: Hodder & Stoughton Ltd, 2004); and Terraine, *The Right of the Line.*

28. Nuttal, "Canadianization and the No. 6 Bomber Group RCAF," 214–15.

29. *Ibid.*, 221.

30. *Ibid.*, 222.

31. Dunmore and Carter, *Reap the Whirlwind*, 12.

32. The story of how and why No. 6 Group came to exist is told in C.P. Stacey, *Arms, Men and Governments: The War Policies of Canada, 1939–1945* (Ottawa: Department of National Defence, 1970), 252–307; and Greenhous and others., *The Crucible of War 1939–1945*, 623–55.

33. Royal Air Force Museum (Hendon, United Kingdom), Harris Papers, A-88, Courtney to Harris, 17 March 1943.

34. Nuttal, "Canadianization and the No. 6 Bomber Group RCAF," 226.

35. *Ibid.*, 668.

36. *Ibid.*, 671.

37. Three Operational Research Section reports were done on No. 6 Group on 10 July 1943, 7 October 1943, and 2 March 1944. They are in the UKNA, AIR14/1794/102386. These words were used in the second report.

38. See the three Operational Research Section reports done on No. 6 Group on 10 July 1943, 7 October 1943 and 2 March1944 in UKNA, AIR14/1794/102386; and Greenhous and others, *The Crucible of War 1939–1945*, 656–88.

39. UKNA, AIR14/1794/102386, Table 3. Report of 10 July 1943.

40. *Ibid.*, Report of 10 July 1943.

41. Royal Air Force Museum (Hendon, United Kingdom), Harris Papers, H 103 File 32E, Brookes to Harris, 21 May 1943.

42. Greenhous and others, *The Crucible of War 1939–1945*, 677–78.

43. UKNA, AIR14/3410, "Bomber Command Report on Night Operations 2–3 August, 1943."

44. *Ibid.*, numbers compiled from nightly reports.

45. *Ibid.*, AIR14/1794/102386, "A Note on Comparative Losses in No. 4 and No. 6 Groups," 2 March 1944.

46. *Ibid.*, "A Further Comment on 6 Group Losses," 7 October 1943.

47. Carter and Dunmore, *Reap the Whirlwind*, 220–21.

5

Murder by Spitfire?
Probing for Mutiny and Indiscipline in Canada's Second World War Air Force

Dean C. Black

"Messer" McPhee[1] was an emotional basket case the night he confessed to having deliberately shot down his own Wing Commander. The senior officer was a stiff Royal Air Force veteran who had been hard on "Messer" in the days leading up to the fateful incident. But "Messer's" reputation was well known to the Wing Commander. "Messer" had been shot down twice in the Mediterranean Theatre without ever having fired on the enemy. On both occasions "Messer's" Spitfires had to be written off. Consequently, "Messer" received a verbal reprimand during a session that left him visibly shaken. The next day, in a swirling donnybrook of Italians, Germans, and Allies "Messer" found himself fifty yards behind an airplane he knew to be piloted by the Wing Commander.[2] Still angry from the ridicule he suffered the day prior, "Messer" let go with one short burst and the Wing Commander's plane blew apart. According to "Messer" it was all over in a few seconds, and there were no witnesses at hand.

Shortly before his death, Spitfire pilot turned author Keith Scott referred to his "'Messer' McPhee" story as "near-truth." Determining just how near to the truth forms an important part of this chapter. Even so, Scott would not be the first military author to stir up controversy by embellishing fiction with fact born of his own wartime experiences. Will Bird, author of *And We Go On*, and Charles Yale Harrison, who wrote *Generals Die in Bed*, both produced First World War memoirs that were criticized for their near-truths. Both memoirs evidently portrayed significant indiscipline, with Harrison describing the shooting death of an officer at the hands of one of his men, allegedly for being too aggressive.[3] Paul Fussell, a respected author and Second World War U.S. Army veteran, described critics of such books as the "loony patriotic type"[4] so as to discourage any and all attempts to sanitize and romanticize war.

Far from romanticizing Second World War life in the Royal Canadian Air Force (RCAF), this chapter explores a possible Air Force example that may be added to the Army experiences provided by Bird, Harrison, and others. Working from large-scale events to smaller but no less significant ones, this investigation builds on the inference from Scott's story that a RCAF fighter pilot deliberately shot down one of his own squadron pilots. Deconstructing the memoirs of another Spitfire pilot — Hugh Constant Godefroy — is central to this effort.[5] The chapter compares Godefroy's memoir-based real-life event to Scott's "'Messer' McPhee." Godefroy's *Lucky Thirteen* account of the loss of one pilot leads one to wonder whether a murder like the one suggested by Scott actually took place. One author has claimed such an event took place during the First World War.[6] Are Godefroy and Scott trying to tell us that such an act also occurred during the Second World War? They would not be alone. One former Royal Air Force (RAF) wing commander, Dizzy Allen, claims a number of pilots in Fighter Command did "get away with murder" during the Second World War, and the context of Allen's claim suggests he is not using a figure of speech.[7]

The ensuing comparison considers first whether or not it was plausible for one pilot to have shot down another from his own side, during the Second World War? It will be shown that, just as Scott has described it, such an opportunity could present itself during air-to-air combat in that twentieth century conflict. It is interesting to note that evidence now points to the likelihood that the legendary legless RAF Ace — Douglas Bader — was inadvertently brought down by one of his own pilots, not by a German fighter.[8] But were there pilots who deliberately perpetrated such an act? We know that on 23 May 1942 a flight of 402 Squadron Spitfires led by Flight Lieutenant Malloy was airborne over the English Channel when another Spitfire suddenly attacked Malloy. Malloy bailed out while his wingman Ian Keltie chased after the assailant. Keltie deliberately shot down the perpetrator, perhaps in retribution for what looked like incompetence, and followed the doomed Spitfire as it crash-landed onto the Hawkinge, England airfield.[9] However, though the incident demonstrates capability, Keltie never tried to conceal his actions. For that kind of incident — the "'Messer' McPhee"-type — further investigation is warranted.

With respect to capability, identification of the skills essential to successfully perpetrate such an act leads to a discussion of one of Canada's more famous Aces from the Second World War — George Frederick "Screwball" Beurling. This discussion of indiscipline could not possibly focus solely on Beurling's extraordinary flying talents while ignoring the other activities for which over time, perhaps somewhat undeservedly, Beurling has also become renowned. And it would be unacceptable for one to attempt to make excuses for Beurling's more questionable indiscretions, notwithstanding claims that some of the Beurling stories have been described as apocryphal.[10] Nevertheless, it is not the intent to insinuate in any way that Beurling is guilty of the act central to this chapter's thesis. To the contrary, Beurling's exploits may be more readily understood in a different context; namely, that his late 1943 appreciation for fighter tactics, resulting in part from his Malta experiences, may have been on the mark more so than his superiors may have been willing to admit.[11] In Beurling's case he may have simply been unable to express himself such that his superiors might be more apt to consider him seriously. Beurling's misdeeds thus become of interest in this study of indiscipline. In the end, because acts of mutiny and related behaviour are arguably among the greatest challenges any military leader can face, an appreciation for the conditions existing in a Canadian fighter squadron, during the Second World War, might be educational for prospective leaders. After all, "[i]f we are to understand the 'leadership perspectives of aerospace power' then we must first understand the human condition in aerospace combat: We must understand the aviators' experience."[12]

What do we mean by mutiny? In some respects it is necessary to distinguish between classic mutinies, or the types of seditious affairs involving handfuls if not scores of personnel, and the mutinous or indiscipline-like behaviour that might have been present within a bomber crew or fighter squadron. Classic mutinies arguably most familiar to the reader might be those fictional and non-fictional cases dealt with in various forms of literature and media, such as the *Caine Mutiny*,[13] and the *Mutiny on the Bounty*.[14] To these naval examples one

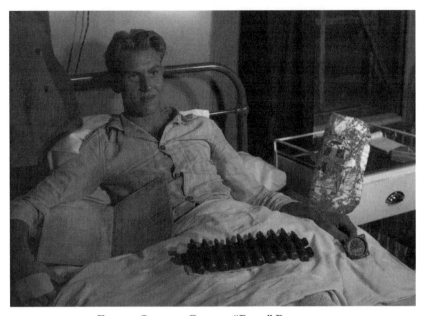

FLYING OFFICER GEORGE "BUZZ" BEURLING
CONVALESCES IN AN ENGLISH HOSPITAL, 1942.
(Department of National Defence, Canadian Forces Joint Imagery Centre PL 10976)

must add the April 1917 nation-wide mutiny of the French Army that followed a five-day failure to rupture the German line and led to 130,000 French casualties.[15] But in answer to the question about what constitutes mutiny, it can be considered, in a most general sense, to be the accepted legal term for almost every refusal to obey orders.[16] While this generality is of some relevance, it is important that we be more specific, so as to understand what may be behind the behaviour central to this chapter.

A more formal definition of mutiny can be gleaned from legal texts.[17] The important point to glean from Chapter 3 to the *Manual of Air Force Law* is that the charge of mutiny did not actually exist. A perpetrator or perpetrators accused of mutiny would, in fact, be charged with other offences described in Section 7 of that manual. Additionally, failure to inform one's commanding officer (CO) of an intended mutiny was deemed sufficient grounds to be charged under Section 7 as well. Mutinous behaviour and indiscipline could thus take many forms but this chapter is particularly interested in how fighter pilots may have dealt with those who were believed to be too aggressive, careless, unpopular, or incompetent. Sadly, space limitations prevent a more thorough analysis of Air Force culture and its relevance to the possibility that a squadron-wide cover up of a pilot's murder, at the hands of another, might in fact be indicative of a unit-scale mutiny in breach of what would otherwise be considered a moral precept, as opposed to a legal order.

Mutinous acts exhibit certain traits. Motive, for example, underpins all mutinies. Messer McPhee sought revenge, wanting nothing more than to get back at his bully of a wing commander. Second, in committing the act a perpetrator typically prefers anonymity although the result normally reflects the desire of personnel other than the perpetrator. Finally, an individual or group willing to commit a mutinous act typically has only one victim in mind, if they plan to victimize anyone at all. However, in many cases the perpetrators want to achieve a certain outcome without violence or injury to any other person than the one deemed to be the problem. A reasonable schema for assessing behaviours central to this paper, thus, considers motive, opportunity/anonymity, and the mitigation of harm. By employing this schema an attempt is made to analyze specific events of relevant behaviour as they unfolded in the RCAF during the Second World War.

The Canadian military has not been immune to mutinous behaviour. Occasionally, poor leadership was a contributing cause, especially in the Army and Navy.[18] However, the RCAF had leadership problems too that contributed to incidents of insubordination, indiscipline or mutiny.[19] With respect to large-scale Canadian Air Force (CAF) mutinies three occurrences come to mind. In January 1919 general demobilization was underway but, despite this, a number of factors began fomenting among disgruntled members of the CAF. At Halton Camp in England, they refused to drill. A British officer had decided that despite the deplorably muddy condition of the drill square he would parade the Canadians. This appeared to be the last straw in a series of events that precipitated the Halton Camp "crisis."[20] This collective action was nearing its end when a similar problem arose at Upper Heyford, when unpaid Canadian aircrew who had been assigned to fatigue duties, denied Christmas leave, and forced to tolerate unacceptable messing conditions for far too long protested. Leadership or a lack thereof, was again an issue. Shortly after the Second World War ended, one of the larger Air Force mutinies took place at Odiham Transport Squadron Station (RCAF) on or about February 6, 1946. Close to 1,500 aircrew fully believed they had not volunteered for further service and could not believe the words of the acting commander-in-chief of the RCAF (overseas), Air Commodore H.B. Goodwin, who claimed that "… most of them would be back in Canada by next September." The action, or inaction, of the men effectively ground to a halt all activities at Odiham, and not a single aircraft left the hangar line for some time.[21]

The aforementioned incidents were relatively large-scale events involving men overcome by boredom and subjected to poor leadership.[22] For smaller events specific to the RCAF it is instructive to look at aspects of individual units. In a fighter squadron, for example, mission success and "[l]ife itself [depended] on the trust and mutual confidence [between the pilot and his wingman]."[23] This cohesion reflected the importance of each man sharing equally in the assumption of risk. Fighter pilots were to be prepared to give up their lives for each other. A wingman was expected to put his leader first, and himself second. Perhaps more important, many a pilot might see his role either as wingman or leader change from mission to mission or day-to-day, especially in periods marked by high casualty rates. Air Vice-Marshal James Edgar "Johnnie" Johnson explained "… the greatest [fighter pilots] have a high sense of duty … and … his pilots [knew] he [would] watch over them and bring them home."[24] But Johnson and some of his peers seemed to appreciate that killing an enemy pilot was a rather impersonal process.[25] Sneaking up behind the unsuspecting enemy was the preferred *modus operandi*. The best pilots have also been described as "back-stabbing assassins."[26] As the war progressed " … most successful pilots … avoided the classic dogfight … [relying instead on] fast [passes] from above taking opponents by surprise, [firing] a close-in burst, then by [disengaging and running]."[27] Bearing in mind such tactics, any effort to apply the traditional code of the warrior to fighter pilots of the Second World War would probably fail.[28] Aircraft technology to that point seemed to favour this type of sniping — the antithesis of civilized killing in combat.[29] As a consequence of these conditions it might be understandable why anything that compromised cohesion between men in these units could in turn contribute to instances of indiscipline, if not insubordination and possibly mutiny.[30] Sometimes the fighter pilot's ego would be enough to destroy that cohesion. "As a group fighter pilots are uniquely arrogant, opinionated and disdainful of anyone except their peer group."[31] Most important, examples exist where some fighter pilots were simply not accepted by their peers. We now turn to such a situation.

Flying instructors were initially hard to come by, during the early part of the Second World War. Most pilot candidates who succeeded in flying training wanted nothing more than to get overseas and fight. The vast majority had their sights set only on a fighter aircraft, and would openly protest when presented with a bomber or patrol aircraft cockpit. Some, however, were motivated toward different goals,[32] while others had to be enticed into the instructor role with promises of rapid promotion.[33] Those with an aversion to combat understandably lobbied for instructor jobs. However, as the war progressed and casualties mounted,[34] some from this group were sent overseas. Not surprisingly, not all fit in well. Some allegedly claimed that by virtue of their advanced rank they deserved better treatment. Having to fly on someone else's wing was an insult, especially if they were of a lower rank. Although there is little doubt these flight lieutenant former instructor-pilots were among the most talented pilots, many understandably knew precious little about air-to-air combat. Wing Commander Hugh Constant Godefroy appears to have described one of these men in his memoirs *Lucky Thirteen*. What is particularly remarkable about Godefroy's description, however, is the reference to a nursery rhyme character. It is an analysis of this reference to which we now turn, in this probe for indiscipline and mutiny in the Second World War RCAF:

> One such individual was sent to the Wing and in no time had generated enormous resentment affecting even the atmosphere of the Mess. The situation resolved itself. On an otherwise *uneventful sweep he failed to return. Nobody had seen what had happened* to him, and nobody seemed particularly curious. The thorn was gone, and overnight the Mess became a different place. Replacements were screened much more carefully from then on. I have always wondered *who shot "Cock Robin."*[35][italics added by author]

Is Godefroy drawing our attention to a possible murder? A clear understanding of the author's intent calls for the passage to be deconstructed, especially in respect of the description of the sweep and the lack of witnesses. The moniker, Cock Robin, also deserves attention. First, the characterization of the sweep, during which Cock Robin goes missing, as uneventful, contrasts sharply with the subsequent claim that "... nobody had seen what had happened." A brief description of fighter air-to-air combat tactics is necessary to illuminate why the two phrases should be considered incongruent. Second, the label, Cock Robin, could be considered a loaded reference unless we believe that a man of Godefroy's intellect and experience accidentally used the metaphor the true meaning of which he was unaware.[36]

Sweeps typically employed formations of four to 12 aircraft. Pilots would weave their aircraft to and fro, intentionally changing heading every five to 10 seconds, to keep a watch so as to spoil enemy attacks. If the sweep was uneventful, as Godefroy claims, then nothing, including enemy fighters, would have interfered with the integrity of their formation. Under these conditions, then, should one pilot fail to return without an explanation, circumstances would seem to point to the others as having turned a blind eye. In Cock Robin's case did those involved choose to obey a code of silence to preserve fighter pilot cohesion? Such a possibility could help to explain an incident that took place on or about 16 February 1943. But before elaborating on that occurrence, other events of interest require explanation.

On or about 13 April 1942 a Canadian pilot named Ron Emberg noted in his log book following an air-to-ground firing practice at Imber Downs, Salisbury Plain, that "[o]ne of the boys mistook spectators for target. Killed 23, Wounded 60."[37] Scratched out ineffectively at the beginning of Emberg's note were the rank and the first three letters of the last name of the pilot at fault.[38] Further probing revealed that also flying that day was a pilot named Charlie Bavis. Bavis apparently had been haunted by a wartime memory so horrible that for much of his life he simply refused to talk about it. However, someone who had been close to Bavis has explained that Bavis named his first-born son after a wartime buddy — Orlan [sic] Roderick Brown — who according to Bavis "... had been shot down by one of his fellow pilots."[39] Brown was lost on 16 February 1943. Was this the incident that haunted Bavis? Was Brown somehow connected to the Imber Downs incident during which one of his fellow pilots killed dozens of innocent spectators? Although it seems unlikely, what should one make of the possibility that a rogue Spitfire pilot may have been seeking to avenge the killing and maiming of countrymen at Imber Downs? In any event, this particular incident offers yet another indication that the issue Scott and Godefroy discuss — the shooting down of one's own — seems plausible. Three pilots, not just Brown, were lost during that fateful 16 February 1943 incident. According to the 540/541 entries of both 402 and 403 Squadrons, oxygen problems were blamed for the losses of Bavis's buddy, Orland Brown, as well as Williamson and Connacher.[40] However, 402 Squadron's account describes two mysterious Spitfires that jumped the massed 402–403 Squadron 21-plane formation.[41] It should also be emphasized that Hugh Constant Godefroy was a member of the 21-plane formation on that 16 February 1943 mission.

When we return to the late 1943 case of Cock Robin, an entry made in the 403 Squadron Operations Record Book, (ORB)[42] for 20 July 1943 reveals:

> F/L [Flight Lieutenant] C.P. Thornton and F/L Southwood were posted to the Squadron wef [with effect from] today, Mr. Southwood coming from 416 Squadron and Mr. Thornton from 402 Squadron.[43]

For the same date 403 Squadron pilot W. (Walter) A.G. Conrad recorded in his personal diary:

> Was on readiness from 8:30 to 1, and 5 to 8 p.m. No show because the weather was bad. Got about three new F/Lts [Flight Lieutenants] in from Canada today — ex-instructors. Getting too many of these types.[44]

It would appear that Conrad was concerned about "ex-instructors" and that his concerns may have matched Godefroy's. A review of 403 Squadron's wartime casualty list reveals that Flight Lieutenant Herbert John Southwood was probably the one Godefroy had dubbed Cock Robin.[45] Furthermore, the ORB for 24 October 1943, the day Southwood disappeared, describes two sweeps:[46]

> Sunday, 24 October, 1943. Today was sunny with a few scattered clouds. Four non-operational sorties were flown on local flying and aircraft tests. There were also two sweeps. On the first sweep, our Squadron became engaged and F/O [Flying Officer] J.D. Browne destroyed one ME-109 and damaged another. F/L [Flight Lieutenant] H.J. Southwood is posted as missing today.

In his logbook Godefroy recorded 1.35 flying hours on Rodeo 280 to the Amiens area during which he saw "50 huns," and another mission — "Ram[rod] 284 to Knocke." Written next to his Rodeo 280 entry is the following message:

> F/O [Flying Officer] Brown [*sic*] — 1 dest[royed].
> 1 damaged S/L [Second Lieutenant] Magwood
> F/O Driver 2 damage[d] F/L [Flight Lieutenant]
> Southwood missing[47]

If one chooses to attribute the loss of Southwood to the uneventful latter sweep — Ramrod 284 — one would clearly denigrate him. Alternately, if Rodeo 280 is selected — during which as many as "50 huns" were seen — then one can avoid denigrating Southwood by acknowledging that he was lost in the presence of a relatively formidable enemy force. Why did Godefroy claim Cock Robin was lost in an uneventful sweep (Ramrod 284?) when Godefroy's own logbook indicates otherwise? A complete accounting for Godefroy's description must address the Cock Robin reference. In fact, regardless of which "sweep" one chooses one is left with the task of accounting for this rather mysterious moniker.[48] Even more disconcerting, perhaps, is the revelation that in the ORB entry J.D. Browne recorded that "after the squadron was vectored onto 'sixty huns' Southwood was last seen proceeding straight and level with some Jerries in eager pursuit." Browne then concludes the entry referring to the "*late* F/Lt [Flight Lieutenant] H.J. Southwood" [italics added by author] and states: "God Rest his Soul." In light of these entries, it is a challenge to figure out why Godefroy claimed that Southwood was only missing, that there were no witnesses, that no one really cared, and that the circumstances were rather benign.

> Who killed Cock Robin?
> I, said the Sparrow.
> With my bow and arrow.
> I killed Cock Robin.

The true identity of Cock Robin, the principal character of the child's nursery rhyme by the same title, has been a curiosity for centuries. The list of candidates includes King William II Rufus, Robin Hood, and even Balder the Norse God, with the most popular tending to be Robin Hood. However, the identity of Cock Robin is of less importance than is the method of his demise. Regardless of the true identity of Cock Robin it is important to understand that death came to each at the hands of a trusted agent by way of treachery.

Can our schema of mutiny help to validate whether or not Cock Robin's demise was the result of a treacherous act at the hands of a trusted agent? As for motive it is clear from Godefroy's reference, and somewhat marginally less so from Conrad's, that a former flying instructor had caused some sort of stir in the unit. According to Godefroy, Cock Robin was not lacking in moral fibre.[49] Something else was amiss. It seems reasonable to infer from the full context of Godefroy's reference that the individual in question may have boasted about his instructional experience and in referring to his rank claimed the right to lead formations, rather than follow. So overly confident might he have been, in his own technical and instructional acumen that others who were expected to serve as his wingmen or lead him into battle may have considered him to be a significant risk until he gained more combat experience. If this former flying instructor's boasting was relentless how far fetched would it be for someone to have decided he must be eliminated?

If Cock Robin's aggression, demonstrated during earlier missions, was of concern to prospective wingmen he would not have been the first 403 pilot to have earned such an assessment. Squadron Leader Alan Deere may have earned that distinction one year earlier.[50] However, the Deere incident of June 1942 would have had no bearing on 403 Squadron one year later, as the squadron's leadership tried to deal with Cock Robin, unless there was someone on strength with 403 Squadron during Cock Robin's time that also witnessed the earlier exploits of Deere when 403 Squadron lost six pilots and seven aircraft. As it turns out there was just such a witness. Charlie Magwood had been serving with the squadron going on two years and would have been in a position to have cautioned his fellow 403 pilots, in late 1943, about not letting the squadron suffer another Deere-type incident, at the hands of a Cock Robin.[51] From the 403 ORB we know that Herb Southwood was far from timid, and that he was an excellent shot. He appears to have scored one FW 190 and could lay claim to damaging another two, by 6 September 1943. Remarkably, however, he seems to have been restricted to flying only as wingman. Despite his 416 Squadron experience it would appear superiors in 403 Squadron were loathe to permit Southwood lead a section or formation of aircraft.[52]

Returning to the original proposition and the matter of opportunity one must ask whether the circumstances prevalent during the mission on which Cock Robin fell were comparable to those faced by McPhee. First it is reasonable to assume anonymity could be relatively assured mindful of the descriptions of air-to-air combat a detailed rehashing of which is not necessary at this point in the narrative.[53] As the reader can well appreciate, it was one rare thing to find a fight, and an even rarer thing to win one, mindful of the earlier description of those opportunities as a series of "whooshes."[54] It would seem, therefore, that engagement of a friendly aircraft could be achieved while preserving anonymity just as easily as one might desire during combat with an enemy aircraft.[55] In fact, one method by which one might increase the chances of not being detected by an enemy pilot would involve removing tracer rounds from one's ammunition bins. The targeted pilot would be less likely to notice that his aircraft was being engaged until rounds impacted his aircraft.

Flight Lieutenant George Beurling, on strength with 403 Squadron at that time, was apparently renowned for such a trick — the removal of tracer rounds — and was extraordinarily confident with his own shooting ability.[56] Within 24 hours of Southwood's disappearance it seems Beurling was promoted to the position of flight commander to replace him. Again, while this is not to suggest that Beurling was in any way responsible for the loss in question, it is intended to show that the skills necessary for the kind of act Godefroy seems to be alluding to were available. Nevertheless, and this is why it is important to discuss Beurling at this juncture, it is Beurling's skills that are highlighted to show that perpetrating such an act would require the most skilled of pilots. There are, as well, no indications that Beurling was even flying on the day Southwood was brought down.

With respect to Beurling's shooting skills, in one famous incident he described in public an encounter that he had with an Italian Macchi fighter pilot, when he was operating out of Malta. Beurling claimed he had complete control of the trajectory of each individual bullet and described how a single round caught the Italian pilot in the face, decapitating him.[57] Another aspect of Beurling's "perverse" behaviour, at the time, was his penchant for breaking formation.[58] Beurling routinely peeled away from his wingmen to pursue single aircraft targets, vehicles on roads, or, in some cases, which seemed to demonstrate a lack of discipline, he would apparently break formation to go after livestock.[59] What is also remarkable about these forays is that Beurling was apparently prone to perform them regardless of the role he may have been assigned for the formation in question. In other words, even where he had been ordered to lead the formation it was not uncommon for him to abandon his duties, leaving the formation to fend for itself while being led by a neophyte Number 2, so as to pursue targets on his own. On one occasion his formation lead — Wing Commander Godefroy — glanced over his shoulder to see Beurling flying inverted in the Number 4 position, as was the case on 18 October 1943 when Beurling nearly lost his life in a high-speed dive after having left the formation without permission.[60] It should come as no surprise therefore, that Beurling's behaviour had "created major tension with his fellow pilots."[61]

On 28 October 1943, Godefroy formally promoted Beurling to the appointment of Commander "B" Flight, thereby replacing the missing Southwood.[62] However, Beurling was apparently not interested in the job. He seems to have rebelled against the appointment fearing too much administration, according to Godefroy.[63] A short while later, he took to low flying in the squadron Tiger Moth, twice passing directly and deliberately over Godefroy's caravan. Although it appears Beurling was acting up over the recent appointment, this was apparently not the first time he had demonstrated such flying judgment. He had developed a reputation for dangerous low flying in previous incidents — one that allegedly scattered a field full of rugby players and another wherein an elderly man who happened to be ambling across an open pasture was apparently knocked down by Beurling's stunt flying.[64] When Godefroy posted a regulation forbidding such activity, on or about 1 November 1943, Beurling appears to have promptly taken off in the Tiger Moth and buzzed his wing commander's caravan for a third time. Godefroy subsequently placed Beurling under open arrest. Minister for Air, Chubby Powers intervened on behalf of the prime minister who apparently had an interest in Beurling. A temporary grounding was imposed, on the renegade pilot, and Godefroy was persuaded to accept the posting of Beurling to 126 Wing and, ultimately, 412 Squadron under the personal care of Wing Commander Buck McNair.

Beurling's second tour with 403 Squadron had lasted barely two months.[65] From 6 September to 9 November 1943 he appears to have incurred the wrath of at least his wing commander, Godefroy, and his CO, Buckham. On one occasion Beurling apparently decided to shoot his revolver at Buckham's pet duck.[66] This was not the only time he fired his weapon at something other than the enemy. While on

Malta Beurling apparently had a penchant for picking off stray dogs and lizards with his revolver.[67] Beurling himself explains, however, that dogs and lizards were legitimate target practice; Beurling would only shoot at them when at a certain distance their size would equal the size of an enemy aircraft at 300 yards, or so. The pet duck incident cannot be so easily explained. On 11 September 1943 Beurling deliberately fired a shotgun at Air Officer Commanding 83 Group Air Vice-Marshal W.F. Dickson's Auster airplane, as it flew overhead while on final approach.[68] However, this had not been the only aircraft Beurling delighted in firing upon.[69]

Buckham was apparently infuriated over the duck incident, and according to Godefroy threatened to kill Beurling if he ever did it again — a credible threat given that Buckham had a Black Belt in judo. The acrimony between Buckham and Beurling, however, is believed to have originated a few weeks earlier. Sometime during the summer the two of them were attending an air gunnery training session at the Central Gunnery School at Sutton Bridge in Lincolnshire. Buckham, the student, is believed to have forgotten his cannons were loaded and his system was armed, when he simulated firing on Beurling, who was instructing him. Beurling's engine was disabled by Buckham's shooting, and he was forced to bail out.[70]

After Beurling unceremoniously departed 403 Squadron he and his new wing commander, Buck McNair, apparently came to a serious disagreement.[71] Beurling is believed to have brought to an early end a four-plane "Ranger" mission when one of his wingmen crashed shortly after takeoff. Beurling may have ignored the order that called for pilots to climb to 1,000 feet before switching over to their auxiliary fuel tank. It was apparently not uncommon for Beurling to ignore such an order.[72] On another occasion in early 1944 Beurling is alleged to have openly defied the authority of his CO by publicly announcing that since the Battle of Britain had ended long ago orders to take turns on "Readiness" were to be ignored.[73] On yet another occasion, despite orders prohibiting him from doing so, Beurling ordered his flight of four airplanes to break formation with the rest of the squadron so that Beurling could do his own thing.[74]

Returning to Beurling's fateful "Ranger" mission, a number of engine failures had plagued 126 Wing, prompting McNair to mandate a procedure to mitigate risk. Pilots had to gain some altitude before switching over to the auxiliary fuel tank to give them time to attempt a restart in the event of an engine failure. On this particular "Ranger" mission, it has been suggested that Beurling and his three pilots took off at low level and despite McNair's order, stayed low. Perhaps upon switching to their auxiliary tanks, the last aircraft in his formation crashed, killing the pilot. Beurling apparently made his way out to the crash scene where he met up with Wing Commanders McNair and Hodson. A heated exchange apparently took place during which Beurling is alleged to have threatened McNair.[75]

In late 1943, Beurling was apparently frustrated with the lack of tactical freedom he had, in comparison to his earlier Malta experiences. Time and again he pined for permission to head out over Germany on his own.[76] The authorities are believed to have relented by authorizing the fateful "Ranger" mission. His earlier habit of breaking formation reflected his desire for greater freedom. That habit, however, was infuriating to Godefroy, and a concern to other pilots in 403 Squadron.[77] Junior pilots were anxious, with the prospect of their lead aircraft, piloted by Beurling, peeling off and disappearing without warning, leaving them to fend for themselves. To make matters worse Beurling's decapitation of the Macchi pilot, coupled with his remarkable ability to pick out and pick off specific Italian pilots who by their reactions clearly demonstrated more refined skills than others,[78] must have been considered extreme by some that were aware of Beurling's apparently unequalled ability to know where each bullet would go, before he pulled the trigger.[79] Additionally, Beurling's public accounts of his exploits may have been considered too gruesome, setting him further apart from other pilots. Beurling's ability to garner the respect and trust of all his peers could have begun to erode, as 1944 unfolded.[80]

However, there were indications that Beurling was probably correct about the most effective tactics to be employed in the West European theatre as 1943 drew to a close. Unfortunately he may have run into a brick wall in the form of a select, conservative few who may have been focused more on running up their personal score and earning post-war glory. Despite professed disgust on the part of British pilots in general and Air Ministry discord in particular, with "the culture of the Ace," the media made great play of RAF and RCAF pilots who were amassing ever higher personal scores — singling out pilots like Bader, Tuck and Johnson as "heroes."[81] These pilots may have believed that one could only succeed in the hunt for such glory if one prosecuted that hunt from the front of large-scale fighter aircraft formations, with the other pilots on hand solely to protect those claiming a legitimacy to act as first shooter. Beurling's own Flight Commander — Cock Robin — may have been hoping to become such a leader.[82] To illustrate, Wing Commander "Johnnie" Johnson was known to acknowledge enemy aircraft sightings made by his wingmen with a terse order for the successful spotter to lead "Johnnie" onto the targets so he could get a shot away, even though he seemed unable to see the targets to which his attention had been drawn. Squadron Leader Godefroy had also gained some success not simply by shooting down enemy aircraft, but by shooting down enemy aircraft he himself had consciously chosen not to reveal to Johnson. Perhaps one might be tempted to excuse Beurling, therefore, for not being able to effectively challenge such perceptions about the best type of fighter tactics, and for having caused so much trouble with his antics that unfortunately continued long after he had been removed from 403 Squadron and 127 Wing.

Evidence exists that many experienced squadron commanders and wing leaders flew to the end of the war without ever having updated the tactics they taught to new arrivals, although fighter combat trends had begun to change.[83] Johnson seems to admit this change took place in his best-seller *Full Circle*, the title of which would seem to imply that the trend in the size of effective formations of fighter aircraft was to decrease, as the end of the Second World War approached, to match the formation sizes that predominated at the beginning of the First World War. Sadly, Johnson successfully avoids giving sufficient credit to Beurling who seems to have been on a crusade to make this tactical trend evident to Air Force superiors.[84]

Beurling probably got along less with his last wing commander, Buck McNair, owing to McNair's fighting style. Johnson and McNair both liked large formations, directing the efforts of their many wingmen like conductors in front of a symphony. But one of McNair's pilots has confirmed that McNair would not enter the fray like Johnson would, chasing after the Huns, but instead preferred to sit atop the fight watching from the heights and radioing instructions to his subordinates.[85] Johnson, on the other hand seemed to prefer lots of wingmen who served as his eyes. Once they told him where the targets were he ordered them to lead him onto them. McNair, however, may have avoided close in engagements after suffering burn damage to his eyes in a previous incident. In either case it seems Beurling felt confined by higher ups who tried to keep him on a short leash. These sorts of tactics could not have been further from the style he had enjoyed while operating over Malta for much of 1942.

Did a real-life event possibly involving the murder of one RCAF pilot by one of his own squadron mates inspire Keith Scott's story about McPhee? On the surface Godefroy's memoir reference to a man dubbed "Cock Robin" would seem to fit the bill. By invoking the legend of Cock Robin in his description of one particular problem pilot, Godefroy left those of us pondering the possibility of mutinous behaviour in the RCAF with a moniker that gives pause for thought. But Godefroy did not stop there. By attributing the loss of the pilot to an uneventful sweep, and by implying that the loss was a morale booster, in the wing, the reader can be forgiven for dwelling on the possibility that Godefroy himself believed that Cock Robin was, as the nursery rhyme suggests, the victim of treachery at the hands of a trusted agent in a fellow pilot. Forty years of hindsight led Godefroy to reflect on Cock Robin's death, and the fact he died without much of a passing positive thought from his peers. Too much confidence may be the most likely explanation for the acrimony Cock Robin apparently created in 403 Squadron during the late fall of 1943. One thing seems certain; at the time Godefroy wrote Cock Robin into his memoirs, he may have believed that the young sprite had been done in by one of his own squadron mates. What remains uncertain is whether or not Godefroy's impressions may have been influenced by the 16 February 1943 incident during which as many as three pilots from 402 and 403 Squadron may have been shot down by two unknown Allied Spitfire pilots. Also uncertain is the role either incident may have played in Keith Scott's short story."

For a fellow pilot to eliminate Cock Robin during a mission aloft, he would have had to rely on certain well-honed skills. Success would have likely called for a few tricks as well, in part to preserve anonymity. After all, anonymity is considered an important characteristic of mutiny. Along with motive, opportunity, and the desire not to harm any other personnel, these traits constitute a schema for assessing such acts. Air-to-air combat of the Second World War can be described as fractions of seconds filled with violence, peppered with brief intervals of silent confusion and panic. Into this mix it has been demonstrated how easy it might have been for one pilot to have engaged and destroyed another of his own, whether in a moment of error or fit of revenge. In McPhee's case we are presented with the latter in the form of a purportedly fictional account of mutiny. In Cock Robin's case we are left to wonder whether or not Godefroy truly believed his pilot had been intentionally done in by one of his own.

Succeeding at such a task would have called for certain skills on which few pilots could probably draw. Upon reflection, however, we see that George Frederick Beurling — one of Canada's more renowned fighter Aces — had what was needed. He had few equals who could designate or pre-ordain where their individual rounds were to impact. Most pilots simply fired at a target's centre-of-mass. Beurling, however, preferred to choose specific parts of his target to disable. Sometimes the parts he chose to engage were biological rather than mechanical. Nevertheless, along with a few others of his calibre, Beurling was attuned to the fighter pilot's *modus operandi* — sneaking up behind a target and destroying it before the enemy pilot had any idea of the danger. By using ammunition belts with tracer rounds removed, Beurling was more likely to surprise his target. Such a trick would also help ensure anonymity, and increase the chances for success.

While motive and anonymity might be more evident, where the Cock Robin and McPhee stories are concerned, the last element of our schema is less so. Mitigation of collateral damage or avoidance of harm to others is more challenging to identify for the aforementioned fighter squadron examples, than it is in larger-scale examples drawn from the Army and Navy experiences. This third element appears to be met if the perpetrator believes that less harm will come to him and those around him if the offending party is eliminated. In this way shooting down McPhee's wing commander and Godefroy's Cock Robin is akin to the shooting death of an overly aggressive officer by his own men, as described in Charles Yale Harrison's *Generals Die in Bed*.

According to Godefroy, Cock Robin's death was a morale booster. The reason appears to have been related to the ex-flying instructor's attitude. Godefroy might want us to believe that Cock Robin fully expected by virtue of his rank and instructional flying experience to lead formations, not follow them. Serving as a wingman was, to him, probably degrading. Unfortunately his lack of combat experience appeared to have led senior squadron authorities to employ Cock Robin in more junior roles much to his chagrin. Interestingly enough, however, his displeasure over these tactics was somewhat akin to that which Beurling was exhibiting, although in Beurling's case it would appear something else was going on.

Like Cock Robin, Beurling, too, appears to have been frustrated with the tactics his superiors held. He was cautioned often not to play the "lone-wolf" since his Malta experiences were, according to those superiors, of no benefit in the enemy aircraft and flak-rich environment of the Western European theatre. Beurling's behaviour leads one to believe he may have disagreed with that assessment.

Spitfires of Number 403 (Wolf) Squadron, Royal Canadian Air Force, likely at Kenley, England, take off in 1943.
(Department of National Defence, Library and Archives Canada PA 115117)

Instead he preferred his own tactical methods, placing more confidence in smaller formations. Consequently, he appears to have worked tirelessly to obtain four advanced fighter aircraft and permission to roam over Europe in a hunt for enemy aircraft. Sadly, Beurling's struggle hit many roadblocks. His fight would eventually create problems and lead to indiscipline. Threatened with court-martial by Godefroy, Beurling was moved to a different wing. Unfortunately, matters did not improve. By April 1944 Beurling had returned to Canada revered for his tally of more than 31 enemy aircraft, but held in disdain by some for the other side of his reputation. Only much later would it seem that his assessment of fighter tactics in 1943 may have been closer to the mark than Godefroy, "Johnnie" Johnson and others appeared to be willing to concede. Johnson's own post-war book, *Full Circle*, seems to confirm Beurling's assessment while at the same time providing a less than complimentary reference to Beurling's superb skills.[86]

This indiscipline-focused study of the human side of air-to-air combat leadership seeks to add to other military studies produced by those with a serious interest in the matter of insubordination, mutiny, and related behaviours. Admittedly, however, it might offer only a partial and possibly unsatisfactory treatment of the subject.[87] Although Colonel Randall Wakelam, the former director of professional development at the Canadian Defence Academy, suggests much can be learned about such aviation leadership challenges from the memoirs of those like Godefroy, even in such accounts important details if not the truth can remain concealed possibly by what Paul Fussell referred to as a tendency to romanticize and sanitize war.

NOTES

1. See Keith Forbes Scott, *Messer McPhee*. This is an unpublished story from a collection of four wartime memoirs found at *www.interlog.com/~kkeith*; and see also Peter Rehak, "WWII Pilot Hated Violence of War: Canadian Flew Spitfires," *National Post*, 3 January 2000, A16.

2. Officers appointed to wing commander (flying) positions were entitled to replace the three-letter call sign on their aircraft with their initials. Robert Stanford Tuck thus had "RST" painted on his airplane.

3. Jonathan F. Vance, *Death So Noble: Memory, Meaning, and the First World War* (Vancouver: University of British Columbia Press, 1997), 193–94.

4. Paul Fussell, *Wartime: Understanding and Behaviour in the Second World War* (New York: Oxford University Press, 1989), ix. Paul Fussell served as Donald T. Regan Professor of English Literature at the University of Pennsylvania. He was also a platoon commander with the 103rd Infantry Division, U.S. Army, during the Second World War.

5. Hugh Constant Godefroy flew with 401 and 403 Squadrons, during the Second World War. He served as the commanding officer of the latter, in 1943, and later assumed the wing commander position (127 Wing) upon James Edgar "Johnnie" Johnson's departure on or about 11 September 1943.

6. Lee Kennett, *The First Air War: 1914–1918* (New York: The Free Press, 1991), 143.

7. Dizzy Allen, *Fighter Squadron: 1940–1942* (London: Granada, 1982), 198.

8. Andy Saunders, "It Happened Here: Who Downed Douglas Bader?" in *After the Battle*, No. 125 (2004), 3–25.

9. Canada, Department of National Defence, Form 540 Operations Record Book, 402 (Fighter) Squadron, Royal Canadian Air Force, 23 May 1942. Operations Record Books can be viewed on microfiche at Library and Archives Canada. Also, confidential email correspondence, 18 February 2005.

10. Don Carlson, "Flight Lieutenant George F. Beurling" in *We Band of Brothers*, Lloyd Hunt, ed. (Ottawa: Canadian Fighter Pilots' Association, 1992), 22.

11. Leslie Roberts, "Kid in the Skies," in Maude Owens Walters, ed., *Combat in the Air* (New York: D. Appleton-Century Company, Inc., 1944), 204. Roberts claims that Beurling might fly seven or eight sorties per day, on Malta, and when he was not flying he would "[bone] up new ideas to be tested in tomorrow's battles."

12. Colonel Randall Wakelam, "Aerospace Power and Leadership Perspectives: The Human Dimension" in *Canadian Military Journal* 4, No. 3 (Autumn 2003), 17–24.

13. See "Excerpts from: The Caine Mutiny (a Novel), The Caine Mutiny Court-Martial (a Play), Herman Wouk," available at *www.english.upenn.edu/~afilreis/50s/caine-mutiny-text.html*; and Herman Wouk, *The Caine Mutiny* (New York: Simon & Schuster, 1985).

14. See Butch Kerr, "The Saga of HMS *Bounty* and Pitcairn Island," available at *www.lareau.org/bounty.html*. Some 2,000 articles and books, five major motion pictures, and many shorter documentary films have looked into virtually every aspect of this mutiny.

15. John Keegan, *The First World War* (Toronto: Key Porter Books, 1998), 329.

16. David Duncan, "Mutiny in the RAF: The Air Force Strikes of 1946," The Socialist History Society Occasional Papers Series: No. 8 (London: Socialist History Society, 1998), available at *www.socialisthistorysociety.co.uk/duncancontents.htm*.

17. United Kingdom, Royal Air Force, *Manual of Air Force Law, Air Publication 804*, (London: His Majesty's Stationery Office, 1933), 2nd ed., 18. The *Manual of Air Force Law* defined mutiny as the collective insubordination, or a combination of two or more persons to resist, or to induce others to resist, lawful Air Force authority; see also Julian Putkowski, *British Army Mutineers 1914–1922* (London: Francis Boutle Publishers, 1998), 9.

18. Between 1942 and 1944 a number of cases of crew sabotage were investigated in the Navy. See Richard Gimblett, "The Post–War 'Incidents' in the Royal Canadian Navy, 1949," in Christopher M. Bell and Bruce A. Elleman, eds., *Naval Mutinies of the Twentieth Century: An International Perspective* (London: Frank Cass, 2003), 246–63.

19. So, too, did the United States Army Air Force. See Bert Stiles, D.F.C., *Serenade to the Big Bird* (London: Lindsay Drummond, 1947), 49; For a Canadian example, see J. Ralph Wood, D.F.C., C.D., *My Lucky Number Was 77: WWII Memoirs of J. Ralph Wood, D.F.C., C.D.*, unpublished memoir found at RAF Hendon. Copy provided to the author by Mrs. J. Ralph Wood of Moncton, New Brunswick, in 2001, 12; and for an example of an Air Force mutiny involving RAF officers

and RCAF non-commisioned officers, or British and Canadians, see Allan D. English, *The Cream of the Crop: Canadian Aircrew 1939–1945* (Montreal and Kingston: McGill-Queen's University Press, 1996), 120, for a discussion of the Cranwell Mutiny.

20. S.F. Wise. *Canadian Airmen and the First World War: The Official History of the Royal Canadian Air Force, Volume 1* (Toronto: University of Toronto Press, 1980), 611.

21. Claude Scilley, "History: As We Saw It," *Kingston Whig-Standard*, February 6, 1999, 4; see David Duncan, "Mutiny in the RAF: the Air Force Strikes of 1946," in *The Socialist History Society Occasional Papers Series: No. 8* (London: Socialist History Society, 1998), available at *www.socialisthistorysociety.co.uk/duncancontents.htm*; and Public Records Office (PRO), AIR 8/790/2157 for a discussion of the Drigh Road RAF Station difficulties.

22. See Julian Putkowski, *The Kinmel Park Camp Riots 1919* (Clwyd, Wales: Flintshire Historical Society, 1989); Desmond Morton, *A Military History of Canada* (Edmonton: Hurtig Publishers, 1985), 166; and J.L. Granatstein, *Canada's Army: Waging War and Keeping the Peace* (Toronto: University of Toronto Press, 2002), 151.

23. Mark Wells, *Courage and Air Warfare* (London: Frank Cass, 1995), 95.

24. J.E. "Johnnie" Johnson, *Full Circle: The Story of Air Fighting* (London: Cassell & Co., 1964, 2001), 275; see Air Vice-Marshal "Johnnie" Johnson *Wing Leader* (Toronto: Stoddart Publishing Co., 2000), 183; see Norman Franks, *Buck McNair, Canadian Spitfire Ace: The Story of Group Captain R.W. McNair* (London: Grub Street, 2001), 2; and Mark Wells, in *Courage and Air Warfare*, 95.

25. See Edward H. Sims, *The Fighter Pilots* (London: Cassell & Co., 1967); and see Bill Olmsted, DSO, DFC and Bar, *Blue Skies: The Autobiography of a Canadian Spitfire Pilot in World War II* (Toronto: Stoddart Publishing Co., 1987), 84.

26. Robert Coram, *Boyd, The Fighter Pilot Who Changed the Art of War* (Boston: Little, Brown & Co., 2002), 42; and Dave Grossman, *On Killing: The Psychological Cost of Learning to Kill in War and Society* (Boston: Little, Brown & Co., 1995), 108–09.

27. Edward H. Sims, *Fighter Tactics and Strategy: 1914–1970* (Fallbrook, CA: Aero Publishers, Inc., 1980), 93.

28. Michael Ignatieff, *The Warrior's Honour* (Toronto: Viking Press, 1998), 117.

29. Grossman, *On Killing*, 181–82. Grossman describes Erich Hartmann's admission that of his 351 kills over 80 percent were inflicted against unsuspecting victims.

30. *Ibid.*, 143–46.

31. Alan Stephens, "Command in the Air," in Peter W. Gray and Sebastian Cox, eds., *Air Power Leadership: Theory and Practice* (London: Joint Doctrine and Concepts Centre, 2002), 1.

32. Olmsted, *Blue Skies: The Autobiography of a Canadian Spitfire Pilot in World War II*, 22.

33. F.J. Hatch, *Aerodrome of Democracy: Canada and the British Commonwealth Air Training Plan 1939–1945* (Ottawa: Canadian Government Publishing Centre, 1983), 115–17; W.A.B. Douglas, *The Creation of a National Air Force: The Official History of the Royal Canadian Air Force, Volume 2* (Toronto: University of Toronto Press, 1986), 230 and 243–45.

34. Forty percent of Canada's sacrifice during the Second World War came from the Royal Canadian Air Force; as many as 17,101 Canadian aircrew lost their lives. Ninety-two percent of aircrew casualties were fatal as compared to 30 percent of Army casualties, and 94 percent of Air Force casualties were flying as opposed to supporting operations from the ground. Allan D. English, *The Cream of the Crop*, 5 and 144; and the Royal Air Force lost 70,253 officers, non-commissioned officers, and aircrew killed or missing on operations of which 47,268 were reported lost by Bomber Command. John Terraine, *The Right of the Line: The Royal Air Force in the European War 1930–1945* (Hertfordshire, Eng.: Wordsworth Editions Ltd, 1985), 682.

35. Hugh Constant Godefroy, DSO, DFC, Croix de Guerre, *Lucky Thirteen* (London: Canada's Wings, Inc., 1983), 194.

36. Although the story of Cock Robin is typically linked to the death of Robin Hood, it has also been "connected to the mysterious murder of William Rufus II, King of England, the unpopular son of the Conqueror, found dead in the New Forest with an arrow piercing his lung." The "Cock Robin" moniker has also been applied to two other mythical figures, information on which may be found at *http://en.wikipedia.org/wiki/Cock_Robin*. Hugh Godefroy married in late 1942 to a Women's Auxiliary Air Force (WAAF) officer named Constance "Connie" Helm. She originated from Castle Douglas, Dumfries, Dumfriesshire, in southern Scotland, not too far from the Kirklees Priory, North Yorkshire, where Robin Hood is believed to be buried. At some point in their war-time courtship, when Godefroy flew to Dumfries often, and after 20 years or so of marriage, Hugh Constant Godefroy and his wife likely paid a visit to the historic site of the legendary bandit's grave. Additionally, Little John apparently returned to his homeland and died near Holderness in East Yorkshire. His grave is described as a tourist attraction, and it is to be noted that the location is close to RAF Catfoss, where a gunnery school was run for most of the war. Godefroy was known to have done some training at Catfoss. See Lieutenant-Colonel Dean C. Black, CD, "Meeting a Legend: An Encounter with Hugh Constant Godefroy, DSO, DFC and Bar, Croix de Guerre," *Airforce* (Summer 2001), 40–42. In a Spring 2002 interview with Charlie Magwood, the last surviving Second World War commanding officer of 403 (RCAF) Squadron, Magwood confirmed the author's assessment of Godefroy as being significantly

more mature than his peers, at the time, simply by adding that Godefroy was a father-figure to almost everyone, such was the quality of his leadership. See Godefroy, *Lucky Thirteen*, 111. Godefroy reflects on the value of attending monthly RAF mess dinners, as he was always impressed with the quality of banter and the guest speakers.

37. Canada, Department of National Defence, Directorate of History and Heritage (henceforth DHH) collection, Ron Emberg, 402 Squadron. Biographical file for Ron Emberg, 13 April 1942.

38. Sergeant (William John Andrew) McLachlan, aged 20. McLachlan was born in Spokane, Washington, thereby making him a citizen of the United States, not Canada, as Martin Gilbert reported, or Poland, as Paul Fussell may have believed. See Dennis C. Bateman, "It Happened Here: Incident at Imber," *After the Battle*, No. A049, (1985), 16–34; See also Martin Gilbert, *A History of the Twentieth Century, Volume Two: 1933–1951* (New York: William Morrow and Company, Inc., 1998), 439; and Paul Fussell, *Wartime: Understanding and Behaviour in the Second World War* (New York: Oxford University Press, 1989), 32–35.

39. Allison and Hayward have spelled Brown's first name as "Orlan." The confidential contact interviewed for this study claimed that Charlie may have been convinced (correctly so) that his buddy's name was Orland. Interview, 10 September 2004; and see Les Allison and Harry Hayward, *They Shall Grow Not Old: A Book of Remembrance*, (Brandon: Leech Printing Ltd., 1996), 80.

40. See *O.K.L. Fighter Claims, Chef für Ausz. und Dizsiplin: Luftwaffen-Personalamt L.P. [A] V Films & Supplementary Claims from Lists Reich & Western Front 1943*. This publication accounts for three Spitfires on 16 February 1943. Two were apparently attacked eight kilometres northwest of Abbeville at precisely the same time, while a third was attacked earlier near Bourseville, east-northeast of Le Tréport. Available at *http://math.fce.vutbr.cz/safarik/ACES/aces1/doc/victories-germany-ww2-1943.pdf*. Additionally, the possibility that Luftwaffe pilots were flying captured Spitfires cannot be ignored.

41. See Department of National Defence, 402 (RCAF) Squadron, Operations Record Book, Form 540/541, 16 February 1943; see also *The RCAF Overseas: The First Four Years* (Toronto: Oxford University Press, December 1944), 80; additionally, John Foreman, *Fighter Command War Diaries: Volume III, January 1942 to June 1943* (Air Research Publications, 2002), 266. Foreman describes the loss of these three pilots and refers to Rodeo 170 as the mission on which they went down. He attributes the loss of two of the pilots to II/JG26; however, the source of his information is unclear.

42. Department of National Defence, 403 (RCAF) Squadron, Operations Record Book (Official War Diary).

43. *Ibid.*, Tuesday, 20 July 1943; and see *416 Squadron History*, (Toronto: The Hangar Bookshelf, 1984), 35 and 38.

44. Personal diary, Walter G. Conrad, quoted with permission.

45. See Fletcher Wade et al., *403 Wolf Squadron: 1941–2001* (Oromocto, NB: 403 Squadron Commanding Officer, 2001), 31 for a list of casualties suffered by 403 Squadron during the Second World War; and for information concerning Flight Lieutenant C.P. "Chuck" Thornton see *The R.C.A.F. Overseas: The Fifth Year* (Toronto: Oxford University Press, 1945), 131. Thornton was shot down on 15 May 1944 while on a 403 Squadron mission to escort Marauder bombers proceeding to Douai. Thornton baled out and was seen running away in an attempt to escape, but other 403 Wolf Squadron pilots (Flight Lieutenant E.C. Williams, Flying Officer J.D. Orr and Flying Officer A.J.A. Bryan) witnessed his subsequent capture by German forces.

46. A caution is appropriate here. Operations Record Books (ORB), or War Diaries, are notorious for their inaccuracy, as are memories. See Norman L.R. Franks, *Royal Air Force Fighter Command Losses of the Second World War: Volume 2, Operational Losses: Aircraft and Crews 1942–1943* (Leicester, Eng.: Midland Publishing Limited, 1998), 7; see Dave MacIntosh, *High Blue Battle* (Toronto: Stoddart Publishing Co., 1990), 3; and see John Foreman, *The Fighter Command War Diaries* (Surrey, Walton-on-Thames, Eng.: Air Research Publications, 2002), 114. It is interesting to note that Foreman claims that Southwood was lost during Ramrod 283, not 284, as Godefroy's logbook suggests.

47. Hugh Constant Godefroy, Wing Commander, personal Royal Canadian Air Force Pilot's Flying Log Book. Godefroy provided the author with a complete copy of his log book in April 2001. Entry made for 24 October 1943. The "F/O [Flying Officer] Brown" referred to was J. Danforth "Danny" Browne — an American.

48. A draft version of the 403 Squadron Operations Record Book (ORB) that appears to be referred to as the "Demi-official War Diary" contains an entry for the 24 October 1943 sweep in question; and see Franks, *Royal Air Force Fighter Command Losses of the Second World War: Volume 2*, 131. Franks's information states that Southwood was [involved in] "Ramrod 283, mid-day. Fighters over Amiens; shot down near Doullens." Godefroy may have recorded it as Rodeo 280 in his logbook. Again, John Foreman's claim matches that of Franks's vis-à-vis Ramrod 283.

49. In an early April 2001 interview Hugh Godefroy confided that he had come across only one bona fide case of "lacking in moral fibre" (LMF), and it was not Southwood. The identity of the pilot is not relevant to this study. See Lieutenant-Colonel Dean C. Black, CD, "Meeting a Legend: An Encounter with Hugh Constant Godefroy, DSO, DFC and Bar, Croix de Guerre" *Airforce* (Summer 2001), 40–42.

50. See Brereton Greenhous, Stephen J. Harris, William C. Johnston, and William G.P. Rawling, *The Crucible of War 1939–1945: The Official History of the Royal Canadian Air Force, Volume 3* (Toronto: University of Toronto Press, 1994), 219–20; see also Lieutenant-Colonel Dean C. Black, CD, "Flying Officer

Knutty, DSO, DFC, DFM, Croix de Guerre Flies Again," *Airforce* (Fall 2003), 64–67; and see Alan C. Deere, D.S.O., O.B.E., D.F.C., Group Captain, *Nine Lives* (London: Coronet Books, 1959), 216–24.

51. By 17 October 1943, the day he left 403 Squadron to command 421 Squadron, Magwood was in his 23rd straight month with the squadron. See 403 Squadron ORB entry for 22 September 1943.

52. See *The RCAF Overseas: The First Four Years*, 110. Southwood claimed as damaged one enemy aircraft over Amsterdam, in August 1943.

53. See Wells, *Courage and Air Warfare*, 37; and, Terraine, *The Right of the Line*, 155. Terraine describes air-to-air fighting as "high-speed, split-second combat and those [pilots] who had [experience] fought at an advantage over those who lacked it."

54. See Group Captain C.F. Gray, "Get in Close," in Christopher Shores and Clive Williams, eds., *Aces High: The Fighter Aces of the British and Commonwealth Air Forces in World War II* (London: Neville Spearman, 1966), 240; and see Grossman, *On Killing*, 30. Grossman cites sources indicating less than 1 percent of all Second World War fighter pilots accounted for 30 to 40 percent of all destroyed enemy aircraft, a finding that suggests the vast majority of fighter pilots either never saw an enemy aircraft during their tour or had the opportunity to engage them only once or twice.

55. See *416 Squadron History* (Toronto: The Hangar Bookshelf, 1984), 38; and see Lloyd Hunt, Ed., *We Band of Brothers* (Ottawa: Canadian Fighter Pilots Association, 1992), 116, for a discussion regarding Beurling's occasional preference for ammunition loads lacking tracer rounds.

56. See H.A. Halliday, "The Lone Eagle of Malta," in Hunt, ed., *We Band of Brothers*, 129; also see Dan McCaffery, *Air Aces: The Lives and Times of Twelve Canadian Fighter Pilots* (Toronto: James Lorimer & Company, Publishers, 1990), 125; for information on the removal of tracer ammunition see Brian Nolan, *Hero: The True Story of the Legendary Canadian Fighter Ace, Buzz Beurling* (Markham, ON: Penguin Canada, 1981), 55 and 68–69. An interview with a 403 Squadron groundcrew member, George Demare, in June 2001, confirmed Beurling's practice of having the tracers removed. Demare lamented having to deal with Beurling's constant checking of work carried out by the (armourers) ammunition technicians; see also Hunt, ed., *We Band of Brothers*, 116; Beurling was also considered somewhat unusual because his guns were harmonized at 250 yards, rather than 350 yards, which was apparently the norm for other pilots. See John Terraine, *The Right of the Line*, 155. Terraine describes the "Dowding Spread," or the emphasis on the importance of harmonization of the guns for 250 yards being deemed more effective, rather than 400 yards, which appeared to be the norm at the beginning of the war; also, Arthur Bishop, *Winged Combat: My Story as a Spitfire Pilot in WWII* (Toronto: HarperCollins, 2002), 91 and 173; see McCaffery, *Air Aces*, 126; and Richard Townshend Bickers, *Ginger Lacey: Fighter Pilot, Battle of Britain Top Scorer* (London: Robert Hale, Ltd., 1962), 114–15.

57. This episode was recorded live, by CBC Radio, in May 1943, and dealt with Beurling's exploits of 27 July 1942 when he downed two Macchi fighters in a single sortie. Beurling's live account is renowned not necessarily for the heroism he displayed but more for what some have described as the macabre description of the harm he visited upon the Italian pilot. See Brian Nolan, *Hero: The True Story of the Legendary Canadian Fighter Ace, Buzz Beurling* (Markham, ON: Penguin Canada, 1981), 83–84; and for another description of Beurling's macabre shooting practices, this one involving lizards see also Lord James Douglas-Hamilton, MP, *The Air Battle for Malta: The Diaries of a Fighter Pilot* (Edinburgh: Mainstream Publishing, 1981),161–62.

58. Squadron Leader Don Carlson, Padre, 127 Wing (Headcorn and Kenley) "Flight Lieutenant George F. Beurling" in Hunt, ed., *We Band of Brothers*, 24.; and the caption to photograph number 80 in James Holland, *Fortress Malta: An Island Under Siege, 1940–1943* (London: Orion Books, Ltd., 2003), 296. Holland describes Beurling as "a brilliant but ultimately flawed man."

59. Carlson, "Flight Lieutenant George F. Beurling," 27; and Halliday, "The Lone Eagle of Malta,"116. Under normal circumstances the least-qualified pilot would be assigned to cover the tail of the most qualified pilot.

60. See Canada, Department of National Defence, 403 Squadron Operations Record Book (ORB) entry for 18 October 1943; and Godefroy, *Lucky Thirteen*, 223.

61. James Holland, *Fortress Malta*, 303.

62. The demi-official war diary states that Beurling took over as flight commander on 25 October 1943, the day following the loss of Flight Lieutenant Southwood; see Franks, *Royal Air Force Fighter Command Losses of the Second World War, Volume 2*, 131; and in an October 2003 interview R.G. "Bob" Middlemiss recalled that it would have been the role of Squadron Leader Buckham to have recommended the promotion for Beurling and the role for Wing Commander (Flying) Godefroy to have approved it.

63. Godefroy, *Lucky Thirteen*, 221.

64. *Ibid.*, 226. Hugh Godefroy placed Beurling under open arrest and advised his superior that he was either prepared to proceed with a court-martial or was prepared to recommend one; see also George J. Demare, "The Beurling I Knew," *Airforce* (April 1996). Demare claims the low flying incident with the rugby players took place during Beurling's first tour with 403 Squadron (16 December 1941 to July 1942). However, R.G. Middlemiss's recollection was that the episode took place in 1943. The demi-official war diary states that Beurling had Flying Officer Tommy Brannagan on board on 17 September 1943 when they " ... buzzed the old man ... nearly frightening him to death."; see *www.constable.ca/beurling.htm* for an account of a low-flying incident while Beurling was on strength with a training unit; and on 11 January 2004 in a confidential interview one veteran recalled that Beurling's troubles began with

Godefroy when the latter received complaints of hazardous low flying from local farmers; and, finally, a confidential 23 May 2004 interview, recalled that it had been alleged that a passenger familiarization flight was what had led to Beurling's final return to Canada, sometime in the early Spring of 1944. On that flight, Beurling apparently took aloft a young WAAF from South Africa who apparently "nearly expired from the scare she received."

65. Monty Berger and Brian Jeffrey Street, *Invasions Without Tears: The Story of Canada's Top-Scoring Spitfire Wing in Europe during the Second World War* (Toronto: Random House of Canada, 1994), 20.

66. Brian Nolan, *Hero: The True Story of the Legendary Canadian Fighter Ace, Buzz Beurling* (Markham, ON: Penguin Canada, 1982), 93.

67. Holland, *Fortress Malta*, 349.

68. Confidential interview October 2003; and Johnson, *Wing Leader*, 187.

69. Demare, "The Beurling I Knew."

70. John Reid, "Aviation Archaeology: Prize Merlin From 26ft Below Ground," in *FlyPast* (April 1987), 32–33. The incident occurred on 8 June 1943. Official records claimed that Beurling bailed out when his engine caught fire owing to a glycol leak.

71. George Beurling with Leslie Roberts, *Malta Spitfire: The Buzz Beurling Story, Canada's World War II Daredevil Pilot* (Toronto: Penguin Canada, 2002), 246. This reprint of the 1943 edition includes a new epilogue written by Arthur Bishop in which Bishop describes the altercation between Beurling and McNair; see Dave McIntosh, *High Blue Battle*, 142. The only accident reported in 412 Squadron for the appropriate time period, in McIntosh's account, was a collision of two Spitfires on the field on 3 March 1944. Flying Officer Berryman apparently received serious burns, but there was no indication Beurling was involved; and see Les Allison and Harry Hayward, *They Shall Grow Not Old: A Book of Remembrance* (Brandon, MB: Leech Printing Ltd., 1996), 841. Flying Officer Zygmant John Zabek, from Hamilton, Ontario, was flying with 412 Squadron when his aircraft crashed five minutes from takeoff, near Seven Oaks, Kent, England. Zabek's engine apparently quit, when he attempted to switch fuel flow from his drop tanks. This flight and Zabek's death occurred on 14 February 1944. Of all the 412 Squadron pilots to perish, or to be shot down, during the period 7 May 1943 to 29 June 1944 (there were 15) only Zabek's circumstances exactly match those described by Arthur Bishop. Indications were that squadrons operating Spitfire IX aircraft had complained of numerous engine failures on switching gas tanks; see Canada, Department of National Defence, 412 Squadron Operations Record Book (Form 541) 14 February 1944. The Ranger mission appears to have been the first, for 412 Squadron. Beurling was leading the four-plane sortie that took off at 1555 hours and landed at 1605 hours. Beurling appears to have flown no more than five additional flights with 412 Squadron before he was repatriated to Canada on or about 9

April 1944; see Norman L.R. Franks, *Royal Air Force Fighter Command Losses of the Second World War, Volume 3, Operational Losses: Aircraft and Crews 1944* (Leicester, Eng.: Midland Publishing Limited, 1998), 15; and Franks, *Royal Air Force Fighter Command Losses of the Second World War, Volume 2*, 134. Franks identifies the aircraft lost on 23 November 1943 as belonging to 411 Squadron and those of 15 January 1944, 24 January 1944, and 28 January 1944 as 412 Squadron. These failures are believed to be the ones that precipitated the order posted by McNair regarding the need to climb to 1,000 feet (300 metres) on takeoff before switching tanks.

72. James Holland, *Fortress Malta*, 347–48.

73. Squadron Leader George Keefer, Commanding Officer 412 Squadron. This apparently was not the first time Beurling publicly questioned Keefer. In a confidential interview it was revealed that Beurling occasionally criticized his commanding officer's decisions, during mission briefings. Despite being told to stop, he continued what he most probably believed was his professional responsibility at the time. Confidential interview, 13 November 2004.

74. Beurling with Roberts, *Malta Spitfire*, 236–47.

75. *Ibid.*, 246.

76. Confidential interview, 10 January 2004. Beurling was rarely seen around 412 Squadron. Many believed Beurling to be in London pleading his case for senior staff to provide him with the proper aircraft and authority to roam the continent freely to hunt for enemy aircraft.

77. See Berger and Street, *Invasions Without Tears*, 24–25.

78. James Holland, *Fortress Malta*, 350. On 27 May 1942, without knowing the man's precise identity but because of the pilot's noticeable prowess, Beurling selected out of the mêlée the Italian Ace Captain Furio Niclot and brought him down. See *Maclean's*, 15 January 1943 reprinted in Michael Benedict, ed., *Canada at War: From the Archives of Maclean's* (Toronto: Penguin Canada, 1998), 107.

79. Grossman, *On Killing*, 128; also see Douglas-Hamilton, *The Air Battle for Malta*, 122–23. Douglas-Hamilton describes Beurling as possessing "the most amazing tricks ... he did not just aim at the enemy aeroplane and fire a long burst, but aimed at one particular vital part of the Hun and gave a very short burst which generally brought it down;" see Holland, *Fortress Malta*, 306. Holland cites sources that explain only one in five pilots achieved "Ace" status (achieved by destroying five or more enemy aircraft) and less than half of those score in the double digits. Holland's sources (see page 306) place Beurling in the top 1 percent of fighter pilots owing to his deflection shooting skills and his amazing eyesight.

80. See Robert Jackson, *Fighter Pilots of Second World War* (London: Arthur Barker

Limited, 1976), 65. Jackson describes a rather unusual incident from July 1944, involving Beurling and Group Captain Adolph "Sailor" Malan, a South African ace.

81. Confidential email correspondence, 13 September 2004.

82. See Godefroy, *Lucky Thirteen*, 193–94.

83. Edward H. Sims, *Fighter Tactics and Strategy: 1914–1970* (Fallbrook, CA: Aero Publishers, Inc., 1972), 179–80 and specifically 18; and J.E. "Johnnie" Johnson, *Full Circle* (Reading, Eng.: Cassell & Co., 1964), the penultimate chapter titled "In Hindsight" explains the circular route fighter tactics have taken through two World Wars, 273–86.

84. Confidential interview, 10 January 2004.

85. Confidential interview 10 October 2003.

86. Johnson, *Full Circle*, 197–98.

87. Randall Wakelam, "Aerospace Power and Leadership Perspectives: The Human Dimension," in *Canadian Military Journal* 4, No. 3 (Autumn 2003), 17–24.

6

AFTER THE EMERGENCY:
DEMOBILIZATION STRIKES,
POLITICAL STATEMENTS, AND THE
MORAL ECONOMY IN CANADA'S AIR FORCES,
1919–1946

Rachel Lea Heide

126 Transport Wing, February 1946

On 9 February 1946, one Canadian newspaper was reporting rumours that Royal Canadian Air Force (RCAF) personnel were on strike in Germany. The commanding officer (CO) of the wing in question denied that any such demonstration was occurring.[1] On the same day the *Vancouver Sun* reported that members of 126 Transport Wing stationed at Uetersen (Germany) had sent the newspaper a letter with "six charges leveled at the air minister." The men felt obligated to exercise their "democratic right" to inform the Canadian public that the government was "giving the people an unfair picture of the status of the RCAF Occupation Army." Those moved to write this letter for publication wanted Canadians to know that "contrary to reports or impressions given in the Canadian House of Commons, we are not the volunteer air force. The overwhelming majority of the volunteers for the Occupation Air Force are in Canada."[2] Much to their consternation, the writers from 126 Transport Wing had to admit that "volunteers for the Occupation Air Force will not (repeat will not) leave Canada to come here (Uetersen) to replace the men desirous of returning home."[3]

   On 12 January 1946, the minister of national defence for air had visited the unit to discuss projected demobilization dates. When Colonel Colin Gibson informed the aircrew that repatriation would not start until 30 June and could take up to the end of December 1946, the men were dismayed. This information from the minister was not "in accord with the impression the Canadian government, the press, and the radio is giving the Canadian people with regard to our status, repatriation, length of stay in Germany, or the date when we expect to return home." (Previous reports had set 31 March 1946 as a target start date). The men wrote: "[T]he lack of a clean-cut, open statement by the government to the people of Canada is causing untold frustration and personal suffering to our wives and our families."[4] These men had proudly served their country as volunteers during the Second World War, but now that the emergency was over, they wanted to be repatriated home. Despite violating military regulations against collective expressions of grievances, 163 men signed the letter intended for public consumption. They did not want families at home believing that they had volunteered to stay away longer. Now that the war had been over for six months, they wanted the government to live up to its obligation and demobilize the civilians who no longer wanted to be in uniform. The action was not spontaneous — they had waited almost an entire month to confront the minister of national defence for air. The aircrew of 126 Transport Wing had not acted alone; protests over slow repatriation policies had been erupting among Commonwealth air forces throughout late January and early February 1946. Now that it was peacetime, enduring wartime conditions and discipline was no longer considered one's patriotic duty. Everyone just wanted to go home.

Disobedience in Canada's Air Forces

According to the National Defence Act, mutiny is defined as "collective insubordination or a combination of two or more persons in resistance to lawful navy, army, or air force authority."[5] Images of mutiny are most often associated with the Navy, and it has not been uncommon to hear of Army units rioting, but collective insubordination is not normally associated with the Air Force. This is not to say that Air Force personnel have never disobeyed orders. Disobedience is simply most often recounted as occurring at the individual level or among small collectivities such as an aircrew. During the Second World War, combat stress kept many individuals from following through with their assigned operations over Europe, despite the threat of being labelled as lacking moral fibre.[6] Some aircrews, once on an operation, decided to avoid certain death by dropping their bombs on the fringe of targets (and hence away from heavy enemy defences), or by jettisoning their bombs in the sea and returning to Great Britain early because of some alleged mechanical failure (such as icing up or an intercom system that ceased to work). Some even resorted to sabotage to keep a plane from getting off the ground: unserviceable hydraulics would keep gun-turrets from operating, and "mag drop" could easily be created by switching off the magnetos and then running up the engine, thus oiling up the plugs.[7]

Although a legacy of mutiny by large collectivities does not exist in Canada's Air Force, its personnel have resorted to industrial action types of protest on occasion. Men in the Canadian Air Force refused to parade and work in January 1919. Ground crews at two stations held sit-down strikes in February 1946. In both instances, the men were not revolting against their superior officers; instead, they were making political statements and prodding the government to fulfill its obligations in regards to promised pay (in 1919) and timely repatriation (in 1946).

In some ways, there are striking differences between the mutinies in Canada's Air Forces and the mutinies in Canada's Army and Navy. Army and Navy demonstrations have always been about restoring or improving acceptable living conditions and challenging officers in command who cared little about their men's welfare and even less about effective communications. In the Air Force experience, effecting change in leadership or living conditions have not been the goals; securing repatriation has been the main focus, and personnel knew that this had to be taken up with political, not military, leaders. Nevertheless, despite the different grievances among the services, there is one important similarity: men from all three services have felt justified in their disobedience because they were upholding a moral economy among their class. Their logic is that leaders must be held accountable when it is felt that they are failing to uphold their obligations and when they transgress what their charges deem to be fair and reasonable treatment in return for faithful military service. The Air Force mutinies of 1919 and 1946 clearly fit into a tradition of defending a moral economy, but the leaders that the men had to confront — especially in 1946 — were not superior officers, but the civilian government.

Theoretical Framework and Literature on Mutiny, Leadership, and the Moral Economy

Literature on military mutinies most often draws conclusions about the deficiency of military leadership and how this precipitates mutinies in the services. Joel Hamby looks at the factors that contribute to refusals to obey, and he explains the role that leadership plays in exacerbating or mitigating situations that could lead to mutiny. A sense of alienation can lead soldiers to refuse to obey orders: they fear that battle will lead to a separation from comrades (soldiers' support network and adopted family). The environment plays a key role in fostering desires to disobey: fear (experienced going into a battle), fatigue (experienced during and after the battle), and boredom (experienced when waiting for the next round of combat) are aggravated by poor weather, unpalatable food, and unreasonable daily military routines. If leave, relief, or rations are not forthcoming as expected, there is a growing sense that leaders have broken an implicit contract with the soldiers. Personal convictions (values) and hope have sustaining and motivating powers; fighting potential diminishes if convictions change or if hope is lost. Combat experience and training can build self-confidence in soldiers. Discipline instills a sense of pride and belonging, but soldiers' consent to be disciplined can be removed if they deem it for a justifiable cause, and if soldiers do chose to break discipline, there is an underlying assumption that there is safety in numbers.[8]

The role of a leader is to influence people, provide purpose and direction, and motivate subordinates to fulfill the mission. Successful leaders filter out negative influences and sustain the group's morale and motivation. Several factors determine how effective a leader can be; the leader's proximity, the intensity of the demands, the legitimacy of authority, and the respect that he or she is able to command. To gain respect, leaders need to form bonds with subordinates, and leaders must be seen as taking active interests in the welfare of their soldiers. If leaders are perceived to be loyal and trustworthy, if leaders can keep the lines of communications open, mutinies can be prevented by pre-emptively removing conditions fostering discontent, rebellion, and mass protest.[9] If formal leadership is deemed to have failed, then the betrayed subordinates will look to informal leaders among themselves, and these *de facto* leaders may convince their fellow soldiers to mutiny as a means of expressing their pent-up displeasure over failed communications and breached contracts.[10]

Allan English argues that examples of individual or aircrew disobedience in air forces of the Second World War were reactions to poor leadership. When the men lost confidence in their leaders, they shirked their duties and focused on preserving their own well-being. Hence, to avoid flying operations over Europe, men would deliberately sabotage their equipment, boomerang (return early), become fringe merchants (bombing target edges), or jettison bombs before reaching targets in Germany. Effective squadron leaders were those who demonstrated their ability to fly operations and who were willing to share the same operational risks faced by their men. When leaders always stayed behind, appeared indifferent to their men's welfare, and treated the crews like expendable attrition fodder, morale sank, lack of confidence became epidemic, and operations lost their efficiency because crews began avoiding their dangerous duties. Wartime commanders needed to exhibit heroic leadership (leading by example and sharing the risks) and technical leadership (specialized knowledge in flying skills). Anything less destroyed morale and fostered acts of undetectable disobedience.[11]

Less often, mutinies are studied as a history from below, as a powerful tool of agency for legitimately disgruntled service personnel. Craig Mantle suggests that military mutinies can be compared with eighteenth century English bread riots because both groups of mutineers were defending what they considered to be their just customs and conditions for existence. According to E.P. Thompson, the poor of eighteenth century England developed a common consciousness from their shared experiences, and part of this consciousness was a notion of a common good in regards to fair, just, and legitimate practices by farmers, millers, bakers, and merchants. When the poor felt they were being exploited, they acted out against the unjust practices, expressing their discontent in food riots (that took place systematically in 1709, 1740, 1756–1757, 1766–1767, 1773, 1782, 1795, and 1800–1801). The aim was not to change the entire economic system, but to target individual transgressors, and restore accepted business practices.[12] Mills were attacked if there were any indications that noxious ingredients were used as substitutes for flour. The poor resented merchants who sold bread to export markets and left the local community destitute. Buyers condemned sellers who would only sell large quantities of flour at a time; those who used smaller measures without reducing bread prices also incurred the wrath of the poor. The collective consciousness of the crowds established a system of morals for their economic setting; when traditional rights and customs were violated and new practices were brought into use that were detrimental to the poor, the crowd would rise up to restore what had once been. They felt justified because they were defending their moral economy.[13]

Mantle argues that this sense of moral economy spurred and legitimized protests in military services. In both Navy and Army examples, military personnel desire solutions to specific grievances concerning quality of life; they are not searching to overthrow the entire military institution. Furthermore, personnel protest only once conditions become unbearable and only when military authorities fail to heed previous warnings that all is not well. Mantle also sees similarities in the idea of a common consciousness being cultivated. Bonds among soldiers, sailors, or aircrew are developed as these individuals share similar experiences and lifestyles. They also develop a collective sense of a common good. When civilians entered the military in both the First and Second World Wars, they willingly surrendered their civil liberties, but in return for disciplined service and obedience, they expected military authorities to carry out their duty of providing the necessities of life and adequate leadership. Canadian soldiers in the First World War, for example, expected adequate rations, water, clothing, and accommodations. They resented financial exploitation by merchants, and they were emotionally dependent on relief from the front-lines and entertainment as pleasurable diversions from life in the trenches. Soldiers also expected competent leaders — those who believed in the sanctity of life, those who refrained from abusing soldiers physically and verbally, and those who were fair and just in their demands and decisions. When needs were not met, when leaders acted immorally, soldiers were driven to riot in protest — for the sake of their self-respect, justified in the name of the collectively established moral economy. Resorting to disobedience was simply a means of reminding the military of its obligations and a means of restoring the fairness, justice, and respect that the soldiers felt had been taken away from them.[14]

According to both Thompson and Mantle, the concept of the oppressed crowds defending a moral economy was a powerful tool of agency that the masses deliberately circumscribed with self-imposed limitations. The goal was not to overthrow the existing system and instigate a revolution; the aim was to restore acceptable living conditions and regain respectful behaviour by those in authority towards those in subordinate positions. Hence, mutinies can be analyzed from both the top-down and from the bottom-up. Lessons can be learned about deficient leadership and what leadership characteristics should be cultivated so as to prevent mutinies. Lessons can also be learned about what constitutes a service's moral economy, what military personnel expect from their leaders in return for their service, and what pre-emptive actions can be taken to not breach the implicit social contract between personnel and the institution, thus avoiding the precipitation a mutiny. Good leaders look out for the welfare of their subordinates, and hence the social contract is automatically upheld. Subordinates are expecting leaders to care for them, and if these unspoken obligations are not met, the subordinates will hold their poor leaders accountable and demand redress. Consequently, leadership and the moral economy are inextricably intertwined in both the creation and prevention of mutinies.

Mutinies in the Canadian Air Force, January 1919

Canadian Air Force personnel in the First World War did not have an air force of their own until just before the end of hostilities. Until the creation of the Canadian Air Force (CAF) in 1918, Canadians served in Great Britain's Royal Flying Corps, Royal Naval Air Service, and Royal Air Force (RAF). Refusal to obey orders was not a tradition for Canadian personnel during the war — their conditions of living were infinitely better than life in the trenches. Nevertheless, once the war was over, some of those awaiting demobilization in the CAF became less tolerant and more vocal about self-interests. The emergency was over, and Canadian personnel at the Halton Camp and the Heyford Detachment in Great Britian wanted better treatment, better conditions, answers about peacetime pay, and assurances about demobilization.

On Friday 3 January 1919, a detail of Canadians attending a trades course at Halton Camp refused to parade. Inquiries the next day revealed that the imperial officer who took a parade on 3 January had shown a severe lack of tact. Although the parade ground "was in a deplorable condition," the officer "began to drill the men before a crowd of young soldiers who obviously took much pleasure in seeing the detail drilling in the mud." In response to this lack of respect and callous amusement of officer and young soldiers alike, the Canadians refused to parade again as a means of protesting their senseless humiliation. The investigating officer recommended having "a reliable officer sent to Halton Camp immediately to take charge of the Canadian details there." With that, he considered the incident closed as he reported to the headquarters of Overseas Military Forces of Canada (OMFC) in London: "the men are working quietly and well at the shops."[15]

The OMFC headquarters in London sent a Captain Ryan to oversee the Canadians at Halton Camp and to replace the previous lax officer who let the trouble brew. The OMFC reported that Ryan had two years experience as a technical officer in France with the RAF; consequently, the general staff believed he was "exceptionally qualified to look after the other ranks … at Halton Camp." On 23 January 1919, Ryan reported to headquarters "that conditions seem much more satisfactory." He did feel, though, that instructors for courses of acetylene welders, blacksmiths, electricians, and engine fitters should be replaced. The RAF instructors were disinterested in their work, and Ryan suspected "this lack of interest [to be] due to the desire for demobilization on their part."[16] Poor leadership and transgressing the men's sense of self-respect lead to the defence of their moral economy at Halton Camp.

The Halton Camp incident was not the only protest Canadian authorities had to deal with. On 7 January 1919, another demonstration occurred, this time at Upper Heyford, and this time, there was a long list of grievances and demands. At 0840 hours, "the other ranks paraded as usual by flights under their non-commissioned officers (NCOs) and the squadron under the regimental sergeant-major. On being given the command to move off to their respective flights to carry on, they refused to move. The NCOs, with exception of the flight sergeants, took the same attitude as the men." When confronted by the squadron's CO, Captain A.E. McKeever, the men refused to carry out technical duties with the squadron until they were guaranteed working pay. Apparently, "on transfer from their [Army] units to the CAF, they were told by Lieutenant Colonel Bishop that they should not lose any pay by their transfer and that technical pay would be given them when they took over technical duties of looking after airplanes to correspond with technical pay given to drivers, cooks, blacksmiths, and various technical men of other Canadian units." The men at Upper Heyford stated very plainly that if the promised working pay was not given them immediately, they would refuse to perform technical duties for the CAF, and they would request to be returned to their Army units. Both the men and the NCOs also wanted to know how long they would be prevented from returning to civilian life: "It has also been asked … if, on return to Canada, they will be forced to remain in the Canadian Air Force for six months after peace is signed or will they be allowed to be demobilized at their request as is apparently the case among their comrades in the various other Canadian units."[17]

Captain McKeever reported the situation to be greatly improved just five days later. Pay and demobilization policy may have been the complaints voiced to justify the refusal to work, but later investigation clearly demonstrated that morale had been low for some time because of poor living conditions. The men had been moved to better accommodations that, according to McKeever, "are as comfortable as one could hope to find any place." This move was necessary seeing as "the quarters which the men were in at the time of my last memorandum have been condemned by the Medical Officer owing to the material on the roof not remaining waterproof after the heavy fall of snow which we had about a fortnight ago." The squadron's commander also put some effort into improving the condition of the men's messing. Consequently, he reported that "the situation with regard to other ranks is greatly improved since my last memorandum…. The work seems to be going along with more vim than it has for some weeks previous to the outbreak."[18]

Despite McKeever's positive update, Major C.M. Marshall's report to the OMFC general staff on 28 January 1919 was anything but glowing. When he visited Upper Heyford on 23 January, he "found the general bearing and discipline of the men … anything but good — their being discontented and slovenly, this being due, in my opinion, to their not being properly commanded and looked after." Marshall also found that two NCOs, "men of very poor type, whose conduct sheets showed numerous previous convictions," had been a bad influence by agitating the men to protest. Marshall had McKeever return the two NCOs to their units to remove their negative influence. Marshall also felt that the men needed more training: "were these men permitted to return to Canada in their present more or less undisciplined and undrilled condition, the impression made would be anything but favourable." Hence, Marshall recommended bringing a drill sergeant-major to be in charge of training. McKeever "heartily endorsed" the suggested changes and improvements.[19]

Nevertheless, Marshall's report to OMFC headquarters at the end of February was another harsh condemnation of Heyford's leadership. Marshall wrote: "[O]n taking over the Heyford detachment on 5–2–19, I found the men generally dissatisfied and slovenly." Marshall made changes to the station's messing, sanitation, discipline, and training. He "called a parade of all NCOs and instructed them in duties and general bearing." He also saw to it that "disciplinary and smartening-up training is carried on each morning from 9 to 10." Because of these changes to living conditions and an increased emphasis on discipline, Marshall was able to write to OMFC headquarters, "I have much pleasure in informing you that the men now appear quite satisfied, and crime has decreased by quite 75 percent."[20] The passing of another couple of weeks saw continued improvement in the men's morale. On 13 March, Marshall described to OMFC headquarters the recreational activities that were being instituted: "sports have been organized, a hut being equipped for training in football, boxing, and wrestling. It is intended in the near future to hold competitions in these sports.... Picture shows are still continued thrice weekly, and at least one technical picture shown during the evening. Permission has been given other ranks to hold a dance." Marshall was not completely satisfied with the state of discipline among the Canadians, but he did feel that improvement was steady, and he could not help but note that "the men seem much more cheerful and contented and appreciate that their comfort and interests are receiving attention."[21]

This is all that the men at Halton Camp and Upper Heyford wanted — to have their plight taken into consideration. Now that the war was over, the sense of urgency and the willingness to bear hardships patriotically had dissipated. These uniformed men wanted to return to their civilian status. The men of Halton Camp wanted some respect shown them and freedom from unnecessary abuse. Their protest was clearly calling for better leadership, and investigators easily saw that the proper solution was appointing a Canadian officer to supervise the Canadian personnel: this fellow countryman and comrade in arms understood the implicit social contract between officers and men better than the imperial officer who humiliated the Canadians publicly in the mud. The problems at Upper Heyford were also rooted in poor leadership and failure to pay attention to the men's general welfare, but it is unclear from the primary records if the men themselves realized this. The complaints they raised were about policy — they were not receiving the pay they had been promised on transfer to the embryonic Canadian Air Force, and they were concerned that their decision to be a part of this new service might result in their having to remain in the military six months longer than their comrades in the Army. Neither of those two concerns could be rectified by their immediate superior officers; these issues had to be dealt with by the policy makers in the military and the government. Although not articulated by the men of Upper Heyford, low morale, questionable living conditions, and poor leadership also played a role in the men's deportment.

Once the discontent was brought to Captain McKeever's attention, he made honest efforts to improve the men's messing conditions and accommodations. Nevertheless, Major Marshall found that McKeever's newly found attention to the men's welfare was not enough. Marshall made further changes to living conditions, created a varied recreational program, and instituted discipline training to counter the men's dissatisfaction and slovenly deportment. Even two months after the protest, after a change of command, and after improved living conditions, Marshall found that "discipline is not yet so good as I would like."[22] Either Marshall had unreachable standards, or the Canadians were just hopelessly lax about discipline. Perhaps these citizens in uniform simply could not see the point of Marshall's fixation on smart deportment since they only wanted to go home and re-establish their peacetime lives. There were no further reports of mass protest while the men awaited demobilization, so it can be seen that attentive leadership and bearable amenities staved off further transgressions, and defences, of the men's moral economy.

Mutinies in the Royal Canadian Air Force, February 1946

As in the First World War, Canadians fighting in the Allied air war between 1939 and 1945 carried off their duties with distinction and determination. Although the Canadian Navy suffered a number of industrial action protests over living conditions and unacceptable leaders, such occurrences did not take place in the RCAF during hostilities. Even once the war had ended and men were kept overseas for occupation duties, RCAF personnel did not feel the need to rise up and try to effect change in their superior officers nor in their living conditions. Nonetheless, in February 1946, RCAF ground crews at two British stations and one German base did feel obligated to demonstrated against the government's demobilization policy and occupation force commitments. Their protest took the form of sit-down strikes, letter-writing campaigns to politicians, and communicating their grievances directly to the Canadian people.

The troubles at the Odiham and Down Ampney RCAF stations were not spontaneous outbursts of discontent expressed by men simply tired of waiting to go dome and grasping for any means of accelerating the process. These frustrations had been brewing for some time, and announcements in January 1946 about demobilization dates had an unintentional effect of acting as a catalyst to the

February demonstrations. On 9 January 1946, Group Captain N.W. Timmerman (the commander of 120 Transport Wing Headquarters at Odiham, Hampshire), held a station parade where he outlined for 437 Squadron the government's policy concerning future occupation commitments in Europe. RCAF personnel were told that squadrons would begin disbanding on 31 March, that RCAF activities would gradually cease through to 30 June, and that most RCAF personnel would be home by early autumn 1946. The station diarist recorded that, "the news was well received, and now that there is a time limit on our stay over here, it is believed that the morale, generally, will show a definite improvement. In spite of all our efforts to provide outlets for airmen's entertainment and welfare, it was difficult to take their thoughts away from the one term: 'when do we go home?'" Two days later, Minister of National Defence for Air, Colonel Colin Gibson, visited the station, and personnel were able to talk with him about repatriation policies, and they were all reassured that they would be home by the fall.[23] Two other RCAF squadrons (435 and 436) making up 120 Transport Wing were stationed at a nearby base — Down Ampney, Gloucestershire. The men at this base were informed on 10 January by their CO, Group Captain R.C. Davis, that 435 Squadron would be disbanding on 31 March 1946, that the entire RCAF occupational forces would be folding-up on 30 June 1946, and that everyone would be home by early September. Colonel Gibson visited Down Ampney on 16 January and "talked to the men and answered their questions on repatriation."[24]

Apparently, the answers given to the ground crews of both stations were not satisfactory, for, on 5 February, the Odiham station diary recorded that, "today, the unprecedented happened in the RCAF at this station — the other ranks mutinied." All personnel had turned out at 0900 hours for the CO's weekly troop inspection (they "put on an excellent show — our best parade to date). After the inspection, though, 1,500 men refused to return to work, thus carrying out their decision, made two weeks previous, to hold a strike in protest of the government's repatriation policies. The main issue for the men had been a published statement by the minister of national defence for air indicating that four-fifths of the RCAF personnel overseas had volunteered to stay in Europe. The men wanted this erroneous figure corrected (only one-fifth of the RCAF occupation forces were volunteers) because "many were receiving letters asking why they had volunteered for occupation service and why they were not coming home to join their families." Consequently, they decided

MINISTER OF NATIONAL DEFENCE FOR AIR COLIN GIBSON ADDRESSES
CANADIAN OFFICERS AT DOWN AMPNEY, ENGLAND, 1946.
(Department of National Defence, Canadian Forces Joint Imagery Centre PL 46523)

they had to clear-up this misconception and take a stand; they told their CO that they would not return to work until the government defined definite repatriation dates and corrected the misinformation about volunteer rates that were being reported by the newspaper and radio media.[25]

Immediate action was taken by the RCAF: the acting air officer commanding-in-chief for overseas — Air Commodore H.B, Godwin — arrived on the station and held a meeting with the strikers at 1600 hours that day. The station diarist reported that, "there was no rowdyism whatsoever, but adequate precautions were taken to ensure that any incidents would be handled expeditiously." Officers at the meeting noted that the men did not ask any new questions; instead, they dwelt on "oft-repeated questions which were discussed with the airmen on previous occasions." Despite promises that RCAF officials would pressure the government to correct the erroneous information being propagated by the media, "the airmen did not seem to derive the satisfaction they desired from the talks by senior officers." Nevertheless, the CO chose to have the station carry on as normal; personnel were not confined to camp, and "entertainments were held as usual." The scheduled dance took place; moving pictures in the airmen's mess were shown; and even "the liberty run to Reading left as usual."[26]

On 6 February, the station diarist recorded, "the airmen are still out." The strikers were staying in their barracks all day, coming out only to get their meals. Those working in essential services remained on duty (cooks, postal staff, service police, and communications personnel), but NCOs, officers, and even the CO had to take over non-cooking duties in their messes. One newspaper reported that, "the strikers are being ignored by air base officers," but it was hard to ignore the sign at the entrance of the men's mess hall: "Our demands are for replacement of every man who wants to go home. Until we get them — no roll call, no work, no nothing."[27] It was even harder not to notice the reporters and cameramen who besieged the CO for more interviews, even though they were disappointed the previous day "at the lack of violence or demonstrations to provide juicy items for their papers." The commander decided not to shun the media, but to follow "a policy of wide publicity." Hence, not only did he give interviews but Group Captain Timmerman allowed the men to give as many interviews as they wished as well.[28]

Wide publicity was exactly what the men wanted — to get their grievances about slow repatriation aired and to get the misinformation about their volunteer status corrected for the Canadian public. Newspapers in Canada widely reported that, "the men said their chief complaints were that while the majority of them have not volunteered for further service, they are being retained against their wishes and that conflicting reports in Canadian newspapers led their families to believe they did not wish to return home."[29] One leading aircraftsman interviewed was openly critical of the Canadian government's recent policy decisions: "We are being kept over here against our will. The government made certain commitments for an occupation force, and it first was planned that these troops would be volunteers. It got them, then sent them home and discharged them. We are not volunteers for the occupation." It did not sit well with them that RCAF personnel in Canada with the same repatriation points standing as personnel overseas were being released first.[30] Frustration over slow repatriation was exacerbated by the news that shipping was being provided for English wives and children of Canadian servicemen wanting to relocate to Canada. Not only were these civilians being given preferential treatment over those who had served on the front-lines, but this transport of wives and children also demonstrated to the men that government claims of shipping shortages were not believable.[31]

A major source of frustration stemmed from the sense they had that their presence in post-war Europe was not essential, was barely necessary. Crews complained that flying new air routes and carrying civilian passengers for British airlines was something civilians should be doing. Functioning as civilian feeder lines and flying civilian officials around northeast Europe was not considered, "now that the war is over, part of their service duties." It really rubbed the men the wrong way that "we are carrying paying passengers [for British Airways], and we cannot get to the continent ourselves on leave."[32] Although most attention was placed on the repatriation demands, there were indications that deteriorating rations quality and quantity was also an issue.[33]

Although the station diary at Odiham ended the day's entry with, "films were shown in the airmen's mess and a bridge tournament held in Canada House," 6 February was not as quiet as it sounded. Rumours had been circulating around Down Ampney, the other 120 Transport Wing station, that personnel would follow the example of their Odiham colleagues. Even though no strike took place that day, the next morning "maintenance personnel left work to attend a meeting ... at 1630 hours." Behaviour of officers and men alike revealed that it was known throughout the station that a strike was in the offing. At the meeting, the station warrant officer passed along a request from the CO for the maintenance personnel to send representatives to meet with him: "a reply was made by them that they would only send representatives if written guarantee could be given by the Commanding Officer that no disciplinary action would be taken." Since this request was refused, between 800 and 1,000 ground crew began a sit-down strike at 1330 hours. Essential services — the switchboard, signals, hospital, flying control, and service police — were kept running. Group Captain Davis met with the men at 1500 hours to hear their complaints, but no progress towards a solution was made. The station diarist recorded that "the airmen were disorderly throughout the meeting." The CO of 120 Transport Wing arrived at 1700 hours and spoke with the men; unfortunately, "a very poor reception was given."[34] Still no progress was made in satisfying the them and ending the strike. The Down Ampney men were serious about pressing their issues. Their strike committee spokesman stated: "We will stay on strike until we are assured that we will be replaced by men from Canada or the occupation force is disbanded." Down Ampney personnel made it clear to the media that their strike was not merely a sympathy strike for their comrades of Odiham: "We are in sympathy with ourselves. There will be no compromise."[35] This resolve of defiance was threatening to spread to yet more stations; newspapers were reporting that similar action might break out among RCAF personnel at the Topcliffe and Leeming stations in Yorkshire.[36]

By the end of 7 February, the RCAF had close to 2,500 personnel on strike, with the ever imminent potential that this number could increase at any moment. Station commanders, because essential services were running at both stations, decided to adopt a "policy of sitting back and allowing the personnel plenty of time to think and use common sense."[37] Officers recognized that the Air Force was very much a "Citizens' Army," and officials realized that the issue was not Air Force leadership, but government higher policy. Hence, "the incident was classed as a strike" rather than the mutiny it technically was.[38] The strikers emphasized this important distinction as well. A leading aircraftsman told reporters, "this is not a mutiny. We have no complaints against anyone in authority here. Our grievance is with the government."[39] The point was reiterated by each group of strikers. When the staff of the orderly room at 120 Transport Wing Headquarters went out on strike on 5 February, "they were most emphatic in pointing out that their action was not decided against the staff officers of the headquarters."[40] When Odiham ground crews began their strike, newspapers quoted an airman as saying, "we have nothing against G/C N.W. Timmerman [the station's CO].... Our main complaints are the repatriation program. We want to go home."[41] The Down Ampney strikers also told newspapers, "we have nothing against our Commanding Officer (G/C Davis)."[42] Since the men were not striking in protest of any superior officer or his demands, they did not consider themselves to be mutineers.

Because the purpose of their demonstration was to bring "the men's plight to the attention of the Canadian government,"[43] the men did not simply depend on RCAF officials and the media to pass along their messages of discontent; instead, they contacted government officials directly. Besides writing their parliamentary representatives, Odiham personnel actually cabled Colonel Gibson, minister of national defence for air, and demanded his resignation: "Your failure to provide replacements for all RCAF personnel overseas reflects your inadequacy to fulfill your duties as Air Minister."[44] Ground crew from Down Ampney boldly telegrammed Prime Minister W.L.M. King with their complaints. On the first day of their strike, they wrote: "'All RCAF transport command in the UK on strike demand immediate change in occupation policy to effect complete evacuation of non-volunteers. Public retraction of Colonel Gibson's erroneous statement that four-fifths overseas personnel are volunteers demanded."[45]

Colonel Gibson made sure that the media reported his responses to the men. First, without hesitation, he admitted that most of the Air Force personnel still overseas were not volunteers: "They were selected for duty."[46] According to Gibson, the uproar caused by the four-fifths figure had been because of the media's misquoting his actual statement: "I stated about four-fifths of the occupation RCAF force was non-volunteer. This figure was erroneously reported in statements reaching the men overseas…. Naturally, they were disturbed at what they thought was misrepresentation concerning their status."[47] Gibson also explained why so many non-volunteers had been kept overseas: since the RCAF had not been recruiting new men since 1944, there was a shortage of ground crews for the occupation force. Because the men felt their presence overseas was not important, the minister reassured all that "their presence is very essential to assist in maintaining control of enemy country."[48] Transport squadrons were responsible for flying medical supplies, clothing, food, mail, and technical equipment to cities in Europe and India. In November 1945, 2.5 million pounds of freight had been transported by RCAF personnel. Although the men saw little merit in transporting passengers to the continent, Gibson explained that this kept squadrons in a state of operational readiness, in case a crisis broke out again in former enemy territory.[49] In response to complaints "that personnel in Canada were being released before overseas personnel with the same point standing," Gibson had to admit that personnel with lower repatriation group numbers were being released, but these men were non-volunteers as well, and in Canada, they were surplus to the needs of the RCAF: "[T]he alternative would have been to retain these personnel in Canada unemployed. It would have been extremely difficult to justify to the Canadian public the dispatch overseas of these non-volunteers."[50] The good news, so Gibson thought, was that 500 replacement ground crew were being sent which would permit the repatriation of some non-volunteers; the first 250 would be leaving Canada the last week in February.[51]

None of the strikers were satisfied with the news of merely 500 replacements; hence, the strikes would continue. On the third day of the protest, strikers at Odiham presented their CO with a three-point ultimatum for him to forward to RCAF headquarters in London.

The men called for "one hundred percent replacement of non-volunteers, investigation into ... erroneous statements by Colonel Gibson that four-fifths of the men overseas were volunteers, [and] continuation of the strike until the Canadian government makes a satisfactory statement on repatriation."[52] With no resolution in sight, the government and Air Force officials began talking tough. On 7 February, the third day of the Odiham strike and the first day for Down Ampney, the minister of national defence for air warned the Air Force personnel that "we cannot tolerate continuance of refusal to carry out normal duties." In the same statement, he threatened that "early repatriation will not be provided for those who take part in serious breaches of discipline."[53] RCAF Headquarters in Ottawa also took on a more threatening stance; officials decided that if the strikers did not return to work by Monday morning, 11 February, then the action would be considered a mutiny, and penalties would be implemented: pay would be stopped, dependents' allowances and post-war gratuities would end, repatriation would be delayed, and court-martial could follow.[54]

Group Captain F.A. Sampson, personnel officer at RCAF headquarters in London, was tasked with announcing these terms in person to the strikers at both stations. The meeting held at the Odiham station Friday morning held no good news for the strikers. The RCAF's commitment would not end until June 1946, the final exit for all RCAF personnel would still be early autumn, and there would be serious consequences if the strike persisted past the Monday deadline. Not surprisingly, "the airmen were discontented."[55] Despite the ominous news, one newspaper reported that "Sampson was given a friendly reception by the men, who after the meeting clustered around him for more than an hour questioning him about individual problems."[56] Sampson's 1500 hours meeting with the Down Ampney strikers did not go as cordially. Down Ampney's station diary noted that Sampson "attempted to address a meeting of [500] airmen but was interrupted frequently by the men."[57] Newspapers described a more colourful exchange between officer and men, one where "shouts ... virtually drowned out [Sampson's] speech." When Sampson assured the strikers that their pleas for speedier repatriation had been brought to the attention of military and government authorities, one man shouted ungratefully, "That's what we want!" Sampson retorted, "I am not here to be insulted." Sampson's mentioning that their CO was their best friend prompted an audience member to yell, "We are not kicking about him." A chorus of boos rang out when Sampson informed the strikers that pay allowances would be stopped and food rations could be cut if the strike did not end by 11 February. After the meeting, one spokesman for the strikers condemned Sampson's intimidation tactics and asked, "Will Canadians at home allow us to starve for the action we have taken?" Down Ampney strikers remained defiant, deciding to continue their walk-out despite the announced consequences.[58]

Nonetheless, RCAF personnel had been given much to think about. Staff at stations in Yorkshire (Topcliffe and Leeming) had great sympathy for the Odiham and Down Ampney strikers because they felt the same way about delayed repatriation. Rumours had even been spreading that strikes were being planned at both stations. At the Topcliffe station, 1,150 men had met Thursday evening to discuss their situation. Instead of striking, three of the men, at the arrangement of their station commander, Group Captain E.H. Evens, would be meeting with Godwin to discuss their repatriation complaints. At the meeting with Godwin, the delegation asked "that the occupation force be disposed of if a sufficient number of volunteers was not available." They explained that misinformation about their volunteer status had caused domestic trouble "between the men and their families at home over the misunderstanding on volunteering." Some men feared that family break-ups might even result. Because of the audience they were given, the men chose to remain at work.[59]

Almost immediately after the visit of Sampson to Odiham, the strikers decided that they would not defy the deadline. One corporal admitted that fear drove them back to work: "To put it bluntly, we went back because we were scared. But at least we 'hotted up' the wires between here and Ottawa."[60] Having decided to return to work although the government had not yet come through with any of the demands, the men at Odiham delivered the station's CO a statement outlining their position:

> On resumption of their duties, the airmen of the RCAF at Odiham wish the Canadian public to know that they are still dissatisfied with statements and actions by the government. They have returned to work solely because they realize that under the circumstances, a demonstration of this sort cannot continue indefinitely, and even now it is still necessary to maintain Canadian commitments overseas. They sincerely hope the people of Canada will not forget

their grievances but will carry on the struggle where they left off.[61]

By Saturday morning, 9 February, approximately 90 percent of Odiham's strikers had returned to work. At 0815 hours Monday morning, all men were on parade, greeted by a smiling Group Captain Timmerman, who told them:"'You've done a wise thing in returning."[62]

The first reaction of the Down Ampney strikers to Ottawa's ultimatum was to remain on strike and refuse to compromise; they wanted a satisfactory reply to the telegram they had sent the prime minister.[63] The day after Sampson's meeting and the announcement that the men's action would be considered mutiny if not over by 11 February, the Down Ampney men's resolve appeared to be weakening. Saturday morning, 100 men from the motor transport division had returned to work. Newspapers were reporting that a meeting of strikers would be held Saturday afternoon, and it was revealed that "the general opinion is that they will decide to follow the example of the ... RCAF ground crew personnel in Odiham, Hampshire, who called off a similar strike yesterday."[64] As predicted, the men accepted the recommendation of their strike committee and reversed the earlier decision to defy the 11 February deadline. Men freely admitted that the decision was taken "because a lot of them have high repatriation numbers, and they aren't going to jeopardize their chances of getting home early."[65] Although they had received no reply to their first telegram to the prime minister, the Down Ampney ground crew sent him another, explaining that they did not consider the issue to be closed:

> Down Ampney ground crew having decided to return to work wish to stress they are doing so firstly because of the threat to stop dependents' allowances as well as airmen's rations, secondly because they believe two principal objectives — airing their grievances on repatriation and correction of false statements at home — have been accomplished. They wish to state emphatically their dissatisfaction has not lessened. They sincerely hope that pressure of Canadian public opinion will force your government to take action on their behalf.[66]

Monday morning, all personnel were assembled for the 0815 parade. The strikes were over.[67]

The officers at the affected stations were surprisingly good natured and tolerant with the strikers. Officers and senior NCOs took over many of their duties to keep the stations running and open for regular flying schedules. They drove motor transport vehicles, handled arriving casualties, carried out maintenance, inspections, and minor equipment repairs, and they worked in the messes as well.[68] The Station Record Book for 120 Transport Wing headquarters recorded that "Officers [are] showing hidden talents during their turn of kitchen fatigue. Never have the dishes been cleaner."[69] Officers performing kitchen duties could even joke with the media about their activities. One Squadron Leader "was up before dawn helping prepare bacon and eggs. He said he had experience in making breakfast for his wife, "but I hope she doesn't expect me to do this all the time when I get home."[70] In the wake of the strike, the CO at Odiham saw to it that amenities for personnel were increased to help make the stay overseas and away from families more bearable. By the end of February, live shows were held in the airmen's mess each night, and twice-weekly, movies were shown there, in the officers's mess, and in the hospital. The station boasted a camera club, musical appreciation hours, as well as badminton, basketball, tennis, and gymnastics facilities.[71] Some discomforts could not be changed, for officials had no control over the poor weather and daily rains that earned Down Ampney its nickname of "Deep Agony."[72] RCAF officials back in Ottawa were powerless to change government policy, nor could they speed up repatriation as the men so badly wanted. The efforts from Ottawa to improve morale appear not only to badly miss the mark, but they also seem to be an amusing misunderstanding of the strikers' real concerns. On 14 February 1946, the Daily Diary of No. 9 Transport Group headquarters in Rockcliffe noted, "As a result of the RCAF strikes in the UK, it was decided to fly approximately 11,000 pounds of ice-cream powder, powdered milk, and chocolate syrup overseas. Liberator 576 departed for Leeming, Yorkshire with the first load of 5,500 pounds."[73] Powdered ice-cream and chocolate syrup — this was not what the ground crews wanted, but what else could RCAF officials do? Their hands were tied by government commitments.

Although Prime Minister King did not respond to the strikers' telegrams, he was opposed to continued occupation commitments. In his diary on 5 February, King wrote: "[W]ord has since come of a 'sit-down' strike of our men in England, bearing out what I had been pressing so hard for over a long time — to get the men back and to stop the nonsense of adding to the size of the forces." King told Colonel Gibson that he wanted a rapid reduction of personnel overseas, but the prime minister and the minister of national defence for air did not see eye to eye on this issue.[74] When Gibson admitted to cabinet that the British were using RCAF transport squadrons to move civilian passengers and commercial freight for profit, King could not believe that the minister not only was in favour of keeping Canadians in Europe to continue these activities, but the minister also wanted to open recruiting again for ground crews. King was at a loss as to how he could get the occupation commitment ended though, "short of tendering the resignation of the entire Cabinet to the Governor General, I doubt if it would be possible to get the defence forces down to the proportions where they should be at the present time."[75]

Just as the strikes were coming to an end, the Air Council in Ottawa was meeting — not to discuss accelerating repatriation, but to prepare an accurate statement of the repatriation policy for the government. On 9 February, the Air Council attempted to provide answers to many of the strikers' questions and complaints. Repatriation policy gave first priority to those who had volunteered for the Pacific Theatre and to prisoners of war and other special compassionate cases. Those who had not volunteered for the Pacific Theatre nor the European Occupation Force would then be demobilized according to their repatriation group numbers as surpluses to occupation force requirements arose. It was deemed that dispatching replacements from Canada for non-volunteers still overseas would not help matters; personnel relieved of employment would still not be able to get home since shipping space was limited. Hence, unemployed personnel in Canada were released, regardless of repatriation group numbers, and personnel overseas were kept in service until RCAF occupational commitments came to an end in June 1946.[76] This was not what homesick staff wanted to hear, but the logic of the policy could not be denied, and the shipping constraints were the determining factor.

Mutinies in the Commonwealth Air Forces, January 1946

The desire to protest the government's repatriation policy was widespread in the RCAF in February 1946. Men at Odiham went on strike for four days, as did those at Down Ampney. Other RCAF stations seriously considered joining the sit-down (Topcliffe and Leeming), and rumours had it that 40 ground crew at the Biggen Hill and Croyden stations were scheduled to walk out on the morning of 9 February (no action was taken).[77] After enduring another month of poor aircraft serviceability, lack of spare parts, winter clothing shortages, and liberty runs in three-ton trucks instead of suitable buses, the men of 126 Transport Wing in Uetersen, Germany, were driven to voice their desire to go home.[78] Hence, as their colleagues in England were striking, the ground crew of 126 Transport Wing collectively signed a letter publicizing their discontent over slow repatriation and misconceptions over their volunteer status.[79] With each passing day, there was increasing solidarity among RCAF personnel. Nevertheless, the idea to strike and voice their discontent over slow repatriation was not their own. Members of the Royal Air Force (RAF) and the Royal Indian Air Force (RIAF) in the Middle East and the Indian Ocean region had been striking in late January, and the RCAF men got caught up in the momentum and atmosphere of protest.

Commonwealth Air Force personnel stationed in the Middle East and Indian Ocean regions had severe environmental hardships that their colleagues in Great Britain and continental Europe did not have to endure. These regions were notorious for tropical heat, a plethora of insects, and debilitating diseases. The stations were also infamous for their poor food and tent accommodations. Adding boredom with peacetime operations, frustration with military routines, fear that all jobs would be taken before demobilization was complete, and a growing longing to see family made for a potentially volatile situation that could erupt into mass mutiny at the smallest provocation.[80] The RAF Drigh Road station near Karachi, India, was the first to experience a breakdown of discipline among the other ranks. The spark was a simple announcement that on 19 January 1936, the CO would be holding a parade where the men were to be dressed in their best blue uniforms (instead of their cooler tropical dress) and where there would be a full kit inspection afterward. Rumblings of displeasure among the men was virtually unanimous — no one relished the thought of parading in the discomfort of their best blue uniform; furthermore, because so much of their kit had long sat in disuse, there was sure to be missing pieces. Word spread throughout the camp that there would be a secret meeting of men, after dark, at the football field. At the meeting, the men decided that they would not parade in their best blue, nor would they parade at all. They would go to the parade ground, dressed in khaki drill uniforms, and tell the CO that they wanted their grievances brought to the attention of higher authorities. On 19 January, they followed through with their breach of discipline, and they got results. The investigating officer sympathetically listened to the demands that the men had prepared for Air Force headquarters in London: They wanted the Air Ministry informed of their complaints over slow repatriation; they wanted permission to correspond with the prime minister and other members of parliament; they wanted a reasonable military routine that had no Saturday parades, no daily parades to work, and no kit inspection; and they wanted improved living conditions with better food and more reasonable hours of work. Within days, meals improved, tattered tents were replaced with new ones, easy chairs appeared, and overtime demands were reduced. It was decided that there would be no more kit inspections or best blues parades, and the demobilization issue was brought to the attention of government authorities. The men were also given permission to write their government representatives. Almost every man below the rank of sergeant signed a petition sent to the prime minister (approximately 1,200 signatures in total), and they had one Member of Parliament visit the station and give ear to their complaints.[81]

The protest at Drigh Road triggered a rash of demonstrations by Air Force personnel in the region, for it appeared that this method worked. Not only were their demands heard and heeded, but the men got away with their disobedience relatively unscathed. Hence, within 11 days of the Drigh Road incident, over 50,000 men in more than 60 units at 22 stations held demonstrations. Lasting anywhere from a few hours to four days, the strikes all had a common theme: the main demand was faster demobilization. Men at the Mauripur camp near Karachi wanted shipping space allotted to RAF servicemen tripled so as to speed up their repatriation. In Ceylon, men at Katunayke, Negombo, Koggala, Ratmalana, and Colombo protested slow repatriation, poor station administration, and the lack of entertainment and sporting facilities. The Cawnpore station in India complained about food, living conditions, slow demobilization, and the injustice of Class B releases where those with skills usable in post-war reconstruction could secure early returns to Great Britain no matter their length of service. The men at Seletar, Singapore walked out of a meeting where officers were touting unbelievable facts and figures; they then held a sit-down strike protesting canteen facilities, accommodations, recreation facilities, and slow demobilization. Discontent had spread to nearby base Kellang in Singapore, but the unrest did not develop into a full-blown strike. Men at Dum Dum, Calcutta, demonstrated against large liners being allocated to transport American servicemen's war brides; this seemed to contradict the Air Ministry's claims that there was a shortage of shipping for getting RAF men home. Other stations that followed suit and received media attention included Almaza (Egypt), Lydda (Palestine), Rangoon (Burma), Poona, and Vizagapatam (both in India).[82] Even the men of the RIAF got caught up in the passion; RIAF personnel went on strike at Cawnpore, Bombay, Allahabad, Jodhpur, and Drigh Road. Besides looking for faster repatriation, these men were also protesting poor treatment by officers and poor food quality. Unrest in India even spread to the Royal Indian Navy where mutinies — some of them violent — broke out in Bombay, Calcutta, Madras, and Karachi. By 1 February, everyone in the RAF had returned to service. Negotiations with the RIAF were still ongoing at the time of the RCAF strikes.[83]

So many frustrated servicemen turned to strikes because this method clearly worked. Food and living conditions improved, and demobilization was accelerated (some calculated that perhaps an extra 100,000 RAF personnel were released as a consequence).[84] Each group was spurred on by previous groups' success without negative consequences. RAF personnel were inspired by strikes in the British Army that occurred in the early post-war period.[85] Canadians also had a recent precedent of a successful strike in the Canadian Army. Bored with the idleness of barrack life, frustrated with poor food and restricted pay, and angry at the profiteering of local business owners, soldiers awaiting repatriation in the Aldershot area of Great Britain rioted on 4–5 July 1945. By the time the violent demonstration came to an end, windows in over 200 shops had been smashed and £15,000 damage had been done. Nevertheless, their expression of impatience paid off. One riot participant claimed without remorse, "We went on strike one day, the next day we got our pay, and on the next day, we were on our way home. It's the only way to get action. Before that, they just kept promising us a chance to get home, but we never got anywhere."[86]

Buoyed by effective precedents in Canadian Army and among Commonwealth flying colleagues, RCAF personnel chose to take a chance and joined in the wave of protest sweeping the post-war services to pressure governments for faster repatriation. Although there were hints that rations and recreation facilities might not have been ideal, this was not the grievance the RCAF wished to air and articulate. Their campaign was to bring attention to much larger issues — slow repatriation, misconceptions that they had volunteered for post-war duties, and the occupation commitments that were part of the government's foreign policy. The men stated clearly that they were challenging the government — not its existence but its unjust policies. They were also emphatic that they had no grievances against their superior officers, and because of this loyalty to the RCAF, the men did not consider their actions to be mutinous. They had served their country and government faithfully during the six years of war. Now that the emergency was over, these civilians in uniform wanted to go home. Not allowing them to return to their civilian lives in a timely fashion was a transgression of their moral economy. Hence, when their family stability was being threatened by official statements that personnel had volunteered to stay overseas and away from family duties, the men exercised their democratic right (as they called it), put on their civilian persona (who they truly were anyway), and protested with strike action and pleas to the Canadian public. They had fulfilled their service duties during the war; now they wanted the civilian government to live up to its obligations in peacetime: repatriate the men now that the war was over.

Mutinies in Canadian Military History

Studying and analyzing mutinies in the military can be a difficult process. Those involved in mutinies — the lower ranks — do not usually keep records of their actions. The mutinies are often spontaneous, and the repercussions can be serious; hence, putting evidence on paper is not always possible and desirable, and admitting to such disobedience is not always socially acceptable. Therefore, researchers must look to the records kept by the officer class. At times, there is an abundance of materials, especially if boards of inquiry were instituted and court-martial was the consequence. On the other hand, some COs kept quiet about the unrest under their watch: it was deemed safer to deal with the problem internally and unofficially rather than report that one had failed to keep control of those under one's command. Canada's military in the twentieth century, for the most part, has been loyal in its service. In the Air Force and the Army, mass demonstrations have been after war has ended and while the men were awaiting demobilization. The Royal Canadian Navy (RCN), on the other hand, has had incidents of industrial action during the Second World War. Air Force strikes in 1919 and 1946 are distinct from riots in the Canadian Army and mutinies in the RCN. There are elements of similarity to Army and Navy action, but there are also major points of dissimilarity as well. Although the culture of mass disobedience is different among the three services, there is one undeniable common thread: those serving had shared a common experience, developed a common consciousness, defined a common good, and were determined to defend the rights they expected as part of their moral economy.

Air Force and Army mutinies shared common motivations: both services were willing to protest slow demobilization when their transient living circumstances simply could be tolerated no longer. The way each service went about expressing their displeasure was very different. While Air Force personnel simply refused to parade or work, soldiers turned to riots and violence to vent their displeasure and pressure the government. Canadian soldiers in the First World War had been promised that they would be home by Christmas 1918. Come March 1919, they were still waiting to get home. Not only had they endured four months of military discipline and barrack life during peace time, but they had had to weather influenza outbreaks in November 1918 and January 1919, an extremely cold winter, and a coal shortage throughout the month of February 1919. There was also a mood of discontent and unrest in the Mother Country (the U.K.) as miners, dockers, sailors, and police held various strikes. Long before March 1919, Canadian soldiers were ready to go home: they believed that those who had been overseas the longest should get to demobilize first, and they felt that all shipping should be made available to transport those who had served their country, done their patriotic duty, and put their lives on hold for so many years.[87] These sentiments erupted in violence at a number of locations, most notably Kinmel Park where on 4–5 March 1919, impatience and tension boiled over into a violent, two-day riot.[88] Despite a number of deaths and courts-martial the goal of early repatriation was achieved by most participants in the wake of this collective action.[89]

Mass disobedience in Canada's Air Force and Navy were similar in that both services chose non-violent means of expressing their displeasure. The immediate goals, though, were different because members of the Navy were not trying to express a point to the Canadian government; striking naval ratings simply wanted to improve their conditions of service with bettering living amenities, better working routines, and better leadership. Their actions and motivations were similar to what they would have done as civilians in the labour force. Naval ratings were not adverse to holding sit-down strikes during times of war. On 19 July 1943, 190 sailors barricaded themselves in their mess deck to protest the captain's cancellation of shore leave — action that he took in response to the theft of a German prisoner's eagle insignia. Upon investigation, it was revealed that the recent leave stoppage was simply a spark lighting a powder keg of grievances that had gone unexpressed: no one felt the complaints would be dealt with sympathetically. Besides protesting the leave stoppage because of the missing insignia, junior ratings resented leave being cancelled for all if even one rating was absent without leave. The protesters complained about being man-handled and verbally abused, and they also felt career advancements were purposely held back for trifling charges. The men demonstrated for the restoration of shore leave, but they also wanted respect and better treatment from the ship's captain. The ship soon became happy and efficient under a new captain.[90]

Lack of confidence in senior officers was behind the January 1945 mutiny on the *Rivière-du-Loup*. This time, the protest was not directed at the captain, but against the unpopular first lieutenant. When they thought they were going to sea without the captain, who had had to leave the ship for medical treatment, 40 ratings locked themselves in their mess decks. The men complained that the executive officer was incompetent: he had let the ship drift off course while escorting a convoy, and he had endangered the entire ship by bringing the engines to a dead stop and turning on the navigation lights (thus potentially revealing their position to German submarines) while investigating an empty craft in the water. The ratings complained about the lack of respect shown to them and the foul language used, and they resented the fact that senior officers were not open to suggestions by capable ratings with respect to routines.[91] Similar incidents occurred on *Reindeer* in November 1942 where sailors protested an overbearing captain, on *Restigouche* in January 1944 in reaction to accusations of theft, and on *Chebogue* in August 1944 where the protest was against the ship's routine. Sit-down strikes had occurred throughout the history of the Royal Navy (RN), and Canadian sailors working closely with the RN adopted this means of bringing grievances to authority's attention for the sake of improving conditions for loyal and hard-working ratings.[92] The

RN tradition easily became part of the RCN's legacy, and the tool of mutiny was used — though circumspectly — during the post-war period and eventually culminated in a series of mutinies that led to *The Mainguy Report* in 1949 and a number of significant reforms in the post-war Navy.

Lessons Learned

At first glance mass disobedience in Canada's Air Force has been markedly different from the culture of protest in the Army and the Navy. First, Air Force strikes in 1919 and 1946 were not violent; the personnel simply remained in their barracks and refused to take part in daily military routines. Second, the strikes of 1946 were not about effecting change in living conditions or opposing their immediate superiors. The RCAF strikers wanted to engage the federal government and press for faster repatriation. The Army's culture of protest has been of a violent nature. During both the First and Second World Wars, Canadian soldiers, too, have wanted to bring about faster repatriation, and they have done so by creating havoc and destruction with riots — and with positive results. To prevent more damage and destruction, the Canadian government responded by getting the riotous men back home and out of the world's eye. Unsatisfactory living conditions and the lack of communication between leaders and subordinates played important roles in fostering discontent and desires to rebel. Mutinies in the Navy were also about changing living conditions and challenging leaders, but this was done with the intention of restoring fair treatment, be it in regards to leave, routine, or respect. The social make-up of the RCN had changed over the course of the Second World War; civilians were brought into the Navy and outnumbered those who had made the Navy their career before the war when training had been done under British tutelage. By the time the war was over, those from the more egalitarian Canadian society resented any sense of superiority that was imported from the British system. This artificial social divide between officers and men lead to a lack of trust and a lack of communications. Consequently, to be heard, sailors felt they had to do so in the form of mutiny.

Although the culture of protest was different for each of Canada's three services, there is a common underlying factor; each incident of disobedience was driven by the perceived need to restore just practices, force superiors to fulfill their obligations, and defend the group's moral economy. Men from all three services had shared common experiences, and through these experiences, they had come to develop a sense of what rights should be accorded them for their service. These rights — and their superiors' obligations — included ensuring good welfare and good leadership for the personnel under their care. Be it the Navy's demands for better leadership and working conditions, the Army's desire for better camp conditions and demobilization, or the Air Force's concern that slow repatriation and misconceptions over their volunteer status would create hardships and heartaches for families, the men in all three services felt they were not being justly rewarded for their service to their country. Just as the crowds did in eighteenth century England when fair prices and practices had to be restored in the bread markets, so too did Canadian servicemen defend what they had defined as their moral economy. Disobedience was a last resort, but it was judiciously used in their self-interest when absolutely necessary.

Lessons can be learned from Canada's experience with military mutinies in the twentieth century. Men and women joining any of the three services do so knowing that there must be obedience and surrender of many civilian attitudes. Nevertheless, in return for this surrender, these men and women expect fair treatment, respect as individuals with something worthwhile to contribute, and good leaders who care about their subordinates. That leaders meet these expectations is neither an unreasonable expection nor that difficult to achieve. Good leadership can prevent acts of mass disobedience. Forming bonds with subordinates by showing concern, respect, and interest in them creates a sense of loyalty. By building trust, leaders can accomplish their role of influencing and motivating subordinates to fulfill their duty. This trust can be built by making certain that subordinates physical and emotional needs are fulfilled, preferably before the masses start complaining about their conditions of service. The key to good leadership, good leader-subordinate relations, and good morale is communications. Leaders need to be willing to listen, and subordinates need to feel free to share their concerns. Leaders need to give subordinates a sense of purpose, and subordinates need to feel that they have an important part to play in the greater mission. History shows that those who are willing to serve their country are willing to endure much hardship in the name of duty and patriotism. Nevertheless, Canada's forces are a civilian military: it has been historically, and it still is today.

Hence, these men and women bring with them the Canadian values of democratic rights, individualism, and an expectation of respect. Consequently, there does come a time when personnel do fight for their self-interests: this occurs when communications break down, when leaders have let their subordinates down, and when reasonable expectations are no longer met. History has shown that leadership and the moral economy are inextricably intertwined in both the creation and prevention of mutinies. History has also shown that without the exigencies of war, Canadian forces personnel are more likely to demand their rights and express their dissatisfaction when the emergency is over.[93]

NOTES

1. Directorate of Heritage and History (henceforth DHH), File 78/47, "Mutiny Charge Facing Airmen at UK Station," Paper Unknown, 9 February 1946.

2. *Ibid.*, "Airmen's Strike," *Vancouver Sun*, 9 February 1946.

3. *Ibid.*, "The RCAF Overseas 'Strike,'" Paper Unknown, 11 February 1946.

4. *Ibid.*, "Airmen's Strike," *Vancouver Sun*, 78/47, 9 February 1946; and quotations from *Ibid.*, "The RCAF Overseas 'Strike,'" Paper Unknown, 11 February 1946.

5. L.C. Audette, "The Lower Deck and *The Mainguy Report* of 1949," in James A. Boutilier, ed., *The RCN in Retrospect, 1910–1968* (Vancouver: University of British Columbia Press, 1982), 236.

6. Allan English, *The Cream of the Crop: A Study of Selection, Training, and Policies Governing Lack of Moral Fibre in Aircrew in the Royal Canadian Air Force 1939–1945* (Kingston, ON: Queen's University Ph.D. Dissertation, 1993), 191–92, 223, 250–51, 263, and 334.

7. Charles Webster and Noble Frankland, *The Strategic Air Offensive over Germany 1939–1945, Volume 2: Try* (London: Her Majesty's Stationery Office, 1961), 196; Charles Messenger, *"Bomber" Harris and the Strategic Bombing Offensive 1939–1945* (London: Arms and Armour Press, 1984), 91; Max Hastings, *Bomber Command* (New York: The Dial Press, 1979), 248; and Norman Longmate, *The Bombers: The RAF Offensive Against Germany 1939–1945* (London: Hutchinson and Company Publishers, 1983), 184–85.

8. Joel E. Hamby, "The Mutiny Wagon Wheel: A Leadership Model for Mutiny in Combat," *Armed Forces and Society* 28, No. 4 (Summer 2002): 577–79 and 581–86.

9. *Ibid.*, 578, 589, 590, and 595.

10. Howard G. Coombs, *Dimensions of Military Leadership: The Kinmel Park Mutiny of 4–5 March 1919* (Kingston, ON: Canadian Forces Leadership Institute, 2004), 8.

11. Allan D. English, "The Masks of Command: Leadership Differences in the Canadian Army, Navy, and Air Force," presented 25–27 October 2002 at *Inter-University Seminar on Armed Forces and Society*, Kingston, Ontario, 6, 17, and 19.

12. Craig Leslie Mantle, *The "Moral Economy" as a Theoretical Model to Explain Acts of Protest in the Canadian Expeditionary Force, 1914–1919* (Kingston, ON: Canadian Forces Leadership Institute, 2004), 3–7.

13. E.P. Thompson, *Customs in Common* (New York: The New Press, 1993), 188, 189, 211, 212, 216, 217, and 246.

14. Mantle, *The "Moral Economy" as a Theoretical Model*, 5–7, 12, 18, 32, 33, 53, and 56–58.

15. Library and Archives Canada (henceforth LAC), Record Group (henceforth RG) 9, Series III B1, Vol. 3430, File D-2-49, Letter from Major J. McCrimmon to CAF Section (OMFC Headquarters, London), 7 January 1919.

16. LAC, RG 9, Series III B1, Vol. 3430, File D-2-49, Letter from General Staff (OMFC Headquarters, Argyll House, London) to Colonel Sadler (RAF School of Technical Training, Halton Camp), 23 January 1919.

17. LAC, RG 9, Series III B1, Vol. 3432, File R-4-49, Memorandum from Captain A.E. McKeever (commanding No. 1 Squadron, CAF Upper Heyford), 7 January 1919.

18. LAC, RG 9, Series III B1, Vol. 3432, File R-4-49, Memorandum from Captain A.E. McKeever (commanding No. 1 Squadron, CAF Upper Heyford), 12 January 1919.

19. LAC, RG 9, Series III B1, Vol. 3068, File A-6-36, Letter from Major C.M. Marshall (Canadian Detachment RAF, Upper Heyford) to Lieutenant-Colonel C.M. Edwards, 28 January 1919.

20. LAC, RG 9, Series III B1, Vol. 3430, File D-2-49, Weekly Report from Major C.M. Marshall (Canadian Detachment RAF, Upper Heyford) to RCAF Section (OMFC Headquarters, London), 25 February 1919.

21. *Ibid.*, Weekly Report from Major C.M. Marshall (Canadian Detachment RAF, Upper Heyford) to RCAF Section (OMFC Headquarters, London), 13 March 1919.

22. *Ibid.*, Weekly Report from Major C.M. Marshall (Canadian Detachment RAF, Upper Heyford) to RCAF Section (OMFC Headquarters, London), 13 March 1919.

23. DHH, Reel 277, RCAF Station Odiham Diary, 9 January 1946, 11 January 1946.

24. *Ibid.*, RCAF Down Ampney Diary, 10 January 1946, 16 January 1946.

25. *Ibid.*, RCAF Station Odiham Diary, 5 February 1946; DHH, File 78/47, "RCAF Strike Still On," *Stratford Beacon-Herald*, 6 February 1946; and quotation from *Ibid.*, "Demand Faster Repatriation," *Ottawa Journal*, 6 February 1946.

26. DHH, Reel 277, RCAF Station Odiham Diary, 5 February 1946.

27. DHH, File 78/47, "Demand Faster Repatriation," *Ottawa Journal*, 6 February 1946.

28. DHH, Reel 277, RCAF Station Odiham Diary, 5 February 1946.

29. DHH, File 78/47, "Demand Faster Repatriation," *Ottawa Journal*, 6 February 1946.

30. DHH, File 78/47, Quotation from "Flyers Refuse to Work Until Demands Met," *Hamilton Spectator*, 6 February 1946; and *Ibid.*, "Replacements Promised as More Men Quit," Paper Unknown, 7 February 1946.

31. *Ibid.*, "1500 RCAF Ground Crew Strike in UK," *Winnipeg Free Press*, 6 February 1946; and *Ibid.*, "Airmen's Strike," *Saskatoon Star-Phoenix*, 7 February 1946.

32. *Ibid.*, First quotation from "Fliers' Strike Discussed by Cabinet," *Ottawa Citizen*, 6 February 1946, File 78/47, DHH; and second quotation from "No Break Yet in Strike of RCAF Airmen,"*Ottawa Citizen*, 8 February 1946.

33. *Ibid.*, "RCAF Strike Spreads; Ottawa Gives Warning," *Vancouver Province*, 7 February 1946; *Ibid.*, "Warning Sent Strikers Repat Chances Reduced by Breach of Discipline," *Toronto Evening Telegram*, 7 February 1946; and *Ibid.*, "Down Ampney Airmen Quit Sit-Down Strike,"*Hamilton Spectator*, 9 February 1946.

34. DHH, Reel 277, RCAF Station Odiham Diary, 6 February 1946; RCAF Station Down Ampney Diary, February 1946, Appendix.

35. DHH, File 78/47, "No Break Yet in Strike of RCAF Airmen," *Ottawa Citizen*, 8 February 1946.

36. *Ibid.*, "Replacements Promised as More Men Quit," Paper Unknown, 7 February 1946.

37. DHH, Reel 277, RCAF Station Odiham Diary, 7 February 1946.

38. *Ibid.*, RCAF Station Odiham Diary, 5 February 1946.

39. DHH, File 78/47, "800 Down Ampney Men Vote to Continue Strike," Paper Unknown, 8 February 1946.

40. DHH, Reel 277, No. 120 Transport Wing Headquarters Station Record Book, 5 February 1946.

41. DHH, File 78/47, "Flyers Refuse to Work Until Demands Met," *Hamilton Spectator*, 6 February 1946.

42. *Ibid.*, "No Break Yet in Strike of RCAF Airmen," *Ottawa Citizen*, 8 February 1946.

43. *Ibid.*, "More Striking Airmen Returning to Duties," *Winnipeg Free Press*, 9 February 1946.

44. *Ibid.*, "Replacements Promised as More Men Quit," Paper Unknown, 7 February 1946.

45. LAC, Manuscript Group (henceforth MG) 26, J1, Vol. 416, Microfilm C9176, 373437, Telegram from Down Ampney Ground Staffs to Prime Minister W.L.M. King, 7 February 1946.

46. DHH, File 78/47, "Demand Faster Repatriation," *Ottawa Journal*, 6 February 1946.

47. *Ibid.*, "Airmen's Strike," *Vancouver Sun*, 9 February 1946.

48. Quotation from *Ibid.*, "Homesick RCAF Unit Will Be Replaced," *Vancouver Sun*, 9 February 1946; *Ibid.*, "Airmen's Strike Halts Movement of Medicine, Food," *Saint John Telegraph-Journal*, 8 February 1946; and *Ibid.*, "RCAF Men Call Off Strike," *Vancouver Province*, 8 February 1946.

49. *Ibid.*, "RCAF Strike Spreads; Ottawa Gives Warning," *Vancouver Province*, 7 February 1946.

50. *Ibid.*, "Warning Sent Strikers Repat Chances Reduced by Breach of Discipline," *Toronto Evening Telegraph*, 7 February 1946.

51. *Ibid.*, "Replacements Promised as More Men Quit," Paper Unknown, 7 February 1946.

52. *Ibid.*, "No Break Yet in Strike of RCAF Airmen," *Ottawa Citizen*, 8 February 1946.

53. *Ibid.*, "RCAF Strike Spreads; Ottawa Gives Warning," *Vancouver Province*, 7 February 1946.

54. *Ibid.*, "Down Ampney Ground Crews Stay Off Jobs," *Hamilton Spectator*, 8 February 1946.

55. DHH, Reel 277, RCAF Station Odiham Diary, 8 February 1946.

56. DHH, File 78/47, "Down Ampney Ground Crews Stay Off Jobs," *Hamilton Spectator*, 8 February 1946.

57. DHH, Reel 277, RCAF Station Down Ampney Diary, February 1946 Appendix.

58. DHH, File 78/47, "Down Ampney Ground Crews Stay Off Jobs," *Hamilton Spectator*, 8 February 1946.

59. *Ibid.*, "Down Ampney Ground Crews Stay Off Jobs," *Hamilton Spectator*, 8 February 1946; *Ibid.*, "800 Down Ampney Men Vote to Continue to Strike, Paper Unknown, 8 February 1946; *Ibid.*, "Down Ampney Airmen Continue Walkout," Paper Unknown, 8 February 1946; and quotation from *Ibid.*, "Virtual Conscription for Canada's Occupation Air Force Has Arisen," *Lethbridge Herald*, 9 February 1946.

60. *Ibid.*, "Down Ampney Ground Crews Stay Off Jobs," *Hamilton Spectator*, 8 February 1946; and quotation from *Ibid.*, "More Striking Airmen Returning to Duties," *Winnipeg Free Press*, 9 February 1946.

61. *Ibid.*, "Down Ampney Airmen Continue Walkout," Paper Unknown, 8 February 1946.

62. DHH, Reel 277, RCAF Station Odiham Diary, 9 February 1946; and quotation from DHH, File 78/47, "More Striking Airmen Returning to Duties," *Winnipeg Free Press*, 9 February 1946.

63. *Ibid.*, "No Compromise: Striking Airmen Ask Resignation of Air Minister," *Sydney Record*, 8 February 1946.

64. *Ibid.*, "More Striking Airmen Returning to Duties," *Winnipeg Free Press*, 9 February 1946.

65. *Ibid.*, "Down Ampney Airmen Quit Sit-Down Strike," *Hamilton Spectator*, 9 February 1946.

66. LAC, MG 26, Vol. 416, Reel C9176, 373416-7, Telegram from Down Ampney Ground Crew to Prime Minister W.L.M. King, 9 February 1946.

67. DHH, File 78/47, RCAF Station Down Ampney Diary, February 1946 Appendix.

68. *Ibid.*

69. DHH, Reel 277, No. 120 Transport Wing Headquarters Station Records Book.

70. DHH, File 78/47, "Down Ampney Airmen Continue Walkout," Paper Unknown, 8 February 1946.

71. DHH, Reel 277, RCAF Station Odiham Diary, Commanding Officer's Summary for February 1946.

72. DHH, File 78/47, "Striking RCAF Ground Crews in Britain Ended Four-Day Stoppage," *Brantford Expositor*, 11 February 1946.

73. DHH, Reel 277, No. 9 Transport Group Headquarters Diary, 14 February 1946.

74. W.L.M. King Diary, 5 February 1946, available at *http://king.collectionscanada. ca/EN/default.asp*.

75. King Diary, 6 February 1946.

76. LAC, RG 24, Vol. 5377, File 45-25-1, Memorandum from Air Marshal R. Leckie (Chief of Air Staff) to Minister, Part 3, "Policy Governing RCAF Personnel Repatriation," 11 February 1946.

77. DHH, File 78/47, "Signs of Weakening Shown by Air Crew on Strike in Britain," *Ottawa Citizen*, 9 February 1946.

78. DHH, File 181.003 (D5041), No. 126 Transport Wing Operations Record Book, Summary for January 1946.

79. DHH, File 78/47, "Homesick RCAF Unit Will Be Replaced," *Vancouver Sun*, 9 February 1946; and *Ibid.*, "The RCAF Overseas Strike," Paper Unknown, 11 February 1946.

80. David Duncan, *Mutiny in the RAF: The Air Force Strikes of 1946* (The Socialist History Society Occasional Paper #8, 1998), Chapter 1.

81. *Ibid.*, Chapters 1 and 2.

82. Duncan , *Mutiny in the RAF,* Chapter 3; "RAF Strikes Overseas: Resentment at Slow Repatriation," *Times* (London), 25 January 1946, 3; "RAF Strikes: Air Ministry Statement," *Times* (London), 26 January 1946, 3; "RAF Strikers Warned: Delay in Repatriation," *Times* (London), 28 January 1946, 4; "RAF Strikes Subside: Government State Awaited," *Times* (London), 29 January 1946, 3; and "RAF Grievances in India," *Times* (London), 1 February 1946, 3.

83. Duncan, *Mutiny in the RAF,* Chapters 3 and 7; "RAF Grievances: Prime Minister's Refusal to Yield to Force," 30 January 1946, *Times* (London), 8; 1 "RAF Grievances in India," February 1946, *Times* (London), 3; DHH, File 78/47, "Down Ampney Airmen Quit Sit-Down Strike," *Hamilton Spectator,* 9 February 1946; *Ibid.,* "More Striking Airmen Returning to Duties," *Winnipeg Free Press,* 9 February 1946; *Ibid.,* "Signs of Weakening Shown by Air Crew on Strike in Britain," *Ottawa Citizen,* 9 February 1946; *Ibid.,* "Will Consider Strike Mutiny if RCAF Men Still Out After Monday," *Saint John Telegraph-Journal,* 9 February 1946.

84. Duncan, *Mutiny in the RAF*, Chapter 3.

85. *Ibid.,* Chapter 8.

86. Hampshire County Council Aldershot Military Museum website, "The Canadian Army Comes to Aldershot," available at *www.hants.gov.uk/museum/aldershot/faq/canada.html*; and quotation from DHH, File 78/47, "Varied Opinions Voices about RCAF Strike," *Saskatoon Star-Phoenix,* 12 February 1946; *Ibid.,* "1500 Airmen Stay on Strike," 7 February 1946, *London Free Press.*

87. Desmond Morton, "'Kicking and Complaining': Demobilization Riots in the Canadian Expeditionary Force, 1918–1919" *The Canadian Historical Review* 61.3 (1980): 336 and 338; and Julian Putkowski, *The Kinmel Park Camp Riots 1919* (Clwyd, Wales: Flintshire Historical Society, 1989), 8–9.

88. Morton, "'Kicking and Complaining,'" 337, 341; and Putkowski, *The Kinmel Park Camp Riots,* 7–8.

89. Coombs, *Dimensions of Military Leadership,* 14–15, 18–19, and 22; and Putkowski, *The Kinmel Park Camp Riots,* 16.

90. Michael J. Whitby, "Matelots, Martinets, and Mutineers: The Mutiny in HMCS *Iroquois,* 19 July 1943," *The Journal of Military History* 65, No. 1 (January 2001), 77 and 90–98.

91. Bill Rawlings, "Only 'A Foolish Escapade by Young Ratings?' Case Studies of Mutiny in the Wartime Royal Canadian Navy," in *The Northern Mariner* 10, No. 2 (April 2000), 63–67.

92. Whitby, "Matelots, Martinets, and Mutineers," 100–02; Richard H. Gimblett, "What *The Mainguy Report* Never Told Us: The Tradition of 'Mutiny' in The Royal Canadian Navy Before 1949" *Canadian Military Journal* 1, No. 2 (Summer 2000), 87.

93. Thank you to Howard Coombs (Queen's University), Timothy Dubé (LAC), Allan English (Queen's University), Mat Joost (DHH), and Randy Wakelam (Royal Military College of Canada) for their helpful suggestions.

7

Matelots, Martinets, and Mutineers: The Mutiny in HMCS *Iroquois*, 19 July 1943

Michael Whitby

A ship at sea is a distant world in herself and consideration of the protracted and distant operations of the fleet units of the Navy must place great power, responsibility and trust in the hands of those leaders chosen for command.

— Joseph Conrad

I had always found that the style of leadership that accorded best with both my own inclinations and operational efficiency was one of treating subordinates with consideration and respect. I had not found that a "tight ship" had to be an "uptight ship."

— Admiral Elmo Zumwalt, USN

0800 — Colours. Hands fall in.
0805 — Hands did not fall in.

THE LAST EPIGRAPH ABOVE WAS how the largest mutiny in Canadian naval history, and perhaps in any navy during the Second World War, was recorded in the log book of the destroyer HMCS *Iroquois*.[2] Protesting a stoppage of leave by their captain, 190 sailors barricaded themselves in their mess decks and refused duty until their grievances were heard by senior officers ashore. But there was more to this mutiny than a crew expressing displeasure at an unpopular superior who had stopped much-treasured leave. The act was symptomatic of the problems of a Navy caught in the midst of unprecedented 50-fold expansion. As young, inexperienced, hurriedly trained volunteer officers and ratings joined the fleet, they collided head-on with the unfamiliar routines, discipline and personalities of the regular Navy. This often produced friction, but in *Iroquois* the combination proved too volatile and brought about a complete breakdown in discipline.[3]

Part One

HMCS *Iroquois* should have been the pride of the Royal Canadian Navy (RCN). More than just the newest addition to the fleet, it was the lead ship of the most ambitious procurement program to that point in the Navy's history, and thus shouldered the heady expectations of Canada's naval leadership. Senior officers, particularly Chief of Naval Staff, Vice-Admiral Percy Nelles, RCN, hoped that the Tribal-class destroyers would strengthen the prospects of a Navy that too often had suffered neglect from politicians and the Canadian public. After winning the procurement of the British-designed "super destroyers" in the rush to rearmament in the first months of the war, Nelles won a fight with his political masters to deploy the Tribals overseas with the Royal Navy (RN) in European waters. There, the chance of action — "traditional" gun-dominated surface action that is, not convoy action — and the accompanying publicity, would be highest. Thus, a lot was riding on HMCS *Iroquois* when it commissioned on a dismal 30 November 1942 in Newcastle, England.[4]

Unfortunately, its initial service fell well short of expectations. As "first of class," and because the Canadian Tribals incorporated key improvements over the original British design, there were more than the usual teething troubles. These, combined with structural problems, personnel shortages and other growing pains, slowed the progress of *Iroquois* towards full operational status. A brief account of what should have been a triumphant maiden voyage to Canada's main naval base at Halifax, Nova Scotia demonstrates how events seemed to conspire against *Iroquois*. After a strenuous work-up with the RN's Home Fleet at Scapa Flow, the destroyer sailed for Halifax on 28 February 1943 — much to the chagrin of senior British officers who were unhappy at losing a valuable destroyer to what they considered a public relations exercise. The passage across the North Atlantic was a rough one and upon arrival *Iroquois* had to put into dry dock for hull repairs. Shore authorities could only muster a small working party, therefore the crew had to perform much of the work themselves, making it impossible for the commanding officer, Commander W.B.L. Holms, RCN, to grant long leave. Holms wrote in his monthly Report of Proceedings that "the morale of the ship's company remained high," but there was grumbling that leave was restricted to short runs ashore, especially since the crew knew they were returning to England and that it would be a long time before they would again have the chance to set foot on Canadian soil.[5]

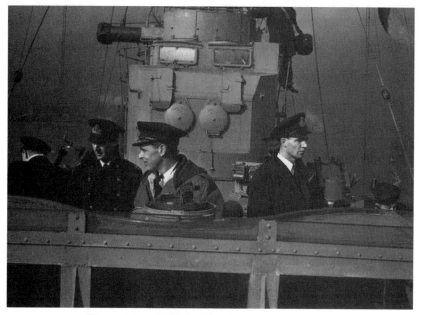

COMMANDER W.B.L. HOLMS (CENTRE) STANDS
ON THE BRIDGE OF HMCS *IROQUOIS*, 1943.
(Department of National Defence, Canadian Forces Joint Imagery Centre R 77)

Bad luck turned worse on the return passage to England. As the destroyer ploughed through the churning seas of a Force 9 gale, two sailors were swept overboard while attempting to rescue a shipmate lying injured on deck. Both were lost without trace and morale plummeted.[6] Further misfortune struck when the destroyer returned to Britain. After finally becoming operational, *Iroquois* again sustained hull damage in heavy seas and again had to put into dry dock. All in all, it was a frustrating beginning. A ship with a strong, professional bond between captain and crew would likely have overcome such adversity but that was not the situation in *Iroquois*. It was an unhappy ship, which only increased the general level of frustration. The root of the problem lay in the poor relationship between the captain and his young, inexperienced crew on account of his rigid discipline and the lack of respect he often conveyed towards his officers and men.

William Boyd Love Holms joined the RCN in 1916. A year later, while attending the Royal Navy College of Canada, he was wounded in the great Halifax explosion, and was thereafter known by the unfortunate sobriquet of "Scarface." His career followed the standard path with sub-lieutenant's courses and capital ship training with the RN, and as a lieutenant he specialized as a "springer" or physical fitness officer. As he climbed the promotion ladder, Holms garnered a reputation as an above average staff officer and a fair ship handler, and in the late 1930s it looked as if his career was taking off when he received four attractive appointments in succession. In 1938, he was selected to be the first commanding officer (CO) of HMCS *Restigouche*, one of four modern destroyers acquired from the RN. After leaving *Restigouche* in December 1939, Holms briefly commanded the training depot HMCS *Stone Frigate* at Kingston, Ontario, before becoming CO of the naval barracks at Esquimalt, British Columbia, the RCN's main training establishment on the West Coast. Then, in November 1942, he was named the first captain of HMCS *Iroquois* — without question the most prestigious sea-going command in the Navy.[7]

This string of favourable appointments marked Holms as a streamer but also contained a flaw, which, through no fault of his, was to a large degree responsible for the problems he would have in *Iroquois*. From the time he left *Restigouche* in December 1939 until he took command of *Iroquois* three years later, the RCN experienced the greatest tumult in its history as the tiny pre-war Navy of a dozen ships and a few thousand sailors exploded to a fleet of hundreds and a strength that would top 90,000. In the words of one historian, thousands of young Canadians were "thrown into totally unfamiliar surroundings, with inadequate training and equipment to fight a deadly enemy."[8] The vast majority of this massive influx of personnel entered as members of the Royal Canadian Navy Volunteer Reserve (RCNVR), or "the Wavy Navy" as it was popularly known, and, like reservists in other services and countries, they generally held values and priorities that were in stark contrast to those of the professional force. Their sense of being Canadian was different from pre-war regulars who had been trained in the RN and who proudly adhered to its customs and traditions; they had a more irreverent and lighthearted approach to discipline; and they had volunteered to fight a war, not to build a career. Through their sheer numbers and their contribution to the war at sea, they slowly changed the basic ethos of the Canadian Navy.

Although the Navy reeled from this massive upheaval at its east coast bases and on the North Atlantic run, Holms was far removed from the tumult at Esquimalt on the relatively quiet British Columbia station. There, the war seemed a distant concern, and peacetime routines and mores held sway. Even when the war came closer to the West coast after Pearl Harbor, there was a marked difference in attitudes at Esquimalt and at bases on the east coast like Halifax, Sydney, and St. John's, which were on the front-line of the Battle of the Atlantic. Senior naval leaders should have recognized this and ensured that Commander Holms received familiarization training before he took over *Iroquois*, as appears to have been done with other officers transferring from the West Coast.[9] That did not happen and it is obvious from the moment Holms assumed command that he was unaware of the vast transformation that had taken place in the Navy.[10]

Part Two

There is a perception in Canadian naval circles that the first captains of the Tribals hand-picked both their officers and key non-commissioned personnel. Moreover, it is held that the big destroyers, upon which the Navy was counting so heavily, had a greater percentage of regular force personnel than other ships.[11] Both perceptions are inaccurate. A comparison with other Canadian destroyers shows that the Tribals had much the same complement in terms of experience and service affiliation — about 80 percent of their crews had never been to sea before and most of the officers were relatively inexperienced reservists. The only significant difference was that the captains of the Tribals were "second-time rounders" with destroyer command time already under their belts, a practice that continued well after the war. As far as captains having their pick of personnel, Vice-Admiral H.G. DeWolf, Canada's most revered naval officer and the first captain of the Tribal HMCS *Haida*, recalled that he was appointed to command with such little warning that even had he wanted to make changes, there was no opportunity to do so.[12] But the perception about the Tribals having hand-picked crews is best dispelled by Commander Holms's comments about his own ship's company.

Within days of taking command of *Iroquois*, Holms complained to the senior RCN officer in the United Kingdom that his officer complement was inadequate in terms of both quality and quantity to handle the heavy challenges imposed on a wartime destroyer. His criticisms started with his first lieutenant — or executive officer — Lieutenant Edward Madgwick RCN, who was also gunnery officer. Holms complained that Madgwick suffered "from chronic seasickness" and that he was incapable of fulfilling his dual responsibilities, an opinion perhaps formed before the war when Madgwick served under Holms in *Restigouche*. Instead of requesting another officer to serve as gunnery officer, Holms asked that "a senior Lieutenant or Lieutenant Commander RCNR[13] be appointed Executive Officer in Madgwick's place with him becoming gunnery officer and flotilla gunnery officer."[14]

Madgwick was inexperienced. He had only three-and-a-half years seniority as a lieutenant and *Iroquois* was his first appointment as first lieutenant, but that was about the same seniority and experience as the first lieutenants of other Canadian destroyers at that stage of the war. On the plus side, however, he had an important qualification that most did not have in that he had completed the RN's arduous Long Gunnery course at Whale Island.[15] In other words, he was suitably qualified, actually well-qualified, for the position of first lieutenant of a Canadian destroyer in late 1942. Like countless other Canadian officers thrust into similar circumstances, all he needed was the opportunity to grow into the job. As it was, Commander Holms's lack of confidence in Madgwick, often expressed openly through shouted criticism, could not have done much for the morale of either Madgwick nor the crew.

Holms had even less confidence in the seven RCNVR officers in his wardroom, who "although keen and interested are most inexperienced and can only be considered as borne additional for training."[16] Although Holms had misgivings about most of them, his evaluation of one officer, the navigating officer, Lieutenant Douglas Bruce, RCNVR, reveals his general attitude towards the "Wavy Navy" and demonstrates how out of touch he was with the staffing situation in the RCN. Holms complained that Bruce "had little sea experience, no destroyer experience, and it is understood that the navigational course carried out by this officer was most incomplete and impractical. The Captain cannot be expected to simultaneously handle and navigate the ship with satisfaction."[17] Because of this lack of confidence, Holms asked Lieutenant W.P. Hayes, a newly promoted regular force officer who was not a qualified navigator, to double-check Bruce's navigation. Hayes later recalled that "the Captain didn't seem to have much confidence in reserve officers; because I was permanent force, I could do almost no wrong." Hayes, who considered Bruce a good navigator, chose not to follow through on his captain's request.[18]

Contrary to Commander Holms's opinion, Bruce had considerable experience for an officer of his rank and position at that point in the war, whether regular or reserve. Indeed, he had more wartime experience at sea than Holms. A pre-war member of the RCNVR, Bruce's seniority as a lieutenant dated to November 1938 and he had seen destroyer duty as a reservist during peacetime. After war broke out, Bruce served in the ex-USN four-stacker HMCS *Annapolis* from November 1940 until July 1941 and, although the destroyer was only operational for three months of that time, Bruce demonstrated enough ability to be appointed first lieutenant of the corvette HMCS *Shediac*. During his nine months in that ship, *Shediac* was assigned to the Newfoundland Escort Force where Bruce was exposed to a wide range of experience on the tough North Atlantic run. That was followed up by the Long Navigation course at HMCS *Kings* in Halifax.[19] Given this record, it is no exaggeration to say that at that point of the war, most commanding officers in the RCN would have enjoyed having a volunteer reservist as experienced and well-trained as Bruce as their third officer.[20]

Holms lodged other complaints about specific personnel and a general shortage of senior ratings but he received short shrift from senior Canadian officers in England and at Naval Headquarters in Ottawa. Captain K.F. Adams, the senior Canadian naval officer in England, minuted to the secretary of the Naval Board, the senior naval administrator, that "it is regretted that the Commanding Officer HMCS *Iroquois* is dissatisfied with the ship's company drafted. Shortages of a minor nature cannot presently be avoided." Adams also noted that some of the personnel about whom Holms was complaining had received good evaluations from previous commanding officers. For his part, the secretary of the Naval Board, curtly informed Holms that "every effort has been made to provide HMCS *Iroquois* with the best ship's company from the personnel available."[21]

Holms's complaints about his crew, and specifically those about his officers, indicate how out of touch he was with the realities of the

OFFICERS OF HMCS IROQUOIS POSE IN AN
UNDATED PHOTOGRAPH ON THE DECK OF THE SHIP.
(Department of National Defence, Library and Archives Canada PA 206875)

mid-war RCN. Another sign of that was his attitude towards routine and discipline. From the time he joined *Iroquois* during the fitting out and commissioning period at Newcastle, Holms ran the ship by a taut peacetime regimen that had long since passed by the wayside in other ships.[22] Each day the crew mustered for Divisions at 0900 and Evening Quarters at 1600. Dress of the day for sailors was No. 3 uniform or blue serge. Captain's rounds were held each Saturday, "even down to the white glove routine."[23] According to *Iroquois*'s chief boatswain's mate, Chief Petty Officer Clement Mann, a veteran of the pre-war Navy, "this type of routine had not been carried out since the outbreak of the war. [By that stage of the war] dress was working rig [dungarees] except for special dutymen. Also by that time blue serge uniforms were expensive and hard to come by."[24] Mann recalls that their No. 3s soon became soiled and worn, but then Commander Holms began to pick them up for sloppy dress. To the relief of sailors on the *Iroquois*, when the ship joined the Home Fleet at Scapa Flow, Rear-Admiral (Destroyers) I.G. Glennie overrode Holms's orders and allowed the crew to wear working rig.[25]

Peacetime routine was one thing — there were always "pusser" captains who went by the book — but the visible contempt that Commander Holms displayed towards his crew was something else again. Mann recalls that "when speaking to individuals one always had the impression he looked at them as inferior beings."[26] Holms showed little tolerance for mistakes, cursing loudly at and sometimes "manhandling"[27] ratings who did not perform to his satisfaction. According to one rating, "One day I was shaken violently by the shoulders and called a 'God damned fool' then pushed heavily against the Chief Gunner's Mate who was told by the Captain to 'throw this bloody thing over the side.' This was caused by the searchlight not elevating due to a mechanical fault when I was ordered to turn it on."[28] Another sailor complained that "Through not spotting an aircraft I was kicked in [the] side and slapped across the right ear by the Captain."[29] As a result, Chief Mann recalls, "when the Captain went down one side of the ship on his walks there was a mass exodus of those who could get away to the other side. I'm sure many of the crew were actually scared of him."[30] And Holms's actions were not directed solely at the lower deck; officers also felt his wrath. On one occasion, when an attempt to secure the ship to a buoy went awry, Holms, yelling loudly from the bridge down to the fo'c'sle, ordered the officers he deemed responsible, including Lieutenant Madgwick, to their cabins.[31] Such action was unheard of and contributed to the general erosion of morale.

One incident particularly rankled the ship's company. "On 23 December 1942," Chief Mann recalls, "we did a practice torpedo run":

> After picking up the torpedo we had to take it around the stern of the ship to the Torpedo Davit. First Lieutenant phoned bridge and asked that the engines not be moved until he gave the all clear, repeated this and received the affirmative. Just as we had the torpedo over the screws, Bridge moved the engines; of course screws hit the torpedo, badly damaged and sank it, at same time chipping one of the screws. We were ordered into the floating dock on Christmas Eve. The Depot Ship had sent around an issue of beer for each ship at Scapa for Christmas Day. On Christmas, Captain ordered beer was not to be issued for punishment at loss of torpedo and our

being in floating dock over Christmas etc. There was
a lot of resentment about this especially because the
blame lay somewhere on the bridge.[32]

As a result, when Commander Holms toured the mess decks
on Christmas Day to exchange the customary compliments of the
season with his sailors, he was greeted by sullen silence. One officer
said he had never seen a ship's morale so low.[33]

The problem was not just Holms's style of leadership; it was the
combination of Holms's style of leadership *and* a young inexperienced
crew. According to one officer:

> He was very difficult man to work for, but so are many
> other Captains of ships, but the trouble in *Iroquois*
> was that our Captain, when thwarted or irritated,
> would completely lose his temper and shout and
> scream in an incomprehensible manner at whatever
> was offending him. A seasoned crew would have
> probably laughed this off, but *Iroquois* did not have
> that luxury and the ship's company grew resentful....
> What was lacking was a Captain who, in addition to
> driving his ship's company hard, could also coax and
> encourage his very green and experienced crew.[34]

Was there anything that the members of *Iroquois*'s wardroom
or lower deck could have done about the situation through official
channels? According to the King's Regulations that governed
discipline in the RCN, "every person is fully authorised to make
known to his superior any proper cause for complaint" but, as the
famous *Royal Oak* courts-martial of 1928 made abundantly clear, that
was not the reality. On that occasion, the captain and commander of
the battleship HMS *Royal Oak* submitted written grievances about
the behaviour of their flag officer. When they were censured for their
action, both officers demanded a court-martial to clear their names
but after a widely publicized trial, both were found guilty of writing
subversive complaints about a superior, reprimanded and removed
from their positions. Their careers were to all intents finished and that
lesson reverberated throughout the Royal Navy, and one can safely
assume the RCN, which was a virtual sub-component of the RN.
Winston Churchill, then chancellor of the exchequer, complained
to the First Sea Lord that "the moral of these Courts-Martial seems

most threatening to all ranks or rating who have to complain of harsh or unjust treatment."[35] Or as one historian succinctly put it: "Making a complaint against a superior officer had always been a risky venture; now it was professional suicide."[36]

In *Iroquois*, there was talk among the non-commissioned officers (NCOs) about making a grievance to Commander Holms about his actions but nothing came of it "because," noted Lieutenant Madgwick, "they were all too scared to bring them up to the Captain."[37] That left the onus on Lieutenant Madgwick as first lieutenant. Indeed, after the mutiny, Vice-Chief of Naval Staff, Rear-Admiral G.C. Jones, insisted that Madgwick was "entitled to bear a share of the blame. If the situation in the ship and his own position, vis-a-vis (*sic*), his Captain, was impossible, it was his duty to represent this fact to higher authority, however distasteful this course might be."[38] Distasteful and unlikely to have produced a positive outcome. If Madgwick had lodged a grievance with Holms, the most likely result, as he later explained at the Board of Inquiry, would have been an outburst that would only have served to make matters worse — remember this was the captain who had once banished Madgwick to his quarters in front of the crew. If Madgwick had gone over Holms's head he would have been accused of disloyalty and, of course, he had the *Royal Oak* example to consider. As it was, *Iroquois*'s first lieutenant did what most officers would have done; carry on with the job as best he could.

Others also apparently chose to let matters run their course. After the mutiny, Canadian officers learned that senior British staff with the Home Fleet had been well aware of the situation in *Iroquois*, but viewed it as a Canadian problem that required a Canadian solution.[39] In the end, that is what happened.

Part Three

Ironically, the mutiny came in the wake of the finest moment in *Iroquois*'s brief service. On 11 July 1943, the destroyer was one of four escorts accompanying the troop convoy "FAITH" across the Bay of Biscay on the way to Casablanca. Late in the evening, three German Focke-Wulf Kondor reconnaissance bombers found the convoy and mounted a devastating attack. Two of the three large troop ships were quickly sunk and *Iroquois* was near-missed. After the enemy withdrew, Commander Holms supervised a rescue that saw some 1,800 soldiers and Air Force personnel pulled from the sea. *Iroquois*'s crew took some 660 survivors onboard their own ship and, amid serious overcrowding, cared for them during the remainder of the passage to Casablanca.[40] Here was something to build upon. The destroyer had finally seen action, and although FAITH had been a dismal defeat, it could in no way be attributed to *Iroquois*. On the contrary, the ship had performed well, fending off air attacks and playing the lead role in the rescue of survivors. Unhappily, there was no opportunity for the improvement in morale to take hold.

On 18 July, while *Iroquois* was re-crossing the Bay of Biscay on her return to Plymouth, six survivors from the German submarine *U-506* were transferred to the ship from a British destroyer. An officer among them asked to have his uniform shirt laundered but upon return it was missing its distinctive eagle insignia, which someone had obviously stolen as a souvenir. The officer was not angry, merely shrugging his shoulders and saying that "this is the cost of the washing."[41] But Madgwick and Holms took the theft seriously, and with good reason. In March 1940, when First Lord of the Admiralty Winston Churchill learned that British sailors had taken a watch, chronometer, and Iron Cross from the captain of the *Altmark* when it was boarded in Norwegian waters, he complained to the First Sea Lord that "Anything of this kind must be stopped with the utmost strictness. No souvenir of any value can be preserved without being reported and permission obtained. Personal property of enemies may be confiscated by the State, but never by individuals."[42] Likely aware that the taking of souvenirs would be viewed unkindly, Madgwick launched a quick investigation but when it failed to turn up the missing insignia he announced over the ship's intercom that if the culprit left it in his cabin nothing more would be said. That was not enough for Commander Holms; he told Madgwick to inform the crew that if it did not materialize, no leave would be granted when the ship reached Plymouth.[43]

By the time *Iroquois* secured to number 7 Buoy in Plymouth Harbour at 1600 hours, July 18th, the missing article had not turned up — it was probably thrown overboard — and, true to his word, Holms refused to grant leave. That was the breaking point. Some of the crew had wives in Plymouth and the remainder, being typical sailors, wanted to go ashore to blow off steam and celebrate their baptism of fire. When Chief Mann circulated around the ship that evening, he detected a lot of discontent and "had a very good idea that something was going to happen."[44] The coxswain came to the same conclusion and, as was their duty, the two senior NCOs informed the first lieutenant of the situation. The three then went to the captain's day cabin where Madgwick voiced their concern to Commander Holms.[45] He would do nothing, and outside of rescinding his order to cancel leave there was really nothing he could do; it was too late. The next morning, in the words of the subsequent inquiry, "a large section of the ship's company of HMCS *Iroquois* refused duty."[46]

The events of 19 July, a dreary rainy day, are best compiled through the reports of Commander Reginald Morice RN, who, as captain (D) Plymouth, had administrative authority over destroyers operating out of that port, and Lieutenant Madgwick. As per normal harbour routine, *Iroquois*'s crew was piped to duty at 0800. Five minutes later, the first lieutenant was informed that almost all junior ratings except stewards and supply ratings had locked themselves in the fore-upper and fore-lower mess decks. After checking the situation for himself, Madgwick "endeavoured to speak to the ratings in the forward messes down the ammunition hoist on the Foxle deck. This had no effect. The First Lieutenant then went back aft and reported to the Captain at about 0830 what had happened. The Captain stated they were to be given one hour in which to produce a spokesman and to fall in. The ratings were informed of this by the Coxswain about five minutes later." The response of the 190 ratings was to chant, like raucous demonstrators, "We want Captain (D)!!; We want Captain (D)!!"[47]

At 0845, while Lieutenant Madgwick was awaiting events in the wardroom, Commander Holms's steward reported that the captain had collapsed: "The Doctor immediately went to his cabin and had him placed in bed suffering what appeared to be a heart attack. In view of this, and the fact that the ship was liable to go to sea at short notice, the First Lieutenant went onboard HMCS *Athabaskan* and reported the situation to Commander G.R. Miles, Captain [and senior Canadian officer present]."[48]

Athabaskan, which had berthed alongside *Iroquois* the previous afternoon, may have been more then just an innocent bystander to these events. Indeed, in the opinion of Commander Holms, its crew was partly to blame for the unrest in his ship. According to his testimony to the official inquiry into the mutiny:

> It is also understood that a disturbance of a similar nature took place in the *Athabaskan* recently, and that a certain number [of ratings] in that disturbance in the *Athabaskan*, are still in the *Athabaskan*. I further

understand that the CO of the *Athabaskan* had asked or suggested to the Staff Officer to the Captain (D), that until the *Athabaskan* had been out and had a shake down, the two ships should not be berthed together.[49]

The disturbance in *Athabaskan* that Holms referred to was a mass leave-breaking in April 1943, and the information about the request not to berth the two Canadian destroyers together almost certainly came from Commander Miles, who had hosted Holms at dinner on the 18th.[50] No other reference to Miles's request to keep the two destroyers apart is extent in the records, but, if it was made, the staff at Plymouth must have been puzzled at the lack of control that Canadian officers thought they had over their sailors.

Holms blamed *Athabaskan* for transforming a buoyant mood in his ship to a sour one:

> I went on deck when the *Athabaskan* came alongside [on the 18th] and heard quite a lot of laughing, and on two or more occasions, I heard references being made by some of my ship's company to *Athabaskan* ratings that 'Why don't they join a fighting ship,' and it all sounded in most pleasant terms.... It strikes me as peculiar that the apparently happy frame of mind changed overnight.[51]

The shift in mood, if indeed there was one, was likely because *Athabaskan*'s sailors got shore leave while *Iroquois*'s didn't! That said, throughout the morning of the 19th, sympathetic sailors from *Athabaskan* passed food, drink and encouragement to their compatriots in *Iroquois* through the forward scuttles.[52] Given that, it is likely they had some influence on events in *Iroquois*, and British and Canadian authorities may have been fortunate that they did not have two mutinous ships in Plymouth harbour that day.

Shortly after Lieutenant Madgwick went onboard *Athabaskan* to explain the situation to Commander Miles, the two officers proceeded ashore to report to captain (D) Plymouth. After confirming that the Canadian ships were not required to sail until later in the day, Commander Morice boarded *Iroquois* to talk to the mutineers. Attached to the door of the forward upper mess was a typed note:

Complaints Registered by Ratings Against Captain

1. Leave stoppage regarding missing eagle.

2. Stoppage of Mess's Leave by one rating adrift.

3. Being talked to in abusive language, cursing, yelling etc., and being man-handled.

4. Possible advancements being held up or cancelled, by trifling conduct charges.[53]

After some delay, Commander Morice and a leading seaman and leading stoker he insisted accompany him, were let into the mess:

> I stepped inside and having ordered silence told the men that I did not wish any of them to speak, and that my future action would depend on their attitude when I had finished what I had to say.
>
> I then commented shortly on the four points mentioned in the paper, told them the proper procedure for forwarding complaints, and said that I had instructed the Leading Seaman and Leading Stoker with me to assist individuals to formulate their complaints and to bring them forward to the Commanding Officer in the proper manner, and that I would instruct him to detail two officers to assist the leading hands in the presentation of these cases. I added a caution on the dangers of putting forward "unjustifiable" complaints, and pointed out the seriousness of "theft" in a ship, and in particular from a prisoner.
>
> After this I informed them that the Captain was sick, that the First Lieutenant had assumed command temporarily in his absence, that the ship was needed that day for service, and that I required an immediate assurance that they would return to their duty forthwith and would give their officers their fullest support. This assurance was given as far as I could see without hesitation and unanimously.[54]

Morice's cool, professional leadership defused the situation. Of course, there was an important mitigating factor in that Commander Holms's medical emergency effectively removed him from the equation. There is no way of knowing whether the 190 ratings would have returned to duty had Holms remained in command, although it seems likely so long as their grievances were presented to captain (D). But there's the rub. There is no telling what might have happened when the hour that Commander Holms gave them elapsed. Would they then have reported for duty? Would Commander Holms have contacted captain (D)? Would the situation have escalated? How would *Athabaskan* have responded? As it was, when Lieutenant Madgwick piped "Hands fall in" shortly after 1100 hours, the crew responded immediately and the ship sailed on operations under his command later that day. Considering what might have occurred, that was a good outcome.

Were the events that transpired mutiny? According to Chief Petty Officer Mann, the sailors involved were careful to ensure that it did not appear that way:

> The crew must have talked among themselves and come up with the only way they could see of getting the attention of Capt 'D' to their grievances. I know they did not consider this 'no-work sit-down' anything like a mutiny and it was done in a way so it would not look like it. All special dutymen went on duty. All rates above AB [Able Seaman] were not included. If ship had been ordered to sea, I'm positive it would have gone.[55]

But if it was intended as a sit-down strike or job action in spirit, it was more than that by the letter of the law. According to the King's Regulations, "the term mutiny implies collective insubordination, or a combination of two or more persons to resist or to induce others to resist lawful military authority." By refusing to respond to repeated orders to turn to, the sailors who barricaded themselves in their mess decks had practised "collective insubordination" and had, technically, committed mutiny.

Part Four

When *Iroquois* returned from an eventful week long patrol in the Bay of Biscay, a board of inquiry convened at Plymouth to investigate the causes of the incident. Captain H.B. Crane, RN, commanding officer of the cruiser HMS *Birmingham*, was president of the board, and Captain Harold Grant, RCN, a Canadian, and Commander Haskett-Smith, RN were assisting. The choice of Grant is interesting as he had been in *Iroquois* on the return passage from Halifax the previous March, and would therefore have had some familiarity with the ship. Moreover, his previous service would undoubtedly have brought him into contact with Commander Holms and some of the other personnel in *Iroquois*.[56]

Over a two-day period, the Board heard testimony from 22 members of the crew, including Commander Holms. The questions put to the three officers who appeared — Lieutenant Madgwick and the divisional officers of the upper and lower forward messes — and the coxswain and the chief stoker, revolved mainly around the subject of whether they had received any formal grievances about Commander Holms before the mutiny. They answered to the negative, although they expressed awareness of more than the normal lower-deck grumbling, and Lieutenant Madgwick admitted that he did not pass that information on to the captain even though Commander Holms had explicitly asked him to do so. In regard to the evident discontent in the ship on the eve of the mutiny, Madgwick testified that beyond the meeting with the captain mentioned previously, he chose not to not press the matter further "because I was rather afraid that if I did, steps might be taken that would reduce leave still further."[57] The ratings called to testify were those who had submitted written grievances on the request of Commander Morice. They gave details about Holms's discipline (see above); however, the board was unable to elicit firm responses when they asked each sailor why they had not grieved about the situation through official channels.[58]

On July 27, the inquiry convened at RN Hospital Plymouth to question a composed and polished Commander Holms. He was shown Lieutenant Madgwick's report on the incident as well as the grievances that had been submitted as a result of Commander Morice's meeting with the mutineers on the morning of the 19th. Holms noted that the complaints came from sailors whose names were often listed in punishment returns. He also emphasised that "at no time has any complaint been brought before me by the ship's company." With regard to "the indefinite charge of abusive language and manhandling," Holms admitted to "nudging" a lookout awake with his toe when he was asleep at his station and occasionally swearing mildly in the fashion of "For God Almighty Sake get a fender out there, you will need it." As to the theft of the German crest, he maintained he was going to investigate the matter further and would probably have restored leave. And besides pointing the finger at *Athabaskan*, he blamed the incident on three ratings awaiting punishment for falling asleep on watch who "had little to lose."[59]

The board was unconvinced and in its subsequent report found "three contributory factors to the refusal of duty." The first was Commander Holms's practice of stopping leave for all members of a mess when one of their number went absent over leave. Second was the complaint that applications for advancement or examinations were "unjustly held up or refused by reason of the applicant having committed some disciplinary offence," although they found no evidence to substantiate this. Finally, there was a feeling among a number of the ship's company that they were being treated unjustly and harshly by the captain, but it is considered that this would, in itself, not have been the subject of complaint by a more seasoned ship's company. There is, however, evidence that the commanding officer did, at times and under stress, show intolerance and an overbearing attitude towards certain of the ship's company.

The board noted that no complaint of this treatment was forwarded by ratings at the time of "alleged occurrences" because of a "general feeling that such complaints would not be dealt with sympathetically." The report concluded, "such fear in no way exonerates the disaffected section of the Ship's Company for not representing their complaints in accordance with the Regulations which had been adequately promulgated and displayed on board."[60]

It is clear from the tone of their report that accounts of life in *Iroquois* left the members of the Board sympathetic with the mutineers. The fact that they referred to Holms's "intolerance and overbearing attitude"[61] certainly indicates that they attached some blame to his style of leadership. C-in-C Plymouth, Admiral Sir Charles Forbes, agreed calling Holms's methods "highly injudicious. In particular, the stoppages of leave of whole messes because of leave-breaking by one member must be regarded as unjust and improper." However, Admiral Forbes considered the crew's means of bringing this to the attention of authorities — through mutiny — to be "reprehensible."[62]

The Canadian naval high command came down hard against Holms. Since *Iroquois* was under the operational control of the RN, senior officers at Naval Service Headquarters (NSHQ) in Ottawa played only a peripheral role during the aftermath of the incident. It appears they received their first detailed information about the incident on 20 July when Commander F.L. Price, the senior Canadian naval officer (London), forwarded a copy of Admiral Forbes's original signal to the Admiralty. In an amendment to the message, Price informed the chief of Naval Staff that it would be a week before Holms's medical condition became clear, but that if a permanent relief was required he would have to come from Canada as there was no suitable RCN officer available in the United Kingdom. Vice-Admiral Nelles's immediate response was to appoint Commander J.C. Hibbard, RCN temporary commanding officer and to transfer Holms onto the books of HMCS *Niobe*, the Canadian staffing depot in England. Before reaching any further decisions, Nelles wanted to know the results of the inquiry.[63]

He and other officers at the top of the Canadian naval hierarchy were dismayed with what they learned. A report to the naval minister written by Vice-Chief of Naval Staff, Rear-Admiral G.C. Jones, and endorsed by Nelles, criticized Commander Holms who, either lacked the ability or was physically incompetent to gauge the extent he could force unorthodox methods to achieve discipline on his ship's company. There is no question that by a threatening and physically intolerant attitude that at times took the form of physical violence, he placed himself entirely in the wrong with his men who awaited their turn to retaliate. Such methods are out of date and render the user liable to any retaliation which may arise.[64]

Jones concluded that Holms's "whole future career has been jeopardised,"[65] which was indeed the case. The chief of Naval Staff met with Holms in Ottawa on 2 September and informed him that he would receive no future appointments to either a training establishment or command at sea. He also persuaded him that it would not be in his interest to request a court-martial to clear his name.[66] Holms served out the war at the Canadian naval mission in Washington, D.C. where he evidently performed well, and, strangely enough, was promoted to captain in 1946. After serving as chief of staff to the commanding officer Atlantic Coast, he retired in April 1948. It must have been a difficult end for an officer, who with *Iroquois*, had been given an appointment with so much promise.[67]

With Holms's fate settled, that of the crew remained. Admiral

Forbes recommended that *Iroquois* be paid off and its crew scattered among other Canadian ships.[68] It appears that the Admiralty was prepared to follow that advice but were persuaded otherwise by *Iroquois*'s new commanding officer. Instead of reporting to the Canadian naval mission in London when he arrived in England, Commander Hibbard went directly to the Admiralty to put forward the case that *Iroquois*'s crew should remain intact and be allowed to prove itself on operations. Although there is no evidence that he was ordered to proceed that way, Hibbard's thinking dovetailed with that of senior Canadian officers in Ottawa. Beyond the personnel upheavals and consequent operational delays that would result from breaking up the crew, such a drastic action would draw attention to the fact that there had been a mutiny in one of the RCN's most prestigious units. That was *not* the type of publicity that Vice-Admiral Nelles and his colleagues sought when they fought to have the Tribals deployed overseas. As it was, Hibbard's persuasiveness won the day, and the Admiralty informed NSHQ that:

> Commander Hibbard has reported to Admiralty and it is recommended that decision on re-commissioning be deferred. Propose that after joining the new CO should take necessary corrective action and should in due course forward report of general conduct of ship together with his recommendations as to whether or not ship should recommission.

That proved a wise decision as *Iroquois* became a happy, effective ship under its new captain. Hibbard was respected throughout the Navy as a talented leader and a good sailor. Moreover, with plenty of experience in the Battle of the Atlantic — both in the fighting at sea and in a training establishment ashore at Halifax — he was well aware of the dramatic upheaval the RCN had undergone during the war. But he was also tough and he did not hesitate to take "corrective action." Lieutenant W.P Hayes recalls that Hibbard's first act upon taking command was to muster the crew by the open list: "each member of the ship's company comes and salutes the Captain and gives his name and number. So that he's under the eagle eye of the Captain who now knows his name and he is being watched. It had a profound effect."[69] Hibbard later reported that the crew "were made to realize the serious nature of the trouble in Plymouth with the consequent discredit to the ship and the ship's company."[70] He also told them

— firmly — that the incident was their fault. But he used more than words to get their attention; 10 ratings deemed to be "mess-deck lawyers" were posted off the ship and, ironically, he stopped all leave for three months.[71]

Iroquois responded favourably. When rear-admiral (D) Home Fleet inspected the ship at the end of August, he reported to the Admiralty that he was satisfied with what he saw:

> It is my opinion that
>
> (a) the ship's company appreciate the seriousness of the action taken by a large percentage of their total,
>
> (b) there will be no further failings of a similar nature,
>
> (c) there is therefore no need to pay the ship off, and
>
> (d) no further action is required.[72]

As Vice-Admiral Nelles had concluded earlier, "a change in Commanding Officers was apparently all that was required to correct a situation that should never have been allowed to arise."[73]

With something to prove, *Iroquois* went on to a successful wartime career. It performed well on several challenging trips on the Murmansk run but its shining moment came in the summer of 1944 as part of Plymouth Command's Force 26 with the cruiser HMS *Mauritius* and the destroyer HMS *Ursa*. Through excellent gunnery and the innovative marriage of tactics and technology — Hibbard was one of the first commanding officers in either the RCN or the RN to conn a force into night surface action from his operations room — *Iroquois* played a critical role in the destruction of German shipping attempting to flee Bay of Biscay ports as a result of the U.S. Army's rapid advance across Brittany and the Loire region.[74] Although its sister ship HMCS *Haida* garnered more publicity and became Canada's most famous fighting ship, *Iroquois*'s wartime record was nearly as good. Certainly, as much as the other ships in its class, it enabled the Tribals to meet the heady expectations thrust upon them by Canada's naval leadership.

Part Five

It remains to place the *Iroquois* mutiny into wider context. There is no question that it gave the RCN a certain reputation. British officers already considered Canadians a wild, unruly bunch who bore watching but the incident resulted in an even closer eye being kept upon Canadian ships serving with the RN.[75] When Commander H.G. DeWolf, captain of the destroyer HMCS *Haida*, paid his respects to rear-admiral (D) Home Fleet at Scapa Flow in September 1943, the meeting opened with a frosty Rear-Admiral Glennie, who had already experienced a mutiny in *Iroquois* and a mass leave-breaking in *Athabaskan*, looking DeWolf squarely in the eye and saying "You won't be having any crew problems in your ship will you?"[76] And, in January 1945, when 47 ratings of the corvette HMCS *Rivière-du-Loup* locked themselves in their mess deck because they mistakenly thought they were heading to sea under command of an unpopular first lieutenant, British naval authorities clamped down hard and sentenced 44 of the culprits to Belfast Gaol.[77]

Of far greater consequence was the impact that the *Iroquois* mutiny had on the RCN. Similar incidents had occurred before. In 1937, sailors in the destroyer HMCS *Skeena* briefly locked themselves in their mess deck to protest a change in ship's routine, and in November 1942 the crew of the tiny armed yacht HMCS *Reindeer* did the same to protest against an overbearing captain — and there may have been others.[78] But the sheer magnitude of a mutiny involving 190 sailors, the fact that it occurred in such a high profile ship and a reaction from the naval brass that sailors could construe as soft, gave the *Iroquois* mutiny notoriety and influence above the others.

Canadian sailors employed similar tactics at least seven times in the next six years:

- In August 1944, sailors in the frigate HMCS *Chebogue* staged mass disobedience over dissatisfaction with the ship's routine.
- In January 1945, as mentioned above, 47 ratings barricaded themselves in the mess deck of the corvette HMCS *Rivière-du-Loup*.
- In the spring and summer of 1947, a series of disciplinary incidents occurred in the destroyer HMCS *Nootka*.

- In August 1947, 40 ratings in the cruiser HMCS *Ontario* locked themselves in their mess deck to bring attention to grievances concerning dress of the day, ship's routine and dissatisfaction with the Executive Officer.
- On 26 February 1949, 90 men locked themselves in the forward mess deck of the destroyer HMCS *Athabaskan II* on account of complaints about dress requirements, the ship's routine and the unreasonable demands of the Executive Officer.
- On 15 March 1949, 83 ratings, including 15 who had participated in the 1947 incident in *Ontario*, locked themselves in the forward mess deck of the destroyer HMCS *Crescent* and posted a list of grievances complaining about the ship's routine and demanding the relief of the Executive Officer.
- On 20 March 1949, 32 aircraft handlers in HMCS *Magnificent* refused to answer a pipe to clean ship. They turned to after the Captain promised to hear their grievances.[79]

There is clearly a pattern here. News, especially of the dramatic variety of mutiny, travels far, fast, and wide — though quietly — in a small Navy, and there is little question that the causes, events and aftermath of the *Iroquois* mutiny were known in the mess decks and wardrooms of the RCN and became a precedent for the incidents that followed. The influence such scuttlebutt could play in sparking mutinies was recognized at the Mainguy Inquiry, which investigated the mutinies in *Crescent*, *Athabaskan II*, and *Magnificent*. A chief petty officer serving in *Crescent* testified that sailors in that ship "followed the [1947] incident that occurred in *Ontario* from hearsay, and acted in a similar manner."[80] And in their final report, the Mainguy commissioners concluded "there was a connection between the incidents in *Ontario*, *Athabaskan*, *Crescent*, and *Magnificent* and each succeeding incident received some pattern and some encouragement from its predecessor."[81] But the hearsay, the connection, the pattern, and the encouragement extended beyond 1947 and HMCS *Ontario*. Louis Audette, one of the three Mainguy commissioners, learned after the inquiry that several ratings who had taken part in the *Iroquois* mutiny participated in the 1947 *Ontario* mutiny.[82] It thus appears that

Iroquois set the example that others followed.

But what example did *Iroquois* follow? There is no doubt that they were following a tradition that existed in the service the RCN was most closely connected to, the RN. Nicholas Rodger, an authority on the social history of the Royal Navy, explains that:

> When other methods failed, mutiny provided a formal system of public protest to bring grievances to the notice of authority. It was a sort of safety-valve, harmless, indeed useful, so long as it was not abused. It was part of a system of social relations which provided an effective working compromise between the demands of necessity and humanity, a means of reconciling the Navy's need of obedience with the individual's grievances. It was a means of safeguarding the essential stability of shipboard society, not of destroying it.[83]

This centuries-old attitude well describes the motives for the mutinies that hit the RCN in the 1940s, but there were also practical examples from the RN that likely raised Canadians' awareness of the efficacy of that form of protest. The 1931 Invergordon Mutiny, where the lower deck of a number of ships in the RN Atlantic Fleet staged mass insubordination to protest a cut in pay, received wide publicity but both the scale and motives behind the Invergordon mutinies were vastly different from *Iroquois*, whose sailors were protesting against an officer, not government policy. Another well-publicized incident in the battleship HMS *Warspite* was closer to the mark. In June 1937, a small group of sailors held illegal meetings to organize a protest about inadequate leave. Word of the unrest reached the press and sparked an inquiry with the result that three officers and a number of ratings were posted from the ship, while three other sailors were discharged from the service.[84]

Even though events such as these occurred years before the incident in *Iroquois*, the use of mutiny as a tool to register protest and affect change would have been known in the wartime RCN because of its close relationship with the RN. During the interwar years and into the Second World War, the RCN and other navies of the Commonwealth were virtual sub-components of the Royal Navy. Their officers and ratings were trained by the RN, operated alongside its various squadrons and proudly followed its customs and traditions. It should not be surprising that mutiny was among the traditions they absorbed. Nor was such transference restricted to the RCN. During the 1930s, the Royal Australian Navy (RAN) was beset by a high level of unrest for reasons related to pay, conditions, and discipline, and although sabotage was often used to express discontent, on a number of occasions sailors refused duty.[85] Given all the above, it seems clear that *Iroquois's* crew were following an empire tradition extending back centuries.

No matter what example was being followed, the string of mutinies that hit the RCN in the 1940s said that the "effective working compromise between the demands of necessity and humanity" that Nicholas Rodger describes, was lacking in too many RCN ships. The situation lingered into the immediate post-war years and was finally rectified by the Mainguy Inquiry that jolted the RCN closer into line with Canadian values, traditions, and character, and that has been credited with transforming the organization into a truly "Canadian" Navy. Indeed, one historian goes so far as to call it "the RCN's Magna Carta."[86] Following that premise, the 190 young sailors who locked themselves in the forward mess decks of HMCS *Iroquois* in Plymouth harbour on 19 July 1943 can be said to have helped the Navy along the road to its Runnymede. That was never their intent, but it should be part of their legacy.

NOTES

1. Reprinted from *The Journal of Military History* 65, No. 1 (January 2001), 77–103.

2. Library and Archives Canada (henceforth LAC), Record Group (henceforth RG) 24, Vol. 7418, Deck Log, HMCS *Iroquois*, 19 July 1943.

3. The *Iroquois* mutiny has escaped attention in Canadian naval historiography. It gained mention in two popular histories of the Royal Canadian Navy (RCN) but only in general, and in Schull's case flawed, terms with no explanation of the long-term causes of the mutiny. See Joseph Schull, *The Far Distant Ships: An Official Account of Canadian Naval Operations in the Second World War* (Ottawa: King's Printer, 1950); and Tony German, *The Sea Is at Our Gates: The History of the Canadian Navy* (Toronto: McClelland & Stewart, 1990).

4. For acquisition and deployment of RCN Tribals see Gilbert N. Tucker, *The Naval Service of Canada, Volume 2* (Ottawa: King's Printer, 1950), 27–29; and Michael Whitby, "Instruments of Security: The RCN's Procurement of the

Tribal-Class Destroyers, 1938–1943," *The Northern Mariner* 2, No. 3 (July 1992), 1–16.

5.   Directorate of History and Heritage (henceforth DHH), HMCS *Iroquois* (1942–1943), 8000, HMCS *Iroquois*, Report of Proceedings, 24 March 1943.

6.   *Ibid.*, HMCS *Iroquois*, Report of Proceedings, 1 May 1943; LAC, RG 24, Vol. 7418, HMCS *Iroquois*, Deck Log, 19 March 1943; DHH, "Canadian Tribal Class Destroyers Built in the U.K."; and DHH, HMCS *Iroquois* (1942–1943), 8000, HMCS *Iroquois* (1942–1943), "Brief Notes Re Operations November 1942–July 1943." These reports were almost certainly written by Lieutenant J. George, an RCN historical officer.

7.   Biographical material from various volumes of the *Canadian Navy List*. Holms passed away in the early 1990s and his personnel files, which contain his S-206 reports, the equivalent of the U.S. Navy's Fitness Reports, will not be opened until 20 years after his death.

8.   Marc Milner, *North Atlantic Run* (Toronto: University of Toronto Press, 1985), xv.

9.   For example, when Lieutenant P.F.M. Defreitas, Royal Canadian Naval Reserve (RCNR), was sent to Halifax to take command of an escort on the East Coast after almost two years command experience on the West Coast (including two deployments to the Aleutians), he was sent out for familiarization training on the North Atlantic. Tragically, he was assigned to the destroyer HMCS *St Croix* and died when it was sunk in September 1943.

10. Biographical information is derived from RN and RCN *Navy Lists* and various interviews held at DHH.

11. That comment is prevalent among Canadian historians and veterans. See, for example, DHH, Biography H, transcript of a November 1986 interview between former naval officer and historian Hal Lawrence and Commodore (Retired) W.P Hayes, 33.

12. Vice-Admiral H.G. DeWolf to author, June 1989.

13. There were two categories of Reserve officers in the Canadian Navy during the Second World War: "Volunteer Reservists," or RCNVR, who had no previous sea experience, and "Naval Reservists," or RCNR, who joined the Navy from the merchant service. One outside observer summed up the rivalry this way: "The Royal Canadian Navy Volunteer Reserve consists of gentlemen trying to be sailors, the Royal Canadian Navy Reserve consists of sailors trying to be gentlemen, and the regular Royal Canadian Navy consists of neither trying to be both!"

14. LAC, RG 24, Vol. 11746, CS384-25-3, Commander W.B.L. Holms to Canadian Officer Commanding Canadian Ships (CCCS), 19 December 1942. CCCS was

the title of the senior RCN officer in Britain before the establishment of the senior Canadian naval officer (London), or SCNO(L).

15. Biographical information is derived from RN and RCN *Navy Lists*.

16. LAC, RG 24, Vol. 11746, CS384–25–3, Commander W.B.L. Holms to CCCS, 19 December 1942.

17. *Ibid.*

18. DHH, Biography H, interview with Commodore (Retired) W.P. Hayes, 28 March 1982, 42–43; and *Ibid.*, interview with Cmdre W.P. Hayes, undated, 33.

19. DHH, RCN *Navy List*, 8000, NHS HMCS *Annapolis, and* 8000, HMCS *Shediac.*

20. Doug Bruce left *Iroquois* in early 1944 for the plum appointment as the first executive officer (XO) of the new destroyer HMCS *Sioux* where, according to historian and naval veteran Hal Lawrence, he was an extremely popular and effective first lieutenant.

21. LAC, RG 24, Vol. 11746, CS384–25–3, CCCS to Secretary, Naval Board, 23 November 1943. Secretary, Naval Board to CCCS and HMCS *Iroquois*, 13 January 1943.

22. DHH, Biography H, interview with Cmdre W.P. Hayes, 28 March 1982, 42.

23. C. Mann to author, n.d., 3.

24. *Ibid.*

25. Amazingly, while the ship was on passage from Newcastle to Scapa Flow, Commander Holms mustered the crew to evening quarters. As Chief Petty Officer (CPO) Mann recalls, "it had been a no-no for quite some time to gather so many men in one area. Lucky no subs." *Ibid.*, 3–5.

26. *Ibid.*, 4.

27. LAC, RG 24, Vol. 4093, C1150–355/11. This was the term used in testimony at the official inquiry. See C-in-C Plymouth, "Board of Inquiry Re *Iroquois* — July 1943."

28. *Ibid.*, Commanding Officer HMCS *Iroquois* to Captain (D) Plymouth, 25 July 1943. This report, written by Lieutenant Madgwick after the mutiny when he was acting commanding officer (CO), lists 10 written grievances filed against Commander Holms.

29. *Ibid.*

30. C. Mann to author, undated, 4.

31. Confidential source. Commodore Hayes describes the situation in *Iroquois*'s wardroom as "a little unhappy." DHH, Biography H, interview with W.P. Hayes, 28 March 1982, 43.

32. C. Mann to author, 5–6. The author is aware of two other accounts of this incident from officers in *Iroquois* at the time of the incident, including DHH, Biography H, interview with James Dowler.

33. Confidential source.

34. Confidential source.

35. Churchill to Bridgeman, 6 April 1928. Quote from Stephen Roskill, *Churchill and the Admirals* (London: Collins, 1977), 60.

36. Norman F. Dixon, *On the Psychology of Military Incompetence* (London: Jonathan Cape, 1976), 273; and for a complete account of the incident, see Leslie Gardiner, *The Royal Oak Courts Martial* (London: Wm. Blackwood, 1965).

37. LAC, RG 24, Vol. 4093, C1150–355/11, Madgwick testimony, C-in-C Plymouth, "Board of Inquiry Re *Iroquois* — July 1943," 8.

38. DHH, 8000, NSS HMCS *Iroquois* (1942–1943), VCNS to Naval Minister, "Disturbance on the *Iroquois* — July 19, 1943."

39. Confidential source.

40. LAC, RG 24, Vol. 3345, HMCS *Iroquois*, ROP, 17 July 1943, 1926-DDE-217 Vol. 1 (Acc 83–84/167).

41. LAC, RG 24, Vol. 4093, C1150–355/11, Lieutenant E.T.G. Madgwick testimony. Quoted in C-in-C Plymouth, "Board of Inquiry Re *Iroquois* — July 1943," 2. Joseph Schull, in his brief account of the incident, maintains that the German officer "raised loud complaints," and insinuates that this reaction forced Madgwick and Holms into their subsequent efforts to retrieve the crest. That interpretation is not borne out by the testimony of Madgwick and others. Schull, *The Far Distant Ships*, 192.

42. Martin Gilbert, *Finest Hour: Winston S. Churchill 1939–1941* (Toronto: Stoddart, 1983), 157.

43. C. Mann to author; and DHH, Biography H, interview with Commodore W.P. Hayes, 28 March 1982, 42.

44. C. Mann to author, 8.

45. LAC, RG 24, Vol. 4093, C1150–355/11, CPO [Chief Petty Officer] William

Montgomery Testimony, "Board of Inquiry Re *Iroquois* — July 1943," 17. Montgomery was *Iroquois*'s coxswain.

46. DHH, 8000, HMCS *Iroquois* (1942–1943), C-in-C Plymouth, "Board of Inquiry Re *Iroquois* — July 1943," 27 July 1943, 1–2.

47. LAC, RG 24, Vol. 4093, C1150–355/11, CO *Iroquois* to C-in-C Plymouth, 19 July 1943. This was written by Lieutenant Madgwick as acting CO.

48. *Ibid.*

49. LAC, RG 24, Vol. 4093, C1150–355/11, Holms testimony, C-in-C Plymouth, Report of "Board of Inquiry Re *Iroquois* — July 1943," 45–46.

50. DHH, Biography M, Miles Diary, 18 July 1943.

51. LAC, RG 24, Vol. 4093, C1150–355/11, Holms testimony, C-in-C Plymouth, Report of "Board of Inquiry Re *Iroquois* — July 1943," 45–46.

52. This information came to light at a recent reunion of *Iroquois* veterans.

53. LAC, RG 24, Vol. 4093, C1150–355/11, Captain (D) Plymouth, "HMCS *Iroquois* — Incidents on 19th July 1943," 19 July 1943. There was a note attached to the doors of both messes. They were identical except that one was typed and in one the word *swearing* is used instead of *cursing*.

54. *Ibid.*

55. C. Mann to author, 8.

56. LAC, RG 24, Vol. 4093, C1150–355/11, C-in-C Plymouth, "Memorandum," 21 July 1943; and DHH, Flag Officer Newfoundland to HMCS *Iroquois*, 28 February 1943, HMCS *Iroquois*, Ships Cards.

57. LAC, RG 24, Vol. 4093, C1150–355/11, Madgwick testimony, C-in-C Plymouth, Report of "Board of Inquiry Re *Iroquois* — July 1943," 2–7.

58. See LAC, RG 24, Vol. 4093, C1150–355/11, C-in-C Plymouth, Report of "Board of Inquiry Re *Iroquois* — July 1943."

59. *Ibid.*, Holms testimony, 45–49.

60. *Ibid.*, 1–2.

61. *Ibid.*

62. *Ibid.*

63. LAC, RG 24, Vol. 11751, CS42–3, SCNO(L) to NSHQ, 20 July 1943; and LAC,

RG 24, Vol. 4093, C1150–355/11, VCNS to Naval Minister, "Disturbance on the *Iroquois* — July 19, 1943," undated but probably 31 August 1943.

64. *Ibid.*, VCNS to Naval Minister, "Disturbance on the *Iroquois* — July 19, 1943," 31 August 1943.

65. *Ibid.*

66. Undated margin note by CNS, *Ibid.*, VCNS to Naval Minister, "Disturbance on the *Iroquois* — July 19, 1943," 31 August 1943.

67. Information derived from RCN *Navy List*.

68. *Ibid.*; LAC, RG 24, Vol. 11751, CS42–3, C-in-C Plymouth to Admiralty, 27 July 1943.

69. DHH, interview with Hayes, 36–37.

70. DHH, 88/7, HMCS *Iroquois*, ROP, 14 October, 1943.

71. *Ibid.*

72. DHH, 88/7, Rear Admiral (D) Home Fleet to Admiralty, 30 August 1943, RCN Narrative, "Canadian Ships with the Home Fleet," 21.

73. CNS to Naval Minister, "Disturbance on the *Iroquois* — July 19, 1943," 31 August 1943.

74. See Bill McAndrew, Donald E. Graves and Michael J. Whitby, *Normandy 1944: The Canadian Summer* (Montreal: Art Global, 1994).

75. For perhaps the best known example of this see Captain Donald MacIntyre's strident criticisms of the RCN escort force in his *U-Boat Killer* (London: Weidenfeld and Nicolson, 1956), 78–82.

76. Vice-Admiral DeWolf has related this story to the author on a number of occasions.

77. See Bill McAndrew, Bill Rawling, and Michael Whitby, *Liberation: The Canadians in Europe 1944–45* (Montreal: Art Global, 1995), 111–12. A Canadian officer, Commander E.D. Tisdall, was on the board of inquiry. This time the crew was broken up.

78. Rear-Admiral Horatio Nelson Lay, *Memoirs of a Mariner* (Stittsville, ON: Canada's Wings, 1982). Lay was *Skeena's* first lieutenant.

79. See *Report on Certain Incidents Which Occurred on Board HMC Ships* Athabaskan, Crescent *and* Magnificent *and Other Matter Concerning the RCN* (henceforth *Mainguy Inquiry*) (Ottawa: King's Printer, 1949) for details of these mutinies.

Besides those listed in this text, in his testimony to the Mainguy Inquiry, the Chief of the Naval Staff referred to a post-war incident in the frigate HMCS *Swansea*.

80. LAC, MG 31, E18, Vol. 21, File 10, L.C. Audette Papers.

81. *Mainguy Inquiry*, 56.

82. L.C. Audette, "The Lower Deck and *The Mainguy Report*" in James A. Boutilier, ed., *The RCN in Retrospect, 1910–1968* (Vancouver: University of British Columbia Press, 1982), 237–39. Louis Audette, a great friend of the Canadian Navy and Canadian naval historians, expanded upon this with the author on many pleasant occasions.

83. N.A.M. Rodger, *The Wooden World: An Anatomy of the Georgian Navy* (Annapolis, MD: Naval Institute Press, 1986), 242–43.

84. For Invergordon see, among many others, Stephen Wentworth Roskill, *Naval Policy Between the Wars, Volume 2* (London: Collins, 1976); Anthony Carew, *The Lower Deck of the Royal Navy 1900–1939* (Manchester, Eng.: Manchester University Press, 1981); David Divine, *Mutiny at Invergordon* (London: Macdonald, 1970); Leonard F. Guttridge, *Mutiny* (Annapolis, MD: Naval Institute Press, 1992); and for the incident in HMS *Warspite*, see Stephen Wentworth Roskill, *HMS Warspite: The Story of a Famous Battleship* (London: Collins, 1957), 166–69.

85. For the situation in the Royal Australian Navy (RAN) see K. Spurling, "Life and Unrest in the Lower Deck of the RAN in the 1930s," *Journal of the Australian Naval Institute*, Vol. 23, No 1 (January–March 1997), 41–48.

86. W.A.B Douglas, *The Canadian Encyclopedia*, Vol. 1 (Edmonton: Hurtig, 1988), 117; see also German, *The Sea Is at Our Gates*; David Bercuson, *True Patriot: The Life of Brooke Claxton, 1898–1960* (Toronto: University of Toronto Press, 1993), 183–86, and William Glover, "The RCN: Royal Colonial or Royal Canadian Navy?" in Michael L. Hadley, Rob Huebert, and Fred W. Crickard, eds., *A Nation's Navy: In Quest of Canadian Naval Identity* (Montreal: McGill-Queen's University Press, 1996), 71–90; and important research on RCN post-war personnel policy is currently being conducted by Captain (Retired) Wilf Lund and Lieutenant-Commander Richard Gimblett.

8

Protestors or Traitors?
Investigating Cases of Crew Sabotage
in the Royal Canadian Navy, 1942–1945

Richard O. Mayne

W HEN THE ROYAL CANADIAN NAVY (RCN) went to war in 1939, it
was anticipated that enemy agents or citizens with radical affiliations
would try to sabotage its warships. Four years later, however, it was
discovered that there was another threat, and so a naval order was
issued that instructed commanding officers (COs) on the procedures
to follow in cases where a member (or members) of the crew had
sabotaged the ship.[2] Such an order was deemed necessary because
naval intelligence officers in St. John's and Halifax had been unable
to solve a string of sabotage attempts where the most likely suspects
were members of the crew. Initially, these officers thought they were
dealing with traitors or even enemy agents, but as they gained more
experience they came to realize that these acts were being committed
by ordinary sailors. At least a dozen cases of crew sabotage were
investigated between 1942 and 1944, and it was suspected that many
more had gone unreported. But investigating these matters was not
easy. As a member of the crew, the saboteur had many advantages —
such as unlimited access to the ship and knowledge of when rounds
were conducted — that made it difficult to determine his identity.
This paper, therefore, will explore the problems that the RCN faced
when it investigated cases of crew sabotage, and argue that these acts
were more likely carried out by sailors with specific grievances rather
than subversive tendencies.

One of the earliest recorded cases of crew sabotage occurred on
HMCS *Eyebright* in early March 1942. During a layover in St. John's,
Newfoundland, *Eyebright*'s generator was undergoing repairs. At the
time of re-assembly it was discovered that someone had removed an

essential part that the repair staff had left unattended in the flats (the ship's main hall or corridor).[3] Although this had caused *Eyebright* to remain alongside for an extra two days, naval intelligence did not respond until three weeks later when something similar happened during repairs to HMCS *Cowichan*'s main fans.[4] Despite the parallels with the *Eyebright* incident, the staff officer (intelligence) in St. John's did not take this matter seriously as he assigned an inexperienced officer to investigate both cases. Quickly overburdened by the task at hand, this junior officer did not interview the crews or repair staff from either ship and even failed to analyze the physical evidence that had been left behind by the perpetrators. Moreover, the determination that a crewmember or members onboard *Eyebright* and *Cowichan* had "sabotaged their ships with the intention to delay sailing" represented the opinion of the ship's officers rather than his own.[5] Based on these findings the investigation was closed.

This was one of Naval Intelligence's earliest encounters with crew sabotage in the RCN, they found the concept disturbing it was concluded that the likelihood of further occurs was remote. Instead, security authorities at the base turned their attention to protecting vessels from outside threats, particularly since it was discovered that there were "cases of people boarding ships and entering Naval Areas with passes signed by Hitler, Tojo, Hedy Lamarr and other enemies of mankind." Although considered an "old and sour joke" such incidents suggested that security at St. John's was lax, and that meant brow sentries needed to "realize the importance of their job and do it properly."[6] Sailors protecting the ship from external threats, however, were ineffectual against crew saboteurs and four months later these same security officers would develop a renewed interest in this subject when two more suspicious breakdowns were reported within days of each other.

Having been tasked as the duty ship on 29 August 1942, HMCS *Wetaskiwin* raised steam in preparation for sailing. After the engine had difficulty turning over, the ship's chief engineer conducted a thorough check and found that someone had deliberately put two pieces of foreign metal in the IP dome, part of the ship's propulsion system. He immediately reported this incident.[7] A few days later, the officers onboard the destroyer HMCS *St-Laurent* were dealing with a similar situation as an examination of the ship's engine revealed that someone had placed metal filings into the lubricants for the pressure system and adjusting block.[8] Quick action and early detection by engine room personnel in *Wetaskiwin* and *St-Laurent* prevented serious damage, and the sailing schedules for both ships remained uninterrupted. But this also meant that naval intelligence had to wait until there was a break in operations before they could conduct a full investigation.

It was not until early October that Naval Intelligence officers in St. John's began to examine the *Wetaskiwin* incident, and their first suspicion was that there was a traitor or enemy agent onboard. As a result, they contacted the Halifax detachment of the Royal Canadian Mounted Police (RCMP) and asked for background checks on the engine room ratings who handled the IP Dome. The RCMP was thorough. Not only did they look for subversive tendencies among these sailors, but also any criminal activities that might make them vulnerable to blackmail. Nothing out of the ordinary was found. All were considered loyal citizens of Canada and although some had previous records for public drunkenness a RCMP Sergeant felt that this just meant they were simply practising to be sailors before actually enlisting.[9] But if it was considered unlikely that the saboteur was either a subversive or traitor, why had he tried to disable the ship? To answer this question the Navy would first need to apprehend the responsible party and they tried to do this through a board of inquiry.

Identifying the saboteur proved more difficult than the board members anticipated. For over two days they listened to testimony from 10 witnesses and reviewed all the evidence that had been secured by naval intelligence. The board found it interesting that *Wetaskiwin* had been an "unhappy ship" and that some crewmembers were more disgruntled than others.[10] The problem was that none of these ratings could be placed in the engine room at the time of the sabotage. In fact, it was impossible to eliminate any member of the ship's company as suspects, because the engine room had been left unattended during silent hours and rounds had not been conducted.[11] Without more evidence the board was unable to draw any firm conclusions other than the sabotage had definitely been perpetrated by a member of the crew with the intention of damaging the engine and making *Wetaskiwin* unseaworthy.

Although the *Wetaskiwin* incident had captured much attention, naval intelligence appeared to have forgotten about the *St-Laurent*. Having returned from escorting convoy ON 133, the *St-Laurent* had been waiting for naval intelligence to send investigators to look into their suspicious engine defects. But on the night of 8 October, their patience ran out as the detection of new foreign material in

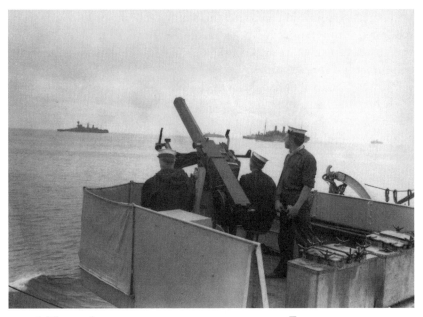

A NORTH ATLANTIC CONVOY MAKES ITS WAY TO ENGLAND IN 1941.
(Department of National Defence, Library and Archives Canada PA 105354)

the lubricating system indicated that the saboteur had struck again. Subsequently, an urgent message went out requesting that an investigation be conducted immediately.[12]

Despite the findings from *Wetaskiwin*'s board of inquiry Naval Intelligence jumped to the conclusion that there was a subversive onboard the *St-Laurent*. Given the size of the destroyer, Naval Intelligence determined that it neither had the personnel nor the expertise to root out the traitor or spy and so turned to the Halifax RCMP, Newfoundland constabulary, as well as the local censor for help. They, too, were "a little appalled at the size of the job" and as a result they then asked for "a little time to organize." These authorities were right to be cautious as the investigation on the *St-Laurent* was massive. First, the entire ship was turned upside down as RCMP officers looked for secret writing materials and unusual equipment of any kind. Next, background checks were conducted on all 40 members of the engine room department, and historical sketches were prepared for the rest of the crew; while the censor examined the ship's mail for hidden codes, secret writing, or some mention of the mechanical problems. Moreover, samples from the lubricating system were sent to two different government labs for analysis that revealed that the foreign matter consisted of welding scale, paint, metal filings, sand, and two pieces of glass.[13]

All this effort produced only one suspect who had sent a coded letter to a woman in Halifax. He was soon cleared, however, when it was ascertained that the only trust this man had betrayed was the wedding vows of another sailor's wife. Finding no evidence whatsoever of subversive activities, the RCMP began to wonder whether an act of sabotage had even been committed, noting as they did that "the personnel of the ship show marked loyalty, not only to their country and the Service, but to their officers." This conclusion was later supported by RCMP marine experts who filed a report suggesting that the substances found in the engine were more likely the product of normal wear and tear. In their final summation it was found that:

> It is not considered that there exists high probability of an act or acts of sabotage having been committed by anyone else. It is felt that physical causes within the ship's system itself, and/or inadvertence during refit at Dartmouth, N.S. and perhaps subsequently, almost certainly explains the occurrences in question and produce all the substances found. It is noted that upon sailing a.m. 8th November, the ship's lubricating system was thoroughly cleaned beyond question. Should a recurrence of these episodes be found upon her return, it is respectfully suggested that investigation may be reopened. Should no recurrence be found, however, it is requested that the writer and D/Sgt. [Detective Sergeant] Wruhleski may be instructed to proceed upon other duties.[14]

Although the naval investigators were beginning to second-guess their assumption that there was a traitor on the *St-Laurent*, they were not so sure that the matter should be dismissed so quickly. In fact, a separate board of inquiry came to the same conclusion, recording that they were of "the definite opinion that a person or persons of the ship's company are responsible."[15] So why did the Navy disagree with the RCMP? Quite simply, they had realized that too many mistakes had been made in the early stages of the investigation. This was also true for the inquiries into the incidents on *Eyebright*, *Cowichan*, and *Wetaskiwin*.

The central problem was that too much time had elapsed between the incidents and the point were the investigations commenced. Although sailing schedules did not always permit a quick reaction, it was determined that naval intelligence had, on average, taken three weeks to send investigators to the ship in question. As a result, testimony from witnesses became less reliable, and much evidence — such as fingerprints — was lost. Moreover, the fact that naval intelligence did not have any experience dealing with crew sabotage led to a number of critical errors. For example, 20 ratings had been transferred from the *St-Laurent* immediately after the second act of sabotage had been committed and were never questioned.[16] Likewise, during *Wetaskiwin*'s board of inquiry the CO, Commander Guy Windeyer, had provided the names of three men he suspected of tampering with the IP dome — remarking that one probably kept watch while the other two committed the act. The day after the abortive sabotage attempt all three of these men had jumped ship just before sailing. Eventually apprehended, they were charged with being absent without leave but their possible link to this case of sabotage was never followed up.[17] This indicated that more thorough investigative procedures were immediately required.

THE TWO EXTREMES: WHILE EXEMPLARY CONDUCT WAS OFTEN REWARDED (IN THIS CASE BY REAR-ADMIRAL MURRAY), SOME SAILORS WITHIN THE LARGER ROYAL CANADIAN NAVY DISABLED THEIR SHIPS AS A MEANS OF PROTEST.

(Department of National Defence, Library and Archives Canada PA 37456)

The original four cases investigated in St. John's had sent a troubling message, as did the belief that many other incidents had gone undetected or, worse yet, unreported. And that led to the uncomfortable conclusion that crew sabotage might be a common, and therefore more serious, problem than anyone had first anticipated. The immediate question, however, was what could be done to stop it. At first naval security and intelligence officers explored preventive measures such as requiring ships to maintain continuous watches in their engine rooms. But it was quickly determined that no ship had sufficient personnel to maintain this routine for sustained periods, and so the idea was subsequently dropped. After discussing several other proposals these security officers came to the reluctant conclusion that "it is not considered that any further steps can be usefully taken which will guard against [the] repetition of crew sabotage."[18] Since prevention was impossible, the other option was deterrence.

Although naval intelligence did not yet understand why these acts were being committed, they had ascertained that some sailors found it an effective means to keep the ship alongside. Any skilled stoker could potentially sabotage a ship in such a way that others would believe that it was a defect in the engine. In fact, even if the saboteur was not an engineer or simply had got careless, the unsuccessful investigations on *Eyebright*, *Cowichan*, *Wetaskiwin*, and *St-Laurent* had set a dangerous precedent. Put another way, these botched investigations showed that it was relatively easy to get away with disabling a ship. In order for deterrence to work the key was not in punishment — sabotage already carried a stiff penalty — but apprehension.[19] Simply put, they needed to catch a crew saboteur and then make an example out of him. As a result, step by step guidelines were established that dictated how future cases of crew sabotage would be investigated.

But the staff officer (intelligence) in St. John's did not think that this was enough, and he told Naval Service Headquarters (NSHQ) in Ottawa as much. According to this report, the best chance the Navy had of catching a crew saboteur was to hand such cases over to the Criminal Investigation Division (CID) of the Newfoundland constabulary. A better option was to bring "a RCMP detachment from Halifax to St. John's for these duties" as it was determined that this move would help avoid jurisdictional problems with a colony that was not yet a Canadian province. Other important recommendations followed, and are worth quoting in full because they identify the difficulties naval intelligence was having when investigating these cases. Whether handled by the Newfoundland CID or RCMP, the benefits of such arrangements were:

(1) The investigation would be carried out from the beginning by men having professional training for the job — Naval Officers do not have this training.

(2) The investigators would be empowered to carry on their inquiries to civilian contacts and in other than Naval establishments. At present, the Police would have to be called to take over any work involving civilians or inquiries ashore such as banks, hotels and in shadowing suspects.

(3) The investigators would be unbiased amongst members of the same ships company and accept no ones word nor be influenced by friendships, acquaintance or rank.

(4) A large force would be available at shore notice.[20]

Although this officer had raised a number of legitimate points, NSHQ was unwilling to hand jurisdiction of these cases over to the either the Newfoundland Constabulary or the RCMP, and so instructed naval intelligence to carry on the best they could. But as future investigations would soon prove, naval intelligence continued to experience difficulties in their attempt to catch crew saboteurs. So much so, that by late 1943, NSHQ finally issued a naval order that gave COs express instructions on how to initiate an investigation in cases of suspected crew sabotage.[21]

Beginning with the convening of a board of inquiry into the "circumstances attending the suspected sabotage in HMCS MELVILLE," naval intelligence investigated at least three other cases of crew sabotage throughout 1943.[22] Between these subsequent incidents and the ones in 1942, a clear pattern had emerged. The instruments of choice were usually metal filings or rags that were then placed in a part of the engine that would result in the ship staying alongside for two or three days. Another interesting aspect of the investigations in 1943 was that naval intelligence had stopped looking for possible traitors among the crew. Unfortunately, without the proper resources naval intelligence was never able to produce a saboteur and this left two important questions unanswered. If these men were not subversives what should they be considered, and why were they trying to sabotage their own ships? Preliminary research suggests that these men can best be defined as disgruntled sailors, and that there are three primary reasons why they took their frustrations out on the ship.

The first possibility is that some of the saboteurs might have been suffering from combat fatigue. Before all the incidents, the ships in question had spent a considerable amount of time at sea, and in some cases even action with the enemy. Moreover, the sabotage was almost always committed during a layover; either just after the ship returned alongside or before sailing for another operation. Take for example, *Wetaskiwin*, which, having participated in the sinking of *U-588* on 31 July, made another two transatlantic crossings (HX 202 and ON 121) and was set for a third (SC 98) before the saboteur struck. Tasked as the duty ship during its brief four-day lay-over, *Wetaskiwin* was in the process of raising steam to go to the aid of a stricken merchantman when the sabotage was discovered.[23] Equally compelling is the fact that the other cases of suspected sabotage in 1942, occurred at peak periods when the RCN was most active on the North Atlantic Run.[24] As a result, the fact that the sabotage was conducted on the engines and was intended only to delay the ship from sailing, suggests that these attempts were the product of overstressed sailors who simply wanted a short break from operations.

Another possible reason is that the sabotage was committed by sailors who were having personal problems at home — such as marriage troubles or an illness in the family — and had been denied a leave of absence or transfer. It was uncovered in two of the 1943 investigations that there were specific crewmembers who were dealing with some type of crisis in their personal life. Both had been denied a leave of absence, and that raised the possibility they had sabotaged the ship in the hopes that it would be interpreted as an engine defect; thereby allowing them to go ashore and tend to their personal matters.[25] As incredible as this might sound, naval intelligence certainly believed it was possible. When compared to the suspected saboteur's alternatives, going "absent without leave" (AWOL) or deserting, temporarily disabling the ship without anyone realizing it was intentional became an attractive option because the chances of getting caught were so low. In contrast, the shore patrol knew the identity of a sailor who had jumped ship from the moment it was discovered that he was missing. And once caught that sailor could expect a punishment that would range from six to eighteen months in jail, along with a deduction in pay, and — in the case of desertion — a dishonourable discharge.[26] But it is doubtful that personal troubles at home can account for most, if any, of the sabotage cases. If this were the primary motivation it would mean that all the saboteurs would have to have families in either the St. John's or Halifax areas, and this seems highly improbable.

Instead, the most likely motive behind most of these incidents was that the saboteurs had a grievance with the CO. This was a possibility in the *Eyebright* incident, as one of the ship's officers had told the investigator that the man most suspected on the ship had "a problem with the CO ... [and] I think he chucked the piece over the side out of spite or not wanting to sail with him anymore."[27] Incidentally, the CO had this suspect transferred the day after the investigator left the ship.

Likewise, it is interesting that the incidents on *St-Laurent* occurred when the ship was in the midst of a command change. While searching for a replacement for the previous CO, Lieutenant-Commander E.L. Armstrong, NSHQ, gave Commander Hugh Pullen temporary command of the ship so that *St-Laurent* could go to sea with a convoy. But the transition from the leadership style of Armstrong (who was popular with the crew) to Pullen's approach was not entirely smooth. As one senior non-commissioned officer observed, "coming from a Captain like Armstrong and running into pusser individual like Pullen, was a drastic change ... he was threatening to run anyone in that didn't have his life-belt on, ... and followed the routine to the book, and all the rest of it ... He had the knack of making everyone hostile."[28] As a result, it is extremely odd that by the time the investigation was finished there had been "apparent sabotage on 3 occasions," all of which had transpired during Pullen's brief period in command.[29] While it is still uncertain whether an act of sabotage was committed, such a coincidence does seem to suggest that a sailor (or sailors) was sending a message that he did not like the ship's new routine.

Ironically, Pullen's relief was Windeyer who had just finished testifying about the incident onboard *Wetaskiwin*. During that testimony, Windeyer had told the board that there was a disgruntled element among the crew, consisting of three engineers and one boatswain mate, who did not like the way he was running the ship.

Windeyer was convinced that these men had tried to sabotage the ship on three separate occasions before the one being investigated, and was frustrated that he was never able to prove his suspicions. As a result, in May 1942 he transferred the ringleader of the disgruntled element off the ship in the hopes that this would prevent any further sabotage attempts.[30] But Windeyer was frank with the board as he stated that he was also tired of this senior engine room rating's constant bickering, and then suggested that the sabotage in August might have been an act of revenge by the remaining members of this group.[31]

Whether these men had legitimate grievances against Windeyer is difficult to determine. A clue, however, can be found in a March 1943 report written by the flotilla engineering officer in Halifax. After inspecting *Wetaskiwin*'s engine room, this officer was greatly disturbed by serious problems resulted from "a lack of supervision and internal organization. The lack of interest shown by the CO regarding the Engine Room Department during inspection was apparent, and also reflected the adverse conditions."[32] While this attitude may have led some in the engine room to dislike Windeyer, it does not appear that everyone onboard shared their resentment. Indeed, accounts on Windeyer's personality vary, as one man who served under him found that "he was very good. A very hard working fellow, very knowledgeable, not quite so pusser ... Every one liked him."[33] While another observed that "he was an interesting man but you had to know your place with Windy. One moment he'd have his arm around you, saying 'Great work.' The next he'd be saying 'Stand at attention when you speak to the captain.'"[34] Other accounts reveal a similar tale, and suggest that Windeyer was a capable, but eccentric officer whose particular command style may have confused and upset some crewmembers. As a result, successful sabotage attempts affected the ship's relative efficiency and therefore would reflect on the individual CO as well.

A similar situation was evident on HMCS *Sarnia* in late 1943, when this ship was hit by two sabotage attempts while in Halifax and a third in St. John's. Suspicion fell on a group of three engineers. According to other crewmembers, these stokers had developed a close bond that was based on their common misery onboard ship. Although naval intelligence also learned that one of these men had been openly hostile to the CO, the investigators were unable to collect enough evidence that would warrant an arrest.[35] The ship's CO was clearly disappointed by the investigation's results, and one month after these incidents he requested that a senior engine room rating be transferred off the ship, stating that "it is thought the standard of discipline would be improved by [his] removal."[36] It would seem that this CO, like others before him, tried to get rid of the ringleader by having him transferred.

Of course, this did not necessarily mean that all these individuals were saboteurs. But this pattern of transferring suspects or ringleaders is strange and suggests that there might have been many unreported cases of crew sabotage within the Navy. With COs apparently taking matters into their own hands, however, there was simply no way to tell. Indeed, the Navy was well aware that a captain was unlikely to admit that a case of crew sponsored sabotage had occurred onboard ship because it "cast on his capability to handle his own affairs." And they had good reason for concern, as at least one staff officer was convinced that the best way to deal with such situations was to draft the "ships company, not least engine room crew, in small groups to other ships or shore estab[lishments]." Such drastic moves, therefore, would serve as a signal to the fleet that there was something wrong on that particular ship and that could translate into an admission that the CO had failed.[37]

But while this sheds light on the reason these acts occurred, the task of placing crew sabotage into a larger context remains. And to do that it is first necessary to explore the Canadian experience with mutiny, which represented a more dramatic expression of sailor protest. Indeed, naval historians have identified a number of commonalties between the string of "incidents" (an RCN euphemism for mutiny) that rocked the Navy throughout the 1940s. Often perpetrated by a sizeable portion of the crew, these mutinies were characterized by sailors locking themselves in their mess-decks until their grievances were addressed. An unpopular change in the ship's routine or a problem with a specific officer — generally the CO or executive officer — was usually at the root of the dissatisfaction.[38] As best demonstrated by the July 1943 case of HMCS *Iroquois*, when a crew of 190 refused to fall in, mutiny was a highly visible and collective act that, as one historian has observed, was akin to "what the Congress of Industrial Organization would have called a 'sit-down strike.'"[39] Moreover, there was little doubt about what the mutineers wanted, particularly since it was not an uncommon practice for some of them to nail a list of their complaints on the door of their messes.

Such an understanding of the Canadian experience with mutiny is important because it makes it possible to draw certain conclusions on crew sponsored sabotage. For example, mutiny was not the only form of sailor protest that shared characteristics with various types civilian labour unrest. In fact, the definition of *sabotage* makes clear that the activities on Canadian warships were more akin to the civilian act of doing "damage to work, tools, machinery, etc. by workmen, against an employer so as to stop production" rather than the word's military meaning.[40] But unlike mutiny, which involved large numbers of discontented sailors, sabotage was an individual act that allowed a sailor or, at most, a small group of sailors to vent frustrations that other crewmembers may not have shared. Given that they obviously did not want to get caught, those who expressed their anger in such a fashion were never in a position to reveal their particular grouse. Put another way, tampering with a piece of equipment would become meaningless if the saboteur risked early detection by nailing up a list of grievances beside his handiwork. Rightly or wrongly, it was also an activity in which suspicion often fell upon a specific trade as it was assumed that sabotaging a ship would require knowledge that only an engineer would possess. Nevertheless, there is little doubt that those who found it an effective form of individual protest did so because it served as a means to relieve stress. Although the Navy did have strong suspicions in a number of cases, no one was ever prosecuted for sabotaging their own ship.

Naval Intelligence continued to investigate suspected cases of crew sabotage through 1944 — including one instance where a depth charge was dropped off the stern of HMCS *Annapolis* when it was alongside[41] — but the fact that a saboteur was never caught was not naval intelligence's fault. Requests to NSHQ for the RCMP to assume jurisdiction indicate that the Mounties had neither the expertise nor the personnel to thoroughly look into the incidents. But their investigations clearly show that these crew saboteurs were not traitors. Instead, it would appear that crew sabotage was indeed a form of protest, the more so since all the documented cases clearly show that the goal was to temporarily disable the ship, not cause permanent damage. While the evidence still suggests that these individuals had a grievance with the CO, it should also be considered likely that combat fatigue played a role; particularly since the pressure of sustained operations undoubtedly added to the saboteur's sense of frustration.

NOTES

1. Reprinted from the *Canadian Military Journal* 6, No. 1 (Spring 2005), 51–58.

2. Directorate of History and Heritage (henceforth DHH), 3266, Canadian Naval Orders, 18 December 1943. For information on enemy subversives and the threat of sabotage on Canadian soil see, Library and Archives Canada (henceforth LAC), Record Group (henceforth RG) 25, Vol. 1967, 1939–867-A, Protection Against Sabotage in Canada, 1939–1943; LAC, RG 24, Vol. 3898, 1035–2–1, Espionage and Sabotage — German, 1939–1943; and LAC, RG 24, Vol. 3899, 1035–3–1, Espionage and Sabotage — Japanese, 1940.

3. LAC, RG 24, Vol. 11942, 1945–300 Vol. 1, Staff Officer Intelligence St. John's to the Captain of the Port, "Suspicious Incidents During Repairs to Ships," 16 April 1942; and DHH, 81/520, 8000, HMCS *Eyebright*, Ship's Movement Cards.

4. DHH, 81/520, 8000, Brief History of HMCS *Cowichan*, n.d.; DHH, HMCS *Cowichan*, Ship's Movement Cards.

5. LAC, RG 24, Vol. 11942, 1945–300, Vol. 1, Staff Officer Intelligence St. John's to Director Naval Intelligence Ottawa, "Sabotage (HMCS *Cowichan* and *Eyebright*)," 17 April 1942.

6. LAC, RG 24, Vol. 11942, 1950–146/25, Vol. 1, Security, Spring 1942.

7. LAC, RG 24, Vol. 11942, 1945–300, Vol. 1, Security Intelligence Officer to the Staff Officer Intelligence, 31 August 1942; and LAC, RG 24, Vol. 11930, NSC 331/114, Vol. 1, Commander (E) W. Morrison, 3 October 1942.

8. Naval Service Headquarters (NSHQ) to Flag Officer Newfoundland Force (FONF), Re: Board Inquiry 09 September 1942 Bearing Deposits HMCS *St-Laurent*, 10 October 1942; and LAC, RG 24, Vol. 11942, 1945–300 Vol. 1, Government Laboratory Analytical Results, September 1942.

9. LAC, RG 24, Vol. 11714, HMCS *Wetaskiwin*, September 1942; LAC, RG 24, Vol. 11942, 1945–300, Vol. 1, Staff Officer Intelligence Halifax to Staff Officer Intelligence St. John's, 30 September 1942; and various RCMP Reports on same file, September 1942.

10. LAC, RG 24, Vol. 11790, HMCS *Wetaskiwin*, Various Documents, March 1941 — March 1942.

11. LAC, RG 24, Vol. 11930, NSC 331/114, Vol. 1, "Board of Inquiry into the Circumstances Attending Engine Room Defects of HMCS *Wetaskiwin*," 2 October 1942.

12. DHH, Ship's Movement Cards, HMCS *St-Laurent*; LAC, RG 24, Vol. 5684, Report of Proceedings for September as well as October 1942.

13. LAC, RG 24, Vol. 11942, 1945–300, Vol. 1, NSHQ to FONF, 2230/29 October 1942 and Staff Officer (Intelligence) to FONF, 16 October 1942.

14. *Ibid.*, J.C.K. McNaught and D/Sgt Wruhleski to FONF, 11 November 1942.

15. *Ibid.*, FONF to NSHQ, 2043/ 27 October 1942.

16. LAC, RG 24, Vol. 5834, NS8000–353/25, Crew lists, September and October 1942; LAC, RG 24, Vol. 11942, 1945–300 Vol. 1, Changes in Complement, October 1942.

17. LAC, RG 24, Vol. 11930, NSC 331/114, Vol. 1, "Board of Inquiry into the Circumstances Attending Engine Room Defects of HMCS *Wetaskiwin*," 2 October 1942.

18. LAC, RG 24, Vol. 11930, 1150–331/114, Vol. 1, Commander (E) Morrison, October 1942.

19. DHH, 81/520/1540–12, Defence of Canada Regulations, 1942.

20. LAC, RG 24, Vol. 11942, 1950–146/25, Vol. 1, Staff Officer (Intelligence) to Flag Officer Newfoundland Force, Procedure for Handling Suspected Sabotage 16 October 1942.

21. DHH, Canadian Naval Orders, 3266, 18 December 1943.

22. Re: DHH, 81/520, 8000, COAC 55-2-1/189.

23. HMCS *Wetaskiwin* Movements from August 1941 to March 1943; and DHH, 81/520, 8000, "A Brief History of HMCS *Wetaskiwin*," n.d. (circa 1965).

24. For the best account of RCN operations in 1942, see W.A.B. Douglas, Roger Sarty, and Michael Whitby, *No Higher Purpose: The Official Operational History of the Royal Canadian Navy, Volume 2, Part 1: 1939–1943* (Ottawa and St. Catharines: Vanwell and Department of National Defence, 2003). Chapters 9 and 10.

25. The ships in question were HMCS *Sarnia* and HMCS *Prince Rupert*.

26. DHH, 82/401, Vol. 4, Men of the Canadian Naval Service Tried by Court-Martial, various dates; and DHH, Vol. 1, King's Regulations and Admiralty Instructions, Chapter 12, Section 6, 252–57.

27. LAC, RG 24, Vol. 11942, 1945–300, Vol. 1, "Suspicious Incidents During Repairs to Ships," 16 April 1942.

28. DHH, Biography M, Report of Interview with Petty Officer William Moodie McLean, by Hal Lawrence, 1 October 1983.

29. LAC, RG 24, Vol. 11942, 1945–300, Vol. 1, FONF to NSHQ, 1415/23 October 1942.

30. LAC, RG 24, Vol. 11569, 27-C-20, "Difficulties — Saturday 16 May," Windeyer to Captain (D) Halifax, 16 May 1942.

31. LAC, RG 24, Vol. 11930, NSC 331/114, Vol. 1, "Board of Inquiry into the Circumstances Attending Engine Room Defects of HMCS *Wetaskiwin*," 2 October 1942.

32. LAC, RG 24, Vol. 11569, 27-C-20, Flotilla Engineer Officer Report on HMCS *Wetaskiwin* to Captain (D) Halifax, 20 March 1943.

33. DHH, Biography M, Report of Interview with Petty Officer William Moodie McLean by Hal Lawrence, 1 October 1983.

34. DHH, Biography M, Report of Interview with Rear-Admiral Daniel Lionel Hanington by Hal Lawrence, n.d. (circa 1942).

35. DHH, 81/520, 8000, HMCS *Sarnia*, various documents, December 1943 to April 1944; LAC, RG 24, Vol. 11942, 1945–300, Vol. 1, "Possible Sabotage HMCS *Sarnia*," Staff Officer (Intelligence) to FONF, 23 November 1943; and *Ibid.*, "Possible Sabotage HMCS *Sarnia*," Staff Officer (Intelligence) to Director of Naval Intelligence, 31 December 1943.

36. LAC, RG 24, Vol. 11942, 1945–300, Vol. 1, Captain D Newfoundland to Captain D Halifax, 2010/5 April 1944.

37. *Ibid.*, Staff Officer notes, October 1942, and LAC, RG 24, Vol. 11942, 1950–146/25, Vol. 1, Staff officer (Intelligence) to FONF, 16 October 1942.

38. Michael Whitby, "Matelots, Martinets, and Mutineers: The Mutiny in HMCS *Iroquois*, 19 July 1943," *The Journal of Military History* 65, No. 1 (January 2001), 77–103.

39. Bill Rawling, "Only 'A Foolish Escapade by Young Ratings?' Case Studies of Mutiny in the Wartime Royal Canadian Navy," *Northern Mariner* 10, No. 2 (April 2000), 59. For more on the post-war mutinies, see Richard Gimblett, "Too Many Chiefs and Not Enough Seaman": The Lower-Deck Complement of a Postwar Canadian Navy Destroyer, *Northern Mariner* 9, No. 3 (July 1999), 1–22; and Richard Gimblett, "What *The Mainguy Report* Never Told Us," *Canadian Military Journal* 1, No. 2 (Summer 2000), 87–94.

40. *World Book Dictionary* (Toronto: Doubleday Canada, 1972), 1812.

41. For more information on *Annapolis*, see DHH, 81/520, 8000, "Brief History of HMCS *Annapolis*," 6 November 1959; and, LAC, RG 24, Vol. 11942, 1945–300 Vol. 1, Security (Intelligence) officer to Staff officer (Intelligence), "Suspected Attempt to Sabotage HMCS *Annapolis*," 10 March 1944.

9

THE V-E DAY RIOTS IN HALIFAX, 7–8 MAY 1945[1]

Robert H. Caldwell

> *People often do things for complicated combinations of reasons…. Causes always have contexts, and to know the former we must understand the latter…. For while context does not directly cause what happens, it can certainly determine consequences.*
>
> — John Lewis Gaddis,
> *The Landscape of History: How Historians Map the Past*[2]

TEN DAYS AFTER THE HALIFAX Victory in Europe (V-E) Day Riots the commanding officer (CO) of HMCS *Cornwallis*, a naval base in rural Nova Scotia, reported that:

> it is considered that the … [*Cornwallis* V-E Day] … story might have been … [different] … had it not been for the fact that the Wet Canteens and other facilities were thrown wide open. The result of the programme was a splendid example of mutual confidence and due respect for law and order.[3]

Cornwallis was typical of the many successful V-E Day celebrations held throughout the Canadian Naval Service, whose 1945 strength was over 90,000 all ranks. In Halifax the story was much different. There were about 18,000 men and women, 23 percent of the Navy, in that city on V-E Day. For about 24 hours, over a two-day period, thousands of those personnel ran amok on the streets of Halifax and, briefly, Dartmouth. Why was this? Why had more than three-quarters of naval personnel behaved well, and the 23 percent in Halifax so badly?

Before the summer of 1945 the official explanation for indiscipline ashore was the high number of small ships in the Royal Canadian Navy (RCN). The findings of the naval board of inquiry on the Halifax V-E Day Riots reiterated this view in May 1945:

> The service of the majority of the seagoing personnel
> has been in small ships, where discipline is necessarily
> less rigidly enforced, due to war conditions, than in a
> peacetime naval organization. While unit discipline in
> the ships may be considered satisfactory, inadequate
> stress has probably been placed on the behaviour
> of libertymen ashore; this would be applicable to
> barracks personnel, a large number of whom have
> served at sea.[4]

Thus, the argument went, small ships provided little opportunity for training and professional development, as compared to big ships, and partially trained sailors drafted to small ships were never instilled with the high sense of discipline that should have been part of their cultural baggage when they went ashore. Officials, however, only resorted to this explanation when there were problems, and they could not explain why tens of thousands of small ship Royal Canadian Navy Volunteer Reserve (RCNVR, or sometimes VR) sailors did demonstrate high discipline ashore, overseas and in Canada, throughout the war. Moreover, apparently satisfied with this single-cause explanation, the official inquiries failed to consider other potentially critical issues,[5] especially those arising from the profound stresses that wartime expansion had placed on the pre-war Navy; on wartime morale, discipline, and leadership; and on the city of Halifax.[6]

The purpose of this chapter is to examine these issues in an attempt to explain more completely the Halifax V-E Day Riots. Part One of this work will examine the immediate causes and events of the Riots, while Part Two will suggest the earlier origins and will examine the unique situation in Halifax. Finally, Part Three will provide some conclusions that suggest a contextual framework to explain the Halifax Riots.

Part One

The Halifax V-E Day Riots demonstrated a breakdown in military good order and discipline, as well as a breakdown in civil-military planning. The events of 7–8 May confirmed that civilian and military activities for V-E Day were conducted independently, and that civilian plans were out of step with the military realities. To make matters worse, with a few exceptions, the military's plans did not meet their own requirements.

Victory in Europe had long been anticipated, but the actual event came without warning. V-E Day was announced by radio broadcast in Halifax about 1030 hours on Monday, 7 May 1945. Civilians were given the rest of the day and the following day off. All stores, cinemas, cafés, and restaurants closed before noon and remained closed until two days later. Thousands of sailors living off-base on "lodgings and compensation," who normally ate in Halifax eating establishments, found themselves without any meal arrangements.

During Victory in Europe (V-E) Day riots in Halifax, Nova Scotia, 7–8 May 1945, a mixed group of Army and Navy personnel relaxes in Grafton Park.

(Department of National Defence, Library and Archives Canada C 79575)

Liquor stores, which had closed as usual on Friday, 4 May, would normally have opened at 1230 hours on Monday, 7 May. No Halifax liquor store, though, opened on either 7 or 8 May 1945, in accordance with the Nova Scotia Liquor Commission's announced V-E Day policy. The commission had informed Rear-Admiral L.W. Murray, commander-in-chief Canadian Northwest Atlantic (C-in-C CNA), of this policy in April.[7]

The three armed services continued to work through the afternoon of 7 May, but canteens were closed. The Navy made no special arrangements for the thousands of officers, sailors, and Women's Royal Canadian Naval Service (WRCNS) belonging to HMCS *Stadacona* and several of the nine other Halifax units, as well as those from ships, whose combined strength totalled about 18,000 men and women. Their "celebrations," based on a parade, were laid on for the next day.[8] During the evening of 7 May, canteens opened briefly, church services were held in the city, and civic officials organized outdoor events, including street dances and fireworks from George's Island. The Navy and Army garrison in Halifax provided equipment and technical support for these events. Otherwise, the city remained closed up.[9]

Thousands of RCNVR reservists, for whom nothing had been arranged and no direction provided, began their own spontaneous, exuberant, and drunken celebration in their canteens on the evening of 7 May. The sailors affirmed their self-image as proud, tough men of the sea who were not to be ignored or trifled with by civil-naval authorities, and who, it will be seen, once again had let them down by not planning on a principle of "mutual confidence."[10] Canteens closed, and as the night progressed, drunken sailors turned their attention to finding more liquor. They became more violent and destructive. Some created diversions to distract the military and civilian police forces away from the real targets — the liquor stores — that crowds then broke into and looted.

The sailors — and later the crowds of soldiers, Air Force personnel, merchant mariners, and civilians who joined them — were allowed to carry on with this behaviour because of the deliberate and well-publicized Police and Shore Patrol policy that permitted crowds to form and did not allow authorities to arrest drunks. Rear-Admiral Murray afterwards told the Kellock Commission that he had developed this policy to protect the Shore Patrol from local civilians who might take offence at any rough treatment of drunk sailors. Murray argued that "the citizens of Halifax ... would say ... here is a man who helped win the war and you are going to arrest him for being a little tight on V-E Day." Judge Kellock no doubt gave voice to the unspoken thoughts of many observers when he referred to the policy as "a rather strange document."[11]

The following afternoon, 8 May 1945, as the official civil-military V-E Day Service of Thanksgiving took place on the Garrison Parade, less than a kilometre away in the lower inner city, the celebratory behaviour started again. The violence escalated, from harmless flag-stealing to window-breaking, for flags, then to looting the window displays, and then to looting the store interiors. Photographs taken at the time showed naval personnel participating in a variety of activities.[12] Some of these young Canadians — chief petty officers (CPOs), ratings, WRCNS, and members of the other armed services — were photographed smiling, sitting on public lawns drinking from looted bottles, and generally enjoying themselves as if at a social or country fair. Other pictures showed the looting. The young ratings, as well as CPOs and petty officers in these images, were clean, fit, proud, and well turned out and often had an exaggerated swagger

DURING VICTORY IN EUROPE (V-E) DAY RIOTS IN HALIFAX, NOVA SCOTIA, 7–8 MAY 1945, RIOTOUS CELEBRATIONS TAKE PLACE ON BARRINGTON STREET.

(Department of National Defence, Library and Archives Canada C 79564)

about them. Discipline, though not obvious, was not entirely absent in these crowds. Time after time during the afternoon officers and sailors spontaneously and bravely reinforced authorities and put themselves "into the breach," holding back mobs at entrances to liquor commissions and department stores.[13]

Despite these efforts at restraint, late in the afternoon the violence escalated. The crowds broke into more liquor stores, continued to loot, and became increasingly unruly. Senior civic officials and military officers in Halifax grew worried. They requested Army reinforcements.[14] At 1800 hours the mayor declared V-E Day to be over and Rear-Admiral Murray, the senior military officer serving in Halifax, accompanied by the mayor, announced that fact from a Royal Canadian Air Force (RCAF) sound truck. As the Halifax streets cleared, rioting began in Dartmouth across the harbour. By 2300 all streets were cleared, and a military curfew was in force.

In the immediate aftermath of the riots, authorities assessed the damage and counted the casualties. Two people had died in the disturbances, a naval officer and a rating, and the physical destruction of the city core had been significant.[15] Less obvious but equally important was the damage done to the Navy's good reputation that had been won in the four gruelling winters of war. And the man in charge of the Navy in Halifax, as well as the East Coast and the North-West Atlantic, lost more than his reputation; he lost his career.

As C-in-C CNA, Rear-Admiral Murray was the only Canadian officer in the three armed services to command an allied operational area. He had the respect and support of the Royal Navy (RN), the United States Navy (USN), the RCAF, and the allied maritime air forces from 1942 onwards. The British had honoured him as a Companion of the Bath (CB) and a Commander of the British Empire (CBE). He was known by thousands of men and women throughout the East Coast anti-submarine warfare fleet. They respected his efforts at managing their operations.

By 1945, however, Murray seemed increasingly out of touch with the fleet and its needs. In speaking to the crews of the recently returned ships *Chaudière* and *Algonquin*, he ignored their exploits and hard-won successes and instead lectured them about conduct, warning them that "he wouldn't have any rowdiness ashore."[16] After the riots, he seemed to drift even further from reality, claiming that while

> [the Riots were] ... regrettable ... [yet they have]
> ... served a very useful purpose. It has put the Navy
> personnel on their mettle and right up on their toes.
> It has been forcibly drawn ... to the officers that the
> ratings are showing much more pride in themselves
> and their appearance ... and much more respect ...
> than before.[17]

Naval Staff Headquarters (NSHQ) did not agree. Murray was blocked from reinstatement or further service in the Canadian armed services or the allied command structure. Until his death the admiral remained obsessed with his treatment following the riots. He left Canada, retired in England, and studied law to pursue his case. Many officers and men who had served with him also never forgot how he had been singled out for punishment.[18] For the sailors — regular and reservist, from upper and lower decks alike — the riots ended the Battle of the Atlantic on a powerful and disturbing note.

Part Two

The purpose of this section is to examine the pre-war background to two assumptions that are central to any understanding of the immediate causes of the V-E Day Riots. The first premise is that the riots represented a failure of the naval command to cope with the personnel and base requirements caused by the wartime expansion. The second assumption is that the riots were a legacy of three years of naval indiscipline in Halifax.

Pre-War RCN Preparation

For all their success in leading the tiny interwar flotillas on either Canadian coast, Admirals Nelles, Jones, and Murray, and their pre-war RCN staff officers, did not respond effectively to the wartime expansion of the Navy. This was partly the result of post–First World War neglect of their service by the government. Perhaps more important, though, was the nature of their training, which was conducted by the RN. Their "big ship time" concentrated on duties and responsibilities at sea, and it was not enhanced with equivalent base administrative experience. The RN Naval Staff College at Greenwich trained RN and RCN officers for RN staff appointments at sea. RCN officers did not hold Admiralty or RN Dockyard appointments. Therefore, they did not have the professional foundation needed to design and develop a complex naval command and shore establishment that could provide leadership for about 15,000 demanding volunteer men and women in Halifax.[19] The narrow and insular experience of the pre-war RCN provided only a limited organizational and personnel model that proved inadequate to the task.[20]

Although RN "big ship" training did not provide adequate preparation to manage service expansion, it did provide an outstanding basis for understanding ships and men at sea. Rear-Admiral Ken Adams, RCN, remembered the importance of the RN fleet training in the interwar years. In 1929, as a lieutenant, he was posted to HMS *Calypso*, a cruiser in the Mediterranean fleet:

> We had a lot of talented officers. This is what makes a Happy Ship as much as anything else. Fair minded, strict and capable officers ... We exercised in every department until we were perfect in everything we did ... confident that we would be able to hold our end up in any situation ... we met the fleet ... It all made sense. The organization of the Fleet as a whole and that of each individual ship was excellent. Every one including the most junior seaman knew what he was doing and why he was doing it. Discipline was strict but always just and fair. Morale was high because of the respect held by juniors for their seniors. I hope I never forget the lessons I learned [with the RN].[21]

Training with the RN also developed character and highly self-possessed personalities. As a result of its emphasis on training for operations at sea, the RN instilled a unique set of values in their officers. According to one interwar description, the RN officer was:

> a man of action and never at a loss. He must make up his mind on every occasion instantaneously and without hesitation, and he must be prepared to take on *any* job at a moment's notice ... in these characteristics lie his strength and his weakness. They make him the finest ships officer in the world, but they render

him unsuitable for work that requires administrative, organizing ... or reflective capacity, and what is more they *prevent him from realizing that there is any kind of work that he cannot do.*[22]

These same values informed pre-war RCN officers who emerged from their training with great confidence in their ability to command, with a strong sense of their own importance and worth, and little or no self-doubt. They were not inclined towards conciliation or consensus-building among themselves or their men, let alone with mere civilians. Some carried grudges against fellow officers.

This temperament and outlook did not mix well with the requirements of the wartime RCNVR that was, in effect, a people's Navy. The thousands of men who made up this force had come of age in the years following the First World War when economic and social upheaval had undermined or altered established hierarchies, institutions and values. The VRs view of the world and their place in it reflected these profound changes. It was characterized by:

> [a] touch of independence, a measure of iconoclasm, a clear contestation of any inherent right to be at the top ... [combined to make] ... a new social heresy. That heresy held that the poor, the lower classes, and even the "lesser breeds" had rights to life, employment, adequate income, good health, a reasonable standard of living, and, where competence existed, to a place and status in the many varied hierarchies of the land.[23]

Yet many RCN officers refused to accept, or even sometimes to acknowledge, that the world had changed. According to Commander Louis Audette RCNVR:

> the [wartime] Navy was in the hands of a scantily educated and largely unimaginative group of Senior Officers who, nevertheless, clearly deemed themselves a very elite group. They found it hard to admit to their councils those who wore lesser school ties. Many of them sought valiantly to perpetuate a state of affairs which had long ceased to exist. Their greatest failing was their persistent attempt to

preserve — or rather to revive — much of what had disappeared with the nineteenth century and which they erroneously thought still to exist in Britain.[24]

Fortunately, not all RCN officers saw these new social views as "heresy"[25] Many of them were young enough not to have had any direct knowledge of the pre-First World War period that some of their superiors longed for. They, like the VRs, had lived with and come to accept social change as normal. For these officers, the unforeseen demands arising from the massive expansion of the RCNVR presented enormous potential. Though this service was separate from their own, the RCNVR provided about 90 percent of wartime naval personnel and, therefore, great opportunities to demonstrate their leadership abilities.[26]

Expansion and the RCNVR

Pre-war RCN officers, serving in the RN or the RCN, had no experience coping with the "new social heresy" that Louis Audette described. The small permanent force RCN, with a minuscule budget, could not have upgraded personnel facilities or improved arrangements ashore even if there had been a demand to do so. But, before the war, there was no demand, because pre-war RCN ratings expected, and received, so little. Commander P.G. Chance, a pre-war officer, remembered the RCN world in 1930's Halifax:

> The only brick buildings were the Admirals' Command offices and the men's wet canteen, known ... as "the little red schoolhouse" ... there was no *Stadacona* Barracks ... sailors were accommodated ... in the yard ... officers [provided] ... for themselves ashore ... [As the Officer of the Day] ... in the wet canteen ... I dared not look right or left as we passed ... the large, silent, group of hardened sailors.[27]

Among these men, claimed pre-war rating W.M. Mansfield, there were those that couldn't read or write, could never pass their ET-1 [Educational Test on joining].[28] Yet morale and discipline seemed unaffected by the generally harsh conditions and spartan recreational and educational arrangements.

After the summer of 1940, this world was turned upside down, when large numbers of RCNVR officers and men were hastily enrolled and appeared for sea duty on the Canadian coasts.[29] These VR officers and sailors enlisted for various personal, social, cultural, ideological, or economic reasons.[30] Once in, different factors impelled them to continue to serve at sea. Attitudes to service at sea and the RCN changed at least twice throughout the war. As these changes took place the VRs created an original identity for themselves, different from anything seen in the pre-war period.[31] Based on an infectious pride — in themselves as individuals and in their service — it was fuelled, rather than depleted by, the harsh wartime conditions of their ships. They expressed their sense of themselves through their tailored uniforms, their ships crests and songs, gun-shield graffiti, and by 1943, they had formed these spontaneous demonstrations of pride into a clear and powerful idea of what it meant to be a VR.[32] How had this happened?

In 1941, the VRs had little more than boundless enthusiasm and a strong loyalty to each other and to their rapidly expanding service. In the winter of 1941–1942 the young VRs responded well to sound leadership from young RCN officers and ratings aboard their new small ships. This harsh period not only enhanced their basic skills, but their survival through it also reinforced their great pride and their enthusiastic amateur ethics. As Lieutenant-Commander Eric J. Downton, RCNVR recalled of this period:

> we were all very young. We were fighting a very crucial battle, but we didn't take it too seriously.... There were the usual tensions and animosities and the living conditions in the [corvette] Mess decks were terrible. You couldn't get hot food, after two days at sea ... the living conditions were appalling ... It was incredible and yet we didn't think of it as hardship It was a challenge. Mainly I recall the very good morale and the sheer physical hardship, in terms of exposure, bad food, cold, wet, and imminent danger ... compared to the professionals in the RN and later the Americans ... we were very ill-trained but the spirit was good and we did the job for which we were needed ... [we were] ... high spirited amateurs, who professionally weren't very good in the RCNVR. I realize now that we weren't very good.[33]

Needless to say, these "high-spirited amateurs" made mistakes but most could be attributed to their inexperience and inadequate training, and their poorly equipped ships, rather than to low morale or poor discipline and leadership.[34] And naval officials were slowly making improvements to conditions afloat and ashore throughout the hard winter of 1941–1942. In modern psychological terms, the combat motivation level of the RCNVR was high, morale remained high, and RCN leadership responded with an equally high level of enthusiasm.

The year 1942 was marked by rapid operational deployment to counter the ubiquitous U-Boat threat. The over-worked escorts fought from the coast to the Gulf of St. Lawrence, to the mid-ocean, and back again. These shifts in operations occurred without warning. As *Paukenshlag*[35] peaked in early 1942, the Canadian escort fleet tasks set by the RN seemed boundless. RCN senior officers had little or no opportunity to make permanent, well thought-out changes. RCN junior officers continued to provide outstanding leadership,[36] and RCNVR officers continued to gain experience.[37]

By the spring of 1943 there was a noticeable change in VR morale. Their enthusiasm waned. The veteran VRs, whose training and discipline had improved during their early winters on the North Atlantic, became disillusioned with the spartan personnel support policies of the RCN, which did not meet VR expectations and were below the standard of the Canadian Army and the RCAF. Improvements afloat and ashore were underway, but not in proportion to the needs at sea, hence they were not visible, and the VRs felt neglected.[38] Disciplinary incidents increased. Hard living in wretched small ship conditions had altered the proud, enthusiastic amateur image VRs had of themselves. Now they also began to work at looking tough; excessive drinking became *de rigueur*, and their great pride was transformed into an aggressive, short-fused, and cocky manner.[39]

Discipline and the RCNVR

During the period 1941 to 1943, the hundreds of newly commissioned Canadian small ships were unable to provide adequate training to complete the development of the rapidly deployed VR officers and sailors. Yet, the volunteer RCNVR officers and men on those small ships developed a highly refined and effective sense of self-discipline and teamwork. A young Canadian diplomat, Charles Ritchie, observed this unusual ethos when he travelled by Canadian Landing Craft to visit troops in Normandy following the D-Day landings in 1944. Ritchie soon discovered that the VRs had developed their own views, which differed from those of the RCN:

> the R.C.N.V.R. hate the Royal Navy as being stuck-up, stuffy and superior. They also hate the [RCN] whom they consider quite rightly to be an imitation of the [RN]. The [RCN] for their part pride themselves on the accuracy of their naval tradition, admire, albeit slightly resent, the [RN], and look down upon the [RCNVR]. These and other naval mysteries have been revealed to me in the course of this visit.[40]

Ritchie was also impressed with the VR leadership style and efficiency:

> Life at such close quarters could be hell, but, in fact, it was carefree and cheerful. It was an efficiently run ship, but not run on any orthodox [RN] lines but in a peculiarly Canadian way — the lack of fuss and feathers, the humour and horse-sense ... This ... was due in part to the officers ... they knew how to run the ship and keep happy a crew of boys of nineteen ... [who] ... were a tough, good natured lot who would have been impossible to manage by spit and polish. They enjoyed every incident and welcomed everything but monotony. It was an atmosphere of youth.[41]

This sense of teamwork was much sought after by the basically trained VR officers in command. As Lieutenant James Lamb RCNVR described:

> The new discipline of the escort groups was based on a team concept, rather than on rank structure; as in a bomber aircraft, officers and men worked in close association in positions that were often interchangeable.[42]

Lamb also wrote that the new wartime discipline was different from:

> The old discipline of the Big Navy ... [the RCN] ... inherited from the Royal Navy was based on an officer class whose education, character, and social background were worlds removed from those of the seamen. On the lower deck, thought was not encouraged; a man did as little as he could get away with, and the whole disciplinary system was geared to produce an acceptable standard of performance from an indifferent crew. It was a system measured in outward show, with lots of stamping and shouting and saluting.[43]

Clearly, by 1943, RCN and RCNVR officers, and their RCN superiors, had to understand that their sailors' effectiveness, afloat and ashore, was suspended in a delicate balance between the culture of the small ships and an informally developed sense of discipline, tempered with excessive alcohol use and the cocky pretence of toughness. All of these conditions existed throughout the Navy. Failure to grasp this reality could lead to trouble, which was seen more in Halifax than any other wartime port.

Halifax and Naval Indiscipline

Halifax was the cradle of a massive naval expansion, as well as the future home of the post-war fleet. Because of this, it was crucial that the Canadian Naval Service establish credible relations in Halifax during the war. This task was more difficult than they first realized. The problem was simple: the Canadian Naval Service was the new kid on the block. In the interwar period, pride of place in the city was shared between the RN and the Canadian Army. The RN had been the naval presence in the port for close to three centuries, and there had been soldiers garrisoned in town since the eighteenth century. By comparison the Canadian Navy had never been of a significant size to matter:

> These traditions prevailed within the extremely difficult wartime conditions in Halifax. The per-

manent residents are too few in numbers, and not quite rich enough, to entertain the 60–70,000 increase in population in their homes. Our facilities for pleasure and entertainment were never lavish, because Haligonians have always been accustomed to entertain at home rather than in night clubs, dance halls, taverns and hotels ... [the city has endured] ... tens of thousands of transient[s] ... and their families. Capital of a small province and a county seat, Halifax is also a railway terminus, a convoy assembly base, a naval [and] ... air base, a military headquarters and a fortress city, a shipbuilding port and a university centre ... Halifax [was like] a town of 3000 with three or four thousand visitors — and a large percentage of them anxious to celebrate.[44]

During the war, Halifax was hopelessly overcrowded with service personnel and temporary civilian workers. Thousands of servicemen, mostly young VR sailors, lived off base using the unsatisfactory wartime expedient of "lodgings and compensation," often three or four to an attic room in an inner city older home.[45] This situation, combined with the complex nature of the city, was an enigma to the armed services at the time, and remains so for the historian today. On one hand there was an acknowledged, well-known, and long-established tradition of liquor smuggling and boot-legging. Conversely Halifax was home to probably the most active and militant temperance movement of any middle-sized Canadian urban area. In 1942 this lobby succeeded in closing down the *Ajax Club*, a privately run institute for ratings.[46] Yet, as if to confound the first two characteristics, hundreds of Haligonians provided help to servicemen, as best they could, in volunteer service organizations in the inner city near the harbour.

From 1942 onwards, incidents of disregard for authority by Canadian naval officers and men steadily increased in Halifax. The pressures of the war and the difficulties of living in Halifax contributed to alcohol-related offences that ranged from "high jinks" to more serious vandalism, destruction of property, and assault. Heavy drinking was a well-known Canadian characteristic.

In June 1942, Naval Minister Angus L. MacDonald asked Rear-Admiral G.C. Jones, commanding officer Atlantic Command (COAC), to investigate disciplinary problems in Halifax, including "excessive drinking by some Naval Officers in Halifax." Curiously, the chief of naval staff (CNS), the naval board and the naval staff — the normal chain of command — were excluded from this investigation. Jones replied to the minister:

> No one suggests that our organization here is by any means perfect, but the faults are almost entirely due to the rapid expansion and the lack of trained officers ... no one can deny that excessive drinking has been indulged in by some Naval Officers. Steps are continually being taken to eliminate these people by dismissal or transfer.[47]

Rear-Admiral Jones added a handwritten note to his minister, "P.S. 'Joe' Connolly is back with some interesting ideas." Commander J.P. Connolly, MC, RCNVR, was the NSHQ director of Special Services (DSS). He was a VR Haligonian lawyer, and CEF veteran, and he had been naval provost marshal in Halifax with Admiral Jones in 1940–1942. He was a close friend of the admiral.

In October 1942 CO *Stadacona*, Captain K.F. Adams, reported to Rear-Admiral Murray (who had just replaced Rear-Admiral Jones as COAC), that the main problems in Halifax were "Discipline ... Morale ... Accomodation ... [and the] RCN Depot."[48] These problems caused further incidents throughout 1943, and early in 1944 Rear-Admiral Murray wrote to his command that "there have been too many cases where officers, who would not think of letting down their ship, have let down the Navy by making a disturbance on shore when in uniform."[49] Several months later R.J. Rankin, managing editor of the *Halifax Herald*, was so concerned about the deteriorating state of naval indiscipline in Halifax that he by-passed Murray and wrote directly to a newly promoted Vice-Admiral Jones, by then the CNS.

Jones responded by once again sending Captain Connolly to Halifax to investigate. He reported on 3 July 44 that there was, "(1) A general deterioration in discipline more or less condoned by Senior Officers (2) Junior Officers appeared to be the worst offenders ... their conduct gives a scandalous example to ratings." Connolly claimed this was caused by: "small ships ... [which] bring ... a distinct relaxation ... when such ratings go ashore ... their failure to observe discipline spreads to shore ratings and those ... [on] training."[50] There was no record of Connolly's meetings with Rear-Admiral Murray while he studied the disciplinary problems on his base. Clearly Admiral Jones trusted Captain Connolly's views on the matter.[51]

Captain Connolly's main contribution was to recommend an overhaul of the Shore Patrol organization. Sadly, between July 1944 and V-E Day, neither Rear-Admiral Murray nor CO *Stadacona* made any effort to integrate Connolly's 1944 revised Shore Patrol arrangements into the Halifax command and staff relationship. As a result, control of the shore patrol fell into a hopeless muddle during the V-E Day Riots. No one seemed to know who the staff officer (shore patrol) was responsible or responsive to, Rear-Admiral Murray and the Area Combined Headquarters staff or to the CO *Stadacona*.[52] After V-E Day, Connolly, by then the successful CO of HMCS *Avalon*, the large base in St. John's, again visited Halifax and reorganized the Halifax Shore Patrol to prepare for V-J Day.

In summary, there had been naval disciplinary problems in Halifax, a city with immense problems of its own, since June 1942. At least twice, in 1942 and again in 1944, officials had advised the naval minister of the situation. In each case surreptitious methods were used to seek solutions, instead of the normal chain of command. These methods, unfortunately, produced only half-hearted efforts to solve problems and failed to provide the necessary continuity or follow-up action between incidents. This was particularly the case with the organization of the shore patrol, the regulatory arm of the naval command.

A Naval Command Failure in Halifax

Between 1942 and 1945 the naval command in Halifax and Ottawa failed to correct the high incidence of naval indiscipline in Halifax. Three factors contributed to this failure. The first was the choice of COs for *Stadacona*. Following Captain K.F. Adams, RCN, an effective CO in 1942 (and who was returned as CO after the riots), NSHQ selected three senior officers, all of whom were "by and large, as unsuitable ... for this appointment ... as could be found."[53] The CO at the time of the riots, the third since Adams, was Captain H.W. Balfour, RCNVR. His plan for V-E Day was defensive in nature, and dwelt on protecting the base property and facilities from his VR ratings.[54] This was an expression of an outdated leadership approach based on fear of the lower deck, and the antithesis of a style based on trust and mutual confidence, which the VR wartime officers and men had come to expect.

The second factor was the lack of effective organization. From

1942 onwards Rear-Admiral Murray and other senior officers in Halifax knew what they needed on their bases, but their efforts were frustrated by the lack of organizational talent available to them. Rear-Admiral Murray, for one, had repeatedly written about the need for discipline ashore, and he had personally advocated the "Divisional System" of man management in the command. Yet he and his staff failed to create an organization that could effectively and professionally administer thousands of sailors undergoing training, working in the dockyard, or awaiting a drafting signal to a ship.[55] They were not helped by a shore patrol organization that was only temporary and not fully trained until 1944.

Finally, the Ottawa–Halifax command relationship was not a healthy one. Vice-Admiral Jones and Rear-Admiral Murray maintained a pre-war grudge and did not communicate with one another, a situation of which the senior officers in the service were well aware.[56] Although operational matters were not impaired significantly by this rift — their staffs did much of this work for them — it had a detrimental effect on the Navy's ability to identify and solve sensitive abstract problems, like civil-naval relations in Halifax. Thus, in June 1944 when the disciplinary situation in Halifax reached crisis proportions, Vice-Admiral Jones sent Captain Connolly to study and make recommendations. Vice-Admiral Jones did not use the normal chain of command or apparently seek Murray's advice beforehand.

Part Three

Conclusions

> *I went ashore [V-E Day in Halifax] and I saw ... there was a hell of a lot of drunkenness ... which was inappropriate ... things were getting out of hand. So I nipped smartly down ... [to] see Jimmy Hibbard [captain (D)] ... He said to me, "I just can't do it, I daren't make a move because Admiral Murray's in town and he will blame me for anything I do wrong" ... there was a lack of direction ... It was nothing to do with training but lack of direction.*
>
> — John Wade, RCNVR[57]

It is tempting, as many people at the time did, to blame the Halifax V-E Day Riots on Rear-Admiral Murray's general approach to command and his actions in the months leading up to May 1945. It would be foolish to deny that his lack of organizational and administrative ability contributed substantially to the crisis. But blaming the riots on the actions or inaction of one powerful commander greatly oversimplifies the complexity of the situation in Halifax in May 1945.

The rapid expansion of the pre-war RCN meant that thousands of untrained RCNVR reservists were given to the Navy for the duration of the war. The VRs were the largest of the three components of the naval service, but they were separate from the RCN and RCNR, which had more training and experience. The VRs had no understanding of naval traditions, nor did they have time to be instructed in the relationship between service traditions, morale, and discipline. Perhaps as a result of these or other circumstances, the VRs created their own culture and identity.

There were good and bad characteristics of the VR culture. VRs had a high sense of pride and team spirit. They demonstrated a strong affinity for teamwork, and a desire for activities based on "mutual confidence." The VRs wanted to feel part of the naval team because they constituted 90 percent of it. The troubling traits included hard drinking, acting tough, drinking-related crime, a three-year habit of crime in Halifax, and a "Them–Us" relationship to those not at sea.

What made these troubling traits potentially dangerous was the fact that some senior RCN officers of an older generation were not equipped to deal with social change as represented by the VRs and their emerging outlook. This senior group was governed by a strong sea-going ethic that did not stress base organization and administration. It is probably not surprising, then, that most of them lacked the ability — and probably the inclination — to administer effectively. Many of them sensed problems, and complained about it, but could not suggest solutions other than a return to the pre-war values. At times there was a longing for the pre-war world. Younger RCN officers, mostly at sea, adapted to the "new social heresy" and at the same time maintained an acceptable standard of discipline on their ships.

These circumstances were common to the whole Navy. Most of the Navy kept on top of the situation, and generally the RCN leadership got the best from their VRs, which helped them to improve their reputation at sea. In Halifax, however, these circumstances collided with existing problems unique to that city. On the civilian side, the city had its own problems: overcrowding with strangers, parochialism, and no tradition of coping with a Canadian Navy of a significant size. At the same time the Navy had failed repeatedly to find effective CO's for Halifax, at least in part because there were not enough good RCN officers to go around. Rear-Admiral Murray, and a succession of mediocre staff officers and base commanding officers, demonstrated an inability to organize the base, and the shore patrol, effectively. Finally the tense Ottawa–Halifax command relationship made handling delicate problems difficult.

This coincidence of circumstances created an explosive situation in Halifax of which officials were well aware. After the disciplinary crisis in June 1944 Captain Connolly predicted "dire consequences" unless changes were made. Little or no action was taken. The V-E Day arrangements indicated that officers such as Rear-Admiral Murray, and his chief of staff, Captain G.R. Miles RCN, were out of touch with the men and women of the Navy in the spring of 1945. Their plans were poorly thought-out and loosely coordinated. No one had the imagination or foresight to make special arrangements based on — "mutual confidence," such as dances, wide-open canteens, unlimited beer and so on. COs simply ordered "Open Gangway" and let their men fend for themselves.

Captain Connolly was the Navy's expert on discipline in Halifax. He had examined the problems in 1942 and again in 1944. He concluded on both occasions that the high level of indiscipline in Halifax was because of the small ship nature of the Navy. He revised his conclusions after V-E Day. Notwithstanding the findings of the board of inquiry, in a *volte-face* Connolly claimed that small ship discipline was higher than discipline ashore:

> large numbers [of sailors] … are returning from sea service [who are] raising the standard of dress and discipline. The latest survey [3 July 1945] shows that Naval personnel who have had sea experience are more highly disciplined and have greater respect for their appearance than the shore going type.[58]

Had Connolly found the real villains — the thousands on "log and comp" — who were an undisciplined aberration of the original, sea-going VRs, with all their troubling traits but without their proud team spirit?

What became clear to everyone was that thousands of Canadian sailors from ashore and from ships projected their highly developed self-images onto *Stadacona* and Halifax on V-E Day. The sailors gave life to their own ideas about behaviour, and they moulded their conduct to fit these expectations. On 7 May, once it became apparent to the VRs that there was no attempt by their superiors to foster mutual confidence, and already knowing that their antics inside and outside *Stadacona* would be ignored and not suppressed, they escalated their drunken high jinks to include vandalism and theft. The VR ratings, including Women's Royal Canadian Naval Service personnel on 8 May, simply reacted in accordance with the image that they had of themselves, and at the same time delivered a final, tragic signal to authorities in Halifax.[59] The message was clear: their needs were those of a wartime people's Navy, which were more complex, and required more adaptation and thought — in other words, forthright leadership — than the needs of RCN ratings in the 1930's.

How should we view the events of the Halifax V-E Day Riots? If the riots were a direct result of the Canadian Navy's failure to administer their men and adapt to their needs, then can we claim that these lapses in command were in turn an inevitable, predictable consequence of the immense challenges arising from explosive? From any point of view, the Navy's tasks were almost impossible. Circumstances were against them; they were required to manage the administrative growth of a large and complex institution — a national Navy — while at the same time fighting that Navy at sea against a wily opponent. Operationally, they were compared with the RN and the U.S. Navy, two naval institutions with centuries of disciplined experience at war and ashore. In Canada, many Haligonians and journalists compared the Navy to the Canadian Army, which was the only fighting service that, in 1939, had an experienced general staff, specialists, and service support capabilities. Clearly these comparisons were unfair. The naval command of the day should be measured against a different standard: "Given their pre-war training and wartime circumstances, how successfully did they manage their part of the expansion?"

Certainly senior RCN officers were not well-prepared to administer the wartime mobilization of their service, to respond to the unique needs of a people's Navy, or to foster sound civil-naval relations. This lapse in preparedness was determined by the training and development of RCN officers before the war. In that sense mistakes made ashore were set up long before the period from 1942 to 1945. Therefore only to the extent that some senior officers failed to see, and adapt, to the new requirements, can they be blamed for their failures managing sailors.

Nevertheless most RCN officers did their best — their own way — and the overall result was successful. When encouraged by the RN, the highly confident and powerful personalities of the RCN officers — although not attuned to administration — provided the perseverance and drive to complete the wartime expansion. They provided hundreds of ships and thousands of voluntary reservists for naval warfare, first in the Atlantic and later in all the allied theatres. No one can question the operational effectiveness of more than 100 RCN fighting ships at sea by 1945. Perhaps Vice-Admiral Sir Peter Gretton RN, put it best, when he claimed:

> There used to be a rather pompous old naval saying, "The impossible can be achieved at once; the miracle takes longer." [Examining] ... the RCN's contribution to the Second World War, one cannot but conclude that the impossible was achieved but the miracles remained elusive ... The average standard of the staff officers at Ottawa was not high enough — there were simply not enough first-rate brains available, and the ships had to be manned ... It is certain that the RCN tried to do too much and thus the miracles were not achieved, but that must be blamed on the politicians as well as the sailors.[60]

In the final analysis, one can suggest that, although the wartime expansion hit the operational mark, the effective administration and organization of naval life ashore in Halifax stood as an example of one of the "elusive miracles" that was unattainable throughout the war. So too, in the category of "elusive miracles," was the reluctance or refusal from some senior officers of an older generation to adapt pre-war perceptions of naval service to the needs of a people's Navy. This refusal of senior naval leaders to adjust to changed conditions exacerbated the wartime frictions experienced by thousands of RCNVR sailors, and indirectly set the scene for the disturbances in Halifax during May 1945.

NOTES

1. Part of this work was published in a substantially similar manner in *The Northern Mariner/Le marin du nord* 10, No. 1 (January 2000), 3–20. I am grateful to the editors of that journal for their kind permission to reuse portions of that article.

2. John Lewis Gaddis, *The Landscape of History: How Historians Map the Past* (Berkeley, CA: Oxford University Press, 2002), 57 and 97.

3. Library and Archives Canada (henceforth LAC), Record Group (henceforth RG) 24, Vol. 11117, File 70–1-6, Captain J.C.I. Edwards, Commanding Officer (CO) *Cornwallis* to the Commander-in-Chief (C-in-C) Canadian North-West Atlantic Command (CNA), 18 May 1945. After the Riots, C-in-C CNA requested that all his COs report on their V-E Day celebrations. The strength of *Cornwallis* was close to 8,000 at the time. Their plan was based on a notion of mutual trust and "confidence," and there were no problems.

4. LAC, RG 24, Vol. 11208, Findings, Naval Board of Inquiry on the V-E Day Riots, page (g). This generalization was revised in an important *volte face* by Captain J.P. Connolly, MC, RCNVR, during July 1945.

5. The Army and the Navy conducted separate inquiries. The Naval Board of Inquiry used the term *factors* and not *causes*. The Commission of Inquiry was ordered by the Government of Canada in an Order in Council, and it was headed by Honourable Justice R.L. Kellock. His public report was widely distributed. Directorate of History and Heritage (henceforth DHH), File 113.3S2.003 (D1), "Report on the Halifax Disorders ..." (henceforth the "Kellock Report, 28 July 45"). The Kellock Inquiry testimonial evidence was not opened to the public until 1997 (henceforth *Kellock Testimony*), at LAC, RG 24, Vol. 5330 and 5331. The commission placed the primary blame for disturbances on naval personnel, and directed that claims for damage and theft be paid by the Canadian government. For later histories, see James M. Cameron, *Murray The Martyred Admiral* (Hantsport, NS: Lancelot Press, 1980); and Stanley R. Redman, *Open Gangway: An Account of the Halifax Riots* (Hantsport, NS: Lancelot Press, 1981).

6. The terms *morale* and *discipline* are used frequently, and in combination, but rarely with full understanding. For the purpose of this study, *morale* is defined as one of the functions that governs how people respond and react to danger. This definition is derived from: John Baynes, *Morale: A Study of Men and Courage* (London: Cassell Books, 1967), Lord Moran, *The Anatomy of Courage* (London: Constable, 1945), and A. Roger Thompson, "Combat Motivation and Behaviour Among Naval Forces: A Discussion Paper," Directorate of Social and Economic Analysis (henceforth DSEA) Staff Note 9/91, NDHQ Ottawa. Chapter 9 of Lord Moran's work has a short chapter, "At Sea." An RCN pre-war definition of *morale* and *discipline*, explained by Rear-Admiral (Retired) K.F. Adams, RCN, is in the "Pre-War RCN Preparation" section, Part II, of that work.

7. The chief commissioner of the liquor commission also had suggested that service canteens be closed on the future V-E Day. Rear-Admiral Murray, on behalf of the three services, had replied to this recommendation arguing that canteens should remain open "to the extent of the limited supplies that would be available ..." Maintaining large stocks of beer and liquor appeared to be a major problem with service canteens. With all the liquor warehouses closed, the canteens would not be able to remain open for long periods. "Kellock Report, 28 July 45," 6.

8. The Civil Defence Committee in Halifax planned the original civil-military V-E Day events only over the period of one day — from 0900 hours until the evening. They did not consider contingency plans detailing what action would be taken if V-E Day was announced, for example, before noon, or during the afternoon before 1600 hours, and so on. Instead, they based their plan on one theoretical day, *vide* the principle that events would divert crowds away from the downtown, and the opportunity it offered for vandalism and crime. Thus the committee agreed, in theory, on a public dance at South and South Park streets, and other entertainments, as well as the Service of Thanksgiving, all for the [Halifax] Commons side of Citadel Hill, away from the downtown. Strangely, then, the committee planned on a harbour fireworks-searchlight-fire boat display for the evening. This was odd, because if the crowds had been diverted from facing the downtown with the early events, they would be required to move to the harbour side of the Citadel slopes, and face the inner city, for the evening displays. Nova Scotia Archives and Records Management, RG 32–102, Series 36C, File C.124, "Brief Outline of Preparations by H.C.E.C. Executive." HCEC stood for Halifax Civil Emergency Corps, and it was known also as the "Civil Defence Committee," 5–7.

9. On the evening of 7 May 1945, at short notice, the officials decided to execute the plan for the outdoor harbour fireworks and light show. They later claimed this was because of a weather forecast that predicted bad weather for 8 May. The armed services reacted quickly with their searchlights and fire-boats. The show went on, and hundreds watched it from the harbour-side — the downtown side — of the Citadel. Thus, crowds were not diverted from the downtown by this event, nor were they diverted by the street dances. The other diversionary entertainments originally planned for the V-E Day were not conducted on 7 May, and few of them, if any, were actually conducted on 8 May. Nova Scotia Archives and Records Management, RG 32–102, Series 36C, File C.124, "Brief Outline of Preparation by H.C.E.C. Executive," 5–6.

10. The term *mutual confidence* was taken from the opening quote by the CO HMCS *Cornwallis*. The term reappears in other naval writing, suggesting that it was a contemporary term in the RCN.

11. See Chapter IV, "Police Forces and Plan for Their Employment," in the "Kellock Report, 28 July 45" 24–28. Kellock's quote was from page 24. Murray's explanation was from the LAC, RG 24, Vol. 5331, *Kellock Testimony*, Vol. 13, 1428–30 (quote from page 1428).

12. The Halifax V-E Day Riots were widely photographed by service and civilian photographers. There is a set of selected black and white photographs at DHH, 113.3S2.003 (D1); and at the NAC. Cine [moving picture] film captured events over time, and the escalation of the violence on 8 May 1945 is apparent in this footage, the best of that is held by CBC Halifax. Film viewed by author 1 June 1998.

13. LAC, RG 24, Vol. 11208, Naval Board of Inquiry, Testimony of Lieutenant R.M. MacLean, CO HMCS *Grou*, 152. *Grou*, a frigate, was in Halifax for a long time being "tropicalized" for Pacific operations. MacLean and an unnamed ordinary seamen defended Eaton's department store from service and civilian looters.

14. After the riots several newspaper editorials compared the Navy with the Army, for example the *Ottawa Journal* wrote: "Why were troops not called out [when] ... uniformed hoodlums ... were ... [rioting]?." Implied here was that the Army was steady and reliable and the Navy were the "uniformed hoodlums." DHH, Vol. 12, 81/520/1440–6, 8000, *Ottawa Journal*, 10 May 1945.

15. The "Material Loss and Damage ..." was briefly summarized in Chapter 12, the "Kellock Report, 28 July 45," 61. "6,987 cases of beer ... 55,392 quarts of spirits were looted from the [several] establishments of the Liquor Commission ... 30,516 quarts of Beer from Keith's Brewery ... In Dartmouth 5,256 quarts of beer, 1,692 quarts of wine and 9,816 quarts of liquor ... [in Halifax] ... 564 firms suffered damage, 2,624 pieces of plate and other glass ... were broken and 207 of these firms suffered from looting in some degree."

16. When HMCS *Chaudière* returned to Halifax in March 1945, the CO, Lieutenant-Commander C.P. Nixon, RCN, remembered that "Admiral Murray came aboard. He evidently knew nothing of our exploits. All he talked about was the conduct of the men ashore ... It went over like a complete wet blanket ... I got [the men] together and thanked them ..." In the same interview Hal Lawrence remembered that "Yogi" Jensen had reported a similar incident when *Algonquin* returned to Halifax. "It was terrible, the admiral's speech to returning warriors. He just warned them that they had better pull their socks up that they weren't in the U.K. now ... It was quite an unsuitable speech." DHH, Biographical File, Interview Captain C.P. Nixon, March 1987.

17. LAC, Manuscript Group (henceforth MG) 30 E 207, Vol. 1, "VE Day," "Murray Papers," Rear-Admiral LW Murray to Captain R.E.S. Bidwell, 15 May 1945, 2.

18. For example, Commodore (Retired) J.C. Littler RCN recently wrote in his published memoir, "Unfortunately, the Halifax riots at the end of the European war caused this finest of Canadian Admirals to take the entire blame for those in command of barracks and dockyard." J.C. Littler, *Sea Fever* (Victoria: Kiwi Publications, 1995), 252. Much of Murray's correspondence, which reflected his life-long concern with his dismissal, is at LAC, MG 30 E 207, Vol. 1. Cameron, *Murray the Martyred Admiral* presented a sympathetic case for

Murray's innocence, partly based — correctly — on the exaggeration of the event by the press.

19. LAC, RG 24, Vol. 5331, *Kellock Testimony*, Vol. 13, 1410. Rear-Admiral Murray was asked if he had ever "satisfied" himself "at any time that your senior Officers had or had not experience in the handling of large concentration camps?" Murray's reply was: "It has never been necessary for me to do so. They have had experience since."

20. The problems on the east coast could only have been solved through greater centralization, in Ottawa, as well as in Halifax. Moreover, greater emphasis in Naval Staff Headquarters (NSHQ) and Halifax should have been placed on the advice of specialists and outside assistance. See this author's "Change and Challenge: The Canadian Naval Staff in 1943," 3 February 1997, and "Admiral Murray and the ACHQ," 11 October 1995, both DHH narratives, DHH. ACHQ is the abbreviation for "Area Combined Headquarters," the joint RCN-RCAF headquarters established in Halifax in July 1943.

21. DHH, Biographical File, Rear-Admiral Kenneth Adams, personal memoir, 36–37.

22. Patrick Beesly, *Special Intelligence: The Story of the Admiralty's Operational Intelligence Centre 1939–1945* (London: Ballantine Books, 1977), 6. The italics were Beesly's.

23. L.C. Audette, "The Lower Deck and *The Mainguy Report* of 1949," in James A. Boutillier, ed., *The RCN in Retrospect 1910–1968* (Vancouver: University of British Columbia Press, 1982), 243. Audette considered the 1943–1949 period as one piece. In other words, from a leadership, morale, and discipline perspective, this period was an unbroken and cohesive experience.

24. *Ibid.*, 236.

25. *Ibid.*, 243.

26. Most the officers and men in the Canadian Naval Service were RCNVR. In January 1945 the all ranks strength figures were: RCNVR — 78,000, RCNR — 5,300, RCN — 4,384. Gilbert Tucker, *The Naval Service of Canada: Activities on Shore During the Second World War, Volume 2* (Ottawa: National Defence, 1952), 274. There is no study that tracks the enrollment into the RCNVR or the RCN through the war. Moreover, apparently many VR ratings transferred to the RCN for six-year periods of service between 1940 and 1942. The author is indebted to Dr. R.H. Gimblett for this insight in May 1998

27. DHH, Biographical File, Commander P.G. Chance, 2 May 1991, Dinner Speech, 2.

28. A.R. Hewitt and W.M. Mansfield, "The Good(?) Old Days," *Salty Dips* (Ottawa: Naval Officers Association of Canada, 1983), 56.

29. The average rate of VR personnel enrolled and sent to the fleet was about 700 men a month. This figure was based on Lieutenant-Commander W.R. Glover's research for DHH on the training demands of the RCNVRs. Discussion with Dr. Roger Sarty, 15 May 1998.

30. David Zimmerman, "The Social Background of the Wartime Navy: Some Statistical Data," in *A Nation's Navy: In Quest of Canadian Naval Identity*, in Michael L. Hadley et al. eds. (Montreal and Kingston: McGill-Queen's University Press, 1992), 256–79.

31. This first scholarly suggestion of a self-image based on a distinct culture was in Michael L. Hadley, "The Popular Image of the Canadian Navy," in *Ibid.*, 35–56.

32. There is a great deal of evidence supporting the high sense of pride of service. For example, in Lieutenant (S) William H. Pugsley, RCNVR, *Saints, Devils and Ordinary Seamen: Life on the Royal Canadian Navy's Lower Deck* (Toronto: Collins, 1945), Pugsley repeatedly stressed pride in his record of the wartime views of the VR Ordinary Seaman: "against the outside world they stood as one [page 54] ... the men are proud of the fact that their discipline is more severe than that of other services [page 66] ... [going ashore] ... you dressed carefully ... to satisfy your own finer instincts of what a matelot should wear [that was] ... a tailor-made job — 'tiddlies' — ... Ratings are ... fussy ... [a sailor said] ... I'm proud of my seaman's uniform ... you can have it tight enough to look good [page 229] ... The seamen are fighting proud of their uniform [page 229]."

33. DHH, E.J. Downton Biographical File, Interview 20 November 1982.

34. Roger Sarty, *Canada and the Battle of the Atlantic* (Ottawa, 1998), 89–90. Sarty cited a report 16 October 1941 that described this dangerous situation, "for the most part [CO's] have not one other officer on whom they can ... rely [upon] ... many of the ships are grossly under manned ... unless urgent steps are taken ... grave danger exists of breakdowns in health, morale and discipline."

35. *Paukenshlag*, or Operation Drumbeat, consisted of the first German submarine attacks off the North America coast in early 1942, after Germany had followed the Japanese lead and declared war against the United States. See W.A.B. Douglas, Roger Sarty, Michael Whitby, et al., *No Higher Purpose — The Official Operational History of the Royal Canadian Navy in the Second World War, 1939–1943, Volume. 2, Part 1* (St. Catharines, ON: Vanwell, 2002), 373–427.

36. DHH, D.W. Groos Biographical File, Letter (name unreadable) from "Ex-MLA, St. Boniface, Manitoba," to Vice-Admiral Nelles, Chief of Naval Staff (CNS), 21 May 1943. "[CO *Collingwood* ... took some [of] the ratings under his care and tutored them for Leading Seaman's rating on the last trip home ... [they] were able to pass their examination. If this condition obtains on other ships then I am free to confess, those in authority deserve the highest commendation for their interest in the ratings." The CO was Lieutenant D.W. Groos, RCN.

37. In a brief social history of the pre-war and wartime Navy, based on eight interviews, James A. Boutilier noted that "Some of the [pre-war RCN] Lower Deck tended to look down upon [VR] officers as inexperienced and amateurish" There were other differences between junior RCN and RCNVR officers: "[RCN] officers were more aloof ... [they] were , well trained but ... distant ... the [VR] officer ... knew a lot but he wasn't afraid to ask [for] more knowledge ... VR's were trying to be an officer without knowing how to be [one] ... [VRs] jumped in there and ran it [well] ... How they got sifted out and did the job I'll never know. I think we were a bunch of lost sheep and I think the RN took a bloody dim view of us." LAC, MG 31, E 18, Vol. 16, 16–2, Audette Papers, James A. Boutilier, "Matelot Memories: Recollections of the Lower Deck in Peace and War 1937–1945," 12–13.

38. LAC, RG 24, Vol. 3997, NSS 1057-3-24, Vol. 1, Acting Lieutenant-Commander D.W. Piers, RCN, "Comments on the Operation and Performance of H.M.C. Ships, Establishments, and Personnel, in the Battle of the Atlantic," 1 June 1943. Also see *Ibid.*, Lieutenant-Commander W.E.S. Briggs, RCNR, "Personal Appreciation of Situation for R.C.N. Ships in United Kingdom," 23 April 1943.

39. In September 1943 Lieutenant-Commander H.E.W. Strange, RCNVR, deputy director of Naval Information, commented on Canadian ratings in Derry. "vice habits of the respective navies ... U.S. ratings seek prostitutes, R.C.N. ratings seek liquor, and R.N. ratings indulge in both ...." LAC, MG 32 C71, Vol. 3, "Equipment on Ship[s]," File 3–12, Part 1," Strange to J.J. Connolly, 21 September 1943. RCNVR rating Frank Curry tried to explain this development: "The dance was a great success ... the consumption of liquor escalated ... the crew [*Kamsack*] took to the streets and battled amongst themselves in a wild, terrifying night of blood ... It was as if all the years of harsh and brutal living conditions had finally turned us into animals ... Often through the long [war] years of despair, our pent-up feelings found temporary release in ... alcohol ... to provide the basis for periodic breakouts ... to return from shore leave to find a good part of the crew roary-eyed drunk and in a vile mood, the ship in turmoil. Who could blame them? The breaking point was often very close ... [small incidents aboard or ashore simply added] ... insult ... to injury." Frank Curry, *War At Sea — A Canadian Seaman on the North Atlantic* (Toronto, 1990), 71–72. On the distortion of VR pride, see Acting Captain J.M. Rowland, captain (D) in St. John's in September 1943, who commented on VR discipline and noted that "There is quite an idea prevalent that one should look 'tough.'" His superior, Flag Officer Newfoundland (FONF), agreed and noted "[what is needed is] a pride in uniform rather than in 'looking tough.'" LAC, RG 24, Vol. 11947, DNF 1700–11 (Vol. 1), Capt (D) to FONF, 2 September 1943; and LAC, RG 24, Vol. 3997, 1057-3-24 (Vol. 1), FONF to NSHQ, 27 September 1943.

40. Charles Ritchie, *The Siren Years: A Canadian Diplomat Abroad 1937–1945* (Toronto: Macmillan of Canada, 1974), 169.

41. *Ibid.*, 171–72.

42. James B. Lamb, *The Corvette Navy: True Stories from Canada's Atlantic War* (Toronto: Macmillan of Canada, 1979), 16.

43. *Ibid.*, 17.

44. DHH, 81/520/1440–6, Vol. 12, David MacLennan, "In Defence of the People of Halifax," *Ottawa Journal*, 22 May 1945.

45. On V-E Day there were over 4,000 naval all ranks living in civilian accommodation on "lodgings and compensation." The *Kellock Report* showed these figures "log and comp" figures: *Scotian* reported 2,639, (page 18), *Stadacona* reported 1178 (page 16). All *Peregrine's* personnel were in barracks. The "Kellock Report, 28 July 45," 17–20. In Captain (D)s files he noted that his shore staff, over 300, were all on "log and comp." See LAC, RG 24, Vol. 11582. This author did not calculate "log and comp" figures for other naval units or the other two services, for example there appeared to be many Army and Royal Canadian Air Force personnel living out in Dartmouth and Halifax.

46. DHH, 87/76, M.A. Thesis, Jay White, "The Ajax Affair: Citizens and Sailors in Wartime Halifax 1939–1945," 39–86; and Jay White, "The Ajax Affair," *Moncton Times-Transcript*, 7 May 1988. The Ajax club was privately organized by outsiders — non-Haligonians. While it existed, the club was an elegant and highly successful wet and dry canteen for ratings only.

47. DHH, 80/218, "Naval Discipline," Vol. 17, F 883/4, MacDonald to COAC, 4 June 1942, F 883/1, and COAC to Minister, 8 June 1942.

48. DHH, NHC, Vol. 14, NSS 1000–5-13, CO RCN Barracks to COAC, 12 October 1942.

49. LAC, RG 24, Vol. 11657, DH 3–2-1 No. 2, Atlantic Command Temporary Memorandum (ACTM) 1979, 25 January 1944.

50. DHH, 80/218, "Naval Discipline," Vol. 17, F 883/4, Connolly to CNS, 3 July 1944. See LAC, RG 24, Vol. 5331, Kellock Testimony, Vol. 11, 1079–1981 for a reference to the "Rankin Incident."

51. In 1991 Dr. Roger Sarty interviewed Katherine Roberts, who was the best friend of "Tillie" Jones, wife of Vice-Admiral G.C. Jones. She advised that "[Jones] was *not* a social person which his wife Tillie was ... To get more information look up Captain Joe Connely [*sic*] — they were best friends. Joe used to attend functions with Tillie when G.C. wouldn't ... I'm under the impression he was the only one G.C. really cared about. Another was Angus L. MacDonald [*sic*] ... All were from N.S ...." Letter Katherine Roberts to Roger Sarty, 19 December 1991, original in Dr. Sarty's own collection, Ottawa.

52. LAC, RG 24, Vol. 5331, Kellock Testimony, Vol. 13, 1423–24.

53. John A. MacDonald to Rear-Admiral C.J. Dillon, 2 March 1965, 81/520/1440–6,

Vol. 12, NHC, DHH. Lieutenant (Paymaster) J.A. MacDonald, RCNVR was the "Captain's Secretary" to the CO. He advised that the chief of Naval Personnel (CNP) had confirmed this opinion of these COs.

54. LAC, RG 24, Vol. 11117, File 70-1-1, CO HMCS *Stadacona* to C-in-C CNA, 8 March 1945. The Naval Board of Inquiry examined this plan in detail when they questioned Captain Balfour, see LAC, RG 24, Vol. 11208, "Naval Board of Inquiry," 86–106.

55. A review of the organization files of the largest Halifax units revealed that solving personnel and disciplinary matters was the major problem facing commanders and staffs during the war. The difficulties were staggering. For example in October 1943, on the eve of an attempt to reorganize the naval command following the implementation of the Area Combined Headquarters, HMCS *Stadacona*'s strength was 11,000 all ranks. Clearly, these numbers were too large for one "unit." LAC, RG 24, Vol. 11541, Files H-1-2-1, H-1-2-8, and H-1-2-4. The files were for C-in-C CNA, *Stadacona* and *Peregrine* respectively. There is related material in LAC, RG 24, Vol. 11009 and 11657, C-in-C CNA organization files.

56. In a 1986 interview describing wartime NSHQ-relations, Rear-Admiral M.G. Stirling, a signals officer, remembered the hate that his director of signals, Acting Captain G.A. Worth, RCN, directed towards Rear-Admiral Murray, RCN. "Sam [Worth] would just tell him to shut up. Sam was by then a Captain. He was senior to [Murray] as a Cadet, and neither of them had ever forgotten it. He [Worth] was not a respecter of persons." In the bipolar world of RCN senior leadership, clearly Worth was a "Jones man." DHH, Stirling Biographical File. There is some evidence that signals between Murray and Jones were sent from duty officer to duty officer on direct teletype. Example dialogue: "Is there an officer there please?" "Yes …" "I have a very important message for CNS which Admiral Murray has asked me to pass to an officer … to be given directly to CNS *with no filed copies* would you mind taking it please" "Yes I am on the … [teletype] … machine … there will be no further filed copy …" DHH, Murray Biographical File, Signal Traffic 14 March 1943.

57. DHH, J.H. Wade Biographical File, Interview Lieutenant RCNVR J.H. [John] Wade and Lieutenant-Commander Glover, 4 February (n.d.), 17–18.

58. LAC, RG 24, Vol. 11117, File 70–1-8, EA to Vice Admiral G.C. Jones to CNS, 3 July 1945, 4. Vice-Admiral Jones was then C-in-C CNA and CNS.

59. The inspiration for the conclusion in the paragraph was drawn from Craig M. Cameron, *American Samurai: Myth, Imagination, and the Conduct of Battle in the First Marine Division, 1941–1951* (New York: Cambridge University, 1994).

60. Vice-Admiral Sir Peter Gretton, "Foreword," in Marc Milner, *North Atlantic Run: The Royal Canadian Navy and the Battle for the Convoys* (Toronto: University of Toronto Press, 1985), ix–xi.

The Post-War "Incidents" in the Royal Canadian Navy, 1949[1]

Richard H. Gimblett

THE ROYAL CANADIAN NAVY (RCN) entered the year 1949 with a certain degree of optimism. It had ended the Second World War as the third largest allied fleet, but within a year demobilization and retrenchment had reduced it to a mere rump of five ships and barely 5,000 men. Recognizing the magnitude of the challenge of re-building the post war fleet virtually from scratch, the assistant chief of naval personnel predicted bleakly that "the training service will be our most important function for the next five years."[2] Three and one-half years later, in February 1949, senior officers of the RCN saw themselves ahead of schedule. Overall strength had been raised to just under the authorized 10,000-man peacetime ceiling, so that, in addition to the aircraft carrier *Magnificent* and the training cruiser *Ontario*, a total of six destroyers were in commission. Although none of the ships could boast full complements, finally there were sufficient hulls in the water to conduct meaningful fleet exercises. For the Navy's spring cruise of 1949, the Pacific and Atlantic squadrons were to combine for fleet manoeuvres in the Caribbean Sea for the first time since the end of the Second World War.

Each of these incidents was defused almost immediately, with the respective captains entering the messes for an informal discussion of their sailors' grievances. Still, something was evidently wrong in the Canadian fleet. Since the sailors had offered no hint of violence, no one used the charged word *mutiny*. Indeed, in *Athabaskan*, the captain was careful to place his cap over what appeared to be a list of demands, so that no technical state of mutiny could be said to exist. But the *incidents*, as they came to be called, constituted a challenge to the lawfully established order of the Navy and warrant the term *mutiny*. Because the incidents transpired in suspiciously rapid succession, they seized the attention of a government and a nation growing sensitive to the spread of communist influence. A communist-inspired strike in the Canadian merchant marine in 1948 sparked fears of subversion in the naval service — indeed, the Liberal government had only just withstood charges by the Conservative leader of the opposition that the federal bureaucracy was overrun by communists. Prime Minister Louis St. Laurent was planning a general election for June 1949, and wanted this latest spectre of the "red menace" also put to rest.[3] The defence minister, Brooke Claxton, ordered a commission of inquiry to investigate the state of the Navy.

The Liberals went on to win the election, and the commissioners presented their deliberations in November 1949 in a volume famous henceforth as *The Mainguy Report*.[4] Its trim length of 57 pages notwithstanding, it remained for nearly 50 years the most incisive examination of a military institution to be undertaken in Canada.[5] It exposed the hardship of general service conditions, described a number of factors critical to achieving good officer-man relations, and outlined a blueprint for reform. Its impact was immediate, and it deserves its description as "a remarkable manifesto" and "a watershed in the Navy's history."[6] Still taught to new recruits of all ranks, and the continuing subject of staff college analysis, the report's findings, recommendations and conclusions remain a potent legacy.[7] The year 1949 is remembered as the one of crisis and reform in the Royal Canadian Navy.

That does not mean, however, that that legacy is all it is presented to be. This chapter will demonstrate that, for all of the universal truths in *The Mainguy Report*, the claims ascribed to it (and by extension to the year 1949), and just about everything else we supposedly "know" of the mutinies in the RCN in that year, except for the facts of their occurrence, are mistaken. The incidents of February and March 1949 occurred for reasons more complex than a simple breakdown in officer–man relationships. In fact, what the report does not adequately reflect are the enormous strains of demobilization and the restructuring of the new peacetime Navy.

REAR-ADMIRAL E.R. MAINGUY SITS FOR A PHOTOGRAPH IN 1950.
(Department of National Defence, John M. Turner, Library and Archives Canada PA 152841)

Background to Dissension

Labour historians have shown that workers tend to strike not to gain some new right, but to recover something lost or threatened. In this there are obvious parallels to naval history, where there is ample evidence to suggest that "mutinous acts remain fundamentally loyal to the *status quo* of the service."[8] This was the case in the series of strikes by the communist-dominated Canadian Seaman's Union (CSU) in

1946–1948, which the Liberal government perceived as the model for discord in the RCN. Indeed, trouble in the merchant marine flared again in April 1949 just as the Mainguy Commission prepared to sit. But where the CSU was fighting for better pay and benefits for its members, and against efforts by the shipping companies to break the union,[9] in the Canadian naval incidents, as suggested by *Crescent*'s captain, "It will be noted that [the] three [conditions] previously considered as all-important; food, pay and leave; are not mentioned. They are eminently satisfactory in the RCN."[10]

What was the *status quo* in the RCN in 1949, and what had occurred to upset it? What had been lost or threatened that the sailors felt compelled to recover through mass insubordination? There was then and is now little disagreement over the initial finding of the commission: that there were no communists in the RCN. It was the subsequent litany of "General Causes Contributing to [the] Breakdown of Discipline" that implied the Navy's post war morale problems were the fault of an uncaring officer corps harbouring aristocratic British attitudes inappropriate to the democratic sensitivities of Canadians. If the commissioners found no organized or subversive influences at work in the naval service, they identified such systemic problems as the breakdown of the divisional system[11] of personnel management (which they attributed to lack of training and experience of junior officers), frequent changes in staffing and routines on board ships with inadequate explanation, a deterioration in the traditional relationship between officers and petty officers, and the absence of a distinguishing Canadian identity in the Navy (as opposed to one described as still too closely linked to the Royal Navy). They laid special emphasis upon the failure in each of the affected ships to provide functioning welfare committees, as prescribed by naval regulations, to allow the airing and correction of petty grievances.[12] They noted also an "artificial distance between officers and men," with the clear implication that this was the result of Canadian midshipmen obtaining their early practical experience in the big ships of the Royal Navy.[13]

None of these "General Causes" should have been the stuff to inspire mutiny, even in its restrained Canadian form of mess deck lock-ins. Reading the report and the volumes of testimony used to prepare it, one is struck, as were the commissioners, by the banality of the men's grievances and their difficulties in articulating them.[14] Neither the absence of welfare committees nor the men's lack of higher education can fully account for the acts of indiscipline or the men's poor attempts at explaining their actions. The spontaneous nature of the incidents and the lack of coordination point to other discrepancies. If the motives for dissension were as widespread as the commission implied, the wonder is not that three ships mutinied in 1949 but that the rest of the fleet did not join them. At the same time the coincidental timing of the incidents, despite the spatial separation, certainly led the minister and the naval staff to presume collusion, and yet none was found. So we are left with two intriguing questions: Were the incidents somehow connected? And why did they transpire at the precise moment they did in 1949?

A "Tradition of Mutiny"

The authors of *The Mainguy Report* acknowledged that, during the Second World War and in its immediate aftermath, the RCN had "grown and shrunk in a manner unparalleled," from a pre-war total strength of 1,585 officers and men to a wartime peak of over 93,000, and back down to the 1949 total of 8,800.[15] They blithely asserted that the "stresses and strains ... accompanying ... every such process ... need no verbal comment," and then proceeded to detail the breakdown of the RCN in the late winter of 1949, as if the service had suddenly dropped at that moment to the bottom of the pit. Brief mention is made of an incident in the cruiser *Ontario* in August 1947, but it was attributed entirely to the character of the ship's executive officer and was considered significant only because the participants were later spread among other ships.

The truth is more complex. Canada's Navy of 1949 was very much the offspring of the service that had fought the Second World War, but was fundamentally different from it. Wartime expansion had been orchestrated primarily through the recruitment of inexperienced civilians into the Royal Canadian Naval Volunteer Reserve (RCNVR) — the "Wavy Navy," so-called because of the distinctive pattern of the officers' rank braid — and because the majority of RCNVR personnel tended to serve in the small-ships of the "corvette navy." With the wartime imperative to crew vessels as quickly as possible, training was kept to the minimum required for safety, and operational effectiveness suffered as a result.[16]

That changed in the last two years of the war, by then RCNVR officers were commanding virtually all the frigates and corvettes fighting the Battle of the Atlantic, and to very good effect. The corollary that has entered the popular historical memory, however, is that the permanent-force RCN abandoned this anti-submarine war to the RCNVRs, in preference to developing a "big ship" fleet of aircraft carriers and cruisers that would constitute the post-war Navy. In truth, there was a great crossover: experienced pre-war RCN officers commanded the *River*-class destroyers that oversaw the convoy escort and support groups, and RCNVR officers and ratings were a major part of the complements of those big ships that operated during the war. More to the point, when the RCN was reduced to a strength of fewer than 5,000 all-ranks in 1946, because of wartime deaths and other dismissals of pre-war "regulars" this in fact reflected an infusion of nearly 4,000 RCNVRs into the post-war force. Improving the "basic" standard of readiness of these officers and men in itself would have rationalized the dedication of the RCN to the training function described above; the recruiting of another 5,000 all-ranks to reach the authorized post-war establishment made it imperative.

A detailed study of the social composition of HMCS *Crescent*, the destroyer that suffered the incident in Nanjing on 15 March 1949,[17] underscores the magnitude of the changes in the RCN. Among other points, the distinguishing feature of the ship's company was its youth. Out of a complement of 14 officers and 187 ratings borne for that cruise, the median age was 22.5, with the youngest being 18.5, and only four were over 35 (including the coxswain and the chief engine room artificer; the captain was only 31). Only 13 ratings had served in the pre-war RCN, while fully half (94) had joined since war's-end; among the officers, only the captain and the two gunners had joined before the war, and the two sub-lieutenants were the only ones (like the captain) who had undertaken comprehensive professional training in the Royal Navy. Translating this into another vague gauge of credibility, of all the senior appointments on board, hardly anyone had more than eight years in the service, fewer than half could claim any truly pertinent wartime experience (especially in destroyers — most were corvette men), and only the captain had filled his present capacity before.

The context simplistically given in *The Mainguy Report* was flawed in yet another respect. Contrary to the impression developed that the breakdown in discipline in 1949 was an isolated event, it was in fact part of a pattern of low-level disobedience that had been practised in the RCN at least since the mid-1930s, probably picked-up by sailors who were frequently rotated (like their officers) for training with the Royal Navy. Because so few ratings in the post-war RCN had served in that period, it is difficult to point to a direct transfer of such knowledge, but the circumstantial evidence that Canadian sailors had been exposed to it is overwhelming.[18] Importantly, that "tradition of mutiny" was well known, understood, and accepted by all ranks throughout the fleet.

The massed expression of protest in the RCN invariably took the form of lock-ins, or "sit-down strikes" as the service's official historian, Gilbert Tucker, styled them.[19] They were spontaneous displays, precipitated by some local event, and undertaken with a view to attracting the attention of immediately superior officers to a problem the sailors believed was within the power of those superiors to correct. The precise cause for protest varied. Most commonly it was conditions of over-work, less frequently it was over issues of welfare specific to the ship (such as food and leave), and occasionally it was in reaction to the intemperate actions of the captain. Only once did the sailors aim to remove the commanding officer (and in that case the captain was clearly unstable), and on only one other occasion did the crew refuse to sail (for convoy duty, but again under a captain in whom they had lost their confidence).

Invariably, large numbers of a ship's company would come together to voice some collective complaint for which there was no other officially sanctioned form of expression. Significantly, their officers recognized the restrictions under which the men operated and appear to have accepted the lock-in as an acceptable form of protest. If the men's demands were at all reasonable (and they usually were), they were acted upon, promptly and without recrimination. No member of the RCN was ever charged with mutiny. The only persons who appear to have earned any significant time in cells were the men who had disobeyed wartime sailing orders. Certainly, no one ever was awarded the punishment stipulated under King's Regulations for the RCN (KRCN) for mutiny — death by hanging.

None of these "incidents," either in 1949 or those preceding them, involved the "the violent seizure of a ship from her officers on the high seas," a display that, according to one naval historian, "may be said to belong to the Cecil B. DeMille school of history."[20] Indeed, the author of that statement, Nicholas Rodger, demonstrated that such incidents "were virtually unknown in the [Royal] Navy." Instead, "collective actions by whole ship's companies ... did happen, and happened quite frequently."[21] The tradition of mutiny in the Canadian Navy, as such, was very much in keeping with that of the Royal Navy, from which the RCN derived so much else of its heritage.

Ships's Companies and the Impact of Change

Having established the incidents of 1949 and the reaction to them as part of a larger pattern, it is time to turn to the substance of *The Mainguy Report*. Fifty years on we have lost sight of the fact that few of the observations and conclusions in it came as a surprise to contemporary officers or politicians. In fact, large portions of it were an almost verbatim repetition of the findings of an internal study into "Morale and Service Conditions" conducted by the naval staff and presented in the fall of 1947 to the minister[22] — the same Brooke Claxton who would receive *The Mainguy Report* two years later. Discontent had been widespread that summer, mostly over the issue of pay. *The Mainguy Report* referred only to the August 1947 incident in the cruiser *Ontario*, but there were also recent incidents

THE HONOURABLE BROOKE CLAXTON (CENTRE) CHATS WITH A SAILOR.

(Alexandra Studio, Library and Archives Canada PA 52462)

in the destroyers *Nootka* and *Micmac* and at the fleet schools in Halifax and Esquimalt. Besides the immediate transfer of *Ontario's* executive officer, the more widespread unrest precipitated significant pay raises that fall and again in 1948. In the time-honoured tradition of the RCN, the men had obtained redress of their grievances.

With the immediate problems of 1947 resolved, the naval staff could turn to the more important task of dealing with the underlying issues. The requirements identified in the Morale and Service Conditions Study ranged from the necessity for adequate quarters (shipboard, barrack, and married), through better pay to be made more equitable among the various trades and branches, to films to be shown at sea, the start-up of a "Lower Deck magazine," the standardization of new entry training, the Canadianization of officer training, and the better application of the divisional system.[23] The majority of these being budgetary considerations, Chief of the Naval Staff (CNS), Vice-Admiral Harold Grant, brought the four main items to the attention of the minister: pay, service accommodation, married quarters, and travel warrants (rail passes for long leave home).[24] Claxton's response is not recorded, but his own depth of concern for the plight of the sailors can be adduced from the fact that travel warrants (made popular during the war but dropped as a peacetime cost-cutting measure) were not reinstated, only a handful of new married quarters were built over the next several years (the number was especially low in comparison to the other services), no new naval barracks would be constructed until late in 1953 (and then only as part of the general Cold War expansion), and the general pay raise was driven only by the imperatives of tri-service equality.[25]

Grant was essentially left to his own devices. Within the strictures of his budget and the physical capacity of the small staff at Naval Service Headquarters (NSHQ), he moved swiftly and effectively. The divisional system already was described in the KRCNs and further bureaucratization of that process evidently was deemed unnecessary. However, a message ordering the institution of welfare committees in all RCN ships and establishments had been promulgated the week before the incident in *Ontario*. When in the fall of 1947 the naval staff looked at re-commissioning HMCS *Sioux*, one of several destroyers held in reserve, the preparatory refit was mandated to include the popular American-style cafeteria messing and the fitting of bunks instead of hammocks.[26] The number of ratings commissioned from the ranks was increased dramatically through 1948, and plans were made to re-open the wartime training establishment HMCS

Cornwallis as a dedicated new-entry training centre. The fleet still was too small to offer any alternative to officer and specialist training with the Royal Navy, but 40 cadets from the naval college HMCS *Royal Roads* were embarked in *Ontario* for the spring cruise of 1948.[27] The glossy naval newsmagazine *Crowsnest* appeared in the fall of 1948. It was immediately popular for its chatty stories of happenings in the fleet, but also contained solid information on directives from NSHQ and the implementation of the various reforms.

It is possible to conclude, therefore, that the Morale and Service Conditions Study undertaken in the fall of 1947 accurately identified many of the underlying sources of discontent in the RCN, and that within months a great many of its recommendations were being implemented. The measure of its effectiveness is that retention and recruiting both improved considerably. Moreover, extensive research has not uncovered a single reference to any sort of incident in the Canadian fleet between that in HMCS *Ontario* in August 1947 and the three in 1949 reported upon by the Mainguy Commission. These developments were not the signs of a service in distress, as the RCN had been in the summer of 1947.

Other than the critical but expensive capital issues of shore accommodation and married quarters, there remained only the requirement "to re-examine the trade group structure as applicable to the Navy." Admiral Grant had promised to do so in his note to the minister, and prominent among the staff action undertaken through 1948 was a fundamental reorganization of the Navy's rank and trade group structure to bring it in line with the establishment and higher pay rates of the Army and Air Force. This was to be effected essentially by splitting the petty officer and chief petty officer rates into new divisions each of 1st and 2nd class. Then, all present leading rates were to be promoted to the new rating of petty officer 2nd class, present petty officers with less than three years seniority would become petty officers 1st Class, and so on.[28] Some stokers grumbled about seamen now gaining the equivalent of their higher technical specialist pay, although seamen resented the promotion of engineering branch members without the requisite leadership responsibilities or capabilities, but the new structure came into effect on 1 February 1949 to general approval.

There was, however, at least one unintended consequence. The social analysis of *Crescent* reveals that, in aggregate numbers, the re-structuring resulted in a change in complement from the authorized 42 chiefs and petty officers to a new total actually embarked of 62, with a commensurate drop in the number of junior ratings from the authorized 150 to 125.[29] Plainly, there were suddenly too many chiefs and not enough seamen to perform the myriad of shipboard tasks.

In the rigidly hierarchical world of a warship's lower deck, this was clearly a disruption to the established order of shipboard life. When *Athabaskan* had to conduct a fuelling in Manzanillo on 26 February 1949, there were too few junior hands to accomplish this labour-intensive undertaking in the humidity, heat, and primitive surroundings of that port. On top of it all, the executive officer had not yet authorized a change to "tropical routine" (with the workday compressed into the 6:00 a.m. to 12:00 noon time period, ending before the heat of the day), and the morning's fuelling was to be followed by a full afternoon's work.

One of the able seamen who struggled with the lines and hoses that morning had been involved in the incident on board *Ontario* in August 1947. He maintains the only connection between the two events was the sudden, overwhelming feeling of frustration at "what was viewed as an unreasonable work environment or treatment."[30] An ill-conceived order from the executive officer, "to put [their] caps on straight" and off the backs of their heads, was sufficient contributing cause to set 90 men in *Athabaskan* to barricading themselves in their mess decks after lunch.[31]

It is easy to envision a similar set of circumstances attending *Crescent* alongside a rain-swept jetty in Nanjing, China the morning of 15 March. Through the previous night, the duty watch had found itself with too few hands to respond to a numbing sequence of misadventures: humping cases of beer for the British embassy ashore to the jetty and then back on board when the lorry failed to appear; replacing the gangplank when it was washed away in the swollen Yangtze current; standing extended sentry guard duty over the ship and the canteen ashore against looters and other hazards of war. The able seaman who would be the ringleader of the incident the next morning told the Mainguy Commission that "we asked [the] PO2 … to ask the coxswain if he would put us in two watches, as it was too much for the small watches we had," but no action was taken on the request.[32] The next morning, faced with the prospect of humping the beer back to the jetty yet again, 83 men responded to the call "out pipes" by locking themselves into their mess.

In both cases, the sailors enjoyed immediate resolution of their demands. Although neither executive officer was sacked, the men did obtain the direct intervention of their captains to address their plight. *Athabaskan* sailed from Manzanillo the same afternoon, but immediately thereafter assumed a tropical routine. The duty watches in *Crescent* were revised, and greater attention was paid to organizing recreational activities ashore. Divisional officers and chiefs and petty officers in both ships adopted a more active interest in the welfare of their men. Just as importantly, no retribution followed. *The Mainguy Report* records that charges of slackness were laid against certain of those involved in *Athabaskan:* "Each case was heard and those who had no reasonable excuse were cautioned," although, as the commissioners further observed, "Caution is not a punishment."[33] In *Crescent*, the captain heard requests from the men, and the most discomfort anyone had was summoning enough courage to face his commanding officer.

The incident a few days later in *Magnificent* demands re-examination. Where the sailors in *Athabaskan* and *Crescent* had been unaware of the other's actions, those in the aircraft carrier were fully aware of the earlier incidents and their apparent success at no personal cost. On the morning of 20 March 1949, the early call to "Flying stations" at 5:30 a.m. was postponed because of suddenly adverse weather conditions. The men were advised they would be piped again at 8:50 a.m., but in the meantime should follow their regular routine, which included breakfast and then falling in to clean ship at 7:45 a.m. The description in *The Mainguy Report* of what followed is most revealing:

> At "out pipes" (0740), the chief petty officer in charge of the aircraft handlers noticed that the only handlers on the flight deck were leading hands. He sent a petty officer [2nd class] below to see what was wrong. The petty officer reported the men were not coming up…. The chief petty officer then went below and found the men sitting around their mess deck in silence. When he asked them if they were coming out he received no reply…. The state of affairs was reported to the Captain. He proceeded to the mess deck…. At the time of the Captain's visit [at 8:10 a.m.], all ratings present in the mess were then employed in scrubbing out their mess deck. This work, which would have been part of the normal duty of most of the men after 0745, was well advanced.[34]

This "incident" in *Magnificent* was nothing of the same scale or intent of those in *Crescent* or *Athabaskan*. It most likely would not have occurred but for the inspiration of the actions in the destroyers. In the tradition of mass protest in the RCN, it would not have received any attention outside the ship were it not for the interest already provoked by the others. There is evidence that this copy-cat incident is more properly understood as the result of personal differences between the executive officer and the air commander — and indeed that it would not have figured in the deliberations of the Mainguy Commission but for previous bad blood between that same executive officer and one of the commissioners.

The wonder then is that only three ships experienced incidents and not the entire fleet. Again, the rank and trade group restructuring offers a plausible explanation. As most of the new senior rates were to be employed at shore establishments, the new structure was never intended to have a major impact upon ships" complements, other than some minor adjustments to ensure all required branch and trade group positions were filled. The temporary increase in the numbers of senior rates in ships would be balanced in short order by the "drafting" or posting process. This is what happened with the Navy's east coast ships, which did not sail until early March, giving time to effect the changes while still in home port. The West coast ships, however, had sailed at the end of January and had to implement the changes at sea with the existing ships' companies and no infusion of replacements. Compounded by the absence of functioning welfare committees in *Athabaskan* and *Crescent*, the result was, if not predictable, at least understandable.

Intent, however, on exposing the breakdown in relations between officers and ratings, *The Mainguy Report* completely overlooked this basic structural problem, restricted as it was to the lower deck. It is surprisingly easy to demolish the further charges in *The Mainguy Report* as to the lack of a Canadian identity in the RCN, the preference of its officers for British ways, the inadequacy of their training in the Royal Navy, and the alleged collapse of the divisional system.

Brief examples must suffice. *Crescent* had been dispatched to Nanjing by the Canadian government precisely for the "prestige" of having its own warship on the scene, and although otherwise indistinguishable from the other British vessels on the station (or the Australian for that matter), the ship proudly displayed standardized maple leaf emblems on its funnel (the commission reported that they had been removed).[35] Instead, for all the fuss made in the report over

"Canada badges" (i.e., shoulder flashes), not one sailor providing testimony to the commission raised that as an issue critical to them, although when queried by the commissioners whether it was a good idea, they of course agreed.[36]

As for the divisional system, evidence from the quarterly reports placed in the personnel records of *Crescent* crewmembers show that it was indeed an institutionalized practice, but a pattern did emerge in that succeeding reports on any individual were invariably written either in a different unit or by a different officer. This suggests that the commission's attribution of the collapse of the system to the poor training of officers was only in part true: although junior officers schooled in the Royal Navy had a good understanding of the working of the system, the ex-RCNVR officers had had only minimal exposure to it during the war. Rather, the breakdown was due more to the frequent turnover of personnel of all ranks through different ships and establishments as they rotated through training billets — a connection the commission failed to make.[37]

One of the committee's better findings was the lack of functioning welfare committees in the three affected ships. Certainly those would have allowed a more effective form of internal communication to possibly defuse tensions. But because the rank and trade group restructuring issue was restricted to the lower deck, the ineffectiveness of welfare committees could only have been a contributing, not a causal, factor of mutiny. Because records from that period were not always carefully preserved, it is impossible to determine whether such committees existed in the other ships of the fleet, and if this played a role in their being spared any unrest.

The Mainguy Report Revisited

The question remains: Why should the memory of events a half-century past be so wrong? There are any number of institutional, political, and even petty personal reasons for this to be so. The main problem, however, is probably historiographical — the entire period between the end of the Second World War and the outbreak of the Korean Conflict is poorly remembered and understood for practically any service, Canadian or allied. Peacetime military administration and bureaucracy is rarely a compelling avenue of investigation. For the five short years, 1945–1950, researchers generally have found it convenient to acknowledge briefly the retrenchment associated with post war demobilization before progressing into the "real" history of the Cold War, starting with the creation of the North Atlantic Treaty Organisation (NATO) in 1949. In Canada, the diplomatic history of the period has been well covered,[38] but, for the RCN, effectively the sole available source has been *The Mainguy Report*.

For all the attention devoted to this document, however, it has never been subjected to rigorous analysis. Two important considerations have been overlooked: first, the otherwise common acceptance that officially sanctioned commissions of inquiry obfuscate as much as they expose; and, second, the general condemnation with which naval officers of all ranks greeted the publication of the report. Not all of these latter misgivings can be dismissed as the ranting of men feeling too personally the sting of its findings.

It is worth noting that Claxton expressed satisfaction in his memoirs with *The Mainguy Report*, making the self-serving claim that "The whole tone strengthened my hand regarding modernization of the treatment of personnel and the further Canadianization of the Navy."[39] The CNS, however, had identified many of the problems plaguing the naval service and recommended solutions to the minister in October 1947. Although Claxton was not forthcoming with the funds required, other than for the immediate expedient of pay, the naval staff was nonetheless able to move ahead on other fronts, including a fundamental reorganization of the lower deck rank and trade group structure. After the rash of desertions and lock-ins of 1947, there were no incidents in the RCN through 1948. Given the progress advanced in so many areas in spite of continued government parsimony, it is possible to conclude that *The Mainguy Report* did not strengthen Claxton's hand, but forced him to follow through on the remaining money matters it also identified. That Vice-Admiral Grant was not fired on the strength of such a damning report can only be explained by the fact that the minister knew his CNS could have brought him down, too. For Grant — ever the stoic archetype of his service — there was perhaps enough in the grim satisfaction of finally obtaining the appropriations needed to rebuild the post war Navy.[40]

The strains of demobilization and the restructuring of the new peacetime naval establishment were far more severe than has been appreciated by subsequent generations. Having discovered perhaps too easily that there were no communists in the RCN, the commission presumed to expand its mandate to find problems between officers and the men. The apparent breakdown in officer–man relationships, culminating in the incidents of 1949, was far more complex than can be explained by simply fixing blame upon an uncaring officer corps steeped in British ways. But the Mainguy Commission's politically driven imperatives blinded it to reporting on conditions that were extant two years previously (in 1947) and obscured the subsequent reforms.

None of this is to say that the Mainguy Commission and subsequent Report were a wasted exercise. Sometimes the obvious must be stated. After the spring of 1949, the Canadian government could no longer ignore the deprivations that peacetime cutbacks had imposed on the naval service. Within the fleet, no one of any rank could any longer claim innocence of the implications of group insubordination. Nor could they sanction the informal resolution of such action, or be indifferent to welfare committees and the divisional system. Proof of this came swiftly. In early June 1949, even as the Commission still was hearing testimony, a group of junior hands in the frigate HMCS *Swansea* — incensed at poor treatment by their commanding officer — locked themselves in their mess. The response was a forceful entry by armed troops, a rapid court-martial of the senior hands, and their sentencing to 90 days hard labour and dishonourable discharge from the Navy.[41] There seems not to have been any similar trouble since.

The "incidents" in 1949 were really only that — discreet events, and not symptomatic of the widespread discontent that indeed had existed earlier. Rather, they fit the pattern of a larger "tradition of mutiny" that extended to other Commonwealth navies. If they were unusual in any way, it was in hastening the end of that tradition — at least in Canada — through the exposure of a formal investigation and an object lesson in the importance of modern grievance resolution practices.

NOTES

1. Reprinted from Christopher M. Bell and Bruce A. Elleman, eds., *Naval Mutinies of the Twentieth Century: An International Perspective* (London: Frank Cass Publishers, 2003), 246–63.

2. Library and Archives Canada (henceforth LAC), Record Group (henceforth RG) 24, NSS 1650–26, Part 1, Minute by Assistant Chief of Naval Personnel (ACNP), 11 September 1945.

3. J.W. Pickersgill, *My Years with Louis St. Laurent: A Political Memoir* (Toronto: University of Toronto Press, 1975), 75–76. See also Reg Whitaker and Gary

Marcuse, *Cold War Canada: The Making of a National Insecurity State, 1945–1957* (Toronto: University of Toronto Press, 1994), especially chapter 14.

4. *Report on Certain "Incidents" Which Occurred on Board H.M.C. Ships* Athabaskan, Crescent *and* Magnificent *and on Other Matters Concerning the Royal Canadian Navy* (henceforth *The Mainguy Report*) (Ottawa: King's Printer, 1949). The report was named for its chair, Rear-Admiral E. Rollo Mainguy.

5. This status was only overtaken by the Report of the Royal Commission of Inquiry into the Deployment of Canadian Forces to Somalia, *Dishonoured Legacy: The Lessons of the Somalia Affair* (Ottawa: 1997).

6. Arthur Bishop, "Save Our Navy: Walter Hose, Rollo Mainguy," in *Salute: Canada's Military Leaders from Brock to Dextraze* (Toronto: McGraw-Hill Ryerson, 1997), 132; and Tony German, *The Sea Is at Our Gates: The History of the Canadian Navy* (Toronto: McClelland & Stewart, 1990), 211.

7. See, for example, William A. Woodburn, "*The Mainguy Report*: A Canadian Sternmark for the 21st Century" (Canadian Forces Command and Staff College, unpublished "New Horizons Paper," 2 May 1997).

8. Peter Archambault, "Mutiny and the Imperial Tradition: The Canadian Naval Mutinies of 1949 and the Experience of Mutiny in the Royal Navy" (University of New Brunswick, M.A. Thesis, 1991), ii; N.A.M. Rodger, *The Wooden World: An Anatomy of the Georgian Navy* (Annapolis, MD: Naval Institute Press, 1986).

9. William Kaplan, *Everything That Floats: Pat Sullivan, Hal Banks, and the Canadian Seaman's Unions of Canada* (Toronto: University of Toronto Press, 1987), 41–71, *passim;* Jim Green, *Against the Tide: The Story of the Canadian Seaman's Union* (Toronto: Progress Books, 1986), 128–284, *passim.*

10. LAC, Manuscript Group (henceforth MG) 31, Vol. 13–2, E18, Louis de la Chesnaye Audette Papers, "Report From Sea," attached to Lieutenant-Commander David Groos (CO, *Crescent*) to Audette, 15 April 1949.

11. King's Regulations for the RCN (KRCN) article 1.02 (xv) provides: "'division' of a ship or fleet establishment refers to the sections into which men serving in the ship or fleet establishment may be divided for purposes of discipline and to facilitate the training and welfare of the men."

12. As ordered in message NSHQ, CANGEN 54, 281445Z/July/1947, and reproduced in *The Mainguy Report*, 26, welfare committees were introduced

> with the object of providing machinery for free discussion between officers and men of items of welfare and general amenities within the ship or establishment that lie within the powers of decision held by the Captain or his immediate Administrative Authority.... They will not repetition not be entitled to discuss questions of welfare or amenity outside the ship nor will they be entitled to

deal with conditions of service, e.g., discipline, pay, allowances, leave scales, etc. Committees were to comprise the executive officer as chairman and representative of the wardroom, the supply officer as secretary, and elected representatives from each of the lower deck messes.

13. *The Mainguy Report*, 32, 37, and *passim*.

14. Audette Papers, Vol. 13–1 "Random Thoughts on Various Subjects Connected with the Inquiry into the Recent Incidents in H.M.C. Ships," (n.d.), 1, and Audette's handwritten commentary throughout the inquiry transcripts on the character and credibility of each witness. See also L.C. Audette, "The Lower Deck and *The Mainguy Report* of 1949," in J.A. Boutilier, ed., *The RCN in Retrospect, 1910–1968* (Vancouver: University of British Columbia Press, 1982), 248.

15. *The Mainguy Report*, 7–8.

16. This story is well documented, most notably by Marc Milner, *The North Atlantic Run: The Royal Canadian Navy and the Battle for the Convoys* (Toronto: University of Toronto Press, 1985); and Roger Sarty, *Canada and the Battle of the Atlantic* (Montreal: Art Global, 1998).

17. Richard H. Gimblett, "'Too Many Chiefs and Not Enough Seamen': The Lower Deck Complement of a Postwar Royal Canadian Navy Destroyer — The Case of HMCS *Crescent*, March 1949," in *The Northern Mariner*, Vol. 9, No. 3 (July 1999), 1–22.

18. Richard H. Gimblett, "What *The Mainguy Report* Never Told Us: The Tradition of "Mutiny" in the Royal Canadian Navy Before 1949," in *The Canadian Military Journal*, Vol. 1, No. 2 (Summer 2000), 87–94.

19. Gilbert Norman Tucker, *The Naval Service of Canada: Its Official History, Volume 2* (Ottawa: King's Printer, 1952), 328–29.

20. Rodger, *The Wooden World*, 237–38.

21. *Ibid*.

22. LAC, RG 24, 83–84/167, Vol. 1, file 4490–1, Box 1596, CNS to Minister, 8 October 1947.

23. *Ibid*., Vice CNS to CNS, 29 September 1947.

24. *Ibid*., CNS to Minister, 8 October 1947.

25. *Department of National Defence Annual Report[s]* (Ottawa: King's Printer, 1949–53) contain annexes detailing the allotment of the departmental budget.

26. LAC, RG 24, NSS 1650–26, part 2, DNPI (director of naval plans and intelligence) to DNC (director of naval construction), "Manning Priorities — Ships Held in Reserve," 17 September 1947; and *Ibid.*, DNC to DNPI, "C- and V-Class Destroyers Comparison of Habitability," 4 October 1947.

27. Department of National Defence, Directorate of History and Heritage (henceforth DHH), "History of HMCS *Ontario*," 19.

28. This "New Advancement Ladder" was described in the second issue of *Crowsnest* (December 1948), 14–15.

29. Gimblett, "Too Many Chiefs," 17.

30. Interview, Able Seaman (Retired) Dick Berg, Markham, Ontario, 10 October 1998.

31. *The Mainguy Report*, 13–14.

32. Audette papers, Vol. 13–12, "Testimony *Crescent*," 1786.

33. *The Mainguy Report*,14.

34. *Ibid.*, 9–10.

35. On the mission, see Richard H. Gimblett, "Canadian Gunboat: HMCS *Crescent* and the Chinese Civil War, 1949," in Ann L. Griffiths, Peter T. Haydon, and Richard H. Gimblett, eds., *Canadian Gunboat Diplomacy: The Canadian Navy and Foreign Policy* (Halifax, NS: Dalhousie University Centre for Foreign Policy Studies, 2000), 77–94.

36. See, for example, Audette papers, Vol. 13–9, "Testimony *Athabaskan*," 250–52.

37. Gimblett, "Too Many Chiefs," 12.

38. See, for example, John Hilliker and Donald Barry, *Canada's Department of External Affairs, Volume 2* (Montreal: McGill-Queen's University Press, 1995).

39. Claxton, "Autobiography," as quoted in James Eayrs, *In Defence of Canada, Volume 3* (Toronto: University of Toronto Press, 1972), 127.

40. A useful biographical portrait of the man has recently been prepared by Wilfred G. Lund, "Vice-Admiral Harold Grant: Father of the Post-War Royal Canadian Navy," in Bernd Horn and Stephen Harris, eds., *Warrior Chiefs: Perspectives on Senior Canadian Military Leaders* (Toronto: Dundurn Press, 2001), 193–217.

41. Audette papers, Vol. 14–3, "Testimony VAdm Grant," 3510; and interview, Leading Seaman (Retired) George MacNair, Ottawa, Ontario, 16 November 2000.

11

The Storm over Unification of the Armed Forces: A Crisis of Canadian Civil-Military Relations[1]

Daniel P. Gosselin

A fundamental policy dispute between the military and the civil authority can only have one outcome: the civil authority must prevail. Otherwise, we could become subject to military dictatorship. There can only be one result in the present controversy between Mr. Hellyer, the minister of defence, and those officers who oppose the next steps in integration of the armed forces, leading to a degree of unification. The policy is the minister's.

— *Ottawa Citizen,* 16 July 1966[2]

Introduction

FORTY YEARS AGO, ONE OF the most important public clashes in Canadian military history surfaced as Minister of National Defence (MND), Paul T. Hellyer aggressively pushed the government's initiative to unify the existing services — the Canadian Army, the Royal Canadian Air Force and the Royal Canadian Navy — into a single service. Although unification of the three services into the Canadian Armed Forces (CF) did not officially become law until 1 February 1968, the civil-military crisis reached its zenith in July 1966 with the public opposition and the firing of Rear-Admiral William M. Landymore, commander of Maritime Command, and the resignation of several general and flag officers, including Vice-Chief of the Defence Staff (VCDS), Lieutenant-General Robert W. Moncel.

The substantial changes that Hellyer instituted to strengthen civil control of the military and the controversy that broke over the merit of implementing the pioneering concept of unification combined to produce the most serious crisis of civil-military relations in Canada since the Second World War.[3] The roots of this civil-military crisis can be traced back to the late 1950s and early 1960s, when defence issues caused the downfall of the Diefenbaker government and strained relations between the military and the politicians.[4] Consequently, Hellyer arrived at Defence in the spring of 1963 with a clear mandate to reform the Canadian military. The new minister had strong views about the need for a comprehensive review of defence policy, and he believed that integration of the command structure of the armed forces was necessary to achieve bureaucratic control of the military, streamline the organization, and reduce the problems of tri-service inefficiencies.[5] Service resistance to his integration efforts between 1964 and 1966 convinced him that only unification of the three services would achieve the objectives he envisioned and truly institutionalize the changes he was seeking.[6] An ambitious politician, he moved aggressively and rapidly to transform Defence and, in doing so, faced major roadblocks along the way.

As opposition to his initiative developed, especially in 1966 and 1967, and senior officers started to opt for early retirement rather than put into service what they perceived to be a flawed policy being implemented recklessly, suspicion and resentment of Hellyer grew. But it was Landymore's "sacking [that] galvanized the battle over Hellyer's plans," a situation that was thoroughly exploited by the opposition parties in Parliament. Anti-unification organizations, formed by veterans and reservists, also started putting pressure on the Liberal government.[7] The press quickly jumped on the controversial issue, and sensationalized it by turning it into a "Revolt of the Admirals." Canadian newspapers saw the crisis for what it truly was; a civil-military relations crisis about the right of the government to assert control over the military.[8]

To this day, however, the dominant perception that remains of the period from 1964–1967 is one of a crisis that was, for the most part, a fight between Hellyer and the officer corps over the potential marginalization of the history, identity, and traditions of the services that unification would provoke. This view is incorrect and represents an incomplete depiction of the debate. There can be no doubt that what was at stake for Hellyer and the government was more than uniforms and traditions: "[T]he issue, I insisted, was civilian control

MINISTER OF NATIONAL DEFENCE PAUL T. HELLYER SPEAKS WITH
ROYAL CANADIAN NAVY OFFICERS IN 1966.

(Department of National Defence, Cardiff, Canadian Forces Joint Imagery Centre PL 66)

of the military. Integration was the policy of the Government of Canada, and it was the responsibility of serving officers to implement rather than oppose it."[9] In contemporary literature, the term *civil control* means that the legitimate responsibility for the direction and actions of the military rests with civilians outside the military/ defence establishment. In democracies, civilian direction is meant to imply direction by elected civilians. This definition does not speak about the moral or ethical foundation for this civilian direction, but it implies that the military has no right to act on its own.[10]

Remarkably, the historiography of the 1960s unification crisis remains limited, and has focused mostly on recounting chronologically the implementation challenges of integration and unification, and the impact on the services.[11] The government-initiated studies of integration and unification in the 1970s and 1980s have tended to focus on the management of defence within the headquarters, on the merits and disadvantages of unification,[12] and on the problems of civilianization of the CF that resulted from Hellyer's initiative.[13] Other assessments have been more limited in scope, such as one study conducted in the early 1970s that analyzed in detail the restructuring of the headquarters and the organization of the regional and functional commands.[14]

Accounts of the 1966–1967 "revolt" controversy have tended to be even more limited, and generally one-sided. David P. Burke's essay, "Hellyer and Landymore: The Unification of the Canadian Forces and an Admiral's Revolt," portrays Landymore as a campaigner ordained to destroy Hellyer and unification in Parliament, and basically lays the blame on the admirals for the unification crisis.[15] In time, Navy proponents and others have provided a counter point to this one-dimensional viewpoint, by stressing the many organizational and operational problems resulting from unification, and by bringing to light Hellyer's single-mindedness and his disregard for professional expertise as he pursued the initiative.[16] Although Hellyer was not the architect of the integrated National Defence Headquarters — created with the merger in 1972 of the two formerly separate civilian departmental and military headquarters, over the years many analysts have argued that it was Hellyer's dominant ideas from integration and unification that ultimately planted the seeds for increased civilianization at the Department of National Defence (DND) and a corresponding loss of military ethos.[17]

By focusing on the contentious organizational changes that unification brought about, or on the sensational Landymore–Hellyer controversy, the more important issue of civil control of the military has been excluded from the discussion, except for two works. R.B. Byers's excellent, but brief, study on civil-military relations focused largely on the role of the military within the Canadian political system, and on attitudes and individual service reactions towards increased civil control. In *Chiefs of Defence*, political scientist Douglas Bland examined the influence of the office of the chief of the defence staff (CDS) on defence policy over the period 1964 to 1994, and, in doing so, touched on many issues affecting relations between the military leaders and the elected politicians.[18] Nevertheless those two studies have been limited in dealing with the fundamental ingredients that combined to produce a serious crisis of civil-military relations.

The purpose of this chapter, therefore, is to examine an important phase of Canadian civil-military relations and to highlight the core issues that pitted Hellyer against his senior military advisers. It contends that, contrary to the prevailing view that opposition to the unification concept arose from a service fight over uniforms and traditions, the unification controversy that took place between 1964 and 1967 was a *bona fide* crisis of civil-military relations in Canada.

This chapter is divided in four parts. The first part reviews the context of the period immediately preceding Hellyer's arrival at DND. This overview sets the stage for the second portion, which is an examination of the main ideas behind the development of the 1964 *Defence White Paper* and the concept of unification, including a review of the specific strategy adopted by Hellyer to implement the government's initiative. The third part outlines the arguments advanced by the senior military officers as they struggled to implement integration and unification, highlights the challenges they faced in their dealings with Hellyer, and reviews the events that led to the tempest of 1966–1967. The politics of civil-military relations are about relations between the state (represented by politicians) and the corps of professional military officers as the two groups discuss issues of defence. Consequently, the final part of this chapter addresses the state of the civil-military debate in the late 1950s and early 1960s, which was pivotal in shaping the views of the key players involved in the unification debate. This part ends by outlining how this crisis eventually developed and why at that particular time.

The Diefenbaker Defence Debacle and Winds of Change

The late 1950s and early 1960s in Canada was controversial period for Canada's military, and it had a significant influence on the new Liberal Government's approach to dealing with defence issues. More important, the nature of the defence issues that surfaced during this period had a profound effect on relations between the politicians and the military leaders in Canada throughout the 1960s and onwards.

A series of separate but interconnected events took place in the period that convinced Hellyer and the Liberal government of the necessity to issue a new defence policy, strengthen civil control of the military, restructure the organization, and implement the concept of unification. Those events included the Diefenbaker government defence policy chaos between 1958 and 1963, the 1962 Cuban missile crisis, and the 1960 Royal Commission on Government Reorganization.

Jon McLin, an analyst of Canada's defence policy of the period, echoed the sentiments of many when he stated that "[t]he years 1957–1963 were a time of turmoil in Canada's defense [*sic*] policy," with many controversial defence issues marking the period.[19] Canadian historian Jack Granatstein was less gracious in his assessment of a period he called a "defence débâcle."[20] The problems that the Diefenbaker government faced at the time centred largely on Canada's military contributions to its North American and North Atlantic alliances.

First, there was the lasting impression that Prime Minister John G. Diefenbaker had been rushed by the military into his decision to establish a joint international command for North American Air Defense (NORAD). The new Conservative government had been elected in late June 1957 and the establishment of an integrated command was announced by both the Canadian and American governments on 1 August 1957. General Charles Foulkes, then the chair of the Chiefs of Staff Committee, even acknowledged to a parliamentary defence committee years later that the military and the new MND, George Pearkes, had "stampeded the incoming [Diefenbaker] government with the NORAD agreement."[21] Second, the cancellation of the CF-105 Avro Arrow aircraft, the selection of the Bomarc anti-aircraft missile, and the acquisition of CF-101B "Voodoo" interceptor aircraft were all highly controversial defence policy and procurement issues that strained relations with the United States. Finally, the re-equipping and changing of the role of the Canadian units allocated to the North Atlantic Treaty Organisation (NATO), with respect to the arming of those aircraft with nuclear warheads, as well as the indecision of the government with regard to the control and deployment of nuclear weapons added to the complexity of the issues being debated between the senior military officers and the politicians.[22] The resolution of several of those contentious defence issues strained relations between the government and its military advisers and eventually affected the solution of other military problems later.[23]

The low point of this period, however, was reached during the Cuban missile crisis of October 1962, after indecision by Diefenbaker and his cabinet led to "the near collapse of civil-military relations in Canada when the control of the armed forces passed briefly out of the government's hands."[24] As Peter Haydon, author of a study on Canada's actions during the crisis, notes, "[t]he shortcomings in the Canadian concept of civil control of the military became evident during the Cuban missile crisis."[25] The lack of coordination between the various levels of the command structure and the high command, including the political executive, became a serious problem. The military response to the crisis resulted in independent action by the services in the belief that the international situation was deteriorating rapidly. Granatstein contends that, over the preceding years, the military "links between the Canadian and American military ... had grown so close that the senior officers [had] placed their service interests and their assessment of the situation ahead of their government's."[26] It is therefore undeniable that the event "had a lasting effect on Canadian defence policy and the structure of the Canadian military" and, as Haydon argues, "indirectly became one of the issues underlying the reorganization of the Canadian Forces introduced by the Liberals in 1964."[27]

The third element that shaped the views of Hellyer and others in government towards the need for greater integration of the services and for increased civil control of the military was the report of the Royal Commission on Government Reorganization. The federal commission — known as the Glassco Commission, named after its chair — had been mandated to review, in the interest of management efficiency, the organization and methods of the federal government. One of the reports of the commission focused solely on DND, because of its large size, composition, and the range and cost of its activities.[28] Hellyer relied to a great extent on the conclusions of the commission "which had done such a splendid job of exposing the waste and extravagance resulting from duplication and triplication."[29] General Jean V. Allard, who became CDS in 1966, related in his memoirs that when Hellyer summoned his senior officers to Ottawa in early 1964, he "wanted to talk about a reorganization resulting from the Glassco Report."[30] In the end, the work of the commission proved to be important because it "was to provide the authority and validity to concepts that others [including Hellyer] would champion later."[31]

Thus, by 1963, the armed forces and the Department were "under increasing strain with no knowledge of where to go."[32] Disparate structures and processes resulting from the existence of three independent services tended to cause confusion within defence administration, through inefficiencies created by duplicate and triplicate organizations, and in a divided command and control structure created by separate headquarters and command formations. Personnel, administrative, and military equipment costs were also rising dramatically to the point that if the current trend in expenditures continued, there would be no money for capital equipment by the end of the decade.[33] It was evident that the military would not get additional funding under the new Liberal government that was elected in April 1963, as Lester B. Pearson's government was definitely more inclined to spend on social programs than on defence.[34]

Events in the years before the Liberals took power in 1963 had brought to the surface an inability of senior military leaders to embrace the new national realities and had highlighted a "divide" between the military leaders and the government's elected politicians.[35] Prime Minister Pearson had concluded that the Diefenbaker "government's mishandling of the defence issues and the resultant disintegration of their ranks was the main reason for their downfall."[36] Pearson also believed the defence department to be a political liability, and that he "was not about to allow what happened to the Conservatives to happen to his government."[37] To Hellyer and his colleagues, it was clear that tighter political control of the armed forces was necessary to prevent similar problems for the Liberals. In short, by 1963 confidence in the direction of the defence policy and how it was being administered at DND was low and "conditions were right for the introduction of new ideas and for a strong minister to push them through a supposedly ossified defence establishment."[38]

Hellyer's Ideas and His Implementation Strategy

Hellyer, who had been influential in the defence debate during 1961 and 1962,[39] arrived at DND after having spent the previous five years as the Liberal opposition defence critic to the Conservative government, and having had the opportunity to immerse himself in the many defence issues that surfaced during the period.[40] Because of his alertness and vigour as a defence critic, especially after the political confusion of the Diefenbaker years, Hellyer had developed a solid reputation and was welcomed at DND.[41] He was a Member of Parliament since 1949, with hopes that his achievements would help him to become an obvious choice to succeed Pearson.[42] He was ambitious, and to bring about the changes he wanted at defence, Hellyer had to act fast.

The minister quickly sent the message that things would run differently at DND. He refused to sign any document in his first 30 days in office; further, he suspended equipment purchases and cancelled outright the Air Force's CF-104 aircraft replacement program.[43] Within a few months in office, Hellyer quickly came to realize that the armed forces was not offering a unified strategic approach to the government in the formulation of defence policy. He was greatly disturbed that "wittingly or otherwise, each service was preparing for a different kind of war." His realization that there was a "lack of coordination at the top" of the defence establishment that had resulted in a "seemingly haphazard determination of priorities" also had a profound influence on him.[44] The defence controversies that surfaced during the Diefenbaker period also confirmed to Hellyer that the three services based their plans and estimates on the assumption that a strong Navy, Army, or Air Force was good and essential for national defence without regard for the needs of the other services.[45] The new minister was determined to address these serious failings, and he used the March 1964 *White Paper on Defence* to start the process of change.

The *White Paper on Defence* outlined most of the concepts that would serve as guideposts to guide Hellyer throughout his tenure as minister. The document was a landmark defence document in many ways, but particularly because "it was an attempt to build a defence policy on a Canadian foundation."[46] To Hellyer, the key elements of this policy consisted of creating one national defence strategy for Canada, a single coherent defence policy, a single war plan, a unified system of command, and a single higher loyalty to the CF.

This policy document was noteworthy for several other reasons as well. While it certainly outlined a vision for defence that Pearson was comfortable with — the prime minister had personally revised the draft and made changes to it, it is important to note that Hellyer had almost single-handedly written the policy, inserting ideas that he firmly believed addressed ongoing defence concerns and could be implemented rapidly.[47] More important, the White Paper made known that the integration of the headquarters and the creation of functional commands "will be the first step towards a unified defence force for Canada."[48] With the concept of unification, Hellyer sought a military establishment that would cease to continually resolve problems and develop policies from a service perspective, and act more from a national perspective. With the release of the White Paper, the government agenda on unification was exposed for all to discuss and challenge, but few really believed that the initiative would come to pass.[49]

Although setting out the basic philosophy and rationale for the unification of the armed forces, the *White Paper on Defence* did not provide an elaborate plan and timeline to progress with integration and achieve unification: "No attempt has been made to set down hard and fast rules for future policy and development.... The paper is a charter, a guide, not a detailed and final blueprint," stated the White Paper.[50] This left the government, and more specifically Hellyer, with the flexibility to make adjustments as he worked out the details and as circumstances dictated, and to proceed towards unification of the CF with few constraints. Finally, unlike earlier integration attempts that were characterized by their haphazard nature and parochialism, this time, the integration of the services — and eventually unification — *was* a government policy to be implemented.[51] Hellyer would often reiterate this point when opposition to integration would intensify.

Understanding the strategy adopted by Hellyer to implement the new defence policy is important as it allows one to better appreciate his priorities as he moved towards unification. It also assists in explaining why the unification crisis did not arise until 1966, two years after the controversial policy was tabled. Hellyer's implementation stratagem was guided by two dominant themes that were central to the achievement of his strategic objectives: those were the requirement to increase civil control of the military and the need to create economies in the defence budget.

Hellyer strongly believed that the mechanisms of civil control of the Canadian military needed a major overhaul, which could be best achieved through a centralization of the control and administration of the CF into one CDS, one single defence staff and one Defence Council. Barely two weeks after the White Paper was presented to the Commons, Hellyer introduced Bill C-90 (*Integration of the Headquarters Staff Act*). Because the existing services were legal entities with the three service chiefs reporting independently to the minister, Hellyer had to proceed through Parliament to amend the *National Defence Act* (NDA). In his address to Parliament he stated that "complete integration of the forces [commences] at the top with the integration of the command structure."[52] Hellyer considered this first step of integrating the top of the military structure "perhaps the most important move in the integration of the armed forces," as it allowed him to rapidly centralize decision-making at DND.[53] He believed that only an integrated staff and headquarters would ensure policy coherence, reduce overhead costs, and realize greater administrative efficiencies. A few months later, in August 1964, Air Chief Marshal (ACM) Frank Miller was appointed as the first CDS.

The Glassco Commission had raised concerns about the excessive military influence of the senior defence military council, the Chiefs of Staff Committee, stating that "the military character of the group raises doubt as to the reality of civilian control if the minister places excessive reliance on it."[54] Thus, building on the recommendations of the commission, Hellyer also moved to strengthen the civil staff under the deputy minister to simplify "the problems of civil control," and to "assist [him] in the control and management of the armed forces."[55] Besides revamping the Defence Council — which resulted in the exclusion of the service chiefs from the council, Hellyer rationalized that "it is essential that there be a strong civil staff in the defence department *outside* the military chain of command for analysing and reviewing military requirements and the use of resources made available for defence." Implied in all these changes at the top of the defence structure was a clear statement by the minister that, from now on, the influence of the senior military advisers would be reduced and more limited to "carry out their military responsibilities."[56]

But Hellyer had more changes in mind for Canada's military forces than simply national headquarters restructuring. He had explained that if Canada was to maintain useful forces to meet its national and international commitments, there were only two choices open to the government: "We had to increase defence spending or reorganize our forces. The decision was to reorganize."[57] As a result, he viewed a major reorganization of the defence forces to be the only means of freeing up resources for future capital equipment acquisitions and building a force structure with maximum flexibility.[58] Hellyer had guessed that with his proposed reorganization "it will be possible to reduce service requirements by 10,000 [persons] without affecting our operational elements," with the aim of increasing the share of the defence budget allotted to capital equipment from 14 to 25 percent.[59] He was convinced that the combination of a major defence reorganization, the establishment of a streamlined bureaucracy, and the modernization of defence management methods would help to achieve the desired economies. Consequently, within the prerogative of his authority as the minister, by 1966 Hellyer had changed the field command structure, creating six functional commands in lieu of the three services' 11 subordinate headquarters.[60]

In spite of the progress made with integration, which had contributed to achieving reduction in duplication and triplication of facilities and services, constant resistance to his integration efforts since 1964 convinced Hellyer that only unification of the services would truly institutionalize the changes he was seeking. To him, unification was "the end objective of a logical and evolutionary progression."[61] Accordingly, in November 1966, Hellyer tabled the bill that would reorganize the existing three services into the Canadian Armed Forces, Bill C-243, *The Canadian Forces Reorganization Act.*

Like Bill C-90, it was necessary for Hellyer to seek Parliamentary approval to change the law and create a single service. The bill received little debate in the House of Commons and was quickly referred to the Standing Committee on National Defence (Defence Committee), which started its hearings in early February 1967. The requirement to enact bills in Parliament forced Hellyer to account to Parliament regularly and publicly for his integration and unification plans. Between 1964 and 1967, Members of Parliament met in special committees and debated both Bill C-90 and Bill C-243, hearing evidence from many witnesses, including senior serving officers who were not supportive of the minister's initiative. Bill C-243 was debated in 55 highly partisan sittings of the Defence Committee in early 1967, and the government ultimately had to set a limit on debate in the House to get final passage of the bill in April 1967.[62]

As he moved decisively to achieve his objectives, Hellyer made his best efforts to influence the policy process to good effect. Unfortunately, the "Machiavellian" tactics he used inside DND between 1964 and 1967 created an atmosphere of distrust between himself and his senior military advisers, culminating with the unification controversy in 1966–1967.[63] Hellyer has been characterized as forthright, self-confident, intelligent, and politically clever; but he was also described as ambitious, arrogant, and in haste to achieve his objectives.[64] As Canadian historian Desmond Morton remarked, Hellyer was "an aggressive man with few of the gentler political graces."[65] Certainly, by 1966, he had lost the complete confidence, trust, and respect of his senior officer corps, and hit troubled waters.[66]

Damn the Torpedoes: Running Too Fast and Too Far?

The senior officer corps that Hellyer encountered when he arrived at DND in 1963 had a completely different background than his own. Although his two immediate predecessors had significant experience in the military, including serving in command positions during the Second World War, Hellyer only had his brief and frustrating experiences as a non-commissioned member with both the Air Force and the Army towards the end of the war.[67] Additionally, Hellyer was not even 40 years old when he assumed the defence portfolio.

Although he may have lacked extensive military experience, Hellyer had compensated by taking opportunities to become acquainted with current defence issues before becoming the minister. For example, in 1961 and 1962 he visited bases in Europe and in the United States, to acquire more knowledge of Canadian military presence and agreements in those areas. Furthermore, when he became minister, he also sought to use ideas from some of his NATO counterparts, including Robert S. McNamara, the U.S. Secretary of Defence under President Kennedy.[68] McNamara had faced his own crisis of civil-military relations during the 1962 Cuban missile crisis when he had a confrontation with the chief of naval operations over the execution of the naval blockade of Soviet ships. McNamara continued to face challenges inside the American military establishment as he attempted to establish civil control over the military through its planning and budget process.[69] At the beginning of his term, in October 1963, Hellyer had visited McNamara specifically to discuss "methods of reorganization."[70] In his memoirs, Hellyer speaks fondly of his relationship with McNamara and the "unspoken bond of kindred spirits" that they shared.[71] Subsequently, in his four years as the minister, Hellyer had many occasions to share his frustrations with McNamara concerning the implementation of unification and to learn lessons from American experiences,[72] as well as to draw strength from other NATO defence ministers who were facing similar challenges within their organizations.

Hellyer's senior military advisers were all hardened veterans of earlier conflicts. For instance, Rear-Admiral Jeffry V. Brock and Landymore had served with distinction during the Second World War, with Brock having also commanded the first naval task group that deployed to Korea in 1951. General J.V. Allard, first commander of Mobile Command who became CDS in July 1966, and the VCDS, Lieutenant-General Moncel, had both commanded brigades during the Second World War, with Allard having also commanded the Canadian brigade during the Korean War. As a consequence, the generals and admirals advising Hellyer were neither bureaucrats nor managers; they were leaders who had reached senior positions in the military because of their extensive operational experience.

On the whole, most officers who testified at the Defence Committee expressed support for integrating several defence functions, such as the headquarters and some support organizations. Even Landymore acknowledged in his testimony to the Defence Committee in February 1967 that he agreed in principle with integration, but stated that the initiative "should confine itself to unification at the top."[73] As integration progressed between 1964 and 1966, and unification efforts accelerated in late 1966 and 1967,

Rear-Admiral William M. Landymore during hearings concerning the Canadian Forces Reorganization Act, Ottawa, Ontario, 1967.
(Department of National Defence, Duncan Cameron, Library and Archives Canada PA 143963)

the main lines of arguments frequently advanced by the officer corps against the initiative principally centred on four areas: the excessive and unnecessary speed with which Hellyer was progressing; the lack of plans to achieve unification; the absence of consultation by Hellyer; and the negative impact on morale that the loss of traditions, identity, and uniforms would have on the services, and the resulting detrimental effect on the operational effectiveness of the Canadian military.

In retrospect, it seems evident that the service chiefs never fully appreciated Hellyer's political timetable nor the mass of changes he had set in motion, particularly with regard to unification. The Pearson government of 1963 was a minority government, conscious that the previous government had lasted only nine months and then collapsed because of controversial defence issues. Accordingly, Hellyer was acutely aware that his tenure as the MND could end suddenly. Another federal election was held in 1965 and, though the Liberals were re-elected with more seats, they failed to gain a majority. By early 1966, he also knew that Pearson would not lead the Liberal Party into another election, and was likely going to resign in 1967. It was evident that Hellyer had definite aspirations to the nation's top political post.

Although some officers, like the CDS, ACM Miller, spoke of accomplishing unification in several years, Hellyer visualized a more accelerated timetable. He had revealed his objective in a circular letter to all members of the armed forces and civilian employees as early as April 1964, stating in part that "[t]he third and final step will be the unification of the three services.... It is reasonable to expect that it will be three or four years before it will be possible to take this action."[74] Senior officers, like Moncel, complained that the "process of unification ... appeared to be moving on an uncharted course at a very, very high speed towards a very, very dim destination." To many officers, Hellyer "speeded up unification solely because it suited his political ambitions."[75] However, to the minister, those arguing that integration was proceeding too fast were those "who have never really endorsed the idea of integration at all and in some cases were adamantly opposed to it."[76] Hellyer knew well that if he wanted to be successful in implementing this defence policy he had to move aggressively and quickly to overcome service resistance and bureaucratic inertia endemic to large organizations like DND. This resolute approach would also demonstrate the seriousness of the government's commitments to transforming Canadian defence.

A frequent criticism made of Hellyer and his initiative was the lack of plan or blueprint for achieving unification.[77] In tabling the 1964 White Paper, the minister had admitted that he had no definite plans beyond the first step, and that these plans would be developed progressively as more integration was taking place and adjustments made along the way. While he had initiated several ministerial study groups soon after taking over as the minister in 1963 to provide a foundation for the *White Paper on Defence*, this time it would be the responsibilities of the "defence staff to work out the problems" of implementing integration.[78] Because unification was a concept that remained to be developed in detail, Hellyer had "made no plan or organizational model available to his colleagues or adversaries," and as a result had left his senior military staff in the dark about his ultimate plans.[79]

Without the benefit of a detailed plan or timetable to assess the long-term implications of unification and with a minority government that could fall at anytime, senior officers opposed to unification likely assumed they had time on their side. Top military advisers counselled Hellyer to adopt a "go-slow policy" and assumed about "five years as a reasonable time to complete the job."[80] They most likely surmised that Hellyer might not be the minister long enough to see unification through and, in any case, that they would be able to block unification at the appropriate time when the plans were more fully developed. This seemed to be the rationale underlying Moncel's explanation to the Defence Committee of his decision to stay after 1964, even when it was then apparent that unification was Hellyer's ultimate goal:

> I took part in it for the time I did in the mistaken belief that possibly I could have some influence and attempt to slow it down…. On no less than six occasions I went to my chief [ACM Miller] and said "I can go on no longer," and in each case he told me, "Wait it out, you have simply got to stay," and I was gullible and I said, "All right, I will wait it out," and I hung on for another month, and another month, and another — the same type of intervention, and we felt surely somebody must listen to what we were trying to say. Finally, it was apparent that the lines were really gone and then there was no point; so I went to my chief and said, "I am out."[81]

Besides the excessive speed of implementation and the lack of a plan to guide unification, one of the most significant criticisms of the unification plan was the totalist attitude that seemed to have been adopted by Hellyer, without consideration of the special needs of the various elements to be unified. Retired officers who testified to the Defence Committee reported evidence of "mistrust, intrigue, hostility, and confusion in DND and CFHQ [Canadian Forces Headquarters]. Officers were asked to write a plan that had no foundation or precedent." Bland contends that Hellyer tended "to be suspicious and even hostile toward those who might question his aims" and that he would use a "series of clever misdirections in order to keep his critics off balance."[82] Senior military advisers were seldom consulted as he developed his unification ideas and "[m]ost senior officers heard about the latest development through press releases issued by Hellyer's personal assistant" or from subordinate officers.[83] Moncel said that, during 1965–1966 when he was VCDS, he had only two meetings with the minister to discuss unification, and he further observed that Hellyer frequently circumvented the CDS and senior military staff to seek advice and find support from more junior military members.[84]

Between 1964 and 1966, an atmosphere of suspicion between the minister and his senior officers developed, with Hellyer losing the confidence of several of his senior military staff well before the crisis of July 1966. Despite this, the minister knew that the group of senior officers he was dealing with was not monolithic, and that each service had its own position on integration and unification, yet another factor that compounded the divisions at the top of the defence establishment. Since the services could not offer coherent "unified" arguments against integration and unification — confirming the point that the minister had been making about lack of strategic unity, Hellyer's efforts to integrate the services were facilitated by this internal divisiveness.

Hellyer could always find other officers to replace the disgruntled who had chosen to depart. The officers who stayed either believed they could best influence the future of the CF by remaining and working with the minister, or were prepared to go along because they envisioned benefits for their service within aspects of unification. General Allard, for instance, saw his appointment as commander of Mobile Command in 1965 as an opportunity to "ensure that the Army would have a strong voice in the wake of integration." He was also convinced that to correct earlier imbalances between the services, he "would have to impose an 'Army' point of view during the integration process." Later, as CDS, he believed his appointment provided an opportunity to positively influence all three services and promote the advancement of francophones at all levels.[85]

It now seems evident that the CDS and the service chiefs were unsuccessful in their efforts to voice objections to the potential adverse impact that integration and unification would have on the operational effectiveness of the forces. Miller, by then retired for nine months, proudly testified to the Defence Committee in March 1967 that "[t]hroughout the period of reorganization [1964–1966] we have maintained our operational capability."[86] At the same time there is no indication that Hellyer was concerned with this aspect of integration. Even though the minister had stated that the "White Paper of 1964 would not have recommended integration … if we had not been certain of the improved capacity of a unified force to meet the demands of modern warfare," operational effectiveness was not a main concern of his defence restructuring.[87] In fact during his address to Parliament for the second reading of Bill C-90, Hellyer stressed that his emphasis for the reorganization was on reducing the duplication of services, increasing efficiency, and strengthening civil control.[88] As Canadian historian David Bercuson has indicated, "[t]he creation of a truly effective fighting force did not figure in the government's agenda."[89] Accordingly, arguments from the service chiefs that unification — including the loss of tradition, identity of the services, and distinct uniforms — would undermine morale and esprit de corps, eventually affecting adversely the operational capabilities of the armed forces, were summarily dismissed by Hellyer.[90] He was more interested in unification as a means to make better use of personnel and to "broaden the opportunities available to service-motivated and expensively trained personnel," reflecting in many ways his own frustrating wartime experience with the services.[91]

With the enactment of Bill C-90 on 1 August 1964, the heads of the three services were eliminated and in their place the CDS had the authority to control and administer the CF. Nevertheless, although the service chiefs had disappeared, the three separate services continued to exist and maintain differences among them that complicated the implementation of common standards.[92] Subsequently, Hellyer said in February 1967 that because "it would be impossible to maintain such an 'integrated force' over a long period of time," the formal elimination of the services and creation of a unified force was the next logical step.[93] In early 1966, senior officers finally realized that Hellyer and the government were serious about unification of the services, and that it was now almost inevitable. During spring 1966, with the single staff and functional commands established, the minister "suddenly speeded things up."[94]

In light of these events, it becomes much easier to place the July 1966 Hellyer–Landymore feud and the ensuing crisis in context. Opposed to unification and Hellyer's methods, a number of officers, such as lieutenant-generals Frank J. Fleury and Moncel, had decided to retire, prematurely, but quietly. However, Landymore, a champion of service efficiency and naval traditions, had continued to openly fight integration and had told the Defence Committee in June 1966 of the many problems that unification was creating for his command and his personnel. Between his appearances in front of the Committee on 23 June and the press on 15 July 1966, events quickly escalated.[95]

According to Landymore, he met the minister on the 24 June, the day following his testimony, and later on 12 July. On both dates Landymore tried to persuade Hellyer to preserve the identity of the Royal Canadian Navy but failed.[96] He was told by Hellyer after the meeting of 12 July that he was being "compulsory retired," or, in effect, fired.[97] With few avenues left to him, Landymore met with the prime minister shortly after, but nothing came out of it.[98] Having exhausted this last channel of appeal, Landymore had taken "every step possible to make known the seriousness of the situation."[99] The next day, back in Halifax and knowing he was leaving the service, Landymore provided an interview to a number of reporters in which he denounced integration and criticized the minister. The story, and Hellyer's reaction to it, appeared in major newspapers across the country on 15 and 16 July, along with speculation that more admirals were about to be fired.[100] Hellyer, who at that time was unsure whether Landymore had broken any service regulations, took the offensive and was quoted as follows:

> It boils down to strictly a matter of whether the military tail is going to wag the dog; whether the Government is going to set and carry out defense [sic] policy or whether it is going to be dictated by a small group of officers. The law of the land puts the military under civilian control and this is the way it's going to be run for a change.[101]

To Hellyer, this issue was one of civil supremacy over the military.

Unfortunately, the furor over the events surrounding Landymore's objections to unification did not end with his retirement in July. Issues pertaining to the minister's apparent prior "censoring" of Landymore's brief that was given to the Defence Committee on 23 June 1966, surfaced in the fall, and again during his testimony of February 1967.[102] But, as Burke notes, "If it had not been a statement made by Hellyer a week later, the Landymore affair might have rested there."[103] Hellyer, tired at the end of a long day of testimony to the Defence Committee in February 1967, when asked if Landymore had been fired because he spoke publicly to the press, retorted that "Admiral Landymore was fired for 18 months of consistent disloyalty to the people he was paid to serve."[104] With the minister's charge of disloyalty — a strong statement he eventually had to retract, the controversy was once more in the national headlines. In the end, seven RCN flag officers retired or were fired in 1966, and two Army generals decided to retire when General J.V. Allard was named CDS in July 1966. By 1967, more than a dozen very senior officers had accepted early retirement or had been fired.[105]

Civil-Military Relations and Pressure for Civil Control

> *The military is jealous of its corporate status and privileges. Anxiety to preserve its autonomy provides one of the most widespread and powerful of the motives for intervention. In its defensive form it can lead to something akin to military syndicalism — an insistence that the military and only the military are entitled to determine on matters as recruitment, training, numbers, and equipment. In its most aggressive form it can lead to the military demand to be the ultimate judge on all matters affecting the armed forces.*
>
> — S.E. Finer, *The Man on Horseback*[106]

During his term in office, Hellyer did more than reorganize the CF and the department; indeed, he fundamentally changed the nature of civil-military relations in Canada. As the MND, he was convinced that the institutional structures in place were not adequate to ensure civilian supremacy over the military. If there were any reservations in Hellyer's mind regarding this issue, there is no doubt that the constant resistance of several senior officers and Landymore's public statements had reinforced Hellyer's belief in the need to enforce civil control of the military. Byers suggests that although "the role of the military within the Canadian political system has been less influential than it is in many [other] states,"[107] and the principle of civilian supremacy has never been impaired in Canada, nevertheless, "the problem of civil-military relationships is one that, in one form or another, all societies have to deal with."[108] Hellyer decided to deal with this dilemma during his time in office.

With the recommendations of the Glassco Commission to support him, Hellyer was convinced that the civilian leadership needed a stronger role in the resolution of defence questions, and this started with the minister. He was of "the view that over the years the military had increased its role to the point where civilian control was being endangered by the inability of the civilians and politicians to assess adequately the proposals presented to them."[109] As a result the policies that he introduced revamped the Defence Council, "shifting the emphasis from excessive reliance on his senior military advisers," created the position of the CDS to "permit an effective exercise of civilian control ... and civilian direction in the carrying out of defence policy," and increased the role of the deputy minister.[110]

The issue of civil-military relations was an important topic of debate in Western militaries and governments in the late 1950s and early 1960s. The early 1950s had seen the public controversy between President Harry Truman and General Douglas MacArthur over the expansion of the Korean conflict and the bombing of Chinese bases. With discussions about the control of nuclear weapons being debated in the United States, political scientist Samuel P. Huntington had published in 1957 his seminal work *The Soldier and the State*, setting out a radical new theory of civil-military relations. Huntington had laid out a proposed pattern of civil-military relations using what he termed as "objective control," which puts forward the thesis that the most effective form of civilian control of the military is that which maximizes the professionalism of the officer corps, by isolating soldiers from politics and giving these officers autonomy within a clearly defined military sphere. He contrasted "objective control" with "subjective control" that aims to maximize civilian power in relations with the military.[111] In the wake of Huntington's treatise, analytical work on alternate theories of civil-military relations emerged in the late 1950s and early 1960s, and, in the aftermath of the Cuban missile crisis, it is certain that Hellyer and his group of general and flag officers had to be aware of this important discussion, and likely had strong views as to where the civil-military divide of responsibility laid.[112]

Although Huntington had his share of critics over the years, with detractors arguing that his work is too narrowly focused and does not represent the true state of civil-military relations, it is certain that his theory would have resonated well with senior Canadian military officers as they struggled with their minister. In his testimony of February 1967 to the Defence Committee, Moncel stressed that the military must "have a very real role to play in offering professional advice to those members of the government who are charged with the responsibility of that particular aspect of it and they do this in a very able fashion."[113] Air Vice-Marshal M.M. Hendrick explained how the military had worked well with the politicians *before* Hellyer became MND: "We also had a feeling ... of confidence that our judgments, our advice, and our technical know-how would be given due consideration by our political masters ... Any of the times I was in the headquarters prior to the present regime [under Hellyer] ... the technical advice and the military opinion of the Chiefs of Staff was given fair consideration."[114]

Thus, it is not surprising that some of the most senior officers felt that Mr. Hellyer had become involved with internal military matters that had normally been considered their prerogative. As one author noted, the establishment of a good working relationship between Hellyer and his senior military advisers was "hindered by different perceptions of the boundaries within which the two groups were expected to function."[115] For instance, Hellyer viewed the decisions relating to the restructuring the military and to the increase in efficiency within his purview. As he had stated in 1964, while "I have no criticism of the men who have served their country in senior military positions," the constitutional responsibility *for changes in organization* is clear and "lies with the minister and the government."[116] As one authority on civil-military relations points out, although debates over force structure and strategy relate to state security, "debates over personnel and organization are at some level debates over how best to ensure that the military is subservient to civilian authority."[117] Between 1963 and 1966, Hellyer changed the division and management of responsibility between civilian leaders and military officers from what had been the norm before his arrival.[118]

Hellyer also questioned the competence, judgment, and objectivity of his senior officer corps. The three Canadian services, while different, were extremely proud of their heritage and traditions, and highly professional. Unfortunately, Hellyer viewed this relatively healthy expression of solidarity to a community as a hardened, unreasoned, and blind commitment to existing doctrine or structure. As he stated in his memoirs, "the services were three separate fiefdoms, each jealous of its own terrain [and] … [t]his sense of division compromised judgment."[119] Bland contends that, by some accounts, in the early 1960s senior officers were so distanced from "the national facts of life" that they had become incompetent advisers and mere advocates for service and alliance interests.[120] Hellyer expected that senior officers would think and act with a national perspective in mind, not close-minded service interests. However, the services (and the senior officers representing them) lacked objectivity in their analyses and, based on their record in advising the government during the defence debacle of the Diefenbaker years, could not be depended on to make unbiased recommendations to the minister. Hellyer believed the wartime experience of his senior military officers was largely irrelevant for the type of difficult defence decisions that needed to be taken. He raised doubts early in his tenure "about the traditional organization and competency of the military" and accordingly tended to disregard the professional expertise of his senior military advisers, which was another element that accentuated the rift between the minister and his officers.[121]

Although there is no doubt that a clear delineation of the boundaries and roles within which the civilians and the military function is central to good civil-military relations, a successful relationship is one based on mutual trust and respect.[122] As one author astutely noted:

> The most desirable civil-military relations in a democracy are not simply those in which civilian leadership almost always prevails . . . [but] those in which there is a nearly altogether candid exchange of ideas between the soldier and the statesman, along with consequent founding of policy and strategy upon a real meeting of minds.[123]

As the gulf between Hellyer and the military widened between 1964 and 1967, senior officers were seldom consulted as he developed his plans and, even more insulting, Hellyer ignored his senior military advisers, bypassing the chain of command and seeking military advice elsewhere. By summer 1966, it is evident that there was much mutual distrust and animosity between the minister and several of his senior officers. Those basic elements of a healthy civil-military relationship — trust, respect, and a candid exchange of ideas — were missing. Their absence was undeniably a key precipitating factor in the unification crisis.

Conclusion

> *The primary purpose of providing for civilian control of the military is to insure that the actions of the military forces of a nation are subordinated to the political purposes of constitutional government.*
>
> — Henry E. Eccles[124]

The civil-military crisis of the 1960s represents one of the most important episodes in Canada's military history, and is best remembered nowadays through accounts of the friction and confrontation between Hellyer and his senior military officers. The so called "Revolt of the Admirals" — a description coined by the press in July 1966 — was not a planned or coordinated revolt, but an attention-grabbing headline to portray the firing and retirement of a number of RCN flag officers.

The Hellyer–Landymore controversy, however, brought to light a continuously deteriorating situation between the minister and his military officers that had existed since the release of the 1964 *White Paper on Defence*. The seeds of discord between the politicians and the Canadian military were planted several years before the arrival of Hellyer as the MND. Unfortunately, because of the publicity given to the July 1966 events and the sensationalist public statements by Hellyer concerning disloyalty of February 1967, informed debate about the merits and disadvantages of the unification proposal was largely marginalized, and was not re-energized until decades later.

The unification debate of the 1960s publicly focused on organizational changes and on the social aspects of the initiative, such as the adverse impact on occupations, uniforms, traditions, and symbols of the three services. While there can be no doubt these elements were an important part of the opposition to unification, this chapter has argued that the unification controversy that took place between 1964 and 1967 was first and foremost a crisis of civil-military relations in Canada. As an editorial in the *Montreal Gazette* observed a few days after the firing of Landymore, "[t]he issues involved may appear to be simple and the consequences of no importance. In fact, the issues are not simple and the consequences are far-reaching and serious."[125] Morton even contends that, to Hellyer and perhaps most Canadians, arguments by serving officers against unification "struck the minister and his chief advisor ... as tantamount to mutiny."[126] The criticism over Hellyer's integration program that gained prominence during the 1966 public controversy, combined with the open resistance of some senior military officers, strengthened Hellyer's resolve to see unification through. With the continued support of Prime Minister Pearson, Hellyer presented himself as the defender of civil authority over the military. When Landymore electrified the debate over unification with his July 1966 press conference, it was clear to Hellyer that this was a struggle over the right of the government to control the military.

By the middle of 1966, civil-military relations in Canada were unhealthy, with mutual trust and respect between the minister and his military advisers absent. However, the blame for the crisis that took place cannot be laid exclusively on Hellyer's personality and methods; the senior officer corps of the three services must also assume a large share of the blame. Primarily, the senior officers were never able to articulate (to Hellyer, to parliamentarians, and to the observing public) in a coherent and unified fashion the deleterious impact that unification would have on operational military activities.[127] More important, senior officers failed to understand the nature of the changes that were taking place within Canadian society and politics, and did not appreciate the impact those fundamental modifications would have on the military, especially in the context of civil control of the military. In short, during this period, the officer corps remained disconnected from the society it was mandated to serve.

In the final analysis, the unification crisis of 1966–1967 was, for all intents and purposes, pre-determined, and culminated as it did because of a continually deteriorating relationship between politicians and military advisers that had started in the late 1950s. From the day of Landymore's press conference in July 1966, support for unification became a casualty of the public confrontation between Hellyer and his senior officers. As one former senior officer stated:

"Within days, the myth of 'great enthusiasm' for unification had been blown sky high,"[128] and, it can be argued, this eagerness never returned in Canada.

NOTES

1. The author wishes to express his appreciation to Jonathan Stone, of the Assistant Deputy Minister (Policy) Group, for his comments in the preparation of this chapter.

2. "Storm Over the Armed Forces," *Ottawa Citizen*, 16 July 1966, 6.

3. In Canada, since the Second World War, it can be argued that there have been four serious crises of civil-military relations. The first occurred towards the end of that conflict and precipitated the conscription crisis; the second occurred during the Cuban missile crisis when civil control of the military nearly collapsed; the third was the crisis over unification and is the subject of this chapter; and the fourth occurred in the mid-1990s in the aftermath of the Somalia incident. For a discussion on this latest crisis, see Douglas Bland, "The Government of Canada and the Armed Forces: A Troubled Relationship," in David A. Charters and J. Brent Wilson, eds., *The Soldier and the Canadian State: A Crisis in Civil-Military Relations* (Fredericton, NB: Proceedings of the Second Annual Conflict Studies Workshop, University of New Brunswick, 1996).

4. J.L. Granatstein, *Canada 1957–1967: The Years of Uncertainty and Innovation* (Toronto: McClelland & Stewart, 1986), 218; and, as for relations between the government and the military, see Douglas Bland, *Chiefs of Defence: Government and the Unified Command of the Canadian Armed Forces* (Toronto: The Canadian Institute of Strategic Studies, 1995), 52.

5. Douglas Bland, *Canada's National Defence: Volume 1 Defence Policy* (Kingston, ON: School of Policy Studies, Queen's University, 1997), 59–61; and Paul T. Hellyer, *Damn the Torpedoes: My Fight to Unify Canada's Armed Forces* (Toronto: McClelland & Stewart, 1990), 36.

6. The term *integration*, before the 1970s, refers to the amalgamation of the headquarters, commands, and support establishments of the three services, while preserving the services themselves as separate institutions. *Unification* means the establishment of a single military service in place of the Army, Navy, and Air Force. David P. Burke, "Hellyer and Landymore: The Unification of the Canadian Armed Forces and an Admiral's Revolt," *American Review of Canadian Studies* 8 (Autumn 1978), 24.

7. Jack Granatstein, *Who Killed the Canadian Military?* (Toronto: HarperCollins Canada, 2004), 80. The most vocal anti-unification organization was the *TRIO Organization* (Tri-Service Identities Organization). See R.L. Raymont,

Report on Integration and Unification 1964–1968 (Ottawa: DND, Directorate of History, 1982), 192–204.

8.   Newspaper front pages and editorial headlines included: "Four Rear-Admirals 'Revolt' in Integration Row," *Montreal Gazette*, 15 July 1966; and "Revolt Against Hellyer: Defiant Halifax Rear-Admiral Sacked," *Ottawa Citizen*, 15 July 1966. On the right of the government, see three editorials from 18 July 1966 that addressed this theme: "The Armed Forces Controversy," *Ottawa Citizen*, 6; "Storm over the Armed Forces," *Montreal Gazette*, 6; and "A Regrettable Protest," *Globe and Mail*, 6.

9.   Hellyer, *Damn the Torpedoes*, 164. Both the adjectives *civil* and *civilian* control were used alternately by Hellyer in documents and speeches, as was the practice during that period. Except for specific citations, the term *civil* will be employed throughout this chapter.

10. Douglas Bland, "A Unified Theory of Civil-Military Relations," *Armed Forces and Society* 26, No. 1 (Fall 1999), 10.

11. See "Unification: The Politics of the Armed Forces," in J.L. Granatstein, *Canada 1957–1967*, 218–42, and Douglas Bland, *The Administration of Defence Policy in Canada: 1947 to 1985* (Kingston, ON: Ronald P. Frye & Company, 1987), 33–55. Additionally, Colonel R.L. Raymont, an executive staff officer to three chiefs of the defence staff in the 1950s and 1960s and an observer to many events, produced three well-researched reports in the early 1980s detailing the origins of integration and outlining the dynamics in play while integration and unification were being implemented. See, specifically, Raymont, *Report on Integration and Unification 1964–1968*.

12. See the following four reports that discuss elements of integration and unification: Department of National Defence (henceforth DND), *Report to the Minister of National Defence on the Management of Defence in Canada*, Report of the Management Review Group, July 1972; DND, *Task Force on Review of Unification of the Canadian Armed Forces*, Final Report, 15 March 1980; DND, *Review Group on the Report of the Task Force on Unification of the Canadian Forces*, Review Report, 31 August 1980; and D.G. Loomis et al., *The Impact of Integration, Unification and Restructuring on the Functions and Structure of National Defence Headquarter*, NDHQ Study S1/85 (Ottawa, DND, 31 July 1985).

13. See Peter C. Kasurak, "Civilianization and the Military Ethos: Civil-Military Relations in Canada," *Canadian Public Administration* 25, No. 1 (Spring 82), 108–29; and Harriet W. Critchley, "Civilianization and the Canadian Military," in B.D. Hunt and R.G. Haycock, eds., *Canada's Defence: Perspectives on Policy in the Twentieth Century* (Toronto: Copp Clark Pitman, 1993), 226–41.

14. Vernon J. Kronenberg, *All Together Now: The Organization of the Department of National Defence in Canada 1964–1972* (Toronto: The Canadian Institute of International Affairs, 1973).

15.   Burke, "Hellyer and Landymore," 3–27.

16.   See A. Keith Cameron, "The Royal Canadian Navy and the Unification Crisis," in James A. Boutilier, ed., *The RCN in Retrospect 1910–1968* (Vancouver: University of British Columbia Press, 1982), 334–42; the memoirs of Jeffry V. Brock, *The Thunder and the Sunshine Volume 2* (Toronto: McClelland & Stewart, 1983); and Marc Milner, *Canada's Navy: The First Century* (Toronto: University of Toronto Press, 1999), 242–61. Bland, in *Administration of Defence*, 50–53, addresses this last theme briefly.

17.   See Kasurak, "Civilianization and the Military Ethos"; General G.C.E. Thériault, "Reflections on Canadian Defence Policy and Its Underlying Structural Problems," *Canadian Defence Quarterly* 22 (July 1993), 8–9; Charles A. Cotton et al., "Canada's Professional Military: The Limits of Civilianization," *Armed Forces and Society* 4 (May 1978), 365–90; and, for an alternate point of view, see Granatstein, *Who Killed the Canadian Military?*, 89–91.

18.   R.B. Byers, "Canadian Civil-Military Relations and Reorganization of the Armed Forces: Whither Civilian Control?" in Hector J. Massey, ed., *The Canadian Military: A Profile* (Toronto: Copp Clark Publishing, 1972), 197–228; and Douglas Bland, *Chiefs of Defence: Government and the Unified Command of the Canadian Armed Forces* (Toronto: The Canadian Institute of Strategic Studies, 1995).

19.   Jon McLin, *Canada's Changing Defence Policy 1957–1963: The Problem of a Middle Power in Alliance* (Baltimore, MD: Johns Hopkins Press, 1967), 3.

20.   J.L. Granatstein, "The Defence Debacle, 1957–1963," in Granatstein, *Canada 1957–1967*, 101–38.

21.   Charles Foulkes's testimony before the House of Commons' Special Committee on Defence, as quoted in McLin, *Canada's Changing Defence Policy*, 45.

22.   *Ibid.*, 123–56; and see also the testimony of General Foulkes, chair of the Chiefs of Staff Committee at the time of the Arrow situation. Standing Committee on National Defence (henceforth Defence Committee), *Minutes of Proceedings and Evidence No. 21*, 16 February 1967, 1267.

23.   McLin, *Canada's Changing Defence Policy*, 45; and Bland, *Chiefs of Defence*, 52.

24.   Bland, *Chiefs of Defence*, 2.

25.   Peter T. Haydon, *The 1962 Cuban Missile Crisis: Canadian Involvement Reconsidered* (Toronto: The Canadian Institute of Strategic Studies, 1993), 207. Haydon was a young naval officer at the time of the crisis and is now a military analyst; his book provides the best account of the Canadian military response to the crisis; and see also Granatstein, *Canada 1957–1967*, 113–17.

26.   J.L. Granatstein, "The American Influence on the Canadian Military," in Hunt and Haycock, *Canada's Defence*, 136.

27.   Haydon, *Cuban Missile Crisis*, 1 and 3–4. In fairness, although Diefenbaker had not authorized any action, MND Douglas S. Harkness did give direction to his military commanders. *Ibid.*, 128.

28.   Canada, Royal Commission on Government Organization (here after *Glassco Commission*), Queen's Printers, Ottawa, Vol. 4, *Special Areas of Administration*, Report 20, January 1963.

29.   Hellyer, *Damn the Torpedoes*, 36.

30.   Jean V. Allard, *The Memoirs of Jean V. Allard* (Vancouver: University of British Columbia Press, 1988), 218.

31.   Bland, *Administration of Defence Policy*, 31.

32.   Bland, *Chiefs of Defence*, 59.

33.   Paul T. Hellyer, "Canadian Defence Policy," *Air University Review* 19 (November-December 1967), 7; and Granatstein, *Canada 1957–1967*, 221.

34.   Ross Fetterly, "The Influence of the Environment on the 1964 Defence White Paper," *Canadian Military Journal* (Winter 2004–2005), 47–51.

35.   Bland, *Chiefs of Defence*, 87–88.

36.   John A. Munro and Alex I. Inglis, *Mike: The Memoirs of the Right Honourable Lester B. Pearson, Volume 3* (Toronto: University of Toronto Press, 1975), 75. Granatstein comes to the same conclusion; see *Canada 1957–1967*, 218.

37.   Bland, *Chiefs of Defence*, 67.

38.   Bland, *Administration of Defence Policy*, 23.

39.   John English, *The Worldly Years: The Life of Lester B. Pearson* (Toronto: First Vintage Books, 1992), 248–50 and 267.

40.   For a brief account of this period, see Hellyer, *Damn the Torpedoes*, 18–27. Hellyer had also served as parliamentary assistant to MND Ralph Campney and also briefly as the associate MND in the cabinet of Prime Minister Louis St. Laurent from April to June 1957. See also Raymont, *Report on Integration and Unification*, 36–37.

41.   Bland, *Chiefs of Defence*, 69.

42.   Milner, *Canada's Navy*, 243. To attest to his personal ambitions, Hellyer ran for the leadership of the Liberal Party and lost to Pierre Trudeau at the 1968

Liberal leadership convention. He resigned in 1969 after a dispute with Trudeau over funding for a housing program, and continued as an independent. After joining the Progressive Conservative, he contested the 1976 Conservative leadership convention, and in 1995 he formed the Canadian Action Party.

43.   Bland, *Canada's National Defence Volume 1*, 58.

44.   Both quotes from Hellyer, *Damn the Torpedoes*, 33–34.

45.   Bland, *Chiefs of Defence*, 16.

46.   Bland, *Canada's National Defence Volume 1*, 59.

47.   Hellyer, *Damn the Torpedoes*, 42–47.

48.   *White Paper on Defence*, in Bland, *National Defence Volume 1*, 92.

49.   As they drafted Liberal defence policy in late 1962, Hellyer convinced Pearson that integration of the services, while not a new idea, was now necessary. In January 1963, three months before the federal election, Pearson made an important speech on defence policy and nuclear weapons for Canada, alluding then to the possible unification of the services: "The three defense services should be fully integrated for maximum efficiency and economy, both in operation and administration." See "New Pearson Stand Backs Nuclear Arms for Canadian Forces," *Globe and Mail*, 14 January 1963, 10.

50.   *White Paper on Defence*, in Bland, *National Defence Volume 1*, 109.

51.   There had been many efforts towards integration before Hellyer arrived at DND. The first meaningful steps in combining the Canadian Forces Headquarters and the DND began with Brooke Claxton, the MND between 1946 and 1954. Determined to streamline the organization and to find efficient ways to meet Canada's defence needs, he introduced ideas that would survive in future white papers, including the concept of unification. Diefenbaker's first MND, George R. Pearkes, continued the trend to amalgamate the armed forces, integrating the medical and chaplain functions, food procurement, postal services, and some recruiting units. He wanted to go further but "did not have much enthusiasm for the practical problems ambitious unification schemes might raise." Bland, *National Defence Volume 1*, 4; and Raymont, *Report on Integration and Unification*, 1–10.

52.   *House of Commons Debates* (henceforth *Debates*), 8 May 1964, 3067.

53.   *Debates*, 8 May 1964, 3065.

54.   *Glassco Report*, Vol. 4, 76.

55.   *Debates*, 8 May 1964, 3068.

56.   Both quotes from Hellyer, *Debates*, 8 May 1964, 3068. Italics added by the author.

57.   Paul Hellyer, "Address on the Canadian Forces Reorganization Act," in Douglas Bland *Canada's National Defence: Volume 2 Defence Organization* (Kingston, ON: School of Policy Studies, Queen's University, 1998), 113.

58.   Bland, *Canada's National Defence Volume 1*, 60.

59.   *Debates*, 8 May 1964, 3066–67.

60.   The six commands included: Mobile Command, which encompassed the Army and tactical air support; Maritime Command; Air Defence Command; Air Transport Command; Training Command; and the Material Command. For a more complete discussion, see Kronenberg, *All Together Now*, and Raymont, *Report on Integration and Unification*, 70–101.

61.   Hellyer, quoted in Bland, *National Defence: Volume 2*, 130.

62.   Raymont, *Report on Integration and Unification*, 233–34. The Committee met between 7 February and 21 March 1967, day of the last sitting of the House of Commons.

63.   This is how ACM Miller described to R.L. Raymont the tactics used by Hellyer to advance integration within the department. Raymont, *Report on Integration and Unification*, 159.

64.   Bland, *Administration of Defence Policy*, 37.

65.   Desmond Morton, *A Military History of Canada*, 4th ed. (Toronto: McClelland & Stewart, 1990), 249–50.

66.   The term *troubled waters* was used by Hellyer in his memoirs. Hellyer, *Damn the Torpedoes*, 85ff.

67.   For instance, Georges Pearkes, MND between 1957 and 1960, was a recipient of the Victoria Cross and had retired in 1945 as a major-general. His replacement, Douglas Harkness, had fought during the Second World War, and in 1943 was awarded a medal for courage while commanding during the Sicilian campaign. Available at *www.answers.com/topic/list-of-canadian-ministers-of-national-defence* (accessed August 2006). Hellyer's service experience — he joined the RCAF for a short period in spring 1944 but subsequently transferred to the Canadian Army because of the shortage of Army reinforcements — frustrated him greatly and brought to light the unnecessary duplication that existed in many areas between the services. While he later said in his memoirs that this experience was probably not a significant factor in the subsequent decision to unify the forces, he admits that "it must have had an effect on the subconscious." Hellyer, *Damn the Torpedoes*, 2–4.

68. Air Vice-Marshal Robert A. Cameron, "Canada's Military Unification: Greater Efficiency or Chaos," *Airforce* (February 1967), 81.

69. For a more complete discussion, see Bernard Brodie, *War and Politics* (New York: Macmillan Company, 1973), 464–73.

70. Granatstein, *Canada 1957–1967*, 223.

71. Hellyer, *Damn the Torpedoes*, 223–24.

72. Some pieces of legislation related to unification of the American services passed between 1947 and 1958. Most of these related to the power of the secretary of defense and the creation of a joint staff. For more details, see Douglas C. Lovelace, *Unification of the United States Armed Forces* (Carlisle Barracks, PA: Strategic Studies Institute, U.S. Army War College, 1996).

73. Landymore, Defence Committee, *Minutes of Proceedings and Evidence No. 21*, 15–16 February 1967, 1073–4 and 1212. To Landymore, this meant "one single chief, one single defence staff, one single budget, a single programme, and single administrative procedures." He had serious issues with integration, notably with the notion of creating the new Training and Material Commands.

74. Hellyer, as quoted in Bland, *Volume 2*, 129. The chiefs of staff also sent open letters to Army, Air force, and Navy personnel. See extracts of those letters in Raymont, *Report on Integration and Unification*, 38–47.

75. Moncel, Defence Committee, *Minutes of Proceedings and Evidence No. 21*, 20 February 1967, 1304; and Cameron, "Canada's Military Unification," 81.

76. Hellyer, *Debates*, 11 April 1967, 14793.

77. Allard, *Memoirs*, 225.

78. Hellyer, as quoted in Bland, *Administration of Defence Policy*, 39.

79. Bland, *Administration of Defence Policy*, 54.

80. Cameron, "Canada's Military Unification," 76.

81. Moncel, Defence Committee, *Minutes of Proceedings and Evidence No. 21*, 20 February 1967, 1345.

82. Bland, *Administration of Defence Policy*, 52 and 36.

83. Milner, *Canada's Navy*, 243.

84. Moncel, Defence Committee, *Minutes of Proceedings and Evidence No. 21*, 20 February 1967, 1345; Byers, "Canadian Civil-Military Relations," 222–23.

Lieutenant-General F.J. Fleury provided the same comments to Raymont, in *Report on Integration and Unification*, 157.

85. All quotes from Allard, *Memoirs*, 236–27 and 248.

86. Miller, Defence Committee, *Minutes of Proceedings and Evidence No. 35*, 20–21 March 1967, 2294–95.

87. Hellyer, "Canadian Defence Policy," 6.

88. *Debates*, 8 May 1964, 3065–69.

89. David Bercuson, *Significant Incident* (Toronto: McClelland & Stewart, 1996), 72.

90. Allard, *Memoirs*, 253 and 261.

91. Hellyer, "Canadian Defence Policy," 7. Quite telling of the importance that Hellyer attached to this specific aim of unification are that the cited comments form part of the concluding sentence to his 1967 article defending unification.

92. Allard, *Memoirs*, 247.

93. Hellyer, Defence Committee, *Minutes of Proceedings and Evidence No. 21*, 23 February 1967, 1579.

94. Cameron, "Canada's Military Unification," 76.

95. The details of the crisis will not be discussed in this chapter. For further reading on these events, see Burke, "Hellyer and Landymore;" "Hard Lying, 1964–1968," in Milner, *Canada's Navy*; and Raymont, *Report on Integration and Unification*, 160–86.

96. Burke, "Hellyer and Landymore," 12.

97. Rear-Admiral Landymore offered these details during his appearance in front of the Defence Committee. See Defence Committee, *Minutes of Proceedings and Evidence No. 21*, 15–16 February, 1067.

98. Unlike today, at that time it was not unusual for senior officers to get access to the prime minister. Rear-Admiral Brock also had an audience in 1964 with Lester Pearson, to no effect.

99. Landymore, as quoted in Burke, "Hellyer and Landymore," 12.

100. Ironically, this same day General Allard was taking over as new CDS, replacing ACM Miller, who was retiring.

101. Hellyer, "Hellyer Assails Admiral for Integration Criticism," *Globe and Mail*, 16 July 1967, 1.

102. Landymore met with the minister and several members of his staff on 22 June in Hellyer's conference room. Although the classified sections of the brief where passed without difficulty, revisions were eventually made by Hellyer's staff to sections of the presentation, the most significant pertaining to personnel. Landymore, although angered by the changes, presented the amended version of the brief. Burke, "Hellyer and Landymore," 9.

103. *Ibid.*, 18–19.

104. Hellyer, Defence Committee, *Minutes of Proceedings and Evidence No. 21*, 23 February 1967, 1622–23.

105. Bland, *Administration of Defence*, 50; and Allard, *Memoirs*, 254. Cameron states that 13 of 15 major appointments changed hands, with nine of the incumbents being fired or taking early retirement. Cameron, "Canada's Military Unification," 77.

106. Samuel E. Finer, *The Man on Horseback: The Role of the Military in Politics* (London: Pall Mall Press, 1962), 47.

107. Byers, "Canadian Civil-Military Relations," 197.

108. Michael Howard, "Introduction: The Armed Forces as a Political Problem," in Michael Howard, ed., *Soldiers and Governments* (London: Eyre and Spottiswoode, 1957), 12.

109. Byers, "Canadian Civil-Military Relations," 199.

110. Hellyer, *Damn the Torpedoes*, 42.

111. Samuel P. Huntington, *The Soldier and the State* (Cambridge, MA: Belknap Press of Harvard University Press, 1957), 80–85. Huntingdon argues throughout this work that "objective control" has only been possible since the emergence of the military professional.

112. The period eventually saw the publication both in the United States and the United Kingdom several seminal treatises expounding theories of civil-military relations. Besides *The Soldier and the State*, see also Michael Howard, ed., *Soldiers and Governments*; Morris Janowitz, *The Professional Soldier: A Social and Political Portrait* (Glencoe, IL: The Free Press, 1960); Finer, *The Man on Horseback*; and for a comparative analysis of these theories, see Peter D. Feaver, "The Civil-Military Problematique: Huntington, Janowitz and the Question of Civilian Control," *Armed Forces and Society* 23 (Winter 1996), 149–178.

113. Moncel, Defence Committee, *Minutes of Proceedings and Evidence No. 21*, 20 February 1967, 1359.

114. Hendrick, *Ibid.*, 1444–45.

115. Byers, "Canadian Civil-Military Relations," 222.

116. Hellyer, *Debates*, 8 May 1964, 3066. Italics added by the author.

117. Feaver, "The Civil-Military Problematique," 155.

118. For a contemporary discussion of the "theory of shared responsibility," see Bland, "A Unified Theory of Civil-Military Relations," 7–26.

119. Hellyer, *Damn the Torpedoes*, 37.

120. Bland, "Who Decides What? Civil-Military Relations in Canada and in the United States," *Canadian-American Foreign Policy* 41 (February 2000). The expression "national facts of life" is from MND Brooke Claxton. See Douglas Bland and Sean Maloney, *Campaigns for International Security* (Kingston, ON: McGill-Queen's University Press, 2004), 75–84, for a more complete discussion.

121. Bland, *Administration of Defence*, 50.

122. Byers, "Canadian Civil-Military Relations,"198.

123. Russell F. Weigley, "The George C. Marshall Lecture in Military History: The Soldier, the Statesman, and the Military Historian," *The Journal of Military History* 63 (October 1999), 810.

124. Henry E. Eccles, *Military Concepts and Philosophy* (New Brunswick, NJ: Rutgers University Press), 175–76.

125. "Storm over the Armed Forces," *Montreal Gazette*, 18 July 1966, 6.

126. Morton, *Military History of Canada*, 252. Hellyer even authorized serving officers who were against integration and unification to testify to the Defence Committee to demonstrate openness about the process and to ensure all objections were heard.

127. During his testimony of February 1967, Landymore discussed many aspects of unification, except operations. He raised the following topics: National Defence Act, promotion opportunity, retirement ages, career service concept, rank structure, uniforms, career opportunities, loyalty, and ultimate state of the armed forces. Landymore, Defence Committee, *Minutes of Proceedings and Evidence No. 21*, 15 February 1967, 1049ff.

128. Cameron, "Canada's Military Unification," 76.

12

The Air Force and Flight Safety: A Culture of Tolerated Disobedience?

Randall Wakelam

There has been a growing acceptance of the philosophy that the first and foremost step to realistic and effective accident prevention is to candidly identify our mistakes. This is a healthy attitude but in the process we must not overlook the fact that more often than not, personnel causes involve the failure of someone to discharge his responsibilities properly.

— Colonel R.D. "Joe" Schultz, Director of Flight Safety 1973[1]

I CANNOT RECALL ONE CASE of a flying-related summary trial or court-martial occurring in the squadrons with which I flew between 1975 and 1987. Indeed, until recently, aviators, and certainly those in Canada in the 1970s and 1980s, did not tend to think in terms of discipline and disobedience when they paused to consider how they went about their daily tasks working around aircraft.[2] This was undoubtedly because air operations, whether actually flying the aircraft, conducting maintenance or providing other types of support, were and remain highly structured activities based largely on rules and regulations. And yet these rules and regulations were regularly breached either by acts of omission or commission. Contraventions did not, however, often, if ever, lead to disciplinary action — the culture of the Air Force was one of tolerance. It was thought better to learn from the mistakes of peers than to punish the transgressions of those who had broken the rules.[3]

This approach would seem a far cry from that taken in the Army and Navy, where, if the rumour mills of the day were to be believed, soldiers and sailors could be and were disciplined for such minor malfeasances as having a dirty weapon during a barracks inspection or not having heaving lines properly coiled. Surely, if these failures in discipline, with clearly potentially dire consequences for individuals and organizations, could result in punishment then the same should have been the case for the Air Force where the failure to follow procedures for the safe operation of aircraft could have catastrophic results.

How is it then that the Air Force appears during these decades to have taken what leadership theory would describe as a laissez-faire approach to discipline? There would seem to be some explanations rooted in the air service's culture. First, as suggested above, leaders have been more interested in finding out about problems and using the results of systematic "flight safety" investigations to educate the rank on file on the sorts of problems that could lead to damage, destruction, injury or death. Second, there has been perhaps a degree of wilful disobedience to flying by the rules. Terms like *pressing on* and *pushing the envelope* suggested to flyers, both young and old, that there was a degree of heroism in getting the machine to go just a bit further, faster or lower. Infractions resulting from these acts generally resulted not in disciplinary action, but in grist for the flight safety system and in new tales to be told and retold at the bar. Indeed, inseparable from the mythology of brave exploits was the presence of strong drink, a holdover from those who flew during the Second World War and the generation that followed.

Paradoxically, these sorts of breaches were not generally evident in the activities of Air Force personnel working in such areas as aerospace control, aircraft maintenance, and logistical and administrative support to flying operations. One is left to wonder to what greater or lesser degree the flight safety program influenced the operating philosophy and practice of these other groups.

This chapter will explore the Canadian Air Force culture of the later Cold War period, the 1970s and 1980s, and to explain the apparent dichotomy between a highly rule-based operation and an apparent disregard for those rules among some aircrew. There is very little literature on flying discipline or disobedience, so the chapter will draw largely on official documents and reports of the period that described the concept and suggest the influence that the flight safety system would seem to have had.[4] It will be necessary, too, to make

A 2004 FLIGHT SAFETY POSTER FROM 14 WING, GREENWOOD, NOVA SCOTIA.

(Department of National Defence, Dawson/Sampson, Canadian Forces Joint Imagery Centre PL 10976)

use of the memories of contemporary Canadian aviators.

Finally, it should be clearly understood that this chapter is not intended as any sort of criticism of the Air Force, aviators or the flight safety system. Rather, it is a partial glimpse of a culture that seemed to prevail during those decades; a culture which while less than perfect was not unlike that of most human endeavour.

Origins

The flight safety program that evolved in Canada during the 1950s and 1960s was based largely on the need to protect scarce resources. By the 1970s a new aviator's first exposure to the notion of flight safety was usually prefaced with the statement that during the Second World War more allied aircraft had been lost to accidents than to enemy action.[5] The basis of the program was to understand what could and did happen by mischance to aviators and to aircraft. To do this, trends had to be captured through statistical study and education programs had to be devised that would show aviators what could befall them in the air and on the ground if they were not focused on the task at hand and operating by the book. To capture the best possible data it was necessary to have full disclosure of safety "occurrences" and to do this it became necessary to formally separate flight safety reporting and investigation from any disciplinary process; otherwise, who would want to implicate themselves in a low flying stunt, a dodgy repair, or a less than precise vectoring of an aircraft around a busy airport? This separation remained in place throughout the Cold War. The 1995 version of the CF Flight Safety Manual stated that in terms of flight safety investigations and reports: "Except as required by QR&O 21.47 [Queen's Regulations and Orders — dealing with injury or death], it is not the purpose of these reports to assign blame."[6] Further; "Investigations do not seek to establish fault or assign blame in the legal sense or to recommend punishment as this is not in keeping with the principles of accident prevention." Indeed, the policy specifically precluded the use of flight safety reports in the preparation of charges, in the conduct of any disciplinary proceedings or in assigning sanctions. This said, the system did not preclude "collateral" investigations for such purposes should these be deemed necessary by the chain of command.[7]

What the concept of flight safety was supposed to engender was clear; one had to be constantly vigilant when working around aircraft, and learning from the mistakes of others was the best way to protect the lives and equipment that the Air Force used to prosecute operations. What was not mentioned seemed, implicitly at least, equally unambiguous; there was no reference to accountability or responsibility other than in coming forward, without risk of punishment, to report what had happened. The flight safety program that began in Canada as early as 1949 was therefore based largely on collecting and disseminating information about aircraft accidents and incidents and not on holding people to account for their actions.[8]

In his message in the first issue of *Crash Comment*, an internal magazine concerned with flight safety, Chief of the Air Staff, Air Marshal W.A. Curtis, put forward that:

> the limited number of personnel and aircraft available to carry out our task, combined with the problems of supply, manufacture and finance, increase the relative importance of each accident. We cannot afford flying accidents. Every effort must be made to eliminate them. I am therefore pleased to introduce the periodical, "Crash Comment," which in replacing the more detailed "Quarterly Accident Summary" will help you, through the experiences of others, to avoid similar accidents.[9]

And in the accompanying "Introduction" the staff provided the background behind the publication. They wanted to combine the statistical data of the previously published quarterly with a somewhat lighter and more readable review of certain accidents and incidents from which others might learn. These errors would be gleaned from "those accidents resulting from disobedience of orders, or a gross carelessness or stupidity…."[10] The editors explained that:

> each issue will contain … under the heading "Of Special Mention," reference to accidents which have brought to light instances of carelessness, disregard of orders or thoughtlessness which have caused or contributed to the accident in question, or while not contributing to are potential causes of accidents.[11]

Nowhere in Curtis's comments or the Introduction was the concept of accountability mentioned. Indeed the editorial lumped disobedience with stupidity as just another cause of problems. This did not mean that those who were involved in flying incidents and accidents were routinely let off and some errors did lead to disciplinary actions although there seemed no consistent application of sanctions. In the first issue of *Crash Comment* a pilot conducted a wheels up landing in a Vampire jet: "It appears the pilot was unable to keep his mind on the immediate problem, which was flying the aircraft. He subsequently received a severe reprimand."[12] Yet in a following issue a pilot committed a similar mistake by raising the landing gear (instead of the flaps) after landing. This "pilot was severely criticized [but not, apparently, disciplined], not only for selecting the wrong lever, but also for attempting to raise the flaps" contrary to operating procedures. In another case a Lancaster was completely written off when on takeoff a crew member raised the landing gear before the aircraft was airborne. "The fact that the aircraft captain failed to carry out a pre-flight briefing relating to the duties of the crewman is considered to be a contributing cause." It was also reported that none of the crew was strapped in during takeoff. But the overall conclusion was simply that: "This accident is an excellent example of what happens when a high standard of flying discipline is not maintained."[13] Three similar accidents — three apparently different correctives. That not all flying mishaps were judged to be acts requiring disciplinary action, or even similar disciplinary action, may well have been akin to leaving the obedience barn door ajar.

Curtis returned at the pages of *Crash Comment* in the following year, this time speaking about things like discipline, obedience to orders, and punishments. He said:

> I have reviewed our flying accidents during the past summer and regret to say that the majority of them have been a result of pilot error that can be traced back to poor discipline. Premature undercarriage retractions, disobedience of briefing orders, running out of fuel, low flying, approaching with undercarriage retracted and unavoidable taxiing accidents are all occasions which strain our resources to the utmost and which on numerous instances have caused the RCAF considerable embarrassment.[14]

The following spring the message was repeated, this time by Air Vice-Marshal A.L. James, air officer commanding Air Defence

Command. Addressing all Air Force personnel, he said, "needless waste by accident, carelessness, negligence or lack of knowledge can detract seriously from our capability." He went on to say: usually, therefore, it will be found that accidents, whether in the air, in the workshop or in the kitchens, are due either to the attempt to do something for which a person is unqualified, disregard of regulations, the lack of good judgment or simply the failure to use plain common sense.[15] Yet by not tackling the issues of disobedience, disciplinary action, and accountability directly what senior Air Force leaders appeared to be saying and what continued to be reinforced by most examples in *Crash Comment* was that disregard for regulations — disobedience — although recognized and disapproved of, appeared to be tolerated in the same way that one could accept accidents precipitated by lack of training or lack of wit.

In 1954 *Crash Comment* changed its name to *Flight Comment* and the new Chief of the Air Staff, Air Marshal C.R. Slemon, focused his comments on the attainment of safe habits: "Whether you fly or provide support services you can learn with advantage from the experiences and knowledge of others."[16] In the editorial the staff of the Directorate of Flight Safety (DFS) stated that the purpose of *Flight Comment* was "to promote the ideals of safer, better flying in the minds of air force personnel, groundcrew and aircrew alike." They continued:

> Our positive conviction is that the air is just as safe as men make it, the responsibility lying directly in the hands of those of you who service our aircraft and those of you who fly them. There is no better way to handle an accident than to keep it from happening. The purpose of "FLIGHT COMMENT," then, is to aid and extend those concepts throughout all phases of RCAF operation.

They invited readers to send in ideas from the field, but they then said that "all letters will be treated 'Confidential'"[17] implying, it could be argued, that the material being submitted might involve some degree of culpability.

There may well have been some culpability in flying operations according to Major-General (Retired) Bob Chisholm whose career began in flying fighters in the 1950s, shifted to helicopters, included command up to the group level and finally deputy command of Air

Command, as well as an appointment as director of flight safety in the late 1970s. He recollects that the fighter pilots were deemed to be "the most likely culprits, since they are the ones who are operating in an environment where "fast and low" is an opportunity." More broadly, Chisholm feels that mixed messages were being sent to aviators:

> From my experience during the period 1956 to 1990, there has been a remarkable change in the nature and environment of air force operations. At the beginning it was apparent that with a combination of WW II veterans and young short service pilots it was an unsafe environment. Leadership from a different era, and the lack of experienced pilots contributed to an unsafe and poorly disciplined environment. Alcohol was certainly abused in part because the officers' messes were the centre of social activities.[18]

Fortunately, says Chisholm, there were some officers who applied discipline and who worried about flight safety; as well, there were means to punish disobedience where such was deemed appropriate. Overall, Chisholm observes that:

> the next generation of air force leaders … emerged from this environment and were influenced by it. Some of the older generation, such as Col[onel] (Retired) Joe Schultz, developed an accident pre-vention system which was highly successful. Whether or not disobedience was a factor in aircraft accidents was the responsibility of air force leadership.[19]

As a result the leaders of the 1970s and 1980s had fairly clearly received some varied, but frequently laissez-faire, messages about how to act and about how to deal with transgressions. The result, debatably, was a culture of passive disobedience where malefactors could go beyond the line of prescribed standards without much consideration for whether or not they were disobeying the rules.

Before moving to those later decades it is perhaps germane to indicate that it was not just the Air Force or the fighter community that had a culture of tolerance. Recounting his early flights as a new naval helicopter flyer, Colonel (Retired) John Lehmann described how he destroyed an aircraft on a "sunny Saturday morning" while conducting his first mutual (two students, no instructor) flight. Practising a manoeuvre called a "quick stop," Lehmann flew his HTL-6 (Bell 47) into the water where it broke up and sank. Later standing before his commanding officer (CO) Lehmann said simply: "I'm sorry, it was an accident." His boss replied: "I'll say it was." To Lehmann's astonishment "… that was it: no board of inquiry, no investigation, no sanctions. The entry in my log book simply states: [Lesson Plan] 20 (incomp)."[20]

Decades of Disobedience

The introductory words of Colonel Joe Schultz, doyen of flight safety through much of the 1970s, were indicative of those who saw the need for leadership. Schultz stated his views clearly in the 1973 edition of the *Annual Aircraft Accident Analysis:*

> Unless we focus our preventive efforts on the underlying causes of personnel failure, we will not decrease the number of personnel caused accidents. This calls for a renewed emphasis on supervision. We must know the strengths and weaknesses of the man, and we must direct of resources to develop in him, the knowledge, skill, and motivation he needs to do the job.[21]

In the same document Vice-Chief of the Defence Staff, Lieutenant-General Chester Hull, a no-nonsense pilot, did not mention the human element when referring to supervision, stating somewhat cryptically that the supervisor "has the ultimate responsibility to make sure that our past mistakes lead to positive and permanent preventive measures for the future."[22] One might well conclude that he was talking more about systemic correction than assigning blame. Ironically it seemed that the flight safety director was taking a somewhat harder line than the second most senior leader in the Canadian Forces. For those aviators who happened to read these comments there could easily have been confusion.

Some of the articles in *Flight Comment* must have been equally perplexing to aviators. A 1975 article entitled "How Sierra Hotel are you?" offered a number of stunts that were indicative of a "hot dog," or S-H, flyer. In one case a flyer earned "5 points for a low pass by the tower; add five if you were lower than the controllers; 10 points if you were so low that nobody knew you did it."[23] Coincidentally, perhaps, in about the same year the retiring commander of a pilot training base would have won the supplemental 10 points had not many staff and students witnessed his ultra low level retirement flight. In fairness, the article did point to the fact that these sorts of manoeuvres were in no way appropriate and that a truly S-H pilot or flyer of any stripe was one who fly well and fly by the rules.

The 1977 *Aircraft Accident Analysis* included another series of remarks. The first was from Chief of the Defence Staff, Admiral R.H. Falls, a former naval fighter pilot, who commented on the higher than normal number of accidents during the previous year. Although he did not want to inhibit the sense of mission accomplishment, he did suggest flyers consider the need to preserve resources. In mild language he underscored the role of the leadership: "The responsibility for safety in our air operations rests as much with those who supervise and manage our air resources as with the 'hands-on operators themselves.'"[24] The new director of flight safety, then Colonel Chisholm, was more focused with his words, pointing out that fully 70 percent of accidents were the result of human error. "The underlying causes can be traced to problems such as poor motivation, inadequate supervision, lack of concern, lack of knowledge and over commitment."[25] The report concluded with a review of trends, focusing specifically on the issue of personnel error. Observers noted that two ways existed to deal with the problem. The first was to accept that "to err is human" and try to make the equipment fail safe. The second, "and to us the only truly valid possibility," was "to begin to mount a serious attack on the problem of human error.... Leadership," the piece continued, "at all levels will be severely tested, motivation [presumably of both leaders and followers] will be required in tremendous quantities."

As part of that attack the Air Force instituted a Flying Supervisors Course. Senior flyers from the various flying communities (fighter, transport, tactical helicopter, maritime and training) were brought together for a review of the philosophy and practice of supervising more junior aircrew. One of the more intense discussions on the course the author attended concerned the legality of allowing non-flying personnel to "manipulate the flight controls" of an aircraft for short periods. Some communities had specifically forbidden the practice, while others didn't really think about it — it had always been done and there seemed no harm in it. In the field, those personnel who were not aircrew enjoyed the opportunity though some of them, says air logistician Colonel Mike Boomer, were not certain of the legality.[26] There seemed a fairly obvious call for ensuring accountability, surely that being the role of supervisors and leaders; yet such terms were not mentioned.

Articles in *Flight Comment* continued to illustrate a similar confusing dichotomy. A piece in 1980 entitled "Pressing Problems" described two Hercules incidents. The author, from the DFS, stated empathetically that he was not "pointing the finger at these two pilots" who had ended up in difficulty when pushing on beyond their capabilities. Instead he said that had they not been so experienced the results might have been worse, and then went on to describe how he himself had pressed the limits too far on occasion. His message was that all flyers should give themselves a margin for the unexpected and was perhaps a softly stated suggestion to fly well within prescribed tolerances.[27] Yet here were three examples of experienced flyers who should have known better, but had erred anyway — and apparently without being held to account. Another article from that year, "Checklist Error," seemed to be a straightforward description of a crew that that become so immersed in their circumstances — "distracted" (to use one of the formal cause factors described below) — that they had failed to complete a check and had as a result oversped all four engines on an Argus maritime patrol aircraft.[28] But within the editorial comments some degree of negligence seemed to be implied: "DFS wishes to compliment the author for his willingness to share this experience with others and his honesty and insight with regard to what was obviously a difficult task."[29] Surely it did not help to have these sorts of veiled innuendos in a magazine aimed at getting at the truth.

This dichotomy was also seen in the units. For example, it was in the same period that a flyer on my base "flamed out" his aircraft (in other words ran out of fuel) just after landing despite that fact that he had passed a suitable refuelling stop only about an hour earlier. It seemed pretty obvious that the flight safety officer would be called upon to prepare the necessary incident report yet nothing was ever said or done about the matter — a matter that was well known along the flight line considering that technicians had had to tow the empty aircraft about a kilometre back to the hangar. In another instance a pilot who had been working in the Operations room overnight went flying the next morning despite being reminded of the prescribed requirement for eight hours of uninterrupted rest. Within an hour of takeoff he had been involved in an accident. In this case an investigation was conducted, but I do not recall any formal disciplinary action.

These then were the sorts of events that were captured either in print or seen in the day to day workings of a flying unit. Some, as had been recounted in *Crash Comment* and *Flight Comment* seemed like legitimate errors, some seemed to be the result of flyers pushing the envelope of their own capabilities, and still others the fairly clear result of noncompliance with orders or, more simply put, disobedience. But who could fault those who lived in a relatively permissive environment where the chain of command did not seem to take serious disciplinary action against culprits and even flight safety personnel who skewed the avowed neutrality of flight safety material with statements with inferences of culpability.

The mid-1980s saw another round of editorial statements from high-ranking flyers. Major-General Larry Ashley, soon to be the commander of Air Command, wrote not about safe and responsible flying, focusing instead on mastering the new aircraft and equipment then coming into service:

> Today, the Air force supervisor must keep himself fully informed of the latest advances in his personal area of expertise, whilst at the same time instilling in the younger airmen the basic principles and tricks of the trade that have served us so well for more than 60 years.[30]

What those principles and tricks might be was left unstated. Earlier in the year, no-nonsense pilot and Chief of the Defence Staff, General G.C.E. Thériault, talked about his pride that 1984 had been a year free of aircraft accidents. He hoped that 1985 would see a repeat:

> These thoughts are more than idle wishes. Here are some ideas on how this can be achieved. Of all of the many ambiguities that go into creating a safe environment for air operations by far the most important is the attitude of the individual airman or airwoman.[31]

Surely, though, there was and is nothing ambiguous about an aviator's attitude. If people were following the intended prescription of the S-H flyer and the counsel of Schultz and Chisholm for strong and effective leadership, then the rank and file, while engaged in high risk operations, should have been operating well inside the appropriate guidelines. The only ambiguity, surely, was in the seeming failure of the chain of command to demand that aviators be accountable for their acts of disobedience or stupidity.

Perhaps the ambiguity existed because, as Major-General (Retired) Fraser Holman, a fighter pilot who commanded at the squadron and wing level before taking on senior appointments at NORAD, describes, it was commonly viewed that flying policy and directives were more guidance than strict orders and that if regulations were disregarded "they were likely thought of little consequence, and probably impediments on mission accomplishment. When balanced with safe accomplishment of a time-sensitive mission, perhaps they could be deliberately overlooked." It was for example a common practice in Europe to climb into cloud (and potentially into other aircraft) without an air traffic control clearance should the weather deteriorate to the point where it was unsafe to continue the flight under visual flight rules.[32] Holman believes however that safe effective operations were at the core of Air Force thinking: "We had reasonably wide latitude within the regulations as to how to accomplish [a mission], and we encouraged initiative while retaining a safe operating environment." Except for gross violations like a case of illegal formation flying which led to a crash and subsequently to a court marshal, Holman says that where discipline was called for "for lesser offences/breaches, other measures could be invoked — verbal warnings, debriefings, review rides with senior pilots and similar less formal methods." But could not these "less formal methods" be misconstrued as an unstated acceptance of day to day disobedience?

If so this might help explain another call, by another director of flight safety for a renewed emphasis on dealing with personnel factors, which were still the cause of 70 percent of accidents and incidents. Colonel Hugh Rose described a new initiative to expand the range of personnel cause factors. He said that: "Troubleshooting personnel cause factors has always been much more difficult [compared to materiel or environmental problems]." He went on to say that only by doing these in depth investigations could the Air Force hope to "understand and correct those conditions which lead to a breakdown in performance...." He wanted investigators to start looking at more than just what had happened, but also why. If one reviews his words with some cynicism, it could perhaps be concluded that Rose was seeking a way to avoid dealing with disobedience. On the other hand he was calling for "a harder look inside the operation," which could well have revealed examples of disobedience.[33]

In fact, the range of personnel cause factors had expanded significantly since the early 1970s and would continue to do so into the 1990s. Table 1 provides the 1995 definitions of "psychological or behavioural" cause factors that could be assigned to personnel whether flying or non-flying. Table 2, on the other hand, shows a comparison of air accidents that had been attributed to flying personnel over a 20-year period. The growth of human factors causes is noticeable, but equally significant is the continued presence of judgment, inattention, carelessness, and noncompliance with orders causes. These, arguably, remained necessary for describing individuals who either wilfully (in the case of noncompliance), or somewhat unwittingly but still actively, went beyond the bounds of what had been mandated or is prudent.

Table 1: CF Air Occurrence Psychological/Behavioural Cause Factors in 1995[34]

Cause Factor	Definition
Boredom	A dull undemanding, repetitive task may result in a *low level of awareness*; as a result, required actions may be omitted in normal operations or during an emergency.
Carelessness	Due regard is not exercised. There is a display of *indifference, laxity, or disregard of established procedures*. This factor is not to be confused with inattention.
Channelized Attention	This factor occurs when a person's *full attention is focused on one stimulus* to the exclusion of all others. This becomes a problem when the person fails to perform tasks or process information of a higher or immediate priority, failing to notice or having no time to respond to cues requiring immediate attention.

Complacency	Complacency as a result of overconfidence, repetition of action, and contentment. The effects of complacency are revealed in a *lowered state of awareness, cursory pre-flight/maintenance checks, and decreased attention to detail.* As tasks become routine, performance become automatic and less attention is paid to detail. Because of past success in mastering the environment, the complacent individual becomes increasingly likely to perform routine tasks casually, rather than planning ahead. Complacent individuals are unaware of the gradual deterioration in performance since their ability for critical self-appraisal has been lost.
Confidence	This factor is normally a positive characteristic that allows one to act with some degree of self-assurance. *Overconfidence or lack of confidence* may undermine one's ability to make rational judgment or decisions.
Distraction	This factor may occur when attention is interrupted by the *introduction of other another stimulus* unrelated to the task being performed.
Expectancy	We anticipate certain environmental cues and tend to search selectively for those cues more actively than others. One extreme of this anomaly occurs when expectancy is so strong that one *perceives cues are in fact are not there*; the other extreme is when does not expect queues, thus *does not detect cues that are there.*
Human Information Processing	This refers to the process of receiving information, assessing its meaning, and deciding on appropriate response. The brain's capacity to process information received from different sources simultaneously is limited, especially when the signals are a short duration and are not anticipated. Can be a *loss of signals* are concurrent with or closely follow, signals already been dealt with.
Inattention	This refers to an *inappropriately low level of attention* to a task or failure to respond to relevant cues. Not paying attention is an accurate description of this aberration since conscious attention must be given to a task.
Judgment	This factor is assigned when one is faced with a choice and the decision, or lack of decision, proves to be wrong, resulting in an occurrence. In this context, judgment involves a *mental reasoning process requiring an assessment of options*, rather than the exercise of skills used in assessing physical quantities like speeds or closing rates. For the determination of cause factors judgment is the metal process used to recognize, analyze, and evaluate all information about the aircraft and the environment.

Motivation	This factor refers to that which stimulates and causes an individual to act. Excessive motivation or under motivation can *degrade one's ability to make rational judgments* or decisions.
Noncompliance with Orders	This factor refers to a *deliberate omission or commission* contrary to published or verbal orders. It should be assigned only for *wilful breaches* of orders, *negligence*, and *deliberate acts of irresponsibility*. The report shall refer to the order in question.
Pressing	This factor is assigned one perceives the need to continue a task beyond personal, equipment or environmental limits, conferring on the task *higher priority than really exists*. Reasons for repressing include self-imposed or peer pressure, or command pressure.
Technique	This factor includes the operation, workmanship, or mechanical skills *below a level that can be reasonably expected* from a person with proper training and experience. Technique involves using skills to assess and react to physical cues such as speeds, distances, closing rates, etc.
Training	Training is the acquisition of the skills, knowledge, and attitudes required to perform satisfactorily. Assignment of this factor would relate to issues such as *insufficient training or inappropriate training*. When assigning this cause factor it is important to remember that responsibility for training rests with the training entity, not with the individual involved in the occurrence. The only exception is the *negative transfer of training*, such as carrying over past procedures to another aircraft; this can be assigned to the individual.
Other	This factor is assigned were none of the definitions above fit the human factor or factors involved. A detailed description is required.

Table 2: Aircraft Accidents with Physiological/Behavioural Cause Factors[35]

Notes for Table 2

1. Accidents are those occurrences resulting in major damage or destruction, injury or death; they do not include incidents that result in minor damage or have the potential to be an accident. In 2004, for example, there were 11 aircraft accidents and 1,585 aircraft incidents.

2. Greyed cells indicate that based on the sources the cause factor in question had not been brought into use. The author determined the grouping of cause factors.

Cause Factor	1973	1976	1977	1978	1979	1980	1981	1982	1983	1984	1985	1986	1987	1988	1989	1990	1991	1992	1993	1994
Disobedience or Discipline-Related Causes?																				
Boredom																				
Carelessness		1	1	1			1	1	1		1	1		1	2		1			
Complacency												1					3	1	4	
Inattention	4	4	8	4	8	2	4	7	3	3	1	1		1	2					
Noncompliance with Orders	2	1			2	2		1			1		1	1		1	1			
Pressing												1					1			
Other Causes																				
Channelized Attention							1		1	1	1	1	1	1	4	1	1	3	1	
Confidence		1																1		
Distraction								2	1					1						
Expectancy											1	1		1	2		2			1
Human Information Processing				1	1			1				1	1							
Judgment	17	12	12	3	8	4	4	9	5	1		2	2	1	5	8	3	4	2	4
Motivation				1									1							
Technique	15	6	7	6	12	3	2	7	7	6	2	3	5	3	4	8	5	4	5	3
Training					1									3						
Other																				

Discipline, unlike flight safety, was not something that related only to the flight line. Both non flyers and flyers could be taken aback by practices in and around the mess. As mentioned earlier it was a place of heavy drinking and other entertainment. Gambling was not uncommon nor was it uncommon to give wives various excuses why their husbands were delayed in leaving the mess.[36] An ultimate mess event, recalls Brigadier-General Rob Clark, an air weapons controller, was the annual Sapsucker weekend where, according to those who had attended, flyers, mostly fighter crews, would arrive at an air defence base, completing very S-H landing sequences, party all weekend and then depart on the Sunday or Monday depending on health.[37] Despite the lingering effects of this extended party it was not unusual for crews to conduct similar S-H departures, though often, according to the myth, while breathing 100 percent oxygen through their facemasks.[38] Was this right? Some aviators did and continue to think not, but others seemed to feel that those who could actually be called on to fight and die in the air were due some leeway, so long as unacceptable behaviour was controlled.[39]

Leeway could also extend off the flight line, but only so far. Many bases had impaired driving checks on Friday nights, but the drunks were generally not charged, rather their keys and vehicles were confiscated sufficiently that they could not get in further trouble.[40] In fairness this approach was on occasion applied earnestly and seriously, particularly in Germany where charges were in fact often laid.[41] But this was not a case so much of the Air Force policing itself but of it acquiescing to larger societal mores that saw drinking, and other mess traditions as incongruent with the expectations of Canadians. Indeed as the 1980s advanced the imposition of societal norms was more noticeable, whereas previously there had often been a reluctance on the part of leaders to provide support to, or just sort out, aviators with serious drinking problems.[42] The same reckoning with Canadian values could be seen in Air Force personnel, including some senior officers, who fell afoul of the law for such acts as fraud.[43]

A Common Air Force Culture?

Much of the literature on the Canadian Air Force of the Cold War suggests that it took its doctrine, organizations, and equipment from American examples. While that may be true, the RCAF's post-war culture was firmly rooted in the RAF experience of the Second World War. The U.S. and British air forces clearly influenced Canada's aviators, so it is of some value to look at recent experiences of those two nations.

The example from the United States Air Force (USAF) is drawn from the 1990s. In 1997 a B-52 crashed during an air show practice. The pilot and crew, composed of that pilot's supervisors, were killed. The crash was widely talked about at the time and it was suggested in the press and by officers well versed with the B-52 community that the pilot was well known for his aggressive flying. Subsequently the DFS in Ottawa produced a short education video entitled "A Darker Shade of Blue." The tape includes a short review of the crash and then extensive comments by the Accident Board president as well as the general officer commanding the base and its flying units. Colonel Michael McConnell, the board president, outlined four case factors. The first was pilot error in that the pilot flew the aircraft "in a manner that violated regulatory provisions and flight manoeuvre guidance" specifically "by exceeding bank angle, speed and altitude restrictions for manoeuvring the aircraft...." The second was crew error, in that the crew allowed the pilot to enter into a stalled flight condition. The third factor was supervision wherein his supervisors had allowed him to continue to fly in spite of poor airmanship. Last came leadership, in that despite direction he had continued to fly overly aggressively. Indeed even having three of his superiors on the aircraft with him had not prevented him from killing himself and them. The comments by the commanding general of the 12th Air Force, Lieutenant-General Thomas Griffith, centred on the notion that "violations of air discipline are aberrations." Aberration this crash might have been, but it was still significant enough for Canada's aviators to distribute the facts to the rank and file and to signal through a rather evocative title that this was a "dark" episode for flyers. Once again, however, there was no commentary by Canadian Air Force leaders to underscore what was clearly a disobedience problem; perhaps they too believed that such acts were aberrations.

Perhaps it was an aberration, but in addition to the video DFS produced a written account of the B-52 accident in the fall of 1998 and a fairly pointed editorial on leadership. The editor, Captain Jay Medves, indicated that bootleg copies of the accident report had generated hot debate when first circulated:

> Rarely have I seen one document provoke so much discussion amongst the leadership. One remark I heard was "interesting, but it couldn't happen here." Not true. A similar scenario is less likely to occur because we are a much smaller air force; not because we are in any way different, better, less susceptible, or less human.[44]

A full edition of *Flight Comment* dealing with discipline followed the next year. With the words "Focus on Discipline" on the front cover the issue included articles from the USAF, U.S. Army, and Royal Australian Air Force. Brigadier-General Charles Burke, the director of U.S. Army Safety, stated bluntly:

Safe aviation operations require elimination of undisciplined actions before they cause an accident. But many times, in the name of "protecting" an aviator's career, we hesitate to hold aviators accountable for breaches of flight discipline, disregard of procedures, and failures to perform to standard.

Undisciplined behaviour rarely corrects itself. It's the commander's job to deal appropriately with violations as they occur.[45]

The issue also contained a commentary by Chief Warrant Officer Bert Lapointe, the formation chief warrant officer for 1 Canadian Air Division. Lapointe observed:

In my career I have seen a lot of great things ... but also a lot of bad habits related directly to a lack of self-discipline which required education and corrective action in the operating procedures. Discipline doesn't have to be authoritative to be effective. It just needs to be incorporated as an integral part of our daily activities.[46]

Here, as we have seen repeatedly, was the flight safety organ pointing the matter squarely towards the leadership of the Air Force.

Most recently, the British services have been in a period of integration and in 2002 a joint flight safety organization, the Defence Aviation Safety Centre, was established and began publication of a new safety magazine *Aviate*. The second issue included a short piece that identified flying as a high risk environment populated by professionals "whose background indicates intelligence, integrity, stability and those who exhibit highly skilled and responsible attitudes." That said the article reported that a recent survey of co-pilots "found them describing their captains as over-confident, arrogant, unpredictable and aggressive, which is classified as exhibiting an 'active-masculine' personality trait." Of interest, the author noted, this trait was equally apparent in female flyers and evident throughout all flying communities.[47] One wonders if there might also be a link to imbedded disobedience for the same author considered the question of conforming and deviating from standards in an article in the following year. Although recognizing the value of non-conformity and adaptability, he concluded that something was "dangerously wrong ... when you find that the culture of your organization is accepting non-standard activities or you find that corners are being cut." "Do not intentionally break the rules; get the system changed."[48] The British flight safety community seemed to be zeroing in on disobedience and another early issue offered some editorial commentary in a piece describing an unauthorized training flight from the early 1950s that had resulted in disciplinary action: "We are more professional than this. Unauthorized flying activities are a thing of the past. Indiscipline is no longer a concern and therefore unregulated flying activities — like those that led to the Wellington accident — are unlikely to happen. Or are they....?"[49] Here once again a flight safety system seems clearly to signalling a need for discipline.

What to Make of This?

Although it seems likely that disobedience, whether explicit or conditioned, did and continues to exist in flying operations and that there have been some at least implicit links to the Air Force's philosophy of flight safety, this chapter provides some reflection on the subject, but also leaves many questions. Little research has been done in Canada on the subject of Air Force culture, so we do not know if the sort of discipline attributed to the Army or the Navy would work or even if it would be desirable in the Air Force. It would, for example, be hard to imagine a young soldier stopping a vehicle from heading out on a mission because he or she felt there was something wrong with it, and yet that sort of technical responsibility is intensely internalized by all members of the Air Force.[50]

Equally, we do not know if the Air Force's seemingly laissez-faire approach to disobedience is just that or is rather a product of risk-taking by leaders that is designed to allow those fighting in the air to have the flexibility and adaptability to ensure mission accomplishment as suggested by Admiral Falls and Major-General Holman. Finding out more about how aviators have and do function and developing an understanding of Air Force culture are essential if leaders are going to ask young aviators, whether flyers or support personnel, to conduct effective and efficient air operations with limited resources in today's complex tactical and operational circumstances.

Finally, because this commentary has generated debate among those who have reviewed it, I would like to indicate that the opinion shared by many, myself included, is that accountability and with it obedience to regulations has improved in recent years. As Major-General Chisholm said:

> my perception is that we now have a much more professional air force than we did 20 years ago. So the question is: what has changed? One might argue that the flight safety system has been effective, and that aircrew and their leaders are now conditioned to be more professional than their predecessors.[51]

NOTES

1. Colonel R.D. Schultz, *Directorate of Flight Safety 1973 Annual Aircraft Accident Analysis* (Ottawa: Canada Department of National Defence, 1973), 3.

2. The term *aviator* is used as the generic equivalent to *soldier* and *sailor*. As such it includes all those wearing Air Force uniforms or working in Air Force organizations. Those aviators involved in flying operations are referred to as *flyers* or *aircrew*.

3. A number of serving and retired officers were contacted in the preparation of this paper. Some supported the thesis, others did not, and still others preferred not to comment. I wish to indicate clearly that the thesis is mine alone; I fully respect the views of all those contacted and any errors in presenting their thoughts is my responsibility alone. The fact that there was no consensus suggests that this is an issue that will require further consideration by senior Air Force leaders.

4. Very little literature exists on the topic of flying discipline. A number of database searches of the Canadian Forces College War Peace and Security catalogue for subjects such as flying discipline or aircrew discipline resulted, in some cases, in no hits whatsoever. Out of more than 600 major papers written by Air Force officers studying at the college during those years, only one was on the topic of flying safety. Unfortunately, this handwritten paper is largely illegible as a result of the transfer process to microfilm.

5. Coincidentally, a review of the papers of Sir Arthur Harris, commander of Royal Air Force (RAF) Bomber Command from 1942 to 1945, reveals that losses resulting from accidents, including low flying, caused frustration. Harris Papers, RAF Museum Hendon.

6. Canada, National Defence, *Flight Safety for the Canadian Forces* (Ottawa: Supply and Services, 1995), 9–10.

7. *Ibid.*, 10–19.

8. All flight safety data are collected based on two categories of *occurrences* (i.e., something happening). An *accident* involves the loss or major damage of an aircraft or death or injury. An *incident* involves minor damage or the potential for any more serious result. Occurrences are further categorized as *air* where activities are related to flying or *ground* where the activities are not in support of flying (i.e., maintenance or refuelling).

9. Canada, Royal Canadian Air Force (RCAF), *Crash Comment* (July-September 1949), i.

10. *Ibid.*, iii.

11. *Ibid.*, iv.

12. *Ibid.*, 1.

13. Canada, RCAF, *Crash Comment* (April-June 1950), 3 and 12–13.

14. Canada, RCAF, *Crash Comment* (July-September 1950), Foreword.

15. Canada, RCAF, *Crash Comment* (April-June 1951), Foreword.

16. Canada, RCAF, *Flight Comment* (Second Quarter 1954), 1.

17. *Ibid.*, 7.

18. Major-General J.R. Chisholm, Email to the author, 29 August 2005

19. Major-General J.R. Chisholm, email to the author, 29 August 2005.

20. Colonel (Retired) John Lehmann, "My First (Potentially Fatal) Helicopter Mishap," *Newsletter of the Venture Association* (June 2002), 3.

21. Colonel R.D. Schultz, *Annual Aircraft Accident Analysis 1973* (Ottawa: Department of National Defence [DND], 1973), 3.

22. Lieutenant-General A.C. Hull, *Annual Aircraft Accident Analysis 1973* (Ottawa: DND, 1973), 1.

23. Canada, DND, *Flight Comment* (Second Quarter 1975), 10–11.

24. Admiral R.H. Falls, *Annual Aircraft Accident Analysis 1977* (Ottawa: DND, 1977).

25. Colonel J.R. Chisholm, *Annual Aircraft Accident Analysis 1977* (Ottawa: DND, 1977), 3.

26. Colonel F.M. Boomer, email to the author, 16 August 2005.

27. Major Jim Stewart, "Pressing Problems," *Flight Comment* (First Quarter 1980), 22–24.

28. *Overspeed* occurs when an aircraft has an airspeed higher than the maximum recommended limits the plane was designed for. The overspeed can occur to the aircraft as a whole or as in this case to the engines where the engine rpm is allowed to exceed the maximum in the same way that a car engine exceeds its redline rpm.

29. Anonymous, "Checklist Error," *Flight Comment* (Third Quarter 1980), 18–19.

30. Major-General L.A. Ashley, "As I See It," *Flight Comment* (Third Quarter 1985), 1.

31. General G.C.E. Thériault, "As I See It," *Flight Comment* (First Quarter 1985), 1.

32. Major-General (Retired) D.F. Holman, email to the author, 15 August 2005.

33. Colonel H. Rose, "As I See It," *Flight Comment* (Fourth Quarter 1985), 1.

34. Canada, *Flight Safety for the Canadian Forces*, 11–8 to 11–11. Italics in original.

35. Table complied from Canada, National Defence, *1973 Annual Aircraft Accident Analysis*; *1985 Annual Aircraft Occurrence Analysis*; and *1988 Annual Aircraft Occurrence Analysis*.

36. Brigadier-General R.H. Clark, email to the author, 16 August 2005.

37. *Ibid.*

38. *Ibid.* These sorts of arrivals were not restricted to Sapsucker. For example, the author witnessed a Tracker maritime patrol aircraft "arrive" for a Moose Jaw air show by flying between two hangars.

39. Boomer email.

40. Holman and Clark emails. I personally remember being very amused when a clearly inebriated chum got only about 50 metres from the mess before going over the curb and subsequently having his keys taken away for the night. He was the object of much derision on Monday morning, but no discipline.

41. I recall one officer who was found guilty of driving while impaired (DWI) and whose promotion was subsequently delayed.

42. Clark email.

43. Major-General Holman conducted a summary trial on an officer accused of shoplifting. In another case a general officer was dismissed from the Air Force for misusing aircraft for personal reasons, as well as padding travel expenses. Similarly, Colonel Boomer recalls pilots during Operation APOLLO getting into trouble for non-flying violations.

44. Captain J.S. Medves, "From the Editor," *Flight Comment* (Fourth Quarter 1998), 1.

45. Brigadier-General C.M. Burke, "Accountability," *Flight Comment* (Fourth Quarter 1999), 15.

46. Chief Warrant Officer B. Lapointe, "Flight Safety and Discipline," *Flight Comment* (Fourth Quarter 1999), 22–23.

47. Peter Adams, "Risk-Taking by Aircrew," *Aviate* (First Quarter 2002), 22–23.

48. Peter Adams, "Are You a Deviant?" *Aviate* (First Quarter 2003), 10–11.

49. United Kingdom, Ministry of Defence, "Fifty Years Ago," *Aviate* (First Quarter 2002), 19.

50. Boomer email.

51. Major-General Chisholm email.

13

When Orders Conflict: A Perspective from the Board of Inquiry — Croatia

Gordon Sharpe

Introduction

T HE BOARD OF INQUIRY — CROATIA (BOI) was convened in July 1999 to examine the medical complaints of a number of Canadian soldiers who had served with the United Nations Protection Force (UNPROFOR) in the Balkans between four and eight years earlier. The specific mission in Croatia, called Operation (Op) HARMONY, that appeared to be giving rise to most of the complaints began in March 1992 and ended in November 1994 and involved a total of five Canadian Battle Groups. A substantial number of the Canadian soldiers who served in Croatia felt that sometime during their tour they had been exposed to some type of environmental contaminants and were now suffering a variety of medical and psychological problems associated with the exposure. They also felt that the Department of National Defence (DND) and Veterans Affairs Canada were paying little attention to their complaints. At least in part to satisfy the media pressure, the chief of the defence staff, with the approval of the minister of national defence (MND), decided to call a military inquiry.

During the course of the inquiry, it became evident that the fundamental cause of most of the medical and psychological issues was not environmental in nature, but more likely related to operational stress. The board expanded its mandate to look at this area and eventually about half of its time was spent looking at this issue.

Although the environmental, medical, and psychological aspects of this operation understandably received the vast majority of the media coverage, there was another facet of the deployment that received little attention — what happens when an order issued through the United Nations (UN) chain of command conflicts with the accepted doctrine and practice of a Canadian force under its command? What happens, personally and professionally, when a Canadian commander is forced to choose between following a legal order from a UN commander and respecting the boundaries of his national mandate? Most notably, regardless of the course of action chosen, can either be considered as an act of disobedience on the part of the commander?

The Croatia BOI merely noted the command dilemma faced by the Canadian commanders, particularly the commander of the third rotation into Croatia, Lieutenant-Colonel Jim Calvin. However, the dilemmas faced by Calvin, and the command decisions he subsequently made, pose questions concerning the nature of military obedience and adherence to a nationally accepted doctrine, when Canadians are operating as part of multinational forces.

Overview

Lieutenant-Colonel Jim Calvin was the commanding officer (CO) of the Canadian battle group in Croatia in 1993 during Rotation (ROTO) 2 of Op HARMONY. He was ill prepared for the situation that eventually materialized on the ground in Croatia, a situation that effectively forced him to choose between following an order from his superior commander in the UN chain of command and following what was effectively Canadian and professional doctrine with respect to maintaining the integrity of his command. His honesty and professional attitude towards accomplishing the mission pushed him into following the direction issued by his UN commander, even though awareness of the serious resource and personnel shortages within his battle group reinforced the validity of the normal Canadian Army doctrine that dictated otherwise. His chain of command nationally was unaware and unhelpful to him in dealing with this dilemma during the deployment, and much of the senior leadership within the Canadian Forces remained unaware of the nature of the operational climate the battle group functioned in for several years afterwards. The situation at the time was further exacerbated by the fact that his Canadian commander within the UN had a dual role; functioning as both a staff officer and a

Canadian commander who lacked both the intelligence assets and staff resources to aid Calvin.

As a result of the decisions he made — some of which were considered retrospectively by a number senior Canadian authorities to be on the verge of mutinous — the mission on the ground was operationally successful, and resulted in a rare UN commander's commendation. In the Canadian context, however, there was no recognition of this achievement until several years after the Battle Group had returned to Canada — in fact, it was not until after the Croatia BOI report called for recognition for this unit that action was initiated. As a commander, Lieutenant-Colonel Calvin was conflicted personally and his troops were put into extremely demanding situations, both physically and psychologically, throughout the entirety of the mission.

After the Canadian Battle Group's return to Canada, the legal and administrative bureaucracies of National Defence Headquarters (NDHQ) began a minute examination of many of the command decisions Calvin had made in the field — indeed they went so far as to launch National Investigative Service probes into several. They appeared to be looking for errors in judgment, omissions, and even commissions of unethical conduct on the part of the leadership of the battle group, most probably as a result of concerns that had been stirred by the public interest in the negative perception of Canadian Forces (CF) leadership during the Airborne Regiment's 1992 — 1993 deployment to Somalia. Although the circumstances of the two deployments were dramatically different, the hierarchy of NDHQ appeared determined to find examples to be made of Calvin and/or some of his subordinates to illustrate the fact that the CF had eradicated the leadership deficiencies of which Canadians had became so aware of during the Somalia Inquiry. Calvin and his troops paid a steep price as a result of this effort, a price that far exceeded the damage done by the combat conditions they endured in Croatia.

The command situation faced by Calvin in Croatia could well be repeated for future Canadian commanders. It is hoped that under similar circumstances the mission could be as well accomplished; however, it would be beneficial if it could be accomplished with fewer stress causalities that occurred in Op HARMONY, and with less unnecessary pressure on the commander. To understand the factors that can lead to similar circumstances, independent of personality and individual leadership ability, it is key find a command and control model and a systematic approach that will permit the challenges of any command situation to be evaluated in detail.

Command and Control Model

The command dilemma that Calvin encountered in Croatia can be appropriately described using the Pigeau and McCann Command and Control model.[1] This particular model has been validated by analyzing a large number of CF command situations and has been introduced to students at the Canadian Forces College for the last several years. This structure links three essential aspects of command, individual competency, legal and personal authority, and extrinsic and intrinsic responsibility, in a three dimensional model. These three factors provide the acronym for this model — CAR — standing for competency, authority, and responsibility.

Competency, as it applies to the abilities required for a military person, is divided into four general categories; physical, intellectual, emotional, and interpersonal. The first two categories, physical and intellectual, are straightforward and have been the subject of the military physical and professional development of leaders since militaries were first organized. The importance of the last two categories, emotional and interpersonal competency, has, however, not been as well understood within most militaries, and certainly not within the CF. Yet, as operational tempo increases with the increased possibility of casualties and resource issues continue to force compromises by senior leaders in terms of force structures, equipment, and training, the facets of emotional and interpersonal competency can become the most important aspects of the CAR model.

This is pointed out by Pigeau and McCann who write that military members are subjected to the full range of negative emotions — guilt, anxiety, anger, frustration, boredom, grief, fear, and depression — but are still expected to command effectively under all conditions. Consequently, Pigeau and McCann suggest that this produces an emphasis on the ability of leaders to develop emotional competency, best described as an individual's resiliency, hardiness, and ability to cope under stress. They conclude that:

> Command demands a degree of emotional "toughness" to accept the potentially dire consequences of operational decisions. The ability to keep an overall

emotional balance and perspective on the situation is critical, as is the ability to maintain a sense of humour.[2]

At the same time Pigeau and McCann propose that while interpersonal competency is more familiar to most military members and has been traditionally interpreted as the ability to communicate verbally and in writing with superiors, peers, subordinates, and outside agencies — they expand these ideas in the CAR concept to include a broader range of social skills, including empathy.

All four competency areas — physical, intellectual, emotional, and interpersonal — played a role in the command circumstances that ROTO 2 of Op HARMONY experienced in Croatia, but applying ideas of emotional and interpersonal competency are critical to understanding the decisions that the CO made while in the area of operations.

Authority is particularly important to military commanders, and was clearly an issue with some of the decisions made by Lieutenant-Colonel Calvin. To a large extent, reservations concerning whether Calvin had exceeded the scope of his authority were the motivation for the retrospective re-examination of his command decisions that took place at NDHQ. The concept of authority as defined by Pigeau and McCann is "the degree to which a commander is empowered to act, the scope of this power and the resources available for enacting his or her will."[3] They further elaborate on aspects of authority, identifying both its legal and personal facets, and show that personal authority–gained through one's personal credibility with superiors, peers, and subordinates — without legal authority is dangerous, while legal authority without personal authority is forced to be rigid and direction based. Command capability is best exercised when both the appropriate legal authority has been assigned and the commensurate personal authority has been developed. An essential element of legal authority, one that is easy to overlook, is the assignment of sufficient personnel and material resources to allow the commander to fulfill his or her responsibilities.

The third category that constitutes command capability is responsibility, defined by Pigeau and McCann as the degree to that an individual accepts the legal and moral liability that goes along with the command. Again, as in authority, there are two components to responsibility. The first one is externally or extrinsically imposed by the legal chain of command, and once accepted, closely resembles accountability. Responsibility applies down the chain of command as well, and demands that the authority, both personal and legal, granted to an individual be used appropriately. When a situation develops where a commander is unwilling to be held accountable for the authority they have been given, some very bad things, such as abuse of authority, can happen.

The other attribute of responsibility is whether it is internally or intrinsically imposed. Intrinsic responsibility is the self-generated sense of obligation that a leader brings to a mission and is traditionally thought of as one's sense of duty. When the degree of intrinsic responsibility is high, but authority is low, as is the case when material or personnel resources are insufficient for the mission, the commander is faced with an ineffectual command situation, and placed under tremendous psychological pressure.

When specific command situations are analyzed using the CAR approach, a three-dimensional plot can be produced that represents a plane upon which a commander exercises his or her command capability. Pigeau and McCann depict this as a command envelope and describe it as balanced if all aspects of the command situation are correct. However, if one or more element of the command circumstance is not correct, then the envelope is described as unbalanced.

A significant advantage of the Pigeau and McCann model is that it provides a consistently enduring framework within which to understand what actually went wrong, or right, with a specific command situation. Simplistically, if a mission fails, the "default position" is to assign blame to the commander. Although that approach can be correct some cases, the rest of the time it tends to obscure serious, underlying problems, and does little to draw out the fundamental lessons that can be learned in order to prevent similar circumstances from developing in the future.

A major advantage of the CAR model is that it focuses on the human element in command, and thus it can be applied to any situation independent of the organizational structure involved. Operations under the auspices of the UN have some complex command and control arrangements, the implications of which are easily missed when looking at the results of these missions. The command situation that the CF battle group led by Lieutenant-Colonel Calvin encountered in Croatia in 1994 is one that involved some serious complications as a result of working within the UN organization.

Deployed Operations and the Impact on
Command and Control

Recently Canadians, and somewhat more slowly, their elected representatives, have been developing an increased sense of awareness of the country's military. However, even before the 2001 terrorist strike on the United States, Canadians traditionally identified with their military units that went offshore to fight, at least with those that could be readily identified as Canadian. While this was typically easier for Army units, it has increasingly become the norm for air and naval forces as well. Operationally, though, Canadian units are more likely to operate as integral parts of larger formations; however, for domestic purposes, the units retain their national identity.

In a paper prepared for the Croatia BOI, Colonel (Retired) Angus Brown describes several examples of the tradition of Canadians identifying with "their" military. This public identification, with at first predominantly Army units, reinforced a similar feeling of identity in the attitudes of Canadian soldiers and their leaders. According to Brown:

> Almost from the first instance when Canadians were deployed in formed military units, there have been strong tendencies to organize, act and fight as Canadian entities. The military accomplishments of Canadians have done a lot to provide a source of national pride and unity for the nation. As Canadians left their home shores, they became more and more nationalistic. This feeling was reflected in their desire to be seen as Canadian, different from others in whatever coalition they were serving at the moment.[4]

What remains a poorly understood and a poorly explained aspect of military deployments for many Canadians is how Canada's military contribution fits into a larger organizational structure. The critical question of how they are integrated into multinational forces when they are sent offshore is often not clear, even to Canadian politicians with oversight responsibilities. For example, some initial confusion was created in 1990 when the then prime minister, Brian Mulroney, stated that the Canadian fighter aircraft would be protecting Canadian ships in the Gulf. Although that was not necessarily a militarily sound operating procedure, the military authorities of the day made every effort to coordinate the disparate activities of the Canadian air and naval contributions in case someone should accuse the prime minister of being inaccurate.

When this lack of understanding of how Canadian contributions are commanded and controlled while deployed extends to senior political or even departmental levels, it can cause significant operational concerns. In the past such misunderstandings have given rise to situations where Canadian military leaders on the ground have been forced to decide whether to live up to Canadian political expectations or to follow potentially contradictory orders that flow down a coalition or UN chain of command — in some cases, orders that even go against Canadian doctrine or practice.

This was the case during the 1990's; Canadians, as a whole, were poorly informed about UN deployments and they were largely unaware that the traditional UN peacekeeping operations had taken on a distinctly different tone. This lack of awareness extended to both the political and military senior leadership. As a result command and control arrangements for deployed Canadian units were not clearly defined and the command and control situation in what frequently became near combat situations could be accurately described as ad hoc.

Even in hindsight, the underlying lack of public awareness of Canadian military involvement in UN operations was, and is, not difficult to understand. In the first place, Canadians were not routinely informed that Canadian troops were deployed to in specific parts of the world, let alone involved in operations where force was commonly required to implement the UN mandate. Not surprising, since often even the military chain of command — distracted and absorbed with budgetary pressures and with public scandal at home — was not well informed of exactly where they were and what they were doing. During a series of interviews in 2003 and 2004 with retired officers who had served at the strategic level of the CF in the last decade of the 1990s, several described their surprise at the intensity of operations Canadian troops had been exposed to during operations euphemistically labelled "peacekeeping" in Croatia. This lack of knowledge as to what was transpiring on the ground in the Balkans was not a result of lack of effort by those involved in the operations. For example, one Canadian general officer who had held a senior UN command position in the Balkans, testifying in front of the Croatia BOI, was clearly frustrated that he was not allowed to brief the senior decision making body in the DND on the events that had unfolded in Croatia during his tour.[5]

At least part of the lack of understanding is because of the assumptions made during UN operations. As Angus Brown describes:

> Canada never gives up full national command of its troops. Nor do other nations. When units are deployed for use in an international force, including UN forces, the commander of that force will be given "operational control." This implies that the force commander is not normally responsible for administration and logistics to support the unit but is authorized to order the operational deployment of the unit to accomplish tasks in support of the purposes for which the force was created and mandated by the UN Security Council.[6]

The term *Operational Control* that Brown refers to allows the UN force commander to employ the Canadian unit in its operationally intended role, it does not, however, allow, the force commander to assign the unit any task other than the one it was assigned to his command to perform, nor does it allow him to change the basic organizational structure of the unit. Brown reflects accepted Canadian doctrine when he argues that even while under the operational control of a UN force commander, a Canadian unit normally maintains unit integrity, as to fail to do so will:

> destroy the integrity of the unit and make it difficult or impossible to command, support or deploy weapons in direct fire support.... a company or a squadron may be tasked individually for a short period of time, but still remaining under the command of the battle group. Long periods, or more complex tasks, will mean that a proportional "slice" of the battle group's other elements (command, support, etc) will also have to be detached. Thus, the integrity of the unit is destroyed, command and support elements are overextended and the possibility of failure or the level of operational risk is increased, both for the

individually-tasked sub-unit and for the remainder
of the battle group.[7]

However this belies the reality of operating in a UN context
which always almost always suffers from a serious lack of resources,
a situation exacerbated by the logistical shortages that many national
contingents assigned to the UN bring with them. What limited
supplies are available through the UN channels are often assigned
to these units from developing nations. From a Canadian national
perspective, the supporting authorities in Ottawa were reluctant
to provide Canadian resources, to include what were perceived as
extra personnel, when the UN was clearly responsible. The resultant
shortages normally have an adverse impact on unit integrity, with
resource restrictions paring the numbers deployed to such a low
level that normal unit integrity cannot be maintained and elements
are, of necessity, piecemealed out to specific tasks, resulting in, "a
reorganization of units to ensure that the minimums are not exceeded.
Unfortunately, units are emasculated and incapable of responding to
any expansion of the risk environment."[8]

The key issue here is the assumption that the risk environment
will not change, because if it does, it can only have two results. Either
the unit will be unable to maintain the required operational tempo
— resulting in risk to the mission, or the level of the individual
soldier's activity will have to increase to the point that severe levels of
operational stress will be generated and the unit will begin to suffer
serious casualties.

Resource constraints also impact the command structure
associated with UN operations. The pressure to keep the number of
personnel deployed on UN operations to the smallest possible number
places major constraints on the deployed headquarters. Accordingly,
during operations such as UNPROFOR, for issues that required
higher levels of authority, a Canadian staff officer in an associated
UN headquarters billet was designated as the Canadian Contingent
Commander. Normal operating procedure for the CF units on the
ground was to refer issues of importance back to Ottawa — to an
NDHQ absorbed in a multitude of other more pressing tasks — to
resolve. According to Brown, this created a situation where:

> there was seldom a superior Canadian headquarters
> in theatre to which the battle group responded.
> The battle group commander was in charge of most

matters affecting his unit and referred administrative or disciplinary matters beyond his power to a nominal Canadian Contingent Commander. If the matter was beyond the limited power of the contingent commander, it was referred to and solved by National Defence Headquarters (NDHQ) in Ottawa.[9]

This process was sufficient for the static, predictable peace keeping operations that had become the norm during the Cold War. Unfortunately for the Canadian soldiers assigned to Op HARMONY, the deteriorating circumstances in the Balkans in the early 1990s resulted in operations that were anything but traditional, and the accepted methodology for establishing command and control led to nearly intolerable conditions for the battle group. Important requests for operational guidance went unanswered or were responded to long after the need had arisen leading to intolerable conditions for the commanding officer, men and women of the battle group.

2nd Battalion Princess Patricia's Canadian Light Infantry Battle Group (2 PPCLI BG) — Op HARMONY

On 4 April 1993 the third rotation of a CF battle group, referred to as Canadian (CANBAT) Battalion 1, based on 2 PPCLI, heavily augmented by personnel from 66 regular and reserve units from across Canada, assumed the responsibility for peacekeeping duties in Sector West of Croatia.[10] Although this was neither the first nor the last Canadian battle group to serve in Croatia as part of UNPROFOR, it was the one that experienced what was perhaps the greatest period of change as this troubled part of the Balkans slipped back into intense ethnic conflict.[11] This battle group began preparing in January 1993, with the arrival in Winnipeg of approximately 550 reservists from across Canada and about 150 or 160 cooks, technicians, medics, and so on to augment the core of approximately 320 experienced PPCLI soldiers from the battalion. In the three months available before the deployment they were subjected to intense training to turn them into a cohesive unit. In the end, an operationally effective battle group of 870 personnel emerged — though with a significant percentage of minimally trained reservists assigned to the rifle companies. Although the training program had started, Calvin was not aware of the degree of danger the battle group would face until he had completed a theatre reconnaissance in mid January, during which he observed a Canadian armoured personnel carrier (APC) being lured into an ambush and destroyed by a Serbian anti-tank rocket.[12] This was his first indication of the nature of what lay ahead, and upon his return to Canada, the intensity and focus of the training changed significantly.

There were three other UN contingents in Sector West aside from the Canadians, the Nepalese, Argentineans, and Jordanians, but they dealt only with either the Serbs or Croats. CANBAT 1, which was also designated as the Force Commander's Reserve, was the only battle group that was responsible for an area encompassing a dividing line between the Serbs and Croats and thus had the most volatile situation. Their mission was to effectively enforce the peace, protect the unarmed and confiscate weapons when they were found. While all the weapons had been, in theory, removed from Sector West, there were still clashes between the two warring factions — ambushes of each other's police forces, anti-personnel mine placements, booby traps, and so on — generally dangerous for the Canadians, but comparatively quiet. CANBAT 1 carried out their

A CANADIAN M113 ARMOURED PERSONNEL CARRIER PATROLS IN CROATIA
DURING UNITED NATIONS PEACEKEEPING OPERATIONS IN 1993.
(Department of National Defence, Sergeant S. Peters,
Canadian Forces Joint Imagery Centre ISC93 5021 32)

mission in this sector for three months before the relative calm was dramatically altered.

Calvin was well aware that at the same time CANBAT 1 was functioning in Sector West, the UN was grappling with how to reassert their credibility and authority in the more explosive southern area of the country. The UN had suffered a severe setback to their reputation earlier in the year when UN troops had withdrawn in the face of a Croatian attack on a power dam. In early July, the UN force commander, General Cot, was party to the signing of an agreement that was intended to create four buffer zones in the region in an effort to de-escalate the fighting in the most hotly contested region of Croatia — Sector South. Unfortunately, General Cot had neither the quantity nor quality of forces he needed in this sector to implement the agreement, and the UN could not afford another failure. Accordingly, he issued a warning order to CANBAT 1 for the Canadian commander, contrary to well-established Canadian doctrine that required unit integrity to be maintained, to be prepared to split the Canadian battalion in half and move it 500 km to the south to reinforce that sector and implement the agreement, while maintaining the same responsibilities in Sector West.

In mid-July the order was implemented, and Calvin split his force, including a slice of the administration and support elements. Not surprisingly, many of the issues that the doctrine predicted began to surface. The operational situation the Canadians were moving into — with half a battalion — was, in the words of a military historian researching the issue for the Croatia BOI:

> in the territory where the Croats and the Krajina Serbs directly confronted one another and, as a result, was bitterly contested by both the Serbs and Croats. Canadian troops often found themselves on the receiving end of artillery shells, small arms, and heavy machine gun fire. The land was littered with anti-tank and anti-personnel mines. Deployed into the middle of the war, the Canadians were often the targets of such weapons in attempts to intimidate the peacekeeping forces.[13]

The personnel situation was so critical that from mid July onwards, all leave except for leave back to Canada, was cancelled for the members of CANBAT 1. For some members, that meant that they went for up to 80 days without a day off in some of the toughest conditions they had ever encountered. Phone contact with families back in Canada was lost once they went south, and environmental conditions deteriorated as they crossed the mountains — temperatures reached into the 40 degrees Celsius range for days on end. Adding to the deteriorating mood was the loss of the first unit member to a road accident in Sector West.

After several weeks the Canadian battle group had begun to reassert the UN presence in the critical areas in the sector — and regain some of the respect the French contingent had lost earlier in the year. The French themselves were trusted by neither side — the Serbs believed they had been at least aware of an earlier Croat attack on them — and thus their utility to the force commandeer was limited. He asked that the full Canadian battle group be moved to Sector South so the UN could move ahead with the implementation of the agreement, and in mid August, the remainder of the Canadian battle group moved to Sector South.

Calvin took advantage of this move to restructure CANBAT 1 to a three-company battle group to facilitate the handover with the three company Canadian contingent arriving in October. The intensity of operations was hard to imagine — as described by Calvin during his testimony six years later at the Croatia BOI:

> we had to maintain the OP [observation post] and we were literally having people going up to the OP, and when the shells started running back to the bunker and things like this. And for four days soldiers maintained their position at that bunker. Now, to be honest, the company commander and the sergeant major maintained their positions there and we tried to rotate soldiers in and out so that any one soldier didn't have to go through the whole period of time. I'm not certain how effective that was. But those were the kind of decisions we had to do if we were going to … [restore the UN reputation] … with the Serbs and get credibility. If they see that every time something happens we run away, we would be no better than the contingent that was there before us. So there was a degree of we had to show that we were there to do our job even if the going got tough and there was also the very real requirement to keep

observation on the Maslenica Bridge.... But I had
to say that down in the B Company area at Miranje
they were shelled. They had OPs that were shelled
regularly and I would say in general that somewhere
in our sector every single day shells were falling.[14]

The last chapter in CANBAT 1's experience in Sector South
was written in the Medak Pocket — a part of the operation that
has been more widely reported on in the last few years. The Medak
Pocket operation started with an intensive Croat artillery barrage
on the town of Medak on 9 September, followed by an attack that
included tanks.[15] The Serbs, initially caught by surprise, eventually
began reinforcing themselves. A standoff resulted with the Serbian
populated town of Medak caught in the middle in Croatian hands.
On the 13 September CANBAT 1, reinforced by two French
companies, was ordered to establish a buffer between the two sides.
On 15 September, they began to move into position to do that.
While moving, one of the Canadian companies came under intense
Croatian fire that the Canadians returned. Eventually the Croatians
withdrew, and the preparations continued to establish the buffer
zone that would require the Croatian forces to leave Medak. In a
face to face meeting, the Croatian commander agreed to withdraw,
but insisted they needed until noon the next day to do it. Waking
up the next morning to the sound of small arms fire and the sight of
smoke rising from several locations, the Canadians realized that the
Croatians were systemically ethnic cleansing the area and destroying
the evidence before they left. At noon, the Canadians moved forward
but encountered a Croatian defensive position complete with a
T-72 tank that had no intention of leaving. Both the Croats and the
Canadians prepared for battle and a tense standoff ensued. Calvin,
determined to move forward and recognizing the Croatian objective
of keeping the world on their side in the larger conflict, brought
up a number of international media to monitor the event, which
immediately diffused the situation and caused the Croats to begin
to dismantle their defences. When the Canadians eventually moved
into the area they found that the Croats had not left a single living
thing in the Pocket — human or animal — and they had not had the
time to completely hide all the evidence of their ethnic cleansing.
The results of the Canadian action were described by Colonel
George Oehring, the Canadian officer who commanded Sector
UNPROFOR Sector South from September 1993 until May 1994,

A MEMBER OF 2ND BATTALION PRINCESS PATRICIA'S CANADIAN LIGHT
INFANTRY STANDS GUARD INSIDE THE MEDAK POCKET IN 1993.

(Department of National Defence, Sergeant Mike Bonin,
Canadian Forces Joint Imagery Centre ISC93 5307 14A)

and then assumed the position of deputy commander of the Canadian contingent until September 1994, when he testified to the Croatia BOI on 10 November 1999:

> First, what was seen as a Canadian success at Medak restored some degree of credibility in the UN, and marked a first for UNPROFOR; that is to say, some land that had been captured by military action had been subsequently surrendered, neutralized and then occupied by the UN. I don't think that happened anywhere at any time in UNPROFOR other than at Medak. The local Serbs were most favourably impressed by the courage, discipline and impartiality of CANBAT 1, and never hesitated to tell me of it, even as I was saying goodbye to them a year later. Even the Croats expressed their grudging admiration for what CANBAT 1 did. One of the operational zone commanders with whom I frequently dealt was often heard to say, "The Canadians do everything professionally."[16]

Command Situation Analysis

The command decisions forced on the Canadian commander of CANBAT 1 in Croatia in 1993 can be described, in somewhat of an understatement, as demanding. During the initial operations in Sector West, Lieutenant-Colonel Calvin's unit operated as a single battle group, coping with the added challenge of working with a large percentage of reservists in operationally trying circumstances. However, the scenario changed dramatically mid-tour when Calvin was asked, as the force commander's reserve, to take actions that were opposed to what he had been trained to expect — and actions that he could reasonable expect would put his soldiers in greater risk of injury than they were already experiencing.

All three axis used in the Pigeau and McCann model — competency, authority, and responsibility can productively be examined to extract information for this analysis. The first category — competency — is particularly worthy of note in this case. There can be no doubt that the first sub-category of competency, physical competency, was extremely important here. The operational tempo was extremely high, particularly for the command element, as soon as Calvin discovered that his early concept of the mission was inaccurate. In essence, the battle group began intense training in mid January 1993, and the pace never slackened until the return to Canada more than nine months later. For many of the soldiers, the last 80 days in theatre were without a day off. In one descriptive overview of the physical environment the CO stated:

> I do believe that stress and fatigue could have played a role in what has happened. I do believe that the severity of our tour was, if not the worst, certainly amongst the very worst in terms of those tours that happened in the early 1990s. A combination of personal danger, extreme fatigue due to lack of leave ... long hours, traumatic stress on individuals, deaths within the battalion produced an overall level of burden on individuals within the unit that it was severe ..."[17]

Clearly, Calvin's physical competency and that of many of his subordinates was a significant factor and had a positive impact on the outcome of this mission.

The second sub-category of competency, intellectual competency, refers to the ability to plan missions, monitor and assess situations as they unfold, draw appropriate conclusions and consider alternate solutions. It also requires the individual commander be able to assess risks to the mission and to the personnel involved in carrying out the mission, and finally, to make appropriate judgments. Above all, since missions frequently change once a force is on the ground, intellectual competency must include creativity, flexibility, and a willingness to learn from experience as a mission progresses. It is apparent that Calvin illustrated the attributes of intellectual competency — when he discovered that the mission was going to be considerably more dangerous than first anticipated, he developed an appropriate training regime to bring the disparate elements of his battle group up to what he considered an acceptable level. The performance of the battle group, including the reservists, in Sector West and later in Sector South, illustrates the effectiveness of the training. Calvin's assessment of and decision to accept the increased risk associated with splitting his unit despite the doctrinal edict against such a move, was a basic intellectual exercise, and one that was key to the eventual outcome.

Physical and intellectual competencies, the traditional areas of attention, were demonstrably important in this operation; however, he less frequently considered area of emotional competency played a significant role as well. Calvin experienced anxiety, anger, frustration, grief, et cetera, during this mission and after his return to Canada as evident in his testimony to the Croatia BOI:

> there is a little bit of an inability to put the tour behind you. I have had people come over to my place and it is still very much a very vivid experience for us all.... many still feel that the system failed them. I think betrayed would be too strong a word, but certainly failed is not. And it is in terms of ignoring the kind of sacrifices that they put them through. It became evident that what we went through was far out of the ordinary than what was expected of what we should have had to do, I believe."[18]

Despite the stress placed on CANBAT 1 by the role they were asked to play as the force commander's reserve with the increased risk, Calvin maintained his ability to make the difficult operational decisions that were required in the Medak Pocket showdown.

Calvin's interpersonal competency, his ability to interact effectively with his subordinates, superiors, and with outside organizations, was severely tested during Op HARMONY. His ability to motivate his subordinates to perform hazardous duties, despite horrible living and working conditions, and the high personal risk involved, was exceptional. Years after the unit returned to Canada, many of his former subordinates still speak of Calvin as the best commander they have ever served under. Equally important to the successful outcome of this mission was his ability to deal successfully with the media and with the Croat military authorities during the Medak Pocket standoff. Overall, the commander of CANBAT 1 displayed extremely high level of interpersonal competency.

Collectively, Calvin displayed competency levels in all four sub-categories that considerably exceed what one would normally expect from an officer with his experience — and this exceptional level of competency was critical to the success of the mission.

Authority, defined by Pigeau and McCann as," ... the degree to which a commander is empowered to act, the scope of this power and the resources available for enacting his or her will,"[19] considered in the two sub-categories of legal (authority assigned from external sources) and personal (earned by virtue of personal credibility), played a large part in this situation. The two sub-categories of authority describe a commander's possible sphere of action, and both are equally important. In this case, Calvin's legal authority was constrained by two things — resources and doctrine.

As pointed out by Pigeau and McCann, the resources available to carry out a mission impact a commander's authority dramatically. In Calvin's case, the resource constraints started well before deployment and continued throughout, becoming most critical when he split his unit in response to the force commander's request. From the shortage of personnel that forced the cancellation of leave for the last three months of the tour to the persistent unavailability of defence stores, resource deficiencies were persistent.

Canadian Army doctrine clearly dictates that unit integrity be maintained to avoid increased levels of operational risk and the overriding risk of mission failure. Calvin, well aware of Army doctrine and practice, was also asked by the force commander to split his unit, which was already under-resourced, into two parts separated by some 500 km and a mountain range. The political significance to the future of the UN of such a move was clear to Calvin, and as the force commander's reserve, he can well have anticipated the request, however, as an experienced Canadian Army officer he would also have been well aware that such an action would seriously push the limits of the operational control authority ceded to the UN force commander, and contradict the guidance inherent in Army doctrine. His legal authority to act in consonance with national command was confused because of the vague role of the Canadian contingent commander in this UN operation, and the lack of awareness on the part of the CF chain of command because of distraction, and the intensity and speed of development of the operation in Croatia. He chose to follow the force commander's order, and his high level of personal authority ensured that his subordinates carried out his direction.

Overall, authority was a key issue in this circumstance, and the combination of resource shortages and the conflicting authority of doctrine and accepted practice placed the Canadian commander in a very difficult personal situation. However, it is evident that both his legal and personal authority was sufficient in this case for the situation. In hindsight, had the resource constraints in theatre been less severe, the doctrinal conflict might have been moderated, but the boundaries of the level of control ceded to UN authorities during UN operations would still have been problematic.

Responsibility, "the degree to which an individual accepts the legal and moral liability commensurate with command," played a significant role both during and after this deployment for both Calvin and many of his subordinates.[20] For Calvin, his personal or intrinsic sense of responsibility for the success of the mission pushed him to obey the order from General Cot to split his force between sectors in Croatia. On the other hand, his strong personal sense of accountability for the consequences of the action on his troops and his extrinsic responsibility to follow Canadian doctrine and professional knowledge, which dictated that his force not be split, competed with this mission focus. He willingly accepted this responsibility and the resultant consequences, and, according to the Pigeau and McCann model, this is a situation that results in "maximal (balanced) command. In this situation, the military organization can be assured that the authority assigned and earned will be treated responsibly in accordance with stated intentions, implied military values and general societal expectations."[21]

Conclusion

When CANBAT 1 was directed to leave Sector West and move into Sector South in 1993, the reputation of the UN in the region was at an extremely low point. The UN had failed repeatedly to fulfill their promise to protect the UN Protected Areas, and when confronted by the threat of violence, UN forces had simply melted away. In the end as a direct result of the actions of CANBAT 1 and the command ability of Lieutenant-Colonel Jim Calvin, the status of the UN in the entire Balkans was enhanced, lives were saved, and subsequent diplomatic actions were allowed to proceed — but at a severe cost to the physical and psychological health of the Canadian troops and the career of a fine officer and leader who behaved exactly as one would predict he would based on the Pigeau and McCann model.

The impact that CANBAT 1 had on the situation in Croatia as a direct result of their commander's decision to set aside accepted Canadian Army doctrine was pivotal in re-establishing the credibility of the UN in the Balkans. Had his actions not demonstrated the resolute intention to enforce the security of the UN Protected Areas in Croatia, the rest of the region would have continued the tumble into violent ethnic conflict. For their efforts, 2PPCLI was awarded a UN Force Commander's Commendation from French General Cot, the first of its kind and one of only three awarded in UNPROFOR's history.

Without doubt, the most important lesson from Op HARMONY in general, and the Medak Pocket in particular, that must be highlighted is that the findings of the Somalia Inquiry were not accurate with respect to the quality of the men and women that the CF were putting in the field to serve the UN. In reality, Op HARMONY demonstrated that the Canadian Army in 1993 consisted of dedicated, competent, well-disciplined soldiers, led by competent, highly capable officers and senior NCOs, operating in a balanced command manner.

Colonel George Oehring summarized the impact that CANBAT 1 had on the situation in Croatia during his testimony to the Croatia BOI:

> The soldiers of 2 PPCLI will never know how much they helped us, the UN and ultimately, the local people even long after their departure and even though I had nothing to do with the conduct or success of their actions…. All this to say, Mr. President, that Canada was well represented in Croatia by a bunch of gutsy, well-disciplined, and well-led young men and women who endured considerable stress and hardship — as did those at home who loved them — and to do the job our government told them to do, but has yet to fully acknowledge. The country owes them at least an understanding that has been too long in coming."[22]

At the point in time that the Canadians involved in ROTO 2 of Op HARMONY were returning home in October 1994, if Canadians thought of the military at all, their attention was focused on what later became known as the Somalia Affair. In this environment, senior DND officials were not in the mood to disclose anything about operations to Canadians that was not absolutely necessary, or to discuss Canadian Peacekeepers engaged in firefights. Although senior UN commanders recognized the Canadians for their valour, they were virtually ignored at home.[23] In the words of their commanding officer, Colonel Jim Calvin, testifying to the BOI:

We were all very proud of what we did. But when we came home, there was no recognition of what we had achieved even though if you talked to anybody in UNPROFOR at that time, they thought we were all bloody heroes. We came back here and it was just you are done.[24]

NOTES

1. Dr. Ross Pigeau and Carol McCann, "Re-Conceptualizing Command and Control," *Canadian Military Journal* 3, No. 1 (Spring 2002), 53–64. This article provides an excellent overview of the command and control model that Pigeau and McCann have developed and validated using numerous case studies from Canadian Forces command experiences. It is particularly effective in looking at command situations where problems have arisen that can appear, on the surface, to be leadership related but have on further analysis proved to be far more complex in terms of causes.

2. *Ibid.*, 58.

3. *Ibid.*

4. Angus Brown, "Command, Control and Intelligence in Peace Support Operations," an unpublished paper prepared for the Board of Inquiry — Croatia (henceforth BOI), and received by the board on 29 November 1999, 4. Originally published on the BOI website and a copy is in possession of the author.

5. Major-General Alain Forand, who was the commander of Sector South in UNPROFOR during 1995, told the BOI: "No, nobody every asked me. Let's put it this way. When I came back I said, 'I am going to put it on paper with the help of some of my staff that were with me over there.' People, I hope they knew it was there because I gave it to some of the people that was with me over there. When they went back — their commanding officer — they knew I had prepared something so I went and gave it. But I was never invited by the headquarters to give a presentation. Even so, they knew because I had spoken to DCDS [deputy chief of the defence staff]. I said, 'You know, I am putting together a presentation on the experience,' because I felt that the worst [was] that [despite all] the Canadians had done there, not only the 2 Van Doos, but all the other Canadians that came before, we never heard about it because it was not Bosnia." Testimony before the BOI, 25 November 1999, 28.

6. Brown, "Command, Control and Intelligence in Peace Support Operations," 3.

7. *Ibid.*, 4.

8.   *Ibid.*, 5.

9.   *Ibid.*, 6.

10. Referred to as Rotation or ROTO 2. The initial deployment 1st Battalion Royal
     Vingtième Regiment Battle Group (1R22eR BG) is referred to as ROTO 0.
     The 3rd Battalion Princess Patricia's Canadian Light Infantry Battle Group (3
     PPCLI BG) was ROTO 1.

11. From March 1992 to November 1994, five Canadian battle groups deployed to
     Croatia.

12. Colonel Jim Calvin made it clear to the BOI that this attack was not by chance:
     "We were going into a theatre where Canadian soldiers could be specifically
     targeted. This was no accident. It wasn't in any way, shape that anyone was
     getting in the way of anything. They had planned an incident. They had drawn
     a Canadian APC and group of soldiers to it and they had attacked that APC."
     Testimony before the BOI, 16 September 1999, 16. Summary of incident from
     Dr. Ken Reynolds, "Canadian Forces Operations in the Balkans, 1991–1995,"
     an unpublished paper prepared for the BOI, 12 September 1999. Originally
     published on the BOI website and a copy is in possession of author.

13. Reynolds, "Canadian Forces Operations in the Balkans, 1991–1995," 5.

14. Calvin, testimony before the BOI, September 16, 1999, 80.

15. About 500 rounds fell on the town of Medak — a village with about 50 homes
     in an area about the size of Parliament Hill in Ottawa — in the first 24 hours.
     Four members of CANBAT 1 were wounded. Calvin, testimony before the
     BOI, 16 September 1999, 87.

16. Colonel (Retired) George Oehring, testimony before the BOI, 10 November
     1999, 12.

17. Calvin, testimony before the BOI, September 16, 1999, 13.

18. Calvin, testimony before the BOI, September 16, 1999, 128.

19. Pigeau and McCann, "Re-conceptualizing Command and Control," 58.

20. *Ibid.*, 59.

21. *Ibid.*, 60.

22. Oehring, testimony before the BOI, 10 November 1999, 17.

23. The force commander was aware of the significance of the Canadian
     contribution and awarded both ROTO 2 and ROTO 3 the Force Commander's
     Commendation. General Cot greeted Colonel Lessard with "The Force

Commander, General Cot, had great confidence in Canadians, mostly because of Medak, of what 2 Patricia did. When he came to visit us, he told us he expected us to do the same." Colonel Marc Lessard, testimony before the BOI, 21 September 1999, 19; and Colonel Jim Calvin was unjustly pilloried by senior officers at NDHQ for his decisions while commanding the Battle Group in Croatia. See Carol Off, *The Ghosts of the Medak: The Story of Canada's Secret War* (Toronto: Random House Canada, 2004).

24. Calvin, testimony before the BOI, 16 September 1999, 129.

14

What Did You Expect? An Examination of Disobedience in the Former Canadian Airborne Regiment, 1968–1995

Bernd Horn

It always felt as if you were sitting on a pressure cooker. In order for it not to blow you always had to make sure it was secure and provide for a control release mechanism.

— Lieutenant-Colonel Richard Dick[1]

THERE WERE MORE THAN A few sobs on the windswept icy Nicklin parade square on Canadian Forces Base Petawawa on the late afternoon of 5 March 1995, as the commanding officer (CO) dismissed the Canadian Airborne Regiment (Cdn AB Regt) for the last time. The event was historic. It was the first time a Canadian military unit was disbanded in disgrace. To many, particularly those serving in the unit, it was a travesty. To others it was anticipated. Their desire to say "I told you so," was only suppressed by their haste in demanding "well, what did you expect — after all, they're paratroopers!"

Regardless of viewpoint, the fact remained that justifiably or not, for the political leadership, some military commanders, and many Canadians, the Cdn AB Regt had come to personify disobedience and a unit out of control. A series of highly publicized and embarrassing incidents for the government and the senior military leadership had pushed them too far. As a result, on 23 January 1995, the minister of national defence (MND) announced the disbandment of the Cdn AB Regt. In the end, the difficulties, particularly the disobedience, was explained as the inevitable problem with a unit of "that type." It was based on a simplistic belief that paratroopers will inherently breed trouble.

As is the case with all such simplistic explanations — they are as inadequate as they are inaccurate. Disobedience in the Cdn AB Regt stemmed from a complex array of factors, many of which extended well beyond the unit itself. In the end, a toxic mix of elitism, favouritism, personnel issues, immaturity, poor leadership, organizational defects, Army culture, misplaced loyalties, and personalities all coalesced to create an environment that often bred disobedience within the unit. However, what is often not understood, or maybe simply ignored, is the fact that spikes in disobedience within the Cdn AB Regt were not anomalies. The troubles in the unit were more often than not directly linked, or the consequences of, externally controlled factors.

To fully understand disobedience in, and the demise of, the Cdn AB Regt it is important to understand the Canadian airborne experience, which has always been a paradox. The paratroopers, who for the greater part of their existence represented the best of the nation's combat soldiers, were largely disliked within the military and virtually ignored in civilian circles, at least until the horrific torture killing of a Somali in 1993 during an operational tour in that country. Up until then, the Canadian attitude to airborne forces had always been schizophrenic and driven by political purpose rather than by doctrine and operational necessity. The failure right from the beginning to properly identify a consistent and pervasive role for airborne forces led to a roller coaster existence, dependent on personalities in power and political expedients of the day. This approach ultimately led to the conditions that allowed the killings to occur, as well as the ultimate demise of the Cdn AB Regt itself.[2]

An examination of the evolution of the country's airborne organizations over the past 50 years demonstrates that the national political and military leaders consistently took an irresolute and confused approach to the requirement for airborne forces. During the early years of the Second World War, the decision to establish a Canadian parachute capability was initially rejected because no clear role for these special troops was visualized. The concept was later accepted but only with the caveat it be kept at a low and decentralized level. The growing American and British interest in airborne forces during the war provided the catalyst for the establishment of a Canadian parachute battalion in 1942, which served with distinction throughout the rest of the conflict but was quickly disbanded at its end.[3]

In 1946, the post-war planners failed to see a place for paratroopers in Canada's dramatically scaled down peacetime Army. Traditional

A CANADIAN AIRBORNE REGIMENT ARMOURED VEHICLE GENERAL
PURPOSE PASSES A HERD OF CAMELS IN SOMALIA IN 1993.
(Jeff M. Speed, Canadian War Museum AN 19940035 001)

anti-military sentiments within the government, compounded by
its enormous war debt, fuelled a drive for economy instead of the
creation of a comprehensive military operational capability that
some of the soldiers wanted. Moreover, the Canadian Government
was responding to voters' preference for social programs in their
desire to return to ordinary pursuits after six long years of war. As
a consequence, the Liberal administration approved only a skeletal
military force designed to provide the framework for mobilization of
a citizen's Army in time of crisis and little else.

However, Canada was not immune from the post-war realities.
The mercurial change in technology during the Second World
War, particularly jet aircraft and nuclear weapons, shattered the
dependence of many nations on geography for security. For Canada,
this predicament was exacerbated by the emergence of two rival
superpowers that sandwiched the Dominion between them. Of
even greater concern, was the realization that the Americans viewed
Canada as an exposed flank. American apprehension for the security
of the North was matched only in Ottawa's concern over Canadian
sovereignty, especially in the northern reaches. To keep the Americans
out of Canada's North, the government realized it must show not

only an intent, but also a capability of guarding the back door. An ill-defined threat to the North, a paranoid giant to the South, and a tight-fisted government that traditionally held the military in disdain, created the quintessential marriage of convenience.

The Canadian Government quickly perceived airborne forces as a political solution to their dilemma. To politicians paratroopers represented a convenient viable force that was capable of responding to any hostile incursion into the Arctic that threatened Canada, or more important, the United States. However, for the government, they also represented an inexpensive means of safeguarding the nation's sovereignty.

And so in the immediate post war period, the reconstitution of an airborne force, now called the Mobile Striking Force (MSF), was rooted in this political reality. Official Department of National Defence (DND) statements described the MSF as a "coiled-spring" of lethality. The truth, however, was substantially different. In the acid test of the real world it became evident that the MSF was a "paper tiger."

The Army leadership consciously maintained this state of affairs. Perhaps realizing that the government was supportive of airborne forces not for the sake of their operational effectiveness, but for the perceived capability that paratroopers represented, some in the Army leadership who were themselves not enthusiastic about parachute troops began to redirect the MSF from its original mandate. Throughout its existence, the MSF was chronically starved of qualified personnel, supporting aircraft, and training exercises. Furthermore, its units were habitually confronted with different priorities, ones that were not ideally suited to the efficient use of airborne forces. Activities such as preparing recruits for the Korean conflict or conducting "all-arms combined training" for the potential European battlefield consistently took precedence over the stated purpose of the MSF, which was the "Defence of Canada."

By the early 1950s the actual military and political indifference to Canada's airborne forces became even more evident with the changing threat to the North. The Inter-Continental Ballistic Missile (ICBM) radically transformed the nature of the menace to North America. The eclipse of the crewed bomber threat over the polar icecap changed the importance of the Canadian North for the United States to merely strategic depth. Predictably, American interest in the Canadian Arctic swiftly dissipated. Canadian activity and concern in the North died almost as quickly.[4]

The effect of this techno-strategic shift on the nation's airborne forces was immense. Already neglected and starved, the airborne capability went into a hiatus in the form of decentralized parachute companies. These were maintained only within the various infantry regiments. The skill was being kept alive, but just barely.

This reorganization from "Airborne Battalions" to "Jump Companies" in 1958 represented the official demise of the MSF. Collectively, the respective parachute sub-units were now designated the Defence of Canada Force (DCF) to underline their "special" role. The continued charade of maintaining a force of paratroops was simply a function of the existing joint security arrangements between Canada and the United States for the defence of North America. For Canada, airborne forces remained the compromise to keep the Americans appeased. For many in the government and in the conventional circles of the military the facade of existence is what mattered. Their ability to respond to a threat, which was largely chimerical in any case, was not deemed important. For them airborne forces represented a classic political expedient.[5]

But as the northern threat in Canada receded, a new menace emerged elsewhere in the world. The late 1950s and early 1960s witnessed an international explosion of nationalistic movements and political unrest. "Brush-fire" conflicts, insurgencies, and wars of national liberation flared-up around the globe. The concept of rapid deployable forces under United Nations (UN) auspices captured the imagination of the Canadian Government that was still euphoric about its new-won international role caused by its diplomatic and military success in the outcome of the 1956 Suez Crisis. Four years later, the emergency in the Belgian Congo reinforced the apparent need for international forces that could deploy quickly to avert the potential escalation of regional conflicts into superpower confrontations.

At the same time, as a result of the changing international security environment, the Americans embarked on a program to better address the "spectrum of conflict" that they now faced. The Americans realized that their existing force structure was not adequate to deal with "limited wars" in distant lands. As a result, the Pentagon now stressed greater strategic mobility, the expansion of Special Forces (SF) to deal with the proliferation of guerrilla type conflict, and the development of an airmobile capability.

The Canadian political and military leadership followed suit. By 1964, the blueprint for a revitalized Canadian Army was based on the concept of a truly mobile force, called Force Mobile Command

(FMC) capable of quick reaction and global reach. Instrumental to this envisioned force was an airborne element that could provide the country with a strategic reserve capable of quick reaction and worldwide deployment.[6]

In 1968, this showcase unit became known as the Cdn AB Regt. However, it owed its existence almost exclusively to the vision and tenacity of the MND, chief of the defence staff (CDS), the FMC (Forces Mobile Command) commander and the FMC deputy commander.[7] Their immediate subordinate commanders were, for the most part, adamantly opposed to the creation of this new unit, particularly at a time when many proud, long standing regiments such as the Queen's Own Rifles of Canada, the Royal Highland Regiment "Black Watch" of Canada and the Canadian Guards were tagged for removal from the Regular Force Order of Battle. The resistance was so great that initially the consensus of the staff at FMC headquarters (HQ) and National Defence Headquarters (NDHQ) was that the plan would never come to fruition (especially if enough obstacles were placed in front of it, while not rejecting the idea outright). As a result, little assistance was forthcoming from various headquarters staffs since most felt it would be a wasted effort.[8]

However, the CDS, General Jean Victor Allard, who developed the idea while he was the Army commander, and his hand-picked successor, Lieutenant-General W.A.B. Anderson ruthlessly enforced their will. As a result, the Cdn AB Regt was established, but with great resentment in the Army at large.[9] Adding insult to injury, it started out as a privileged organization. It was given formation status with direct access to the Army commander and it was spared the tedium of national taskings such as providing personnel to run reserve training or to act as instructors at CF or Army training establishments. This simply added to the undercurrent of resentment and anger among many senior Army officers. As a result, although its creation was characterized by great passion and high ideals by a few senior Army officers and politicians, by the late 1970s it suffered from the same ailment of its predecessors. The larger military establishment and the Army in particular, never fully accepted the existence or designated role given to the Cdn AB Regt, and as a result continually tried to marginalize it.

This is not totally surprising. The paratroopers' mandate was as elusive as it was inclusive. There existed a wide variance in its stated purpose. Military briefings and official DND press releases described the unit's role as everything from an international "fire-brigade," a national strategic reserve, a stop-gap to buy time for heavier mechanized reinforcements to deploy to Europe, to a UN-ready force. As an afterthought, political and military planners also claimed that the Cdn AB Regt was also ideally suited for Defence of Canada Operations (DCO). In fact, Anderson's guidance directed that the Cdn AB Regt was to be organized and equipped to perform a variety of tasks including:

a. Defence of Canada;

b. The Standby role in response to the UN;

c. Peacekeeping operations;

d. Missions in connection with national disaster;

e. "Special Air Service" (SAS) type missions;

f. Coup de main tasks in a general war setting; and

g. Responsibility for parachute training in the Canadian Forces.[10]

The fact that each one of its multiplicity of roles was mutually exclusive was simply ignored by nearly everyone.[11]

The inability to fully rationalize the role, structure, and relevancy of the Cdn AB Regt simply increased the resistance to its survival within the Army. During the 1970s, its existence was marked by changing priorities in both relevancy and role. It went from an independent formation tasked as the national strategic reserve to simply another "conventional" unit within an existing brigade. It became the target of continual malevolent debate within the Army and the hostage to the individual impulse of those in power. As a result, its strength, both in terms of personnel and organizational integrity, was insidiously whittled away.

By the 1980s, the lack of a clear, credible, and accepted requirement for Canadian airborne forces proved to be a difficult obstacle to overcome. As Canada's role in the world turned away from Europe and towards different goals of foreign policy, the Canadian Armed Forces underwent a self-definition crisis. This was manifested by shrinking budgets and declining personnel levels. The

Cdn AB Regt found it difficult to convince its political and military masters of its relevance. Furthermore, the more its advocates (those commanders who had been young subalterns in the early days and had now percolated to the senior echelons) attempted to prove its utility, by assigning it new tasks or reinitiating old ones, the more they highlighted its greatest weakness. It had no credible or consistent role that made it indispensable.

This lack of organizational support had a direct impact on the state of the Regiment. The continual erosion of its status and institutional support was paralleled by a decrease in postings to the Regiment of the vital experienced leaders and soldiers from the other regiments who were responsible for feeding the Cdn AB Regt with personnel. The Regiment now began to receive young soldiers, some right out of basic infantry training. These individuals were much less mature than the seasoned corporals of the unit were used to. Their youth and immaturity, combined with the airborne mystique and the distinctive maroon beret, created an explosive mix. Moreover, an inability to recruit the necessary number of senior non-commissioned officers (NCOs) willing to volunteer for airborne service necessitated keeping those who were willing — individuals who were not always the cream of the crop. Their agreement to serve, however, often meant a promotion they most likely would never have received otherwise, or at least not as quickly.

More damaging yet, was the problem associated with the parent feeder regiments. When the chair and/or members of the senior councils of the feeder regiments were not supporters of the Cdn AB Regt they would, not surprisingly, restrict the quality and number of officers posted to serve in the Airborne. Worse yet, the feeder infantry regiments saw in the Cdn AB Regt a home for their malcontents and trouble-makers — a sort of reform school. Often, the Airborne was seen as a place to "tame" them or at least an easy way to get rid of a problem, while at the same time meeting the personnel quota that they were responsible to fill. As a result, troublesome members would often be sent to the Airborne and conveniently forgotten. An Army study revealed that the Cdn AB Regt had to "rely almost exclusively on the good will of the parent regiments for troop replacements."[12] Although on one level this meant that the Cdn AB Regt reflected the Army as a whole, practically, it evolved into a unit that had more than its fair share of troublemakers and individuals who were "rough around the edges." Unfortunately, chronic personnel shortages, because not enough Army personnel, particularly senior NCOs, volunteered for service with the Airborne because of its reputation for hard soldiering, meant the unit had to accept anyone they were sent or go short.

As if this was not bad enough, the appointment of the regimental commander also became a "political" issue. Command was rotated and passed not to the best individual available, but the choice of the regimental senate of the feeder infantry regiment whose turn it was to provide the commander. Often, it became a consolation prize for an officer who was not deemed worthy to become a CO of one of the conventional infantry line battalions of the respective feeder infantry regiment.[13] In sum, these factors resulted in a number of weak leaders, some more than others, being responsible for harnessing the energy, positive and negative, of a group of self-selecting, young, aggressive soldiers imbued with a sense of elitism and indestructibility.[14]

Not surprisingly, by the mid-1980s there were severe disciplinary problems in the Cdn AB Regt. Disobedience, insubordination, assaults, weapon thefts, linkages to criminal motorcycle gangs were just some of the manifestations.[15] One serving member at the time recalled the sense of anarchy. He confided, "it is a bad sign when officers are threatened by the troops. You clearly have a problem."[16]

Just as disturbing, and a key cause of the disobedient behaviour, was a distinct non-sanctioned airborne ethos and culture, which was promoted by some elements within the Regiment's NCO corps, centred on an elitist, macho, renegade attitude. Loyalty was defined in terms of the airborne itself, often to a particular clique therein. Moreover, airborne service became an end in itself. Service to Canada and the public, as well as appreciation for national policy and the concept of the greater good was rejected. Outsiders were shunned and considered only worthy of contempt. Soldiers would not salute a "LEG" (a pejorative term for non-airborne personnel that means "lacking enough guts") officers on bases. Worse yet, their chain of command would do nothing to discipline their soldiers if a complaint was actually received.[17] There existed a "we/they" attitude that became a part of the airborne cohesion. However, it undermined obedience. Not surprisingly, this overall lack of discipline fostered an unofficial attitude that authority, especially the chain of command outside of the Regiment, was a target to be defied.

This airborne sub-culture also fuelled an unofficial chain of command centred on the "old timers," particularly NCOs. Because of their long service in the airborne, often seven or more years (a function of the necessity to keep those willing to serve), they became the guardians of the airborne ethos. They defined what being a paratrooper meant — and socialized new members. Often, newly arrived senior NCOs and junior officers would look to these "airborne veterans" as role models. Colonel Ken Watkin observed that a major problem developed when officers tried too hard to be privates because they wanted to be accepted by the men.[18] Often questionable behaviour, disciplinary infractions or disobedience was overlooked and ignored by the neophyte airborne supervisors because of a desire to fit in. "You're in the Airborne now," quickly became a nuanced rebuke that inferred non-acceptable behaviour within the Regiment.

However, these problems were also a reflection of the larger malaise in the Army.[19] In the Spring of 1984, then Brigadier-General R.I. Stewart, the commander of the Special Service Force (SSF) addressed his command:

> The problem in a nutshell is that we have far too many cases of ill-disciplined behaviour, assault, disobedience, disrespectful behaviour; theft of private and public property by soldiers; impaired driving offenses; vehicle accidents; inadequate control of stores; ammunition/pyrotechnics, weapons and equipment that result in loss or theft; and a general laxness in properly controlling soldiers, all which contribute to an erosion of disciplined/ soldierly behaviour. We have in many cases lost our regimented pattern of behaviour and our standards of performance are seriously in jeopardy. The danger of allowing standards to slip is self-evident. Once started on the decline, the process picks up momentum and reaches a point when we have no junior leaders who comprehend the standard and it is then impossible to reverse the process.[20]

By the summer of 1985, the problem in the Army had reached such a state that the CDS agreed to the commission of an investigation titled the *FMC Study on Disciplinary Infractions and Antisocial Behaviour with FMC with Particular Reference to the Special Service Force and the Canadian Airborne Regiment*. This probe became known informally as the "Hewson Report," named after Major-General C.W. Hewson, the chief of intelligence and security, who was the chair of the board of inquiry.

Its aim was to review disciplinary infractions within the Army and investigate the factors that led to the excessive antisocial behaviour. The terms of reference, guidelines, and investigative team were left to the Army, which in turn entrusted the inquiry to a group of "loyal" Army officers and staunch Airborne supporters who, needless to say, were anything but critical of the Army or the Cdn AB Regt.[21] They concluded that there appeared to be a higher number of assault cases in the two infantry units in the SSF (1 RCR and the Cdn AB Regt) compared to the remaining infantry units in the rest of the Army.[22] The FMC team then went on to rationalize the behavioural issues within the Cdn AB Regt to a combination of factors such as the absence of junior leaders, the immaturity and lack of experience of some of the replacements sent to the Regiment, and the semi-isolation of Canadian Forces Base Petawawa itself, which failed to provide an adequate number of drinking establishments and other off-base social outlets that could absorb the large single-male population of the base.[23] The final report declared, "there is no cause for alarm or requirement for precipitate action."[24] It went on to argue, "there appears to be a lower incidence of serious pathology and violent behaviour in the Canadian Forces than in the Canadian population at large."[25]

The Hewson Report had no real effect. The chair, Major-General Hewson himself, later conceded, "I know of no specific action that resulted from our study."[26] A strong CO in the wake of the report, however, seemed to put a temporary lid on the problems, but by the early 1990s, disciplinary troubles once again raised their ugly head. This time, they would not be so easily brushed aside. By the summer of 1992, Canada's decision to participate in a UN mission to Somalia, which eventually evolved into the American led peace-enforcement operation known in Canada as Operation Deliverance, allowed pro-airborne senior Army officers in influential positions within the CF hierarchy to pull strings to ensure that the Cdn AB Regt would be the unit sent to fulfill the Canadian commitment. Although the paratroopers were not the ideal unit to deploy (i.e., they were already scheduled to undertake a Cyprus rotation and they had no light armoured vehicles) they received the nod anyway, simply because their benefactors wanted them to have the choice operational mission.[27] However, the storm clouds began to gather as the Regiment began its preparatory training. Discipline problems, a lack of Regimental SOPs and overly aggressive behaviour by 2 Commando raised the concerns of the brigade commander. However, these problems were largely waved away by the same senior military commanders who had cleared the path for the Regiment's assignment.[28]

In theatre overall, the Cdn AB Regt performed superbly for the most part and earned the praise of U.S. commanders, UN envoys, and non-governmental organization (NGO) representatives for their efforts and success at both securing their sector and delivering humanitarian aid.[29] However, there was also a dark side. Once in Somalia, many of the concerns about discipline and professionalism that were raised during the predeployment training came to the surface. Undeniably, the flaws were attributable to poor leadership at the NCO and officer level. This was a direct outgrowth of the problems that had been identified earlier but not corrected. Very quickly it became evident that some elements within the Cdn AB Regt Battle Group (Cdn AB Regt BG) were mistreating Somalis who were captured while illegally entering the Airborne compounds to steal.[30]

The frustration of the paratroopers is unquestionable. The Somali population was not always appreciative of the soldiers' efforts on their behalf. The paratroopers were exposed to rock throwing, shootings, protests, spitting, and constant thievery. The Cdn AB Regt BG compounds became natural targets; night after night, looters and thieves would slip through the razor wire barrier and steal anything and everything. Those thieves who were apprehended were turned over to local authorities, only to be released without sanction. For the paratroopers the incessant ingratitude and hostility, from the very people they were there to assist, was difficult to understand and accept.[31] Nonetheless, the reaction of many, seemingly condoned by the officer and NCO corps, was unacceptable.

Through the course of the whole operation Canadians killed four Somali nationals and wounded many others. Some of the deaths were unquestionably avoidable. One such killing occurred on 4 March 1993. Increased security at one of the Cdn AB Regt BG camps resulted in gunfire as two would-be thieves attempted to escape. Initially, the shooting was termed justifiable within the Rules of Engagement by a unit-controlled investigation. However, continuing allegations by one of the contingent's medical officers, who professed that the death of one of the interlopers was the result of a deliberate execution style killing eventually raised some disturbing questions.[32] Although these allegations have never been conclusively proven or refuted, the shootings themselves have been declared unjustifiable. The carefully planned ambush operation obviously was "designed to send a strong message to would-be infiltrators that any attempt to penetrate the perimeter of Canadian installations would be met with gunfire."[33]

As disturbing as these allegations are, they are not the only ones. Mixed messages reverberated through the Airborne compounds in Somalia. Not only was a questionable shooting quickly dismissed and the participants praised, but there existed a perception that abusive behaviour was ignored and not punished. This outlook became prevalent in some elements of the Cdn AB Regt BG. This was due in part to the fact that mistreatment of prisoners was condoned by some officers and NCOs within the Canadian contingent. In sum, this laid the groundwork for the defining moment of the Somalia mission

On the night of 16 March 1993, an apprehended teenaged looter, Shidane Arone, was systematically beaten to death while in the custody of 2 Commando. What made this tragedy even harder to understand is the fact that throughout the beating, which lasted several hours, many soldiers, senior NCOs, and officers either heard the cries or actually dropped by the bunker and witnessed the beating in progress; yet, no one stopped it until it was too late.[34]

Initially, the death was explained away as the result of injuries sustained during capture. However, the sergeant leading the patrol that apprehended Arone refused to accept that explanation. Subsequently, one of the guilty individuals, Trooper Kyle Brown brought forward evidence and explained what had happened. The other perpetrator, Master Corporal Clayton Matchee, was subsequently arrested. The matter was kept low-key. To that point no word was released to the public and senior political and military decision makers felt they could control the situation. Top officials in DND learned of the death within 48 hours of the event, yet it appeared that a decision to contain rather than disclose information was taken.[35] However, while in custody Matchee attempted to commit suicide and his body being taken for medical treatment was witnessed by a reporter who quickly learned the full story.

As the incident became national news an overwhelming wave of enmity, by both the public and other military personnel, swept over the paratroopers.[36] Its impact was enormous. Even those senior military commanders who for years showed preferential treatment towards the Cdn AB Regt and who had previously dismissed their antics with a "boys will be boys" attitude now abandoned them fearing for their own careers.[37]

A POINT OF ACCESS TO THE SANDBAG BUNKER IN SOMALIA WHERE MASTER
CORPORAL CLAYTON MATCHEE TRIED TO HANG HIMSELF IN 1993. MILITARY
POLICE SIGNS PROHIBITING ACCESS ARE POSTED ACROSS THE ENTRANCE.
(Jeff M. Speed, Canadian War Museum AN 19940035 016)

Not surprisingly, the media put DND and the CF under a
microscope with devastating effect. That single event itself was
numbing and the failure of so many to do anything to stop the
beating, remains inexplicable. Incredibly, the tragedy magnified.
The appearance of an attempt to cover-up the incident outside as
well as inside the Regiment spoke volumes about serious failures in
the military and political chain of command at DND. The military
leadership decided to deal with the continuing criticism by formally
establishing The Board of Inquiry (BOI) — Canadian Airborne
Regiment Battle Group (informally named the De Faye Commission
after its chair, Major-General Tom De Faye) to "investigate the
leadership, discipline, operations, actions and procedures of the
Airborne Battle Group."[38] The board presented its Phase I Report in
late summer 1993, and much like the Hewson Report, said that there
was no real cause for alarm. But this failed to placate critics within or
outside of DND.[39]

The disciplinary and leadership problems evident in the Airborne
in the early 1990s, and specifically during the pre-deployment
period and during the unit's time in Somalia from October 1992 to

May 1993, were reminiscent of problems identified as early as the beginning of the 1980s. Moreover, the increased scrutiny of DND now revealed other disturbing problems.

Simply put, the Cdn AB Regt's problems seemed to be a direct a reflection of the larger long-term failure in the Army and the CF — specifically, the inability, or reluctance, to take the necessary steps to make hard decisions ensuring the stability of the institution. The CF officer corps placed a priority on acquiescence instead of critical thought, on a tolerance for the secretive machinations of regimental councils who were largely unaccountable, and on the parochial interests of individual services and corps, and they provided the government politically acceptable solutions instead of sound military advice. These issues, added to the anti-intellectual officer corps that was unable to recognize and react to the changing social and geo-political environment, led to a collective abrogation of responsibility and strategic impotence in regards to correcting the problems that were evident in the Cdn AB Regt and the CF long before Somalia. Peter Desbarats, one of the Somalia Inquiry commissioners, noted that the "Airborne was only the most brutal manifestation of the disease. Amputating it did nothing to resolve the real problems except to allow the leadership to pretend that they had cured it." He summarized that "this was more dangerous than doing nothing."[40]

Even after the return of the Regiment to Canada, the issue of the torture murder never fully disappeared. Courts martial and ongoing commentary kept the subject alive. Two high-profile disciplinary incidents by 3 Commando (Cdo) paratroopers serving in Rwanda in the summer of 1994 simply fuelled the fire. In the first case, two off-duty paratroopers became drunk in their quarters and decided to become "blood brothers." The resultant cuts to their palms required only a few stitches, but the resultant furor in the press brought unneeded publicity. The second, and more serious lack of judgment, transpired when a section second-in-command, although tasked to provide security for a local building, allowed several soldiers not on duty, to consume beer and discharge shotgun blasts at the large stone structure they were protecting. Needless to say, this incident quickly exploded in the media and brought renewed criticism of the Regiment.[41]

But these were mere preludes to more ominous events. On 15 January 1995, the CTV television network broadcast excerpts from a homemade video, made by soldiers of 2 Cdo during their tour in Somalia, on the nightly news. Several members were shown making racial slurs and behaving in an unprofessional manner. Media reaction was sharp, as was the subsequent political anger. Once again, the recurrent Somalia issue catapulted the Cdn AB Regt into the public and political spotlight. The mortal blow, however, came three days later when another amateur video depicting a 1992, 1 Cdo "initiation party" was aired. The tape exhibited 1 Cdo paratroopers involved in behaviour that was degrading, disgusting, and racist in nature and contrary to CF rules and regulations. Its release embarrassed the government and the CF yet once again. It also completely destroyed any remnants of the Regiment's image. As a result, the MND announced the disbandment of the Cdn AB Regt in disgrace, on 23 January 1995.[42]

The political and senior military leadership quickly promulgated a consistent message to the public. They maintained, the troubles experienced, and the embarrassment caused to the nation's government and military institution, were inherent, and inescapable, as a result of the existence of an "airborne" organization. The disciplinary problems, allegations of wanton violence, racist innuendo, elitist attitudes, ties to U.S. paratroopers in the American "Deep South," and connections to the "paras" of the notorious French Foreign Legion, were all presented as clear manifestations of the claim. Paratroopers, it seemed were simply unsavoury characters, if not born killers.[43]

Political motives aside, this rationalization to explain disobedience within the Cdn AB Regt is grossly inadequate. The answer is complex and a combination of internal and external factors. Initially, the Regiment itself must take responsibility for its failings. It allowed the "airborne mystique" and cult of the elite to impact on its culture and behaviour.[44] Justifiably or not, the members of the Regiment, as well as the CF at large, considered the paratroopers an elite.[45] They were entitled to special orders of dress and distinctive clothing items, allowance to wear unique insignia, extra pay, privileged access to the chain of command, allowances for special courses, a greater number of foreign exchanges for training, exemption from routine taskings, as well as the element of parachuting. In addition, they were far fitter, and normally more proficient in field skills than their counterparts in the regular infantry battalions.

Their unusual status, combined with the self-selecting nature of the unit (i.e., individuals had to first pass the basic parachutist course and then volunteer for the Regiment), plus their reputation for extremely demanding and tough exercises and physical fitness regimes, developed both a cohesion and arrogance that created the airborne as a "group apart." Their intense "esprit de corps" and elitist sentiment that was nurtured by the group, and both promoted and tolerated by the chain of command, allowed the Regiment to devolve into an exclusive club that shunned outsiders. This created an "us against them" attitude, which manifested itself in complete disregard for, and overt disobedience to, the external chain of command, as well as military rules and regulations in general. One senior officer recalled, "we acted independently and did what we wanted to do." But this was only part of the problem. "Furthermore," he added, "we got away with it."[46]

As is often the case with special type units with extremely high levels of cohesion — discipline and the enforced adherence to the tedious rules and regulations of the "conventional army" were normally lax. Moreover, airborne officers and senior NCOs were loathe to discipline one of their own for petty offences committed against a "LEG" or in violation of normal military protocol (i.e., saluting a non-airborne officer), which were more often than not discounted as "chicken shit rules" not worthy of attention by "real soldiers." As such, the internal chain of command often fostered a "we're above the law attitude" that seeped into member behaviour and conduct. This bred a culture that later in the Regiment's life, morphed into a cancerous underground ethos that imbued resistance to any authority — including that of the Airborne chain of command.

The lax approach to discipline and dismissive attitude towards external organizations and individuals are problematic by themselves. However, staffing practices proved to be another key factor in disobedience within the Cdn AB Leadership. The early philosophical intent that only the seasoned, mature, and deserving be allowed to serve in the Cdn AB Regt to provide additional challenge and act as a leadership nursery served the Regiment well in the early years. But, as explained, the recruitment pressures and continuing erosion of support for a "special and privileged" unit over the years resulted in a less than desirable rotation practice. By the late 1970s, some young immature soldiers right out of battle school were sent to the Regiment. These youngsters, who inherently by their youth and occupation of choice were prone to bravado and macho posturing, now fortified by the vaunted maroon beret and fuelled by the airborne mystique and its legacy of aggressive, daring, and fearless action, became trouble waiting to happen. Adding to the problem was the lax environment and contemptuous attitude towards outsiders. This seemingly permissive attitude provided little restraint and in many ways set a tone, if not a socialization process, that almost encouraged members to flaunt convention.

More corrosive yet to the discipline of the Cdn AB Regt was yet another staffing practice — dumping. Many of the COs of feeder battalions of the parent infantry regiments who were obligated to post a set number of personnel to the Cdn AB Regt every posting season often used the opportunity to rid themselves of troublesome individuals. As such, the Regiment became a form of reform school. Once again, the prevailing attitude and lax discipline provided those already prone to flouting rules and regulations to prosper. Worse yet, because of their experience and time in, they became role models for the young soldiers who had just joined the CF and the Regiment.

The faulty staffing practices had another negative consequence that directly contributed to disobedience in the Cdn AB Regt. Because of chronic personnel shortages and a reluctance to order personnel to serve in the Regiment — those willing could stay in the unit for as long as they chose. In some cases, to fill the necessary rank structure they even received promotions that they may not have received, or at least not as quickly, had they not remained in the Regiment. As a result, many individuals who did not "fit in" a regular battalion remained within the Regiment. These "long timers" became the continuity. They were the holders of the airborne ethos and socialized new members in the unit. They defined what being a paratrooper meant. Part of this definition included the disregard for "petty rules and regulations." In the most extreme cases, underground parallel chains of command emerged that defined loyalty only in terms of small inclusive sub-groups within the Regiment. Open acts of defiance, such as the display of banned rebel flags and the stonewalling of authority were demonstrated.

The greatest significance of the defective staffing of the Regiment, however, was the impact it had on leadership. There are several dimensions to this. It is important to point out that many exemplary individuals of all ranks served in the Regiment. However, there were some who were far from exemplary. It was not unknown for officers and senior NCOs to be dumped as well. In these cases, weak leaders were either unwilling or unable to enforce rules. Often they simply acquiesced to those with time-in, because of incompetence, or efforts to fit in and get by.

Conversely, in some instances, these leaders were strong personalities but poor leaders and caused problems of their own. Within a unit climate that provided little structure or control over its sub-units, which often acted independently, an officer could run a "regime" that created frustration, if not injury, to his subordinates. With little recourse, soldiers often turned to disobedience, such as damaging personal property (e.g., slashing a bivvy bag, or torching a vehicle) as a sign of protest or as a signal that the leadership had gone too far. In this case, disobedience was a direct result of weak leadership throughout the chain of command. It was symptomatic of a laissez-faire attitude and misguided belief that strict discipline was somehow "unairborne."

The other element at play, often ensnaring even the strongest of leaders was the desire to fit in as an airborne warrior and be accepted by the more experienced personnel. The airborne mystique and allure of the maroon beret are powerful motivators. Newly arrived individuals wish to conform. Very quickly, they become acclimatized and become part of the problem. They accept the persona and all that it entails.

And so, a number of factors created an environment conducive for disobedience. Unfortunately, the normal safeguards such as a chain of command that enforces normal military protocol and rules and regulations as part of its normal military ethos was not in place. What added to this problem was another leadership failure — one at the most senior levels of command. The senior chain of command for almost the entire lifespan of the Cdn AB Regt inexplicably tolerated the Regiment's poor conduct. It turned a blind eye to incidents and general behaviour and attitudes. The conventional wisdom posited that you had to allow for such behaviour because the airborne was more aggressive — a bit wilder. Senior commanders maintained a "boys will be boys" attitude. Instead of demanding a higher professional standard, which should be expected of a supposed elite, and providing the necessary talent, the Army leadership acquiesced to, if not endorsed, the airborne attitude and disposition. As such, they directly contributed to disobedience within the Cdn AB Regt.

All these factors were instrumental in creating the conditions for disobedience in the Cdn AB Regt. However, another factor that must be considered is the pervading climate and composition of the CF throughout the history of the Cdn AB Regt. In essence, the Cdn AB Regt was the most evident symptom of a larger problem. After all, by its composition it reflected the larger Army as a whole. Although some internal dynamics did fuel disobedience, for the large part the Cdn AB Regt's disciplinary record mirrored that of the larger Army. A report by the Special Service Force (SSF) pointed out that the demise of the

Cdn AB Regt was "due not to operational deficiencies but to a failure in application of the personnel system" over the long run.[47] During a telephone interview with the editor of the *Esprit de Corps* magazine, Lieutenant-General Reay made reference to the Regiment's poor disciplinary record. The editor quickly challenged him on singling out the Cdn AB Regt. In response, Reay had to concede that if any of the other Army "regiments were held up to the same microscopic scrutiny it would produce the same damning results."[48]

This was the element that was ignored. The Cdn AB Regt was not an aberration. It was not different. It was representative of other Army units in regard to discipline. During the Somalia mission, the SSF commander reported, "historical records and comparative records of disciplinary problems showed no disturbing trends, certainly nothing worse than other Infantry and Combat Arms units."[49] Similarly, the De Faye Commission also concluded, "in terms of numbers of disciplinary infractions, the state of discipline in the Canadian Airborne Regiment was similar to that of other infantry units."[50] Colonel A.R. Wells, a former director general of security at NDHQ said that the number of incidents reflected in Military Police Reports "compared favourably to those of its [Cdn AB Regt] sister infantry battalions in the Special Service Force, and that its disciplinary rate was consistent with the other infantry battalions in the Army."[51] Moreover, Colonel Walter Semianiw acknowledged that the commander's investigation, initiated as a result of the hazing videos in January 1995, similarly documented that the Regiment's record was "normal, no worse than any other unit."[52] Furthermore, Major-General J.M.R. Gaudreau testified before the Somalia Commission in October 1995 that the problems faced by the Cdn AB Regt were in fact typical of those faced across the entire military structure of Canada.[53] This in turn was reinforced by an internal Land Forces Command (LFC) report that acknowledged, "every regiment has at least one serious incident in its history which has discredited the honour of the [respective] regiment."[54]

Statistical analysis also challenged the myth that all airborne units are worse behaved than others. An examination of the record of summary trials for many National Defence Act (NDA) offences, for all LFC infantry units, from 1988 to 1993, revealed that the Regiment was never the unit with the highest number of trials/offences. In fact, it was well within the average for each given year.[55]

In addition, other Canadian military units deployed overseas also had a plethora of problems that were conveniently overlooked as a result of the controversy swirling around the Cdn AB Regt. For example, many of the Canadian contingents that deployed to the Former Yugoslavia experienced disciplinary difficulties, particularly in relation to drunkenness. Examples abound: 2 Service Battalion had their CO and regimental sergeant-major and many soldiers returned during their tour in Yugoslavia for proven malfeasance or alleged misconduct; and soldiers in the Royal Canadian Dragoons gave their unit the nickname "Chargebat" because of the high number of charges that had been laid against soldiers for disciplinary infractions. Elsewhere serious questions were raised about lost equipment and vehicles during tours; and another national scandal erupted in 1994 as the result of the questionable behaviour of 60 Canadian peacekeepers at the Bosnian Bakovici mental hospital. Cambodia and Haiti were equally fraught with incidents of scandalous and unprofessional behaviour that included black market activity, corruption, drunkenness, and prostitution. The operational scandals overseas were matched at home by scandals of unethical behaviour, particularly the misuse of public funds, as well as opulent spending practices by senior military officers at a time when the country faced a financial crisis as a result of its burgeoning national debt.[56] This brief overview is not meant to be comprehensive. Neither is it designed to be a condemnation, nor exoneration, of the military or its personnel. It is, however, a reminder that the Cdn AB Regt was not an aberration.[57]

And so, disobedience in the Cdn AB Regt cannot be simply explained away as an inevitable byproduct of creating an airborne unit or some genetic defect common to paratroopers. It was the explosive mix of a large number of factors. Poor leadership, faulty staffing practices, and the powerful effect of elitism, which was not properly managed, as well as the prevailing Army culture of the time, all combined to create an environment conducive to disobedience. In the end, this climate eventually destroyed the Regiment. As such it stands as a powerful case study that is worthy of consideration and study.

NOTES

1. Interview with author, 15 April 1998.

2. For a complete account of the Canadian airborne experience, see Bernd Horn, *Bastard Sons: An Examination of Canada's Airborne Experience, 1942–1995* (St.

Catharines, ON: Vanwell, 2001); and Bernd Horn and Michel Wyczynski, *In Search of Pegasus — The Canadian Airborne Experience, 1942–1999* (St. Catharines, ON: Vanwell, 2000).

3. See Bernd Horn and Michel Wyczynski, *Paras Versus the Reich: Canada's Paratroopers at War 1942–45* (Toronto: Dundurn Press, 2003); and Bernd Horn and Michel Wyczynski, *Tip of the Spear: An Intimate Portrait of the First Canadian Parachute Battalion, 1942–1945* (Toronto: Dundurn Press, 2002).

4. See David Bercuson, *True Patriot: The Life of Brooke Claxton* (Toronto: University of Toronto Press, 1993); Bernd Horn, "Gateway to Invasion or the Curse of Geography? The Canadian Arctic and the Question of Security, 1939–1999," in Bernd Horn, ed., *Forging a Nation: Perspectives on the Canadian Military Experience* (St. Catharines, ON: Vanwell, 2002), 307–34; "A Military Enigma: The Canadian Special Air Service Company, 1948–49," *Canadian Military History* 10, No. 1 (Winter 2001), 21–30; and Horn, *Bastard Sons*, Chapters 3 and 4.

5. See Horn, *Bastard Sons*, Chapters 3 and 4.

6. See Lester B. Pearson, Directorate of History and Heritage (henceforth DHH), File 112.11.003 (D3) — Box 3, "Force for U.N.," *Foreign Affairs* 35, No. 3 (April 1957); *Ibid.*, Lieutenant-Colonel R.B. Tacaberry, "Keeping the Peace," *Behind the Headlines* 26, No. 1 (September 1966), 7; *Ibid.*, "Appreciation and Proposed Options for the Structure of the Canadian Army Field Force 1965–1970 Period," 5 April 1965, 2; DHH, File 90/452, Canada, *Rationale for Canadian Defence Forces* (Ottawa: DND, 14 May 1968), 29; General Jean V. Allard, *The Memoirs of General Jean V. Allard* (Vancouver: University of British Columbia Press, 1988); Paul Hellyer, *Damn the Torpedoes: My Fight to Unify Canada's Armed Forces* (Toronto: McClelland & Stewart, 1990); and Horn, *Bastard Sons*, Chapter 5.

7. Forces Mobile Command (FMC) was one of the functional commands that arose from efforts to unify the Canadian military in the 1960s and was for all intents and purposes the Canadian Army. In the early 1990s it was renamed Canadian Forces Land Force Command. Horn, *Bastard Sons*, 98–110.

8. See Horn, *Bastard Sons*, 120. The perception held by FMC and Department of National Defence Headquarters (NDHQ) staffs had a real effect on the Regiment. During the initial period of the Regiment's establishment, it suffered from a dearth of equipment. This was because the various staffs made no serious effort to locate or obtain equipment as no one thought the Regiment would actually be formed. It was not until the actual stand-up that a concerted effort was undertaken.

9. "General Allard," Rochester recalled later, "was determined it would happen." He further added that Lieutenant-General Anderson, the FMC commander, "was convinced." Rochester readily admitted, however, that "no one else seemed to be." He also remembered being told as late as February 1968, "by

a very senior officer, who was a friend of mine, that I might as well forget it because the Airborne Regiment would never be formed." Colonel D.H. Rochester, "Birth of a Regiment," *The Maroon Beret*, 20th Anniversary Edition (1988), 34; and Horn, *Bastard Sons*, 120.

10. "Formation of the Canadian Airborne Regiment — Activation and Terms of Reference," 15 May 1967, 3. Colonel (Retired) Michael Barr Personal Papers.

11. See Library and Archives Canada (henceforth LAC), RG 24, Vol. 23491, File 1901–2, Part 1, Department of National Defence (DND) Message, "CANMOBGEN 098 Comd 2549, dated 022030Z December 1966; DND Message, CANCOMGEN 022, dated 111600Z April 1968, *Organization Mobile Command*; "Approval of MOBCOM Forces Structure Concept;" Canada, *CFP 310 (1) — Airborne, Volume 1, The Canadian Airborne Regiment* (Ottawa: DND, 1968); "Formation of the Canadian Airborne Regiment — Activation and Terms of Reference," 15 May 1967, 2; and Horn, *Bastard Sons*, Chapter 5.

12. There is overwhelming consensus on this issue by former Airborne personnel who served in leadership positions (i.e., regimental commanders, commanding officers [COs], officers commanding, regimental sergeants-major [RSM], commando sergeants-major [CSM]. All conceded that there were many, blatant, instances of weak personnel being posted in. In the same vein, it was noted that the calibre of replacements was often directly related to the COs and RSMs of the dispatching units. Not surprisingly, there was agreement from those interviewed that those COs and RSMs without Airborne experience were more likely to unload weak or "problem" personnel. See FMC, *Mobile Command Study — Report on Disciplinary Infractions and Antisocial Behaviour with Particular Reference to the SSF and the Canadian Airborne Regiment* (henceforth *Hewson Report*), September 1985, 46; "Manning — Canadian Airborne Regiment," 9 October 1985, *Information Legacy*, Evidentiary Exhibits; and Major-General Tom DeFaye, Board of Inquiry — Cdn AB Regt BG, Phase 1, Vol. 11, 16–30, H-1/6, and K.

13. See Horn, *Bastard Sons*, Chapters 6 and 7.

14. Lieutenant-Colonel Lorne O'Brien, a former 3 Commando commanding officer, believed, "You had to run herd on them [the soldiers] all the time." He likened it to a professional athletic team. "You keep them pumped-up but that comes with certain problems," O'Brien explained, "you have to let steam off judiciously and you have to be ruthless with discipline." When the "screws were loosened," he revealed, "it [Airborne Regiment] had enormous problems." Interview with author, 14 April 1997. The Regiment's last commander, Colonel Peter Kenward agreed. He was convinced that "more rigid control, if not a tight rein is required because of the high level of energy in the ranks. Things can go adrift, and as a result leadership by example and being in people's face becomes very important." Interview with author 4 October 1996.

15. Incredibly, a 1 Commando motorcycle club, called the "Para Nomads," with known connections to the Hells Angels existed within the Regiment and

seemed to be tolerated by senior leadership. Brigadier-General Ian Douglas acknowledged, "We knew from the SIU [Special Investigations Unit — military] and the OPP [Ontario Provincial Police] that they [Para Nomads] were tied to the Hells Angels." Douglas's attempts at eradicating the "club" were largely frustrated. The 1 Commando CO at the time insisted that it was just a Royal Vingtième Regiment (R22er) club and that the members had a legal "right" to participate. Douglas stated that the problem was eventually solved by making it difficult for the motorcyclists to come onto the base and slowly posting the participating members back to their parent regiments. Interview with author, 18 March 1998. Brigadier-General Beno, Major-General Gaudreau, and Major-General Stewart all asserted that weapon thefts in the Regiment in the 1980s were "inside jobs" and were linked to the "motorcycle club." Interviews/ letters to author.

16. Confidential interview. Specific incidents include the booby-trapping of an officer's office with an artillery simulator wrapped with nails, as well as the later well-known burning of an officer's car on the parade square in 1990 and that of a senior NCO in 1992.

17. Interview with Lieutenant-Colonel Watkin and Lieutenant-Colonel Bradley, 4 June 1998 and 15 September 1997 respectively. The derogatory term *LEG* originates from the Second World War. Regular infantry wore canvas "leggings" as part of their uniform. The "elite" paratroopers were spared this ordeal. They were issued with high cut "jump boots," into which they could tuck their uniform trousers. Needless to say, the paratroopers quickly christened their brethren with the contemptuous label of *LEG*. A more contemporary version translates the meaning to "lacking enough guts."

18. Interview with author, 15 September 1997.

19. See Peter Desbarats, *Somalia Cover-Up: A Commissioner's Journal* (Toronto: McClelland & Stewart, 1997); David Bercuson, *Significant Incident* (Toronto: McClelland & Stewart, 1996); Donna Winslow, *The Canadian Airborne Regiment: A Socio-Cultural Inquiry Society* (Ottawa: Commission of Inquiry into the Deployment of Canadian Forces to Somalia, 1997); and Horn, *Bastard Sons*, Chapter 7.

20. R.I. Stewart, "Discipline, Soldierly Behaviour and Leaders Responsibilities," 7 May 1984. Accessed from Major-General Stewart's personal papers.

21. See *Hewson Report* and Covering Letter. For additional details, see Horn, *Bastard Sons*, 172–74.

22. Although statistically 1st Battalion The Royal Canadian Regiment (1 RCR) had a greater incidence of assault cases than the Airborne, the study team dismissed this as an unexplainable anomaly. The fact that 3 Commando, The RCR component of the Airborne Regiment, had the highest number of incidents of assault within the Airborne also seemed to go unnoticed.

23. *Hewson Report*, 51–54.

24. *Ibid.*, Executive Summary, 1. This one line underscored the importance of the study, namely to prevent the disbandment of the Regiment.

25. *Hewson Report*, 51.

26. Canada. *Dishonoured Legacy: The Lessons of the Somalia Affair: Report of the Commission of Inquiry into the Deployment of Canadian Forces to Somalia* (henceforth *Somalia Commission Report*), Transcript of Evidentiary Hearings, Vol. 2, 3 October 1995, 361.

27. See Horn, *Bastard Sons*, Chapter 8.

28. See *Ibid.*, 193–95.

29. See Berel Rodal, *The Somalia Experience in Strategic Perspective in a Free and Democratic Society* (Ottawa: Commission of Inquiry into the Deployment of Canadian Forces to Somalia, 1997), 1; and Horn, *Bastard Sons*, 198–201.

30. Letter, Brigadier-General E.B. Beno to Colonel J.S. Labbé (commander Canadian Joint Task Force Somalia), 8 April 1993. See also "General Urged Troops to Lighten Up," *Globe and Mail*, A6; Allan Thompson, "Wider Airborne Violence Revealed," *Toronto Star*, 6 October 1996, A1; and Beno, "Treatment of Somalis in the Custody of the Canadian Airborne Battle Group," Brigadier-General E. Beno personal files and records (henceforth *Beno Papers*).

31. *Somalia Commission Report*, Transcript of Evidentiary Hearing, Vol. 7, 23 October 1995, testimony of Dr. Menkaus (academic specialist on the Horn of Africa), 1266–1352; and Peter Worthington, "Private Brown," *Saturday Night* (September 1994), 34.

32. According to the report of Major Armstrong, "the deceased had been first shot in the back and subsequently "dispatched" with a pair of shots to the head and neck area. Major Armstrong considered that the wounds were consistent with the Somali being shot as he lay wounded on the ground." *Information Legacy*, Report of the Commission of Inquiry into the Deployment of Canadian Forces to Somalia CD ROM of evidence, testimony and documents (henceforth *Information Legacy*), Executive Summary — Mission Aftermath, Record 2874. Master Corporal Petersen testified that he observed that "the dead Somali's neck was blown out, his head was gaping open at the back of the skull and his face was sagging to one side." *Ibid.*, Report of the Commission of Inquiry, Vol. 1 — March 4 Shooting, Record 2871.

33. *Information Legacy*, Report of the Commission of Inquiry, Vol. 5, 4 March — Findings, Record 9569. The commission was scathing in its comments of the handling of the incident. It asserted that actions both within theatre and by the command structure in Canada were negligent in ensuring a proper investigation was conducted. See also Jocelyn Coulon, *Soldiers of Diplomacy:*

The United Nations, Peacekeeping, and the New World Order (Toronto: University of Toronto Press, 1994), 97.

34. Peter Worthington, *Scapegoat: How the Army Betrayed Kyle Brown* (Toronto: Seal Books, 1997), 116–35; Worthington, "Private Brown," 35–36; Brian Bergman, "A Night of Terror," *Maclean's*, 28 March 1994, 26–28; and "Brutal Allegations," *Maclean's*, 7 March 1994, 13. Major Seward the OC of 2 Commando later wrote in his diary, "it is my intention to openly and readily state that I did order Somali intruders to be abused during the conduct of apprehension and arrest." *Information Legacy*, Report of the Commission of Inquiry, Vol. 1, Record 3026. See also George Shorey, "Bystander Non-Intervention and the Somalia Incident," *Canadian Military Journal* 1, No. 4 (Winter 2000–2001), 19–28; and Horn, *Bastard Sons*, 196–98.

35. See *Information Legacy*, Report of the Commission of Inquiry, Vol. 1, "MGen Boyle's Analysis of the De Faye Report, Record 3160 and Hearing Transcripts, Vol. 95, testimony of Colonel Haswell 18480–18555. Colonel Haswell, then a staff officer in the Director General of Public Affairs (DGPA), later testified that "we recommended that we should get this information out as quickly and completely as possible because the Public Affairs branch felt that early disclosure would reduce the negative impact on DND." But he revealed that that the overriding concern at the moment "at very high levels in the Department [was] that nothing be done to interfere with the leadership run." This affected the release of information. The chief of staff of Kim Campbell, then the minister of national defence (MND), acknowledged that he was informed of the death only hours after it occurred and Campbell herself stated she was briefed around 17 March. As early as 22 January 1993, and again on 1 March 1993, because of the expected leadership candidacy of the MND for the position of prime minister, the deputy minister, Robert Fowler, had reminded members attending the daily executive meeting that it was necessary to exercise "extreme sensitivity in all matters relating to public statements, speeches, press releases." See Luke Fisher, "On the Defence," *Maclean's*, 26 July 1993, 16; David Pugliese, "HQ in Somalia Coverup," *Ottawa Citizen*, 14 June 1997, A1; D'Arcy Jenish, "What Did He Know?" *Maclean's*, 15 April 1996, 17–18; "Colonel Cites Politics in Delay over Somalia," *Globe and Mail*, 14 September 1996, A1; and David Pugliese, "Military Hid Murder to Shield Kim Campbell, Inquiry Told," *Ottawa Citizen*, 14 September 1996, A1/2; and *Information Legacy*, Report of the Commission of Inquiry, Vol. 1, Passage of Information about the March 4th Incident, Record 2888.

36. Mistreatment of Somalis by other military international contingents later caused scandals in countries such as Belgium, Germany, and Italy. Allegations included mental and physical abuse, beatings, as well as the killing of captured thieves. Relative to the other contingents in Somalia and elsewhere, the Canadian cases of mistreatment and killings may have appeared minor, but its impact reverberated through Canadian society and shook the conception Canadian soldiers had of themselves . See Andrew Duffy, "Now It's Belgian Soldiers," *Ottawa Citizen*, 12 April 1997, 1; Raf Casert, "Somalia Scandal Sparks Belgian Review," *Ottawa Citizen*, 18 April 1997, A10; "Now Belgium Rocked by Somali

Scandal," *Toronto Star*, 12 April 1997, A18; "Burns, Shocks Given Somalis Italian Says," *Toronto Star*, 7 June 1997, A21; and Vera Haller, "Italy's Somalia Scandal Grows," *Ottawa Citizen*, 15 June 1997, A5. See also Coulon, *Soldiers of Diplomacy*, 98–99.

37. See Rodal, *The Somalia Experience in Strategic Perspective in a Free and Democratic Society*, 1 and 70; and Horn, *Bastard Sons*, 226–27 and 253–55.

38. The board was established on 28 April 1993. After running off course, over budget and over time, the MND shut the commission down in March 1997. The *Board of Inquiry (BOI) — Canadian Airborne Regiment Battle Group* (henceforth *BOI Cdn AB BG*), Phase 1, Vol. 11, Appendix 3 to Annex A, 1/5.

39. The *BOI Cdn AB BG*, unlike the *Hewson Report*, did not placate the critics in or out of the military. An internal DND review considered the final report as flawed. Major-General Jean Boyle, then the associate assistant deputy minister (Policy and Communications) and chair of the NDHQ "Somalia Working Group" conducted an assessment of the study that pointed out in July 1994 that "a close reading of the De Faye board's report, comparing it with information from courts-martial testimony, would reveal that were weaknesses and, more important, significant discrepancies in the De Faye board's findings and recommendations, on which the CDS was basing a number of reforms." He further noted that certain conclusions did not appear to be borne out by the actual testimony heard. Moreover, Boyle felt that there had been enough evidence before the De Faye board to suggest that leadership problems reached up the chain of command right to the Canadian Joint Force Somalia Command. In addition, Boyle acknowledged there were documents that revealed direct attempts to cover up facts behind the 4 and 16 March 1993 incidents. He finished by concluding that the most pressing issue regarding the Canadian Airborne Regiment was leadership. *Information Legacy*, Report of the Commission of Inquiry, Vol. 1, "Major-General Boyle's Analysis of the De Faye Report," Record 3160.

40. Desbarats, 3. See also Bercuson, *Significant Incident*, 242; Winslow, 8; and *Information Legacy*, Letter Commander LFCA to the CDS/MND, "Report Fact Finding Mission Into the Canadian Airborne Regiment," 22 January 1995, 2. Lieutenant-General Foster, a former Airborne and Army commander, also thought that the Airborne Regiment's problems were really a manifestation of problems that existed throughout the Canadian Forces. Moreover, he blamed the Army for failing to deal with the flaws at the root of the Airborne's demise. Interview with author, 6 June 1998. Similarly, Lieutenant-Colonel Lorne O'Brien, a long-serving Army officer and former paratroop commander, said what many were too frightened to admit. He declared that if in fact there was a problem in the Airborne, then there was also a problem in the entire regimental system. O'Brien pointed out that by its very nature the Airborne was the sum of the parts of the line infantry regiments. Interview with author, 14 April 1997.

41. Interestingly, the master corporal in charge was newly posted-in. He had a solid reputation. Many involved in the unit felt his poor judgment was a direct result

of trying to fit in. DND News Release, NR-94,039, "Negligent Performance of Duty in Rwanda," 16 September, 1994; Bruce Wallace, "Fighting a Reputation," *Maclean's*, 30 January 1995, 17; Interviews with participants and witnesses.

42. CBC and CTV Nightly News, 18–21 January 1995; *Somalia Commission*, Transcript of Evidentiary Hearing, Vol. 49, 20 February 1996, testimony of General De Chastelain, 9917–18; Scott Taylor and Brian Nolan, *Tested Mettle* (Ottawa: Esprit de Corps Books, 1998), 207; Luke Fisher, "Canada's Shame," *Maclean's*, 30 January 1995, 14; Dave Rider, "Video Outrage," *Ottawa Sun*, 19 January 1995, 4; and Horn, *Bastard Sons*, 228–37.

43. Cotton, "Military Mystique"; Winslow, 138–141; Peter Cheney, "The Airborne Story," *Montreal Gazette*, 22 January 1994, B1 and "Canada's Rebel Soldiers," *Edmonton Sunday Journal*, 30 January 1994, D1.

44. See Bernd Horn, "A Law Unto Themselves? — Elitism as a Catalyst for Disobedience," in Craig Mantle, ed., *The Unwilling and the Reluctant: Perspectives on Military Disobedience in the Canadian Forces* (Kingston, ON: CDA Press, 2006).

45. *Hewson Report*, 23–27; *BOI — Cdn AB Regt BG*, Phase 1, Vol. 11, 19 July 1993, K-1/9; and Winslow, 126–35.

46. Interview with author, 15 April 1998.

47. Brigadier-General N.B. Jeffries, "Future Airborne Capability," 30 January 1995, 3.

48. Editorial, *Esprit de Corps* 4, No. 2, 9. See also Peter Worthington, "A Blind Eye to a Regiment's Sins," *Ottawa Sun*, 1 August 1996, 11.

49. Brigadier-General Ernie Beno, "The Somali Affair," 2. Accessed from Beno's personal papers.

50. *Cdn AB Regt BG — BOI*, Phase 1, Vol. 11, Annex C, C-5/8.

51. Canadian Airborne Forces Association (CAFA) Written Submission Number 2 to the Commission of Inquiry into the Deployment of Canadian Forces to Somalia, February 1997. Accessed from Beno's personal papers.

52. Interview with author, 1 December 1997. Lieutenant-Colonel Ferron also attested that the Regiment did not have a reputation worse than anyone else in the Brigade before the hazing video. Interview with author, 8 April 1998. See also *Information Legacy*, Letter Commander LFCA to the CDS/MND, "Report Fact Finding Mission into the Canadian Airborne Regiment," 22 January 1995, 2.

53. *Information Legacy*, Hearing Transcripts, Vol. 3, 5 October 1995, testimony of Major-General Gaudreau, 560.

54. Land Force Command (LFC), "Estimate of the Impact to Re-Establish 1 Canadian Parachute Battalion," 28 February 1994, 2–3.

55. *Information Legacy*, Evidentiary Exhibits, Summary of Court-Martial Offences, Period 1 January 1988 — 31 December 1992, Document Control No. 000226, DND Document No. 200146. As with all statistical data, there is a degree of unreliability because of interpretation. For instance, the data given contains an inherent danger. Often a high number of trials are viewed as a sign of ill discipline and a unit out of control. However, the converse is likely. It could be demonstrative of good control and a no-tolerance approach. Conversely, a low number of charges could be indicative of a lax, laissez-faire approach where the leadership is weak and reluctant to alienate its subordinates. The use of this data must be weighed in conjunction with the other evidence. Further indications of the scope of problem was evidenced in a former SSF commander's observation during the period 1992–1993. He observed that in regard to drug problems, the soldiers returning from Germany were the main concern in Petawawa. Ernie Beno, "Attitudes and Values," 2. Accessed from Beno's personal papers.

56. For example, see DND News Release NR-96.111, 27 December 1996; "The Rise and Fall of an Officer," *Ottawa Citizen*, 10 April 1998, A4; Jack Granatstein, *Who Killed the Canadian Military?* (Toronto: Harper Flamingo Canada, 2004), 155; John A. English, *Lament for an* Army (Concord, ON: Irwin Publishing, 1998), 7, 64–65; and Scott Taylor and Brian Nolan, *Tarnished Brass* (Toronto: Lester Publishing Ltd., 1996); Major Robert Near, "Divining the Message: An Analysis of the MND and Somalia Commission Reports," in Bernd Horn, ed., *Contemporary Issues in Officership: A Canadian Perspective* (Toronto: CISS, 2000), 65–91.

57. See "Court Martial Held Without Public Notice," *Globe and Mail*, 9 July 1997; *Report of the Board of Inquiry into the Command, Control and Leadership of CANBAT 2*, dated 15 November 1996; Taylor and Nolan, *Tarnished Brass* and *Tested Mettle* (Ottawa: Esprit de Corps Books, 1998); "Shamed in Bosnia," *Maclean's*, 29 July 1996, 10–12; Worthington, *Scapegoat*, 314–15; Desbarats, 4–5; and Winslow, 72–74. *Esprit de Corps* magazine also ran a running critique of any and all foibles present in the CF in virtually every issue of its publication from 1993 to the present.

APPENDIX

COMPLETE TABLE OF PRE-UNIFICATION AND POST-UNIFICATION RANKS OF ALL SERVICES

Canadian Forces Maritime Command	Royal Canadian Navy	Canadian Forces (Force Mobile Command, Air Command)	Royal Canadian Air Force	Canadian Army
Flag and General Officers				
Admiral	Admiral	General	Air Chief Marshal	General
Vice-Admiral	Vice-Admiral	Lieutenant-General	Air Marshal	Lieutenant-General
Rear-Admiral	Rear-Admiral	Major-General	Air Vice-Marshal	Major-General
Commodore	Commodore	Brigadier-General	Air Commodore	Brigadier
Officers				
Captain	Captain	Colonel	Group Captain	Colonel
Commander	Commander	Lieutenant-Colonel	Wing Commander	Lieutenant-Colonel
Lieutenant-Commander	Lieutenant-Commander	Major	Squadron Leader	Major
Lieutenant	Lieutenant	Captain	Flight Lieutenant	Captain
Sub-Lieutenant		Lieutenant	Flying Officer	Lieutenant
Acting Sub-Lieutenant	Sub-Lieutenant	Second Lieutenant	Pilot Officer	Second Lieutenant
Naval Cadet	Midshipman	Officer Cadet	Officer Cadet	Officer Cadet

Non-Commissioned Personnel				
Chief Petty Officer 1st Class	Chief Petty Officer 1st Class	Chief Warrant Officer	Warrant Officer Class I	Warrant Officer Class I
Chief Petty Officer 2nd Class	Chief Petty Officer 2nd Class	Master Warrant Officer	Warrant Officer Class II	Warrant Officer Class II
Petty Officer 1st Class	Petty Officer 1st Class	Warrant Officer	Flight Sergeant	Staff Sergeant
			Sergeant	Sergeant
Petty Officer 2nd Class	Petty Officer 2nd Class	Sergeant	Corporal	Corporal
Master Seaman		Master Corporal	Leading Aircraftsman	Lance Corporal
Leading Seaman	Leading Seaman	Corporal	Aircraftsman	Private
Able Seaman	Able Seaman	Private (Trained)		
Ordinary Seaman	Ordinary Seaman	Private (Basic)		

Table was accessed at *www.canadiansoldiers.com/mediawiki-1.5.5/index.php?title=Table_of_Ranks_and_Responsibilities.*

Glossary

AOI	Aircraft Operating Instruction
APC	Armoured Personnel Carrier
BG	Battle Group
BOI	Board of Inquiry
BS	Bullshit
C-in-C CNA	Commander-in-Chief Canadian Northwest Atlantic
CAD	Canadian Air Division
CAF	Canadian Air Force
CANBAT	Canadian Battalion
CAR	Competency, Authority, and Responsibility
CASF	Canadian Army Special Force
CB	Companion of the Bath
CBC	Canadian Broadcasting Corporation
CBE	Commander of the British Empire
Cdn AB Regt	Canadian Airborne Regiment
CCF	Co-operative Commonwealth Federation
CDA	Canadian Defence Academy
CDS	Chief of the Defence Staff
CEF	Canadian Expeditionary Force
CF	Canadian Forces
CFLI	Canadian Forces Leadership Institute
CFHQ	Canadian Forces Headquarters
CGS	Chief of the General Staff
CID	Criminal Investigation Division

CMHQ	Canadian Military Headquarters
CNS	Chief of Naval Staff
CO	Commanding Officer
COAC	Commanding Officer Atlantic Command
CSR	Combat Stress Reaction
CSU	Canadian Seaman's Union
DCF	Defence of Canada Force
DCGS	Deputy Chief of the General Staff
DCO	Deputy Commanding Officer
DFC	Distinguished Flying Cross
DFS	Directorate of Flight Safety
DND	Department of National Defence
DSO	Distinguished Service Order
DSS	Director of Special Services
DZ	Drop Zone
ET-1	Educational Test
FMC	Force Mobile Command
GOC	General Officer Commanding
GS	General Service
HMCS	His Majesty's Canadian Ship *or*
	Her Majesty's Canadian Ship
HQ	Headquarters
KRCN	King's Regulations for the Royal Canadian Navy
LEG	Lacking Enough Guts
LFC	Land Forces Command
LMF	Lack of Moral Fibre
MC	Military Cross
MGO	Master General Ordnance
MND	Minister of National Defence
MO	Medical Officer
MSF	Mobile Striking Force
NATO	North Atlantic Treaty Organisation

NCO	Non-Commissioned Officer
NDA	National Defence Act
NDHQ	National Defence Headquarters
NGO	Non-Governmental Organization
NORAD	North American Air [Aerospace] Defense
NP	Neuropsychiatric
NRMA	National Resources Mobilization Act
NSHQ	Naval Service Headquarters
OMFC	Overseas Military Forces of Canada
Op	Operation
OP	Observation Post
ORB	Operations Record Book
PTSD	Post-Traumatic Stress Disorder
QR&O	Queen's Regulations and Orders
RAAF	Royal Australian Air Force
RAF	Royal Air Force
RAN	Royal Australian Navy
RCAF	Royal Canadian Air Force
RCMP	Royal Canadian Mounted Police
RCN	Royal Canadian Navy
RCNVR	Royal Canadian Naval Volunteer Reserve
RFC	Royal Flying Corps
RIAF	Royal Indian Air Force
RN	Royal Navy
RNAS	Royal Naval Air Service
RSM	Regimental Sergeant-Major
ROE	Rules of Engagement
SF	Special Forces
S-H	Sierra Hotel
SOP	Standard Operating Procedure
UN	United Nations
UNPROFOR	United Nations Protection Force
U.S.	United States
USAF	United States Air Force
USAAF	United States Army Air Force

VC	Victoria Cross
VCDS	Vice-Chief of the Defence Staff
WRCNS	Women's Royal Canadian Naval Service
1 Cdn Para Bn	1st Canadian Parachute Battalion
1 RCR	1st Battalion, The Royal Canadian Regiment
2 PPCLI	2nd Battalion, Princess Patricia's Canadian Light Infantry
3 Para Bde	3rd Parachute Brigade
6 AB Div	6th Airborne Division

CONTRIBUTORS

Dr. David Bercuson is a Canadian labour, military, and political historian who has published academic and mainstream texts on a range of subjects, focusing primarily on modern Canadian politics, Canadian defence and foreign policy, and Canadian military history. A prolific author he has written, co-authored, or edited more than 30 books. As well, he writes regular columns for *Legion Magazine* and the *Calgary Herald*, among other publications. Furthermore, he periodically does political commentary for CBC and CTV Television. He is currently a professor of history at the University of Calgary and director of The Centre for Military and Strategic Studies at the University of Calgary.

Lieutenant-Colonel Dean C. Black joined the Canadian Forces in 1977, graduating from the Royal Military College in 1981 with a baccalaureate in applied science. He flew tactical helicopters for 21 years, accumulating more than 3,600 hours. After commanding 403 (Helicopter) Operational Training Squadron, Black served as a defence analyst with the Director General Strategic Planning at National Defence Headquarters for three years. He earned an M.A. in war studies with the Royal Military College at Kingston, Ontario, and is a graduate of the Canadian Forces Command and Staff Course, Canadian Land Forces Command and Staff Course, and the Aerospace Systems Course.

Robert H. Caldwell served in the Canadian Army for 35 years. He finished senior technical and staff officer courses in the United Kingdom at Shrivenham, Camberly, and the Joint Warfare

Establishment at Old Sarum. In 1987, after completing an M.A. in war studies from the Royal Military College, he was employed as a researcher and historian at the Operational and Research and Analysis Establishment, later followed by service with the Directorate of History, in Ottawa, where he has been a part of the Naval History Team for the past 14 years. During this period, he has written extensively on the Royal Canadian Navy in the Second World War. He is currently the Canadian representative on the first Combined Operations naval history project, working with historians from the United States, Britain, and Australia. His research focus for this effort will be the Canadian Navy in the Arabian Sea and Gulf from 1991 to 2003. This four-power project will publish its findings in 2007.

Howard G. Coombs retired from active duty with the Canadian Forces in 2002. He is a graduate of the United States Army Command and General Staff College, where he was one of 11 students to earn the designation U.S. Army Master Strategist in 2001, as well as the U.S. Army School of Advanced Military Studies, which awarded his master's degree. Currently, he is a doctoral candidate at Queen's University in Kingston, Ontario; a teaching fellow at Queen's; research associate of the Canadian Forces Leadership Institute, Kingston; part-time instructor at the Canadian Forces College in Toronto; and a reserve officer commanding the Princess of Wales's Own Regiment, an infantry unit based in Kingston.

Dr. Allan English has taught various courses at the Canadian Forces College since 1998. He is an adjunct associate professor of history at Queen's University, where he teaches a graduate course in Canadian military history. His latest book, *Understanding Military Culture: A Canadian Perspective*, was published by McGill-Queen's University Press.

Dr. Richard H. Gimblett is the command historian of the Canadian Navy, which he served for 27 years in ships of various classes on both coasts, notably as combat officer of HMCS *Protecteur* for operations in the Persian Gulf during the war in 1991. He subsequently co-authored the official account of that conflict under the title *Operation FRICTION: The Canadian Forces in the Persian Gulf, 1990–1991* (Dundurn Press, 1997). More recently, he published *Operation APOLLO: The Golden Age of the Canadian Navy in the War Against*

Terrorism (Magic Light, 2004). Gimblett has also participated with the Directorate of History and Heritage in writing *Volume 1 (1867–1939) of the Official History of the Royal Canadian Navy*. His various affiliations include president of the Canadian Nautical Research Society and adjunct professor of history at Queen's University in Kingston.

Major-General Daniel P. Gosselin is the director general of international security policy at National Defence Headquarters. Some of his recent assignments include chief of staff for the CF Transformation Team, commandant of the Canadian Forces College, commander of the CF Joint Operations Group, and chief of staff for Headquarters, Joint Task Force Southwest Asia during Operation APOLLO. A graduate of the Advanced Military Studies Course and the National Security Studies Course, he holds a B.A.Sc., an M.A.Sc., an M.P.A., and an M.A. in war studies, and is now undertaking a Ph.D. in military history at Queen's University.

Rachel Lea Heide is a doctoral candidate with the Department of History at Carleton University. She is in the last stages of completing her Ph.D. dissertation entitled "Politics, Policy, and the Professionalization of the Royal Canadian Air Force, 1919–1958." Her research interests include Air Force organization, training, leadership, morale, accident investigation, and government policy between the First World War and the Cold War (the subject of her dissertation), as well as current Canadian defence policy, peacekeeping intelligence, expeditionary Air Forces, continental air defence, and the war on terrorism. Currently, she is a professor of Canadian history at Algonquin College in Ottawa and a distance learning instructor at the Royal Military College of Canada and the Canadian Forces College Joint Reserve Command and Staff Course. Besides being a pre-doctoral fellow with the Centre for Security and Defence Studies at Carleton University, she is also an associate Air Force historian with the Office of Air Force Heritage and History at 1 Canadian Air Division in Winnipeg. As of September 2006, she joined Defence Research and Development Canada's Centre for Operational Research and Analysis as a defence scientist/strategic analyst.

Colonel Bernd Horn is deputy commander of Special Operations Forces Command and the former director of the Canadian Forces Leadership Institute. A seasoned infantry officer with command experience at the unit and sub-unit level, he was the commanding officer of 1st Battalion, The Royal Canadian Regiment (2001–2003); the officer commanding 3 Commando, the Canadian Airborne Regiment (1993–1995); and the officer commanding "B" Company, 1 RCR (1992–1993). Horn has authored, co-authored, edited, and co-edited 20 books and numerous articles on military affairs and military history. He is also an adjunct associate professor of history at the Royal Military College of Canada.

Lieutenant (Navy) Richard O. Mayne has published extensively on topics relating to the history of the Canadian Navy. A serving officer in the Canadian naval reserve, he is a member of the Directorate of History and Heritage's Post-War Naval Team and is currently finishing his Ph.D. at Queen's University. His dissertation focuses on the procurement of the Canadian Navy's DDH 280 Destroyers. His book, *Betrayed: Scandal, Politics and Canadian Leadership*, which explores the events leading up to the wrongful dismissal of Vice-Admiral Percy W. Nelles, was published by University of British Columbia Press in October 2006.

Brigadier-General (Retired) Gordon Sharpe served as an air navigator in the Canadian Forces from 1965 until his retirement in 2001. Over the course of his career he was posted as a navigator, staff officer, and commander at squadron level, and was air component commander during the Winnipeg flood in 1997 (Operation Assistance). In August 1997 he returned to Ottawa to assume the responsibility of director of air strategic plans. It was during this period that he served as the president of the Board of Inquiry — Croatia and chaired a special review group for the Chief of Defence Staff examining the issue of leadership during Operation HARMONY (Croatia). Promoted to the rank of brigadier-general in May 2000, he retired from the Canadian Forces in April 2001 and now serves as a special adviser to the CF/DND ombudsman on post-traumatic stress disorder (PTSD) and environmental exposure. He is also a member of the board of directors of Thales Canada.

Colonel Randall Wakelam retired from the Canadian Forces in 2005 after 36 years of service. Between 1977 and 1987 he flew Twin Hueys, amassing 3,000 flying hours and holding appointments as flight safety officer, tactical instructor pilot, operations officer, and flight commander. From 1991 to 1993 he commanded 408 Tactical

Helicopter Squadron, and between 1993 and 2002 he served at the Canadian Forces College, holding a variety of appointments that included director of warfare studies. While at the college he was a lead designer for the Advanced Military Studies and National Security Studies Courses. After retirement he retained his links to the college as a part-time instructor and returned to the institution as director of curriculum (a full-time reserve position) in 2006. He is a graduate of the Canadian Land Forces Command and Staff Course and the Canadian Forces Command and Staff Course, and completed his Ph.D. in history at Wilfrid Laurier University in 2006. His research interests include air warfare, command and leadership, and military education.

Major Richard J. Walker retired from Regular Force Army service in 1996. He holds the British Combat Team Commander and CLFCSC Kingston Qualification (1982) and is a graduate of CFCSC Toronto (1991). As a political historian, he has taught a variety of American history courses at Wilfrid Laurier University and the University of Ottawa. His forte is Canadian civil-military relations, and he has published and presented along the academic lines of his doctoral dissertation, *The Political Management of Army Leadership: The Evolution of Canadian Civil-Army Relations 1897–1945*. Currently, he is serving as a reservist with the Land Staff as the Army ethics officer and is the author and principle manager of the Army Ethics Program (AEP).

Michael Whitby is senior naval historian at the Directorate of History and Heritage, Department of National Defence. Among many works, he has has recently co-authored Parts One and Two of *The Official History of the Royal Canadian Navy in the Second World War* (Vanwell, 2003 and 2006), edited *Commanding Canadians: The Second World War Diaries of AFC Layard, 1943–45* (University of British Columbia Press, 2005), and co-edited *The Admirals: Canada's Senior Naval Leadership in the Twentieth Century* (Dundurn Press, 2006).

Index